TRANSNATIONAL AND COMPARATIVE CRIMINOLOGY

TRANSNATIONAL AND COMPARATIVE CRIMINOLOGY

Edited by
James Sheptycki and **Ali Wardak**

with the editorial assistance of
James Hardie-Bick

London • Sydney • Portland, Oregon

First published in Great Britain 2005 by
GlassHouse Press, The Glass House,
Wharton Street, London WC1X 9PX, United Kingdom
Telephone: + 44 (0)20 7278 8000   Facsimile: + 44 (0)20 7278 8080
Email: info@cavendishpublishing.com
Website: www.cavendishpublishing.com

Published in the United States by Cavendish Publishing
c/o International Specialized Book Services,
5824 NE Hassalo Street, Portland,
Oregon 97213-3644, USA

Published in Australia by The GlassHouse Press,
45 Beach Street, Coogee, NSW 2034, Australia
Telephone: + 61 (2)9664 0909   Facsimile: +61 (2)9664 5420
Email: info@cavendishpublishing.com.au
Website: www.cavendishpublishing.com.au

British Library Cataloguing in Publication Data
Sheptycki, JWE
Transnational and comparative criminology
1 Criminology – Cross-cultural studies
I Title II Wardak, Ali
364

Library of Congress Cataloguing in Publication Data
Data available

ISBN 1-90438-505-2
ISBN 978-1-904-38505-9

1 3 5 7 9 10 8 6 4 2

Printed and bound in Great Britain

Dedicated to students of criminology everywhere

List of Contributors

Biko Agozino was born in Nigeria in 1961. He earned a first class honours degree in Sociology from the University of Calabar, Nigeria, in 1985. Later he taught for two years as an Assistant Lecturer in the same department before proceeding to Trinity Hall College, University of Cambridge, where he completed the Master of Philosophy degree in Criminology in the Faculty of Law, 1989–90. He then undertook PhD research on black women and the criminal justice system at the University of Edinburgh (1990–95). He is currently the Series Editor of the Ashgate Interdisciplinary Research Series in Ethnic, Gender and Class Relations. He is on the editorial board of *Jenda*, a journal of culture and women's studies, the editor of the African Journal of Criminology and Justice Studies and an Associate Editor of *Passages: A Journal of Transnational and Transcultural Studies*. His publications include *Black Women and the Criminal Justice System: Towards the Decolonisation of Victimisation* (Ashgate, 1997 (reprinted 1998)) and *Counter-Colonial Criminology: A Critique of Imperialist Reason* (Pluto Press, 2003). His co-authored research report (with Unyierie Idem), *Nigeria: Democratising a Militarised Civil Society* (London, Centre for Democracy and Development, 2001), was recently a finalist for the Outstanding Medal on Development Research, Global Development Network, 2003 and he is co-editor (with Anita Kalunta-Crumpton) on *Pan African Issues in Crime and Justice* (Ashgate, 2004). Biko is currently an Associate Professor in Social Relations at the Cheyney University of Pennsylvania.

Janet Chan, BSc, MSc, MA (Toronto), PhD (Sydney), is a Fellow of the Academy of Social Sciences in Australia. She is currently Head of the School of Social Science and Policy at the University of New South Wales. Her research interest has been in the critical theorising of reforms and innovations in criminal justice, including criminal trial, sentencing, penal policy and policing. She has published extensively in these areas and has also served as research consultant to numerous government bodies in Australia. Her recent publications include *Changing Police Culture* (Cambridge University Press, 1997); *e-Policing: The Impact of Information Technology on Police Practices* with Brereton, Legosz and Doran, Queensland Criminal Justice Commission, 2001); *Managing Prejudicial Publicity: An Empirical Study of Criminal Jury Trials in New South Wales* (with Chesterman and Hampton, NSW Law and Justice Foundation, 2001); and *Fair Cop: Learning the Art of Policing* (with Devery and Doran, University of Toronto Press, 2003).

Hazel Croall is Professor of Criminology at Glasgow Caledonian University. She was formerly Senior Lecturer and Head of Division of Sociology at the University of Strathclyde and she has taught a variety of criminology courses. She is the author and co-author of the texts *Crime and Society* (Longman, 1998) and *Criminal Justice in England and Wales* (Longman, 1998) and has published widely in the area of white collar crime. Her publications include *Understanding White Collar Crime* (Open University Press, 2002), chapters in books and articles in journals, including the *British Journal of Criminology, Crime, Law and Social Change*, the *International Journal of Risk, Security and Crime Prevention* and the *Journal of Financial Crime*. Her main interests in respect of white collar crime are in its conceptualisation, exploring aspects of victimisation and the use of sanctions.

Adam Edwards is Senior Lecturer in Criminology at Cardiff University. He was formerly Director of the UK Economic and Social Research Council Research Seminar Series on Policy Responses to Transnational Organised Crime and, in this capacity, addressed the United Nations Congress on Crime Prevention and the Treatment of Delinquency, Vienna, April 2000. He has published widely on such topics as the politics of crime control, organised crime, crime prevention and crime control policy transfer in various journals, including the *British Journal of Politics and International Relations; Contemporary Politics; Crime, Law and Social Change; Crime Prevention and Community Safety: An International Journal; International Journal of Risk, Security and Crime Prevention; Security Journal.* He has also produced two co-edited volumes entitled *Crime Control and Community* (with Gordon Hughes, Willan, 2002) and *Transnational Organised Crime* (with Pete Gill, Routledge, 2003).

Felipe Estrada taught Criminology in the Department of Criminology, Stockholm University, Sweden up to December of 2004. His PhD dissertation, 'Juvenile crime as a social problem – trends, media attention and societal response', was published in 1999. During 2000–01 he worked as secretary in the Swedish welfare commission that was set up to draw up a balance sheet for welfare in the 1990s. This task included an examination of the connection between living conditions, social exclusion and victimisation. He has published widely in the *Journal of European Social Policy,* the *British Journal of Criminology* and the *European Journal of Criminology.* Currently he is also editor of the *Journal of Scandinavian Studies in Criminology and Crime Prevention.* In January 2005 Dr Estrada began research on criminology and social exclusion at the Institute for Future Research in Stockholm. That work continues until the end of 2008.

Narayanan Ganapathy is an Assistant Professor in the Department of Sociology at the National University of Singapore. He has an MA in Criminal Justice from Brunel University in the UK, and a PhD in Sociology from the National University of Singapore. Selected publications include 'Policing minority street corner gangs in Singapore' (2002) 12(2) *Policing and Society* 139–52; 'Rethinking the problem of policing marital violence: the Singapore perspective' (2002) 12(3) *Policing and Society* 173–90; and 'Conceptualising community policing, crime prevention and criminology' (2000) 33(3) *Australian and New Zealand Journal of Criminology* 266–86. Dr Ganapathy is a member of the Editorial Board of the *European Journal of Criminology* and has served as an academic consultant to the Singapore Police Force and the Singapore Prison Service. Between September and December of 2003 he was a visiting Fulbright Scholar at the University of Nebraska at Lincoln. His research and teaching interests are criminology, sociology of crime and deviance, sociology of law and policing, juvenile justice, criminal gangs and domestic violence. He is currently working on a project that examines victim experiences of policing in domestic violence in the Singaporean context.

Jo Goodey was awarded a PhD from the University of Hull in 1995. From 1994 to 2000 she was a Criminology lecturer at the Universities of Sheffield and Leeds, after which she took up a Research Fellowship at the United Nations Office on Drugs and Crime in Vienna. She is currently working as a consultant for the UN's International Narcotics Control Board, and is an Associate Fellow of Leeds University's Centre for Criminal Justice Studies. She has published many journal articles and book chapters on a diverse range of criminological and victimological subjects, from fear of crime and masculinities through to trafficking in women for Europe's sex industry. She is co-editor with Adam Crawford of the book *Integrating a Victim Perspective Within Criminal Justice* (Dartmouth, 2000) and is European Editor of *Critical Criminology.*

Carol Jones is Professor of Law and Comparative Criminology in the School of Law, University of Glamorgan, South Wales. She is currently an Associate Fellow at the Centre for Study of Contemporary China, City University, Hong Kong and was a Lecturer in the Department of Sociology at the University of Hong Kong from 1990 to 1995. She was a Lecturer and Research Fellow in the Faculty of Law, University of Edinburgh from 1984 to 1990. She earned her PhD at both the Department of Social and Political Science, Cambridge University and the Centre for Socio-Legal Studies, Oxford University. She has published widely on a diverse range of comparative legal topics. Publications include: 'The Asian mode of production or politics by legal means: law's articulation with socialism in modern China' in Gillespie, J and Nicholson, P (eds), *Socialism and Legal Change: The Dynamics of Vietnamese Renewal and Chinese Reform* (Melbourne, Cambridge University Press, 2004); 'Politics postponed: law as a substitute for politics in Hong Kong and China' in *Power, Capitalism and the Rule of Law: Legal Institutions in Eastern Asia* (Routledge, 1998); and 'Capitalism, globalization and the rule of law: an alternative trajectory for law in China' (1994) 3 *Social and Legal Studies* 195–221.

Michael Kempa is a member of the Department of Criminology, University of Ottawa, Canada. He is interested in understanding how and why particular governance initiatives arise, take hold and spread when and where they do. This theoretical work is intended to be strategically useful towards enhancing democratic governance on the ground. He engages this problem through the empirical window of trends and developments in policing, with a particular interest in transitional political contexts. This interest is reflected in his PhD thesis, which examines the policing reform process underway in Northern Ireland as part of that territory's broader peace process. He has begun to publish on these themes, often with colleagues, in the *British Journal of Criminology, Policing and Society*, the *European Journal on Criminal Policy and Research*, the *American Annals of Political and Social Science, Transformation: Critical Perspectives on Southern Africa*, and the *Nigerian Law Enforcement Review*. Practical aspects of this research programme have begun to be developed in collaborative policy reports to the Law Commission of Canada and the Jamaican Ministry of National Security. Michael teaches theories in criminology, policing in modern society, and a special topics seminar course that addresses the role of the criminologist in studying and engaging criminal justice reform in transitional political contexts.

Paul Norman is Director of International Programmes at the Institute of Criminal Justice Studies, University of Portsmouth. Paul is an interdisciplinary political scientist researching regional police co-operation, international criminal justice organisations and the work of the EU and G8 in international policy making. His current research interests focus upon regional co-operation in the southern African region, counter-terrorism after September 11th and the role of the UN.

James Sheptycki was born in Regina Saskatchewan and grew up in various parts of the Middle East and south-east Asia. He is currently Associate Professor of Criminology at York University, Toronto, Canada. From 1994 and 1998 he was a post-doctoral research fellow in the School of Law at Edinburgh University, where he undertook research on transnational policing in the English Channel region. His PhD research on the policing of domestic violence was undertaken as at the London School of Economics between 1986 and 1991. He has published widely on criminological topics, such as domestic violence, serial killers, money laundering, organised crime and transnational policing in various journals, including the *British Journal of Criminology*, the *British Journal of Sociology*, the *Canadian Journal of Sociology*, the *International Journal of the Sociology of Law*, the *European Journal of Criminology* and the *European Journal of Crime, Criminal Law and Criminal Justice*. He has produced an edited volume entitled *Issues in Transnational Policing* (Routledge, 2000) and is the author of two research monographs: *Innovations in Policing Domestic Violence* (Avebury, 1993) and *In Search of Transnational Policing* (Ashgate, 2002). He was also editor of *Policing and Society* from 1997 to 2003.

Anne-Marie Singh currently teaches Criminology at Ryerson University, Toronto, Canada. She holds a Masters in Criminology from the Centre of Criminology, University of Toronto and a Doctorate in Sociology from Goldsmiths College, University of London. She has considerable experience in South Africa, where she conducted fieldwork between 1995 and 1999 for her PhD on the reconfiguration of policing in the post-Apartheid period. During this time she contributed to numerous policy papers on policing transformations in post-Apartheid South Africa as a research associate both at the University of Cape Town and at Technikon South Africa. She has also been a researcher with the Centre for Urban and Community Research at the University of London where she assisted in the evaluation of a local city challenge project. She is currently researching the place of coercive techniques in contemporary practices of rule.

Bill Tupman is a lecturer in Politics at Exeter University, UK. He is an associate research fellow at the Institute of Advanced Legal Studies in London, England and a member of the editorial board of the *Journal of Financial Crime*. He has published numerous articles on financial crime and policing in journals such as the *Journal of Financial Crime*, the *Journal of Money-laundering Control* and *Information and Communications Technology Law*. In 1999 he published a book (with Alison Tupman) entitled *Uniform in Diversity: Western European Police Services in the 1990s* (Intellect, 1999). In addition to matters concerning corruption and financial crime, his research interests extend to supranational policing arrangements as a response to organised crime and terrorism. As a political scientist he is particularly interested in relationships between Eastern and Western Europe with regard to crime, the *Schengen acquis* and Justice and Home Affairs matters in the European Union.

Ali Wardak was born in Afghanistan and is a graduate of Kabul University in Law and Jurisprudence. He received his PhD degree in Criminology from the University of Edinburgh, where he also worked as a tutor of Criminology and Criminal Justice (1992–95), and as a research fellow (1995–96). In January 1996, Dr Wardak joined the University of Glamorgan as a full time lecturer in Criminology, where he played a central part in founding the BSc (Hons) Criminology and BA (Hons) Criminal Justice awards, and is now Reader in Criminology. From June 1997 until July 2001 he held the post of Criminology and Criminal Justice Awards Leader at Glamorgan; and between August 2001 and September 2003 he was seconded to the directorship of a large Home Office funded research project that looked at the criminogenic needs and probation experiences of black and Asian offenders in England and Wales. Wardak's teaching interests in criminological theory, comparative criminology, 'race', ethnicity and crime are closely tied with his research interests. His papers, articles, book reviews and interviews have been published in the *British Journal of Criminology*, the *Howard Journal of Criminal Justice*, the *Journal of Crime, Law and Social Change*, the *Journal of Culture and Religion*, *Planet*, *The Guardian*, *Asia*

Express, India Weekly, Al-Majallah and *golwg*. He is the author of *Social Control and Deviance* (Ashgate, 2000) and is co-author of *Afghanistan's Political and Constitutional Development* (2003 ODI/DFID); and *Black and Asian Offenders on Probation* (Home Office, 2004). Dr Wardak proficiently speaks, reads and writes in English, Pashto, Persian/Dari and Arabic.

Lars Westfelt completed his PhD dissertation in 2001, entitled 'Crime and punishment in Sweden and Europe, a study in comparative criminology'. This was undertaken in the department of Criminology at Stockholm University, Sweden. In the field of criminology, his main focus has been on comparative criminology and crime theories. He is now working in the area of gambling research at SoRAD (Centre for social research in Alcohol and Drugs), Stockholm University. The gambling research project he is the director of at present concerns the community impact of introducing casinos in Sweden. Previous publications include: *Brott och straff I Sverige och Europa. En studie i komparativ kriminologi* (Kriminologiska institutionen, Stockholm: Stockholms Universitet).

Jennifer Wood has a doctorate in Criminology from the University of Toronto and has taught in the areas of policing, crime prevention and trends in governance. She is currently a Research Fellow at Security 21: International Centre for Security and Justice, Regulatory Institutions Network, Research School of Social Sciences at the Australian National University. She also functions as the General Co-ordinator of the Project for Safe and Just Communities in Argentina that is sponsored by the Canadian International Development Agency and administered by the Centre for International Studies, University of Toronto. She is currently working with Clifford Shearing and Peter Grabosky (Australian National University) and Victoria Police on an ARC Linkage grant devoted to developing and assessing models to guide the mobilisation and co-ordination of state and non-state resources in the governance of security. Publications include: 'Nodal governance, democracy, and the new "denizens"' (with Clifford Shearing) (2003) 30(3) *Journal of Law and Society* 400–19; 'Reflections on the governance of security, a normative inquiry' (with Clifford Shearing) in (2000) 1(4) *Police Practice: An International Journal* 457–76; and 'Reflections on the evolution of the concept of private policing' (with Clifford Shearing, Michael Kempa and Ryan Carrier) (1999) 7 *European Journal on Criminal Policy and Research* 197–223.

Peter Young is currently Professor of Criminology in the Department of Criminology at the University of Hull, UK. There he teaches on undergraduate and postgraduate courses in criminal justice. His distinguished academic career includes having been Director of the Centre for Criminology and the Social and Philosophical Study of Law at the University of Edinburgh; Head of School of Law at the University of Edinburgh, Member of the Parole Board of Scotland, and Director of the Institute of Criminology at the University College, Dublin. His research interests are in the comparative study of long-term crime rates and the sociology of punishment. His publications include *The Power to Punish* (edited with David Garland, 1983, Heinemann/Gower); *Crime and Criminal Justice in Scotland* (The Stationary Office: Edinburgh); 'Crime trends in Scotland since 1950' (with David Smith) in Duff, P and Hutton, N (eds), *Criminal Justice in Scotland* (Ashgate); and 'The fine as an autopunishment: power, money and discipline' in Duff, P and Hutton, N (eds), *Criminal Justice in Scotland* (Ashgate).

Contents

Introduction:
Transnational and Comparative Criminology in a Global Perspective

James Hardie-Bick, James Sheptycki and Ali Wardak

Any criminology worthy of the name should contain a comparative dimension. The contents of cultural meanings that are loaded into the subject of criminology are too variable for it to be otherwise. It is fair to say that most of the important points made by leading scholars of criminology are comparative in nature. It is just that the basis of comparison is often relatively narrow. For example, the hyphen that both separates and binds the phrase 'Anglo-American criminology' implies an obvious basis for comparison, although it remains within 'Anglophonia'. British criminology invites comparison between England, Wales, Northern Ireland and Scotland, even if the differences are too often disregarded by criminologists there. Federal systems such as Australia, Canada and the United States offer a good basis for comparative work and European criminology provides ample room for comparison, with added richness due to wide linguistic and national variability. At a real stretch comparative criminology would go for total global reach and try to touch upon matters of criminological concern on all the major populated continents of the world. Such an undertaking is rare indeed.

In fact, the criminological canon, as exemplified by the growing ranks of criminology textbooks that populate the shelves of university bookstores, has not taken much notice of global developments in its domain. Not, at least, until very recently. Issues such as the campaigns on the high seas against piracy and the slave trade (early forms of transnational policing) are most often given short shrift in criminology texts (if they are covered at all), as are contemporary issues like that of despoliation of the high seas due to toxic waste dumping or illegal fishing. Most criminology textbooks have a national focus, with perhaps a chapter on comparative criminology at the end, or a chapter on the 'globalisation of crime' in the middle, and usually a nod in the direction of early European criminologists – such as Adolphe Quetelet, Gabriel Tarde, Cesare Beccaria and Jeremy Bentham – at the beginning. In short, although criminologists are comparative by nature, they are also very often rather ethnocentric and quite parochial (see Sparks, 2001).

However, there has long been a significant vein in academic criminology that has aimed to be fully comparative. Hermann Mannheim's monumental two volume *Comparative Criminology* (1965) set the pace initially and remained, apart from a smattering of journal articles scattered across a variety of academic journals, the only significant landmark until Beirne and Nelken's (1997) edited collection admirably consolidated that literature. More recently, Gregg Barak (2000) put together a quite remarkable collection examining crime and its control in 15 'nations'.[1] Yet another example of the new interest in matters both transnational and criminological is Philip Reichel's *Handbook of Transnational Crime and Justice* (2004) which looks at the phenomena of transnational crime, and compares various national and international efforts to 'combat' such phenomena. Post-9/11, criminology became global, just as the business of crime, crime definition and crime control became matters of global concern.

Criminologists have questions of their own to ask when it comes to globalisation. The term is a difficult one. It is used to speak to different audiences, often about different institutions, processes and concerns, and for a variety of different reasons. The basic questions of comparative criminology (Why do some societies have lower crime rates? What are the differences and similarities in crime definition and control across social and cultural frontiers? How do theoretical models relating to crime translate across cultures?) are not merely academic exercises. Crime, along with a number of other issues such as war and peace and the environment, has become a public issue globally. Moreover, crime is a matter of concern at every level of governance, from the city neighbourhood to the pinnacles of the global system in such institutions as the IMF, the G8, the OECD and the United Nations. New categories of transnational crime have emerged. The passage of many international conventions has created a catalogue of them: organised crime and corruption, crimes against the environment, human trafficking and international sex tourism, to name but a few. Then too, the mobility of populations, and especially the ability of diasporic communities to maintain cultural and familial links over intercontinental distances, means that social life is not so bounded by national borders as it once was. This is an era of 'global cities' or 'multicultural cities'. As social life is lived transnationally, so too is crime manifest transnationally. As traditional comparative criminology, practised by the likes of Hermann Mannheim, is confronted by what we may refer to here loosely as the processes of transnationalisation, it changes in interesting ways. Part of the reason for this book is to explore those changes.

How to proceed beyond this point is not obvious. Some criminologists have tried to envisage or create a cross-cultural theory that would explain and predict all categories of crime. Others have aimed to test the degree of cross-cultural consensus about core categories of crime, or to compare the trajectories of crime rates in different national contexts. Still others are interested to see how this or that theoretical concept (risk, for example, or capitalism) can be used to think about

---

1 In Barak's book, each 'nation' is examined in a separate chapter, and chapters are grouped under three headings. The book thus considers six 'developed nations' (the United States, Germany, United Kingdom, New Zealand, Taiwan and the Netherlands); three 'post-traditional nations' (Ghana, Nigeria and the Navajo Nation) and six 'developing nations' (Brazil, Poland, Russia, Iran, China and India). This is a cross-national comparative study which attends to the historical records and territorial developments of crime and crime control at a fairly macro level of analysis (ie, using statistical indicators about crime, politics, economics, and society generally). The book moves between local and global perspectives and makes efforts to highlight specific and changing local conditions, such as ethnic diversity, population growth, politicisation of crime, extent of urban development, global economic marginality, and inequality, in each place. The details are fascinating, but one conclusion reached is that there can be few unambiguous generalisations about crime and crime control arising out of detailed comparison. How could it be otherwise when the unit of analysis (the nation) and that which is to be explained (crime) are both mired in ambiguity? Barak, however, has no difficulty in concluding that crime and crime control are growing and expanding enterprises worldwide. We concur.

crime in different times and places. Much of the comparative literature is limited to the OECD countries (the economically developed countries), and this begs questions about crime in places that are more peripheral to the circuits of transnational global capital. Then too, as David Garland has so eloquently described, the criminological enterprise is a particularly robust institution in countries that have experienced persistently high crime rates (Garland, 2001). It is not surprising to find that most criminologists know comparatively less about countries with low crime rates. The advent of the International Crime and Victimisation Survey, and a host of other studies analysing a variety of criminal justice statistics, has begun to add quantitative weight to the programme of comparative criminology (see Estrada and Westfelt, and Young this volume). Such advances raise methodological and interpretive challenges that need to be confronted head on.

The rhetorical import of the term 'globalisation' has prompted other criminologists to move away from comparative concerns *per se*. Instead some have begun to concentrate attention on specific forms of transnational crime (for example, Beare, 2003; Edwards and Gill, 2003). Until relatively recently, practically the only criminological topic that was explicitly transnational in focus was drug trafficking. This is no longer the case. A variety of social practices have become defined as matters of transnational or global crime concern and thriving new areas of criminology have been established. These raise new theoretical and practical issues with which traditionally nationally focused criminologists are ill-equipped to deal. Then too, when it comes to transnational and comparative criminology, the difficult problem of cultural relativism eventually comes to the fore. What is the status of criminological knowledge in a global context? Criminologists need to be sensitive to the differences in the cultural meanings of what constitutes 'crime', especially since criminological thinking remains a mode of thought which still maintains its Enlightenment roots. Ultimately, there is the problem of governance, for some people are going to want to ask ameliorative questions about the problem of crime. How do we make things better? It is not that criminology is necessarily a utopian pursuit (see Young, 1992), but even the most pessimistic criminologists need some hope if they are not to lie awake at night. Transnational and comparative criminologists are quite rightly concerned about what is to be done. The answers to such questions are not easy, and never more so than when the context is global.

These are all difficult and worthy topics of enquiry, but since there is no established paradigm for transnational and comparative criminology it is necessary to invent one. This book is an attempt to do so, or at least it is an attempt to move criminological discourse in that direction. The collection strives to show some of the central issues in comparative and transnational criminology and on as wide a geographical canvas as possible. We rejected from the outset the idea that a project such as this could be harmonised by the imposition of a particular theory. Criminology is interdisciplinary in nature, and transnational and comparative criminology are all the more so. Recognising this, our aim has been opposite to those criminologists who seek to provide a single overarching point of view or neat analytical structure. It is not that we reject such efforts as somehow completely unfeasible. Perhaps there really is something like the global risk society. Maybe the punishment-deterrence relation is a universal cultural expectation. Possibly, via a globalising war on crime rhetoric, we could bring an end to organised crime and corruption. However, we were not comfortable with the idea of imposing theoretical blinders on our readers as foregone conclusions. Instead, we wish to display variation in approaches to criminology, so that readers can engage in comparison for themselves and come to their own conclusions about the utility of the various perspectives. In putting together this collection, we were mostly interested in how criminology's global context encourages the transgression of boundaries: national, cultural and theoretical. In summary, we believe that the paradigmatic approach to transnational and comparative criminology ought to be broadly interdisciplinary, catholic in taste and open to new insights in the pursuit of justice and humanity.

In order to help make sense of the contributions to this volume, four themes have been used to organise the presentation of chapters. These are, in order of appearance: comparative criminology, area studies, transnational crimes, and transnational control responses. In the following sections of this introduction we briefly describe each of the chapters that we have grouped under these headings and try to draw out what, for us at least, are the most interesting points. We end our introduction with reference to Janet Chan's chapter, which addresses the changing nature of criminological thought in the contemporary period. As editors, we fully acknowledge that what is being left out of our summary account of each chapter probably says as much about us as editors as it does about individual contributors. We hope, nevertheless, that the following summary will help to orient the reader and encourage them to read closely, compare, contrast and transgress in their own process of discovering what makes up transnational and comparative criminology in a global context.

Comparative criminology

A good starting point for comparative criminology would be to confront the problems associated with the validity and reliability of data on crime rates and victimisation. Although some students of criminology resent it, even while others become too obsessed by it, quantification is an important element in the criminological enterprise, albeit only one. We offer here three chapters which exemplify what might be called, without any negative inference, traditional comparative criminology. The opening chapter in this section is by Felipe Estrada and Lars Westfelt. It is an analysis of crime trends in Europe over the course of the latter half of the 20th century. However, the chapter is not concerned to show the trends in an unproblematised fashion, as if the lines on the graphs speak for themselves. Estrada and Westfelt identify the 'continuity problem', that is, the difficulties associated with comparing statistical series over time. Since categories of official crime (and the way they are counted and measured) change from time to time, analysis of statistical series may lack continuity. Estrada and Westfelt also identify the 'congruity problem' which relates to a general problem in the cross-national comparison of crime statistics. There are differences in legal, statistical, and cultural definitions of crime. These differences mean that there may be a lack of congruence between different countries' categories of crime and therefore in how crime is counted and measured. None of this makes the data entirely useless,

Estrada and Westfelt show, since these problems can be partly controlled for in the process of interpretation.

They also show that it is especially important to be able to triangulate official criminal justice system statistics against alternative statistics. Crime surveys, self-reporting, hospital emergency room admissions and coroners' reporting all offer alternative sources of information about crime trends, and Estrada and Westfelt carefully explain the necessary caveats that should be made before using these data. This discussion has general methodological import that can only be understood by careful engagement with the chapter itself. All we would wish to emphasise here is their conclusion that there has been a clear trend towards increasing levels of crime in Western Europe over about a 50 year period. However, they also show that the trend is not linear, and that there is a levelling off from about the mid-1980s. Using alternative sources of data, they show that trends in violent crime especially exhibit this levelling off. Estrada and Westfelt's analysis is remarkable. They argue, in part, that public perceptions regarding increasing risks of violent crime are fanned by a sensationalist media. They suggest that, while actual levels of violent crime have not been greatly increasing, people's tolerance has changed. Citing the ideological shift from a treatment ideology to a neo-classicist focus on just deserts, they account for the perception of increasing levels of violent crime, at the same time that a less alarming statistical picture is emerging. Contradictory impulses have led to an increasing propensity to report acts of violence, which in turn has led to a situation exhibiting all the classic characteristics of a deviancy amplification spiral. This suggests that crime control policy in Europe is at least partly fuelled by alarmism. It follows that comparative criminologists should, without being overly sanguine, be cautious in their interpretations of statistical data so as to provide an accurate picture and avoid fuelling an overreaction.

Criminologists have pondered changes in crime rates ever since the Belgian Adolphe Quetelet undertook to analyse the first nationally compiled statistics in France at the beginning of the 19th century. The use of national crime statistics by academic criminologists must be undertaken with caution for, as Peter Young explains in his contribution, these data were not invented with a view to providing theoretical understanding, but rather as an instrument for the control and management of populations. Young reviews the reasons why criminologists need to approach national criminal statistics with some caution, but goes on to show how they can throw real light on issues of genuinely academic interest. Using data from Scotland and Ireland, he shows how the production and interpretation of criminal statistics are intertwined. Such intertwining has consequences for the practices of penal welfarism, aetiological questions about the relationship between crime and social structure, and other theoretical and practical concerns as played out in strictly national contexts. All of this becomes particularly interesting when comparative criminologists and governmental programmers seek to use national crime statistics for the purposes of 'benchmarking'. In so doing they thus confront issues of philosophical and sociological import that can only be properly answered by reference to particular data. Further, the cross-national comparison of national crime statistics is becoming a feature of transnational governance, of the control and management of populations transnationally. Young's analysis of two specific jurisdictions provides both particular and general lessons that help to promote an understanding of how academic criminology fits into this picture.

Comparative criminology invites much more than a comparative analysis of crime trends across jurisdictional boundaries. It also requires thoughtful reflection. Enlightenment assumptions still lie at the heart of the culture of the modern West. These assumptions are, *inter alia*: the unity and inherent rationalism of humanity, the individual as the creative force in society and history, the superiority of the West, science as truth, and the belief in social progress. The culture that harbours these assumptions is now in a state of crisis. Signs of cultural turmoil are everywhere: in the resurgence of religious fundamentalism, in the declining authority of key social and political institutions, in the enfeeblement of political ideologies and parties, and in the cultural wars over literary and aesthetic canons and paradigms of knowledge (Seidman, 1998, p 1). But exactly how does such a 'crisis' affect the criminological imagination?

This turmoil is connected to the difficult question of 'relativism'. If truth simply depends on one's point of view, and each perspective is equally as valid as the other, how can the criminologist find a way to proceed in an intelligent and critical manner? In his contribution, James Sheptycki argues that sociological and philosophical reflection is central to the comparative spirit. However, he does not advocate an unfettered relativism and argues that, precisely because there are no universally accepted definitions of crime, comparative criminologists need to do more that simply insist that crime is a relative concept. Relativism seems complacent and ill-placed when confronting the brutal reality of violence and crime globally. This echoes Cohen (2001) who has argued that the ideas of what he calls the postmodern cultural left are dangerous. According to Cohen many of the ideas relating to the relativistic nature of morality and values are:

> ... simply ludicrous. And as long as they remain in seminar rooms, conferences and *curricula vitae*, they are harmless fun. But when they circulate noisily in middlebrow and even mass culture, they begin to supplement the inventory of denials available to the powerful. This was not intended. Nor, of course, do tyrants have to read postmodernist philosophy to get the moral go ahead for doing what they have always done. But tyrants too live today under the meta-rules of globalisation and reflexivity. They need new and better stories – designer accounts to offer in the General Assembly, to visiting plenipotentiaries from the IMF, the World Bank and WTO, and even the fact finding mission from Human Rights Watch. (2001, p 280)

Sheptycki suggests that the way to proceed is to take the aggregate science of criminology seriously, including its relativistic second thoughts, in order to judge truth as earnestly and absolutely as can be, always subject to revision. He ends cautiously suggesting that transnational and comparative criminologists seeking to interpret and act in world of flux and change might find at least some existential ground by reference to human rights philosophy: what is fear and suffering for one is fear and suffering for another.

Area studies

The contributions that make up our first section, as different as they are from each other, all pertain to traditional issues in comparative criminology. If that is all there was to it, we might not have been so interested to undertake the project that is this book. As academic criminologists, we have observed that students of criminology (among which we count ourselves) are quite often unaware of the broad facts of geography and history that make the task of comparative criminology so interesting. The second section of this collection is our way of trying to address this problem. As we see it, in order to undertake comparative criminology in a global context, it is necessary to devote time to understanding how the cultural and political histories of different regions of the world serve to establish distinctive points of view about criminology and its object. But criminologists are not necessarily aware of Latin American political and economic history, or the anthropology of Muslim customary law, or how the geography of 'Eastern' Europe affects its place in global illicit markets, or any one of a myriad other relevant knowledges outside of the 'core' disciplinary competences of criminology (however any particular criminologist might choose to define 'core competence'). In section two, we therefore offer a series of studies from different regional perspectives. These incorporate non-criminological knowledge(s) into the analysis where the authors consider it relevant to do so.

Ali Wardak's study of social control in Saudi Arabia takes the vocabulary of social control theorists from the West and applies it to the structures of formal and informal social control in one of the most devoted Muslim countries of the world. In addition to providing much needed background understanding of what makes Saudi society tick, Wardak also shows the fruitful utility of using Western theoretical notions for studying other cultures. At the heart of this chapter, however, lies a prosaic criminological question, and that has to do with how we understand the apparently low crime rate in Saudi Arabia. The answer is complex and it has to do with the way that formal, semi-formal and informal social control mechanisms and institutions work on, and through, individual people and, further, how these three levels of social controlling interrelate with each other. Ultimately, the embedded Saudi system of social controlling is challenged by processes of globalisation of which it is a part. Symptomatic of this are emerging discourses about women's unfreedom, the conditions of foreign guest workers, and how Saudi Arabia is configured in the global Muslim Diaspora. Wardak gives a sense of all of this and more. In asking questions about the balance of freedom and control in Saudi Arabia, Wardak is doing no more, or less, than criminologists ought to do in respect of their own cultures. Let us be clear and say that comparative criminology is not about casting aspersions. We do not believe that comparative and transnational criminology has any role to play in the so-called 'clash of civilisations'. Rather, our view is that criminology, like another mode or topic of academic enquiry is, at heart, a way of coming to terms with ourselves.

Those used to operating on the bad edge of the world system are apt to be critical of academic criminological discourse as it is practised in the universities of the advanced capitalist West. Biko Agozino's consideration of West Africa is a case in point. He offers a post-colonial critique of the criminological gaze as it pertains to that region. His analysis is shot through with elements of postmodern irony, but his contribution to this collection also works to fill in the details – historical, political, legal, journalistic – that potential students of transnational and comparative criminology do not often have at their finger tips. Regardless of what labels might be applied to his analysis, and to what theories the author himself refers, there can be little doubt that the chapter represents something other than Western ethnocentric criminology. Especially when read alongside other contributions to this book, this chapter should work to promote a better understanding about issues of crime and violence in regions that are peripheral to global capitalism. More often than not, the situation in places like West Africa is simply incomprehensible to criminologists. If nothing else, Agozino shows that it need not be.

This contribution is followed by another chapter that considers transformations in the police apparatus of post-apartheid South Africa. Anne-Marie Singh's analysis of these processes leans on an entirely different theoretical understanding. She uses the governmentality literature to cast light on how neo-liberal principles, operating in connection with local and contingent factors in South Africa, have served to recast in specific ways both state and private institutions' claims to the capacity to organise coercion. She shows how private corporations and private interests in South Africa have remained world leaders in legitimising their own capacities for mustering organised violence in the maintenance of a particular social order viz: the South African manifestation of neo-liberalism.

It is worth stressing again that comparing and reading across the different chapters in this book can be productive of insights the contributors themselves did not foresee. It is by so doing that the reader will discover that the whole is, indeed, more than the sum of the book's parts. For example, how different would our understanding of the contrasts between Western and Southern Africa be if these authors had traded analytical lenses? There is no reason to suppose, at the outset, that one part of Africa is better understood through the theoretical perspective of post-colonial theory and the other by reference to governmentality. What differences do theories make to our understanding of the brute facts of crime and crime control in different parts of the world? What differences do the facts make to the choice of theory? These seem to us to be obvious questions to ask – and we hope that through the readers' own process of reading, reflection and synthesis they might discover their own answers.

The next chapter in this section considers Singapore, a famously orderly and disciplined society. The darker side of this is that successful and comprehensive regulation may provide a justification for essentially repressive laws: the Singapore solution. Narayanan Ganapathy's examination of this island state's policing casts light on the impossibility of detaching crime and criminal justice data from their social, economic and political contexts. He questions the usefulness of separating issues of 'crime' from 'crime control', particularly in a paternalistic and authoritarian regime. The relationship between crime and crime control is quite central to the concerns of comparative criminology. Ganapathy argues that any investigation into, and appreciation of, the crime problem must necessarily evaluate the sources and constructions of knowledge on the nature and extent of crimes as well as the objectives of crime control in *particular* socio-historical periods. As readers will learn, this is especially important in the Singapore context because the state police are the only agency that has the resources and legitimate authority to collate and communicate information about crime (especially quantitative information) to the general populace. In the absence of alternative sources of data, knowledge of the crime problem and processes of crime control in Singapore are primarily state-defined and ideologically propagated. Having said that, Ganapathy's critical realism also shows that there are contradictory impulses present in Singaporean society. While he eschews simplistic talk of 'police models', he does show that, in Singapore, policing tends to be readily aligned with the 'authoritarian' model of policing where a strong political dynamic dominates a weak social dynamic. At the same time, he shows that Singaporean policing also displays features of Anglo-Saxon community policing based on the idea of policing by consent. When it comes to policing in Singapore, there is a space between, and that offers a vantage point for critical reflection and analysis.

Singapore is one place where East meets West in the frenzy of consumerism. In the contemporary period, the People's Republic of China is undergoing a different process of transition, as the formerly Maoist state hitches its productive capacities to the requirements of global capitalism. Carol Jones' descriptive analysis of this process of change shows how the response to crime in Maoist China (always a highly politicised affair) has changed over the recent past. The result is not, as the Chinese authorities might articulate it at present, a distancing of politics from crime. Criminal law in China remains politics by other means. In all societies, crime and law are partly shaped by history, tradition and culture. But they are also shaped by how regimes harness these to alter or preserve the status quo. China is often spoken of as 'different from the West', and its relatively low crime rates are often attributed to its Confucian heritage, which is said to emphasise harmony, stability, social solidarity and consensus. In their search for the recipe for the crime-free society, criminologists may become mesmerised by such talk, and Jones' chapter is a useful antidote to this. Confucianism has been rehabilitated by the Chinese state, and its supposed reverence for hierarchy, strong leadership and authoritarian rule has been used to legitimise the use of strong measures against anyone and anything which challenges the regime. While this has the superficial appearance of something quite exotic and different, Jones' close attention to the details of the case reveals that the war on crime in China describes the policing of anything which threatens China's economy, be it economic crime, public protest, demonstrations and strikes, or other types of 'traditional' crime. How different is this really from the practices of zero tolerance policing in North America? The devil is in the detail, of course, but it does seem possible to say that, like many Western countries, China is caught in a crime control spiral from which escape will prove extremely difficult. Observing China's emergence as the penal workshop of global capitalism and comparing it with developments elsewhere, one of the conclusions that comparative and transnational criminologists might draw is that the governance of crime, and indeed governance *through* crime, has become global.

The transnationalisation of crime governance is not new. It has been ongoing for some time, and as we observe the process of building transnational institutions for that aim to governmentalise 'global crime', we observe an interesting convergence between the theoretical discourses of international relations and criminology. International relations realism meets criminological realism. Transnational criminologists have made a crucial interdisciplinary leap. The disciplinary difference is that criminologists have traditionally been concerned with the internal order of states, whereas international relations theorists have traditionally been concerned with order between states. In a world that has gone global, the boundaries between the internal and external order of the state have become blurred. Realist theories pertaining both to international relations and criminology intersect, as do the practices implied by the theories, and normative questions about the nature of police power become clearly recognisable as common to both disciplines. This observation reinforces a central theme of this volume: that transnational and comparative criminology are intertwined and interdisciplinary.

Transnational crime issues

It is probably true to say that, historically, nothing coloured public discourse about global crime more than the concept of organised crime, although terrorism has eclipsed the term somewhat of late. Theorising about the organisation of crime is difficult and fraught, and yet there is a tendency to use the words 'organised crime' unproblematically, as if everyone were talking about the same thing (this is also true of the term 'terrorism'). We did not set out to address this specifically when looking for contributions on transnational crime, but that is the way things turned out. In retrospect, this is hardly surprising since, during the late 1990s and early part of this century, specific categories of crime (involving transnational illicit markets, economic crime, financial crime and illegal immigration, to name some of the more obvious) became such important issues in transnational governance. These types of crime are organised, in the sense that they require some collective action, a division of labour and pursue the rational aim of profit making (albeit by illegal means). Criminological thinking ought to be up to the task of analysing these forms of criminality as they go transnational. After all, critical consideration of the concept of the phenomenon goes back at least to Morris and Hawkins' classic essay 'Organised crime and God' (1969), while it is well over a quarter of a century since Mary McIntosh wrote the definitive essay on the social organisation of crime (1975). However, as has been argued in a number of recent contributions to the literature (Beare, 2003; Edwards and Gill, 2003), when it comes to thinking about the organisation of crime in a transnational context, there is a danger that more nuanced discussions will be jettisoned in favour of no nonsense 'tough on crime' rhetoric. Such rhetoric is of little practical value since it merely results in the advocation of simple solutions to complex problems.

Here we present a selection of chapters on organised crime, white collar crime, corruption and sex trafficking, and each shows somewhat different perspectives on the organisation of transnational crimes. As the theoretical language shifts, the object (organised criminality) also changes. In the not too distant past, authors of criminological textbooks would routinely bemoan the lack of emphasis on 'crimes of the powerful'. One question that might be asked after reading the chapters collected here is: what do criminologists understand by 'power' when they talk about crimes of the powerful and how has this changed as a result of globalisation? Organised gangsters have a kind of power in (but perhaps not over) illicit markets. Politicians and white collar professionals have access to a different kind of social power and so to different criminal opportunity structures. The confluence of illegal immigration and the sex industry operates at a specific juncture of social power that is different again. Criminologists of a transnational and comparative bent need, we think, to continue to refine their conceptual vocabulary in order to describe better the various conjunctions of criminal opportunity manifest in a global context. As the chapters presented here also show, these are not purely academic matters. Issues of governance and policy derive from these definitional issues.

Our first chapter in this section, by Adam Edwards, focuses on what we might call 'traditional organised crime' which emphasises the linkages between global and local illicit markets. Edwards probes the 'glocality' of subterranean criminal networks participating in transnational clandestine markets. This highly nuanced analysis emphasises the importance of understanding the context of criminal opportunity and carefully abstains from warfare rhetoric to instead pursue other policy options. Edwards' interest in transnational illicit markets can be nicely contrasted with Hazel Croall's discussion of white collar crime. She explicitly plays on the analytical distinction between 'organised crime' and 'white collar crime'. Among other things, she asks how we might evaluate the global impact of the latter and, in so doing, grapples with the question: is globalisation criminogenic? She argues that many economically and socially harmful activities find space to flourish in the climate of deregulation and have become morally justifiable in the context of global neo-liberalism. But she also notes that many of these harmful activities are not necessarily defined transnationally as criminal. In coming to terms with these chapters, readers will see how a fairly long-standing debate within criminology has been extended into its present transnational context. Bill Tupman's chapter reinforces questions about the ambivalence of the control response (transnational and otherwise) when it comes to crimes perpetrated by persons of respectability. He proceeds from an avowedly interdisciplinary perspective to look at the political structures of opportunity that shape the transnational practices of corruption and tries to understand how these are activated at the individual level through the application of game theory. He also surveys the institutional responses to corruption developed in the Americas and in Europe during the latter years of the 1990s and up to the present. Ultimately, he shows that policy makers' neglect of the theoretical discussions, and the coincidental irresolution with which the many institutions of transnational governance have treated the problem, has allowed corruption to flourish. This, in turn, has been detrimental to the institution of trust, which is itself vital for the support of markets and democracy that are supposed to be the beneficial outcomes of globalisation.

The last chapter in this section, by Jo Goodey, presents an analysis of the development of policy and practice within the territory of the European Union for answering problems of so-called human trafficking, especially in the context of the sex industry. This is a very particular manifestation of organised illicit activity. In part, she shows how strictly criminological thinking in policy making may disadvantage victimological concerns, ultimately compromising the aims of policy. Her analysis of policy measures regarding sex trafficking reveals a tension between victimological and criminological approaches to the phenomenon. Criminology inscribes different practices than victimology and each differentially affects the possibility of just and humane policy outcomes. When concern for victims is outweighed by determination to punish offenders, the social basis of social policy (transnational and otherwise) is affected in important ways. This problem is manifest transnationally because institutions of transnational governance, not least the European Union, act as conduits for ideas about what constitutes best practice in the social response to the participation of illegal immigrants in the illicit and semi-licit sex trade. If nothing else, Goodey's work in this field might help to shift discussion about the transnationalisation of the sex industry away from its limited focus on crime and border controls to include concerns about the humanity of its victims.

These are all pressing issues, especially for an up and coming generation of criminologists. Distilling them down into one or two essential points risks distorting the ambiguity with which each of our contributors has struggled. Nevertheless, it is probably safe to say that all of them would agree that the choice of theoretical vocabulary matters for how we understand what passes for the 'objective facts' of transnational crime; that several disciplinary perspectives, rather than one master discourse, contribute to better criminological understanding; and that ultimately, good policy ought to take some account of people's intuitions about justice and humanity. Agreeing on this much does not make things any easier. Policy making (and non-making) is ongoing in the institutions of transnational governance and this has implications for how 'the crime problem' is manifest globally. Again it seems necessary to emphasise that criminological expertise is considerably challenged in this environment, a point to which we shall return in our conclusion.

Issues in transnational control responses

Quite a bit of the discussion that emerges on the back of previous chapters concerns what is to be done regarding the problem of transnational crime and, indeed, crime considered in its global context. In part four of this collection we offer some selections that shed theoretical and empirical light on the control institutions themselves.

Firstly Jennifer Wood and Michael Kempa develop the theme of policing as new nodal governance. According to this view, recognising the 'plural', 'multi-laterised' or 'nodal' nature of policing has opened up new conceptual spaces regarding policing governance and the governance of policing. The concept of nodal governance signals recognition that policing and security are guaranteed by both the formal public institutions of criminal justice and by organisations within civil society. It aims to rejuvenate the ideals of democratic policing for a contemporary context in which the global and the local have become inextricably linked. The conception is particularly used to highlight the options of harnessing private and non-profit institutions, which have the potential to further public safety, human rights and conflict resolution. Policing through new nodal governance is democratic policing. Formal policing institutions necessarily play a role at the strategic planning levels and policing agencies are encouraged through this approach to continue to develop along the lines of community policing models mapped out over the past two decades. However, it differs from previous versions of community policing because it begins with an acknowledgment that public policing capacity needs to be enhanced via an enhanced interface with external institutions in the private and non-profit sectors, and also acknowledges the global-local simultaneity of much policing activity. Policing governance is not law enforcement. Lest the idea of plural nodes of policing leading to a just and humane social order seem utopian, it should be stressed here that the conceptual work presented here draws on observations about policing in very difficult social and political circumstances, for example in Northern Ireland and South Africa. The goal of imagining how democratic policing can be built in such situations could scarcely be more challenging, but it is not necessarily impossible. In the recent past many countries have been undertaking attempts at transition to democracy. In places such as Brazil, Argentina, Ukraine, Nigeria and South Africa, policing and other criminal justice agencies have been subjected to processes of transition and reform towards more democratic forms (International Council on Human Rights Policy, 2003). All the while, in established democracies as well as in less favoured nations, there is an evident discordance between the theory and practice of democratic policing (Human Rights Watch, 2003). While the goal may seem illusive, the alternative is the further destruction of social capital by ever more militarised policing and ever harsher penal regimes (Mendes *et al*, 1999).

Theories about the democratic capacities of new nodal governance are being worked out practically every day. How policing might evolve transnationally over the coming years is difficult to predict. Perhaps future developments will continue on similar trajectories, and so futurologists might content themselves with the overview offered here, by Paul Norman, of the evolution of Euro-policing during the tumultuous decade of the 1990s. He shows that the security consciousness of Euro-policing easily pre-dates the declaration of a worldwide war on terrorism signalled after the events of 11 September 2001. Concerns about (in)security have long underpinned the continuous expansion of the net of Euro-policing outwith the confines of the European territory, as well as the refinement of that net within that territory. This ought to raise questions about the democratic accountability of the institutions of transnational policing (Sheptycki, 2002a; 2002b; 2004). Readers will have to decide for themselves to what extent panels of unelected experts and governmental technicians are best placed to make decisions about how best to provide for human security, locally, transnationally and globally.

Paraphrasing David Smith's editorial in the first issue of the *European Journal of Criminology* (2004), comparative criminology has a distinctive role that sets it apart from common sense opinion, and this has never been more true than it is in the contemporary (transnational) context. Globally, criminology does not have a single coherent, integrated body of knowledge or practice, nor should it. Criminology depends on the input of scholars from many disciplines. Students of criminology all contribute to a continuous renewal of the collective understanding of crime and crime control, and recombine it with new knowledge in a more or less systematic effort to build on it. Everyone has a stake in both security and freedom and it is just as well that we all work to understand the complex processes that influence the balance between them. That is why we do not impose simple answers to the questions raised in this book, but rather encourage readers to think for themselves. That is, in our view, what criminological scholarship is about.

Conclusion

A frequent problem with edited collections is that they end but they do not conclude. We have chosen to round off this collection with a chapter by Janet Chan, which has been adapted from an earlier article published in the *Australian and New Zealand Journal of Criminology*. Her conclusions are her own, of course, but we adopt them as ours. Her chapter offers a detailed overview of the state of criminological theory under conditions of globalisation and reflexive modernisation. This is a complex undertaking and any who are interested to get to grips with transnational and comparative criminology will be repaid handsomely by engaging with her argument.

Globally, criminology operates amidst countervailing tendencies. In the contemporary period there is a palpable decline in the authority of academics in many fields, not least in criminology. At the same time, Chan shows, using empirical examples, that criminologists can successfully educate policy makers and the general public about the dangers of mindlessly importing foreign solutions to local crime problems. Criminologists can also successfully educate with regard to transnational trends and global developments in their field of expertise. The many cross-currents of globalisation exert strong pressures on societies around the world and some of the negative manifestations of this are within the purview of criminology. Transnational and comparative criminology is in its infancy as an academic pursuit. It is coming into a world that is inclined to doubt its efficacy and is therefore puny in comparison to the many other interests that shape the nature and quality of both global governance and governance globally. Nevertheless, it is by studying the local and the particular, by relating what they find to an understanding of the general and the global, and by acting transnationally, that criminologists are able to influence the future turn of events, promote what is good about global society and contest some of its less desirable influences.

We embarked on this book project in 2001, after talking about it for several years, and did so with a good deal of trepidation. Criminology – that is the putative science for defining, measuring and governing 'the crime problem' – is, we believe, now thoroughly implicated in the project of globalisation. Academic criminology is only slowly beginning to develop the theoretical sophistication to be able to participate fully in this global discourse. Academic criminologists are writers and thinkers and, for the most part, they are far from the action. And yet the day of the armchair criminologist is over, if indeed there ever was such a time. It can be clearly seen that too much crime and violence is taking place before the very eyes of world society, which neither spares applause nor sheds virtuous tears before reaching for the remote in order to change channels. There are remarkable scholars who dare to leave the television and the wired world in order to delve into the real world of transnational and comparative crime; we cite Gunst's outstanding book *Born fi' Dead: A Journey Through the Jamaican Posse Underworld* (1995) as one example. However, even while it is seldom created within the sound of real gunfire, transnational and comparative criminology has begun to shed much needed light on a perplexing subject.

In trying to put together a collection of readings that would answer the need for a comparative and transnational criminology capable of playing a positive role globally, we shared similar concerns to those expressed here by Janet Chan. How will academic criminologists both contest and test the appropriateness of various practical options and encourage theoretical diversity, while at the same time not risking that the discipline will degenerate into a fog of competing claims and counterclaims amidst an overabundance of theoretical frameworks? This collection is the result of our efforts. We are not alone in attempting to take criminology out of its traditional parochial confines inside national states. Many are now awakening to the global possibilities of criminological discourse. It remains to be seen what the lasting consequences of all of this will be.

References

Anderson, M, den Boer, M, Cullen, P, Gilmore, B, Raab, C and Walker, N (1995) *Policing the European Union*, Oxford: Clarendon

Barak, Gregg (ed) (2000) *Crime and Crime Control: A Global View*, London: Greenwood Press

Beare, M (ed) (2003) *Critical Reflections on Transnational Organized Crime, Money Laundering and Corruption*, Toronto: Toronto UP

Beirne, P and Nelken, D (eds) (1997) *Issues in Comparative Criminology*, Aldershot: Ashgate

Cohen, S (2001) *States of Denial: Knowing About Atrocities and Suffering*, Cambridge: Polity

Deflem, M (2002) *Policing World Society*, Oxford: Clarendon

van Dijk, J (1999) 'The experience of crime and justice', in Newman, G (ed), *The Global Report on Crime and Justice*, New York: OUP together with the United Nations Office for Drug Control and Crime Prevention

Edwards, A and Gill, P (eds) (2003) *Transnational Organised Crime: Perspectives on Global Security*, London: Routledge

Garland, D (2001) *The Culture of Control: Crime and Social Order in Contemporary Society*, Oxford: OUP

Gunst, L (1995) *Born fi' Dead: A Journey Through the Jamaican Posse Underworld*, New York: H Holt

Human Rights Watch (2003) *Human Rights Watch World Report 2003*, New York: Human Rights Watch

International Council on Human Rights Policy (2003) *Crime, Public Order and Human Rights*, Versoix, Switzerland: International Council on Human Rights Policy

Mannheim, H (1965) *Comparative Criminology*, two volumes, London: Routledge and Kegan Paul

McIntosh, M (1975) *The Organisation of Crime*, London: Macmillan and the British Sociological Association

Mendes, E, Zuckerberg, J, Lecorre, S, Gabriel, A and Clark, JA (1999) *Democratic Policing and Accountability: Global Perspectives*, Aldershot: Ashgate

Morris, N and Hawkins, G (1969) 'Organized crime and God', in Morris, N and Hawkins, G, *The Honest Politician's Guide to Crime Control*, Chicago: Chicago UP

Reichel, P (ed) (2004) *The Handbook of Transnational Crime and Justice*, London: Sage

Seidman, S (1998) 'Introduction', in Seidman, S (ed), *The Postmodern Turn: New Perspectives on Social Theory*, Cambridge: CUP

Sheptycki, JWE (2002a) 'Accountability across the policing field: towards a general cartography of accountability for postmodern policing' 12(4) *Policing and Society Special Issue on Police Accountability in Europe* (Guest editor, Monica den Boer) 323–38

Sheptycki, JWE (2002b) 'La problème de la responsabilité et de l'action policière sous tous ses aspects: pour une cartographie générale de la responsabilité en matière de police à l'ère postmoderne' 48 *Cultures et Conflits*, Hiver, 81–108

Sheptycki, JWE (2004) 'The accountability of transnational policing institutions: the strange case of Interpol' 19(1) *Canadian Journal of Law and Society* 107

Smith, D (2004) 'Editorial: criminology in the wider Europe' 1(1) *European Journal of Criminology* 5–16

Sparks, R (2001) 'Degrees of estrangement: the cultural theory of risk and contemporary penology' 5(2) *Theoretical Criminology* 159–76

Young, P (1992) 'The importance of Utopias in criminological thinking' 32(4) *British Journal of Criminology* 423–37

Part I

Comparative Criminology

International Crime Trends: Sources of Comparative Crime Data and Post-War Trends in Western Europe[1]

Lars Westfelt and Felipe Estrada

Introduction

Comparative analyses of crime trends show that the level of crime has increased in practically all Western European countries during the post-war period (for example, Gurr, 1978; Wilson and Herrnstein, 1985; Smith, 1995; Westfelt, 2001). There are however a number of problems associated with the study of crime over a period of several decades. The task is not made easier by the additional cross-national comparative element. Official crime statistics are the most accessible source of data and, therefore, also that which the majority of comparative analyses are based on. As we will show in this chapter, however, their use is problematical. Our knowledge of longitudinal changes in reporting behaviour, as well as judicial and policing practices, is all too often unsystematic and incomplete. It is therefore wise to nourish a healthy scepticism in the face of claims that crime statistics actually describe 'real' crime trends.

The aim of the chapter is to present and discuss the available data relating to crime trends in Western European countries during the post-war period (1950–99). The first section opens with a discussion of different methodological approaches for the study of international crime trends. This section goes on to examine sources of comparative crime data such as Interpol and the International Crime Victims Survey (ICVS). We outline the availability, strengths and weaknesses of various kinds of official and alternative crime data. Thereafter, we illustrate a number of the methodological issues involved in using empirical data on crime trends in Western Europe. Here, three sub-sections deal specifically with the overall crime trend and trends in violent crime and youth crime.

Methodological issues for comparative analyses of crime trends

This section examines some methodological issues associated with comparative research in crime trends. The first relates to the choice of countries to be included in the comparison, the second to the collection of data and the third to the type of data that are to be employed.

The most similar v the most different approach

As regards the question of which countries are suitable for comparison, there are two fundamental approaches. The 'most different' approach looks to include countries whose structure and culture are as unlike one another as possible, whereas the 'most similar' approach seeks to compare countries that are alike one another in these regards (see Teune, 1979; Marshall and Marshall, 1983; McClintock

---

1 This chapter is mainly based on Estrada (1999, 2001) and Westfelt (2001).

and Wikström, 1987; Lieberson, 1991; Tranøy, 1993). The literature contains a number of different recommendations as to when one of these methods is to be preferred over the other. The 'most different' method is often deemed appropriate where the approach is more deductive and where the objective is to test the generalisability of a given theory. When the objective is instead to build up a theory by means of induction, the 'most similar' approach is recommended (Marshall and Marshall, 1983). According to McClintock and Wikström (1987), the 'most different' approach may be preferable where theories are to be examined by means of hypothesis testing. When findings with relevance for crime policy are sought, on the other hand, the 'most similar' approach may be more appropriate. In addition, these authors suggest that in the context of a policy study, it may be of interest to examine the different ways in which countries deal with crime, whereas in a 'theoretical study', interest is focused more on how differences between countries are associated with variations in crime.

When it comes to explaining similarities and differences, it has been suggested that the correct choice will depend on the outcome of the dependent variable. If, for example, one is looking to explain a difference in crime trends (the dependent variable), then a sample of countries that are similar to one another in other respects (independent variables) is appropriate since, in theory, this allows one to ignore these similarities and to limit the number of differences that might be chosen as possible explanations.[2]

Similarly, the 'most different' approach is to be preferred when it is similarities in the dependent variable that are to be explained. This approach then minimises the congruencies that might possibly explain the similarities in the dependent variable. In a situation where the outcome on the dependent variable is unknown and itself constitutes the objective of the initial phase of a study, this line of reasoning cannot of course be applied. In the context of a broad study involving a large number of countries, the 'most similar' strategy might be employed in connection with the initial sample, after which different methods or approaches may be used to guide subsequent, smaller samples (Tranøy, 1993, p 27).

Meta-studies

A sensible way to begin a comparative study is to take advantage of the analyses already carried out by researchers in the relevant countries; that is, to conduct a kind of meta-analysis. It is reasonable, after all, to assume that such researchers know a good deal about the factors that affect their domestic crime statistics. The validity of a meta-study will depend upon whether its conclusions are grounded in adequate descriptions of crime trends in the various countries included. It is vital that these descriptions are sufficiently representative. The issue is the degree to which the studies referred to contain all the relevant information available in the countries in question. Researchers often have differing opinions. How are we to know that the researchers whose studies form the basis for the meta-analyses are those whose work best represents the available research in these countries? The honest answer is that we can't be certain. Insofar as researchers have similar chances of getting their analyses published, a review of databases ought to produce a

---

2   This might be described as amounting to an automatic 'standardisation' of variables.

reasonably undistorted sample. One might still object that analyses of national crime trends are often not intended for an international audience, and that they are therefore rarely published in international scientific journals. An important part of a comparative meta-analysis therefore involves contacting researchers from the different countries in order to improve the availability of relevant data. Meta-studies are of necessity based on data that was produced for other purposes. For this reason, the indicators used and the periods studied often vary to a certain extent between the different countries.

Available data

Crime statistics

The study of crime trends over the post-war period requires indicators that extend over time of course. Official crime statistics constitute the only available systematic source of data of this kind. The primary sources of international crime statistics are Interpol, HEUNI (UN), WHO (UN) and the Council of Europe (Newman, 1999). Whilst a number of countries have conducted victim surveys with the objective of charting the general population's experience of criminal victimisation, comparing data across these surveys is difficult, and the furthest these data extend back in time is to the mid-1970s. It is only since the end of the 1980s that attempts have been made to produce internationally comparable victim surveys (van Dijk *et al*, 1990; van Dijk and Mayhew, 1993; Mayhew and van Dijk, 1997; van Kesteren *et al*, 2000).

The validity of official crime statistics as an indicator of both crime trends and the amount of crimes committed has been discussed at length within the field of criminological research. The problems associated with the dark figure, that is, the relationship between the number of reported offences and the 'actual' number of offences committed,[3] as well as those associated with changes in legislation and policy, are well known within the field and must be given due consideration. One general conclusion as to the validity of official crime statistics, for which the literature provides substantial support, is that (police) statistics provide a better picture of trends in *serious* (traditional)[4] offending. Which is to say that the relatively large proportion of unreported crimes are to a substantial extent comprised of offences where the value of the loss or damage involved is low and/or where physical injuries are minor (for example, Huang, 1993; Coleman and Moynihan, 1996).[5]

---

3 Important factors assumed to have an effect on the propensity to report crime include: the nature of the relationship between victim and perpetrator; the seriousness of the offence; the general attitude towards crime; and whether or not the object of the crime is covered by an insurance policy.

4 The term 'traditional crime' refers primarily to violent and property offences. It might be added that the majority of these offences are offences that for the most part only come to the attention of the police when they are reported by the public. By contrast, many so called modern offences are instead such as must be 'discovered' by the police in the course of their work in order to be recorded.

5 There are a number of exceptions, however. Two examples include serious offences where the persons involved are close to one another, and crimes that take place within groups where levels of criminal involvement are high. For a discussion of results from victim surveys and self-report studies on the propensity to report crime in different countries, see, for example, Skogan (1984).

Comparing crime statistics across different countries does nothing to reduce the level of problems associated with this indicator. Some researchers are highly sceptical about the possibilities of carrying out such comparisons (for example, Scott and Al-Thakeb, 1980; Wilkins, 1980). Others contend that the task is made practicable by focusing the analysis on *trends* rather than *levels* (Council of Europe, 1982; Archer and Gartner, 1984; Bennett and Lynch, 1990). The point of departure for the present work is that basing an analysis on trends in time series, rather than on crime levels, makes it possible to conduct comparisons.[6] Isolated annual fluctuations are also excluded from the analysis. The basic assumption made in the comparative analysis of crime trends is that possible shifts in these trends are to be interpreted as representing real changes if the legal and statistical conditions on which the statistics are based may reasonably be excluded as an explanation.[7] At the practical level, however, the difficulty lies in collecting a sufficient amount of 'background information' relating to the international statistical series that are to be included in the analysis. This constitutes one of the reasons for excluding isolated annual fluctuations from the analysis; the risk for making erroneous interpretations is diminished when the focus of the analysis is directed solely at the overall trends. What then are the most important problems that arise in connection with an analysis of trends in crime statistics from different countries? First and foremost, it may be noted that such an analysis includes the dimensions of both time and space. In order to frame the problems in terms of these different dimensions, two constructs have been borrowed from the literature in this area (von Hofer, 1991; Westfelt, 2001):

(1) *The continuity problem* – relates to difficulties associated with comparing statistical series over time (see the examples presented below).

(2) *The congruity problem* – relates to all the problems associated with comparing statistics across different countries. Simply choosing not to focus on crime levels does not mean that one avoids all the comparability problems associated with comparative analysis. It is important to identify differences in legal, statistical and cultural definitions of crime in order to be able to find comparable offence categories. The objective is naturally to achieve as great a degree of similarity as possible in the content of the categories to be compared (see the examples presented below).

In addition, three additional factors should be mentioned, all of which have a fundamental effect on statistics. These are *statistical conditions, legal conditions,* and *real world conditions.* The following figure cross-tabulates these conditions with the two dimensions described above (Westfelt, 2001):

---

6 There are crime types for which cross-national comparisons of levels are in fact possible. Such crimes are those for which alternative data sources are available and/or for which the propensity to report is very high.

7 The term 'real changes' also refers to shifts in the propensity to report crime. The dark figure problem is not quite so difficult to deal with in relation to analyses of trends, however, as it is in relation to comparisons of crime levels. When comparing levels, the proportion of crimes that remain unreported has to be the same across the countries included in the comparison. Trend comparisons, on the other hand, only require that the proportion of unreported offences is more or less constant over time.

Table 1: Cross-tabulation of methodological problems and conditions affecting crime statistics.

	Continuity problem	Congruity problem	
Statistical conditions	Changes to (formal) rules governing the collection and production of statistics as well as the (informal) application of these rules over time.	Differences between countries regarding the (formal) rules governing the collection and production of statistics as well as the (informal) application of these rules.	A
Legal conditions	(Formal) changes in the formulation of legislation/legal process and (informal) changes to praxis over time.	(Formal) differences between countries regarding legislation and legal process and (informal) differences relating to their application/praxis.	B
Real world conditions	Changes in the propensity to commit offences, the opportunity structure, likelihood of detection, reporting propensities, etc.	Differences between countries regarding the propensity to commit offences, the opportunity structure, likelihood of detection, reporting propensities, etc.	C

The term 'statistical conditions' relates to (formal) rules for the collection and production of statistics and the (informal) application of these rules. One example from this area would be changes over time, or differences between countries, in the rules for how various offences are counted and the way such rules are applied (see the examples presented below). The term 'legal conditions' refers to a country's legislation and the way legal procedures are formulated (formal) and to praxis in these areas (informal). Examples might include the opportunities available to the police to exercise various forms of discretion and police policy in general. The term 'discretion' is used to refer to the police's capacity to choose whether or not an offence should be investigated/recorded; the extent of this discretionary power is in turn dependent on different legal traditions (for example, Sveri, 1988; Kangaspunta, 1995; Kommer, 1995). Naturally, the way the police prioritise the use of their resources, and their exercise of discretion, will affect the statistics. It is only possible to talk about real world conditions once controls have been conducted for these other factors (that is, A and B are prerequisites for C). Examples of such conditions are the propensity to commit offences, the opportunity structure, control, the likelihood of detection and reporting propensities. Thus, these conditions include the factors that are viewed by theories to be the causes of crime (and of the reporting of crime).

In the ideal data set for trend comparisons, all problems associated with dimensions A and B (in the model) would be controlled. In reality, of course, this is impossible. The most difficult factors to control for are probably the differences and changes of an 'informal' nature (von Hofer, 1991). Differences between countries, and changes over time within the same country, with regard to praxis within the justice system (the police and courts), and the application of rules for the collection and production of statistics, may be difficult to measure and therefore also difficult to know very much about.

Alternative statistics; victim surveys, self-report survey, hospital admissions and cause of death data

For a couple of decades now, victim surveys have been conducted in several, but unfortunately in nothing like all, European countries, asking a random sample of the general population about their experiences of criminal victimisation. One obvious advantage with these surveys is that they are independent of the relevant country's judicial system and official statistics. These surveys have therefore shown themselves to constitute an important complement to the official crime statistics. They are not without problems of their own, of course. The sources of error involved here include the use of small samples, for example, large attrition rates, and under- and over-reporting. Two basic types of victim survey can be distinguished; one comprises the national surveys, whose objective is to follow levels and trends in victimisation in individual countries, the other comprises the international survey, whose objective is to compare different countries with one another. This latter project goes under the name the 'International Crime Victimisation Survey' (ICVS) and to date, four such surveys have been conducted in 1988, 1991, 1995 and 1999 (van Dijk et al, 1990; van Dijk and Mayhew, 1993; Mayhew and van Dijk, 1997; van Kesteren et al, 2000).

The samples employed in the international crime victim surveys are relatively small (approximately 2,000 individuals per country, but for several countries the completed response rate is as low as 1,000). The size of the samples drawn for the national victim surveys are generally somewhat larger (the series presented later in this chapter are based on annual interviews conducted with between 4,000 and 12,000 individuals/households). Employing a sample to draw conclusions about an entire population is always associated with some degree of uncertainty, but this level of uncertainty decreases the larger the sample that is used. This means that the findings of the ICVS are less suited to estimating actual levels of victimisation in the various countries involved. Cross-national comparisons of victimisation levels are also difficult to make on the basis of the national victim surveys, however. Here the problem is primarily related to the fact that the operationalisations of crime differ between the surveys employed in different countries. One example of this is that the series for violent crime measured in Sweden includes muggings, whereas in England it relates only to assault (Farrington and Wikström, 1993, p 149). In Finland, the same series is restricted to violence resulting in physical injury (Aromaa, 1998).

A further problem with victim surveys is that not all potential respondents can be reached by means of an interview. There is a risk that certain groups, such as those living in poverty and marginalised individuals, will be excluded from the survey. One particular problem associated with attempts to compare levels of victimisation across different countries is that of variations in the proportion of the population with access to a telephone. Another related problem is that certain of the persons contacted do not wish to be interviewed. In certain of the countries included in the ICVS surveys, levels of this kind of attrition have been very high (comprising up to 70% of the sample). The average level of attrition for the first three surveys amounted to 43%; in the most recent survey, this figure stood at 36% (van Kesteren *et al*, 2000, p 116). When it comes to interpreting survey findings, the essential question is that of whether the attrition may be regarded as more or less random, or whether it is selective. If different categories of people are counted among the attrition to a varying extent in the countries studied, comparability will be seriously affected.

In the majority of victim surveys, data on criminal victimisation are presented using two different measures: prevalence and incidence. The term 'incidence' relates to the number of incidents/offences that the respondents have been exposed to, whilst prevalence data relate to the proportion of persons with experience of criminal victimisation. In some of the empirical examples presented below, both these measures have been used. Prevalence data may be regarded as being somewhat more reliable, for which reason these have been used as the principal measure. The reason prevalence data are somewhat more reliable is that an additional degree of uncertainty is introduced when the number of incidents/offences is estimated. One problem relates to the risk for overestimation as a result of double reporting: if a number of individuals are victims of the same event, then this event is counted several times. Another problem is that the risk for memory lapses may be assumed to be greater when the number of incidents is to be reported.

In addition, there are problems associated with the 'correctness' of respondents' answers. 'Incorrect' answers may result from several different causes. Amongst others, these include misunderstood questions, memory difficulties, untruths and an unwillingness to answer questions deemed to be sensitive. A certain level of over-reporting may also result from so called telescoping effects. This refers to the phenomenon of respondents reporting incidents that occurred prior to the recall period covered by the survey (for example, 'the previous year'). This might be caused by a desire to please the interviewer or more generally to give socially desirable answers. Under-reporting may result for the same reasons, but it is more often caused by an unwillingness to answer questions of a sensitive nature, such as may relate to sexual assaults and violence perpetrated within close relationships (Walby and Myhill, 2001).

Self-report surveys also constitute a good alternative means of measuring the extent of and trends in crime. These are associated with similar advantages and problems as the victim surveys. An additional limitation, however, is that studies of self-reported offending most often focus on crimes committed by juveniles. Unfortunately, there is at present only one study that has attempted to describe the extent of various criminal behaviours among young people in different countries, namely the International Self-Report Study (ISRD) (Junger-Tas, 1994). To date, a second wave of the ISRD has not yet been conducted, which makes comparisons over time impossible. On the other hand, a number of Western European countries have conducted national self-report surveys that do allow for comparisons over time. Both Finland and Sweden have conducted four national surveys covering the period 1995 to 2001 (Kivivouri, 2002; Ring, 2003). In Sweden, there are also a couple of more local studies that have examined trends over time, of which the most interesting compares offences committed by young persons in 1971 and 1996 respectively (Ward, 1998; Chinapah, 2000). In Denmark, one local self-report study has been conducted in three waves in 1979, 1989 and 1999 (Balvig, 2000). In Holland, a national self-report study has been conducted biannually since 1988 (Estrada, 1999).

Once source that is not used very often, but which can often provide valuable information on violent offences, is hospital admissions data. Several studies have described violent crime on the basis of cross-sectional surveys of patients admitted to accident and emergency departments as a result of violent injuries (for example, Cherpitel, 1993; Shepherd et al, 1993; Brink, 1999). One problem is that data relating to patients with violent injuries are often geographically restricted and another problem is that longer time series are more or less non-existent. One of the advantages associated with this source of data, on the other hand, is that they show a good deal of the more serious violence that is never reported to the police or recorded by victim surveys. There is thus a clear potential here for the creation of interesting and comparable series describing violent injuries in different countries. This chapter presents a series of data on violent injuries from Sweden.

Statistics relating to fatal violence are often seen as the most reliable indicator of the trends in violent offending, since few cases will be unreported. Trends in fatal violence can therefore be used as verification for trends in types of violent offences characterised by a somewhat larger dark figure (Doob and Sprott, 1998; von Hofer, 2000). With regard to fatal violence, it is essential to differentiate between cases where a homicide has been attempted and those that have actually resulted in death. These categories are combined far too often. The point of using fatal violence as an indicator is its robustness in relation to changes in the way society reacts to violence. Attempted murder is an arbitrary categorisation sensitive to changes in the general perspective on violent acts. The homicide trends witnessed by Holland's police statistics constitute an example of this. Data relating to longer term trends are only available with the offence of attempted homicide included. For those years where it is possible to separate attempted homicides (1983–94) it can be seen that the series including attempted homicides increased by a factor of 70%, whereas the series with attempted offences excluded increased only by 15%. Thus, series including attempted homicides should not be compared with statistical series where these attempt offences are not included.

The discussion above has shown that analyses of international crime trends based on a single statistical indicator are often fairly unreliable. In short, any attempt to produce an ideal description of international trends should be based not only on official crime statistics, but should also utilise other statistics, such as victims studies and cause of death statistics, that are less affected by changes in the criminal justice system or in the methods used to produce the official statistics.

Further, the available data are most suited to describing and comparing crime trends across different countries and not crime levels. Where possible, a presentation of the domestic debate regarding crime trends and the reliability of the data contributes to the analysis by making it possible to judge the relative worth of the various indicators. Validity should thus be seen as less satisfactory for those countries where descriptions are based on the analysis of a very few indicators, such as 'persons convicted of all offence types'. In those cases where the description is based on a number of sources including alternative statistics, and where a discussion of crime trends is included, validity is much improved.

International crime trends in practice: exemplifying three different approaches to the study of post-war crime trends in Western Europe

It is well established that the number of criminal offences registered in the official crime statistics was much larger in the year 2000 than it was in 1950. Post-war criminological research into crime trends has accordingly been dominated by descriptions of an ever increasing population of offenders (see for example, Wilson and Herrnstein, 1985; Killias, 1995; Smith, 1995). In more recent times, however, an alternative description, highlighting a levelling off in this trend during the 1980s has gained currency in some circles (von Hofer, 1985; Kyvsgaard, 1991; Joutsen, 1996; van Dijk, 1997; Estrada, 1999; Westfelt, 2001). Two models can be formulated to describe these trends:

(1) The linear upward trend (the usual description).

(2) An initial increase followed by a levelling off (the alternative description).

Since these models differ only in respect of the second half of the period under study, the following analysis focuses chiefly on those trends that have characterised the last three decades. The question to be answered is which of these two models best describes the trends in crime in Western Europe.

This section employs three different methods for conducting international comparisons of crime trends in order to illustrate the methodological issues discussed in the first section of this chapter. The presentation begins by presenting the overall crime trend in Western Europe during the post-war period. The sample of countries has been chosen on the basis of a 'most similar' approach and the analysis is based on crime statistics collected by the authors themselves, which are then compared with alternative data from international and national victim surveys. The second sub-section relates to trends in juvenile crime in Europe. Here too, the study is based on a 'most similar' approach and employs a number of different sources of data. The difference here, however, is that the analysis is based on a meta-study. The final sub-section employs several different sources of data to examine European trends in violent crime.

The overall crime trend

Figure 1 presents the trend in offences reported to the police in nine Western European countries. At the general level, the trend appears to be similar across these different countries. Note that it is not appropriate to analyse level differences in this context as a result of differences in legal and statistical conditions between the countries examined. None of the countries presents a stable or decreasing trend during the post-war period. All countries have recorded increases in crime. On the whole these trends are dominated by theft and criminal damage. Trends in two of the countries have periodically differed somewhat from the remainder. In Austria, the number of reported offences increased at a somewhat slower rate than in the other countries up until the end of the 1970s (see Gurr, 1978; Hanak and Pilgram, 1991, p 93). England and Wales witnessed a substantial increase in the number of reported offences between 1989 and 1992 (Joutsen, 1996; see also Tham, 1998). The similarly dramatic decrease over the following period might be interpreted as constituting a case of 'regression towards the mean', that is, that the series is retreating from extreme levels towards more 'normal' values. For the most part, however, there are substantial similarities across the countries and the pattern during the 1990s indicates that the crime trend in Western Europe appears to have shifted direction. The figure shows that none of the series lies at a higher level at the end of the 1990s by comparison with the beginning of this decade. In the majority of the non-Nordic countries, the slow down can be distinguished as early as the second half of the 1980s, whereas this levelling off does not begin until the 1990s in the series from the Nordic countries. These results correspond with the second of the two models (Model 2) described above.

Figure 1: Total number of registered offences in nine European countries, 1950–97, per 100,000 of population.

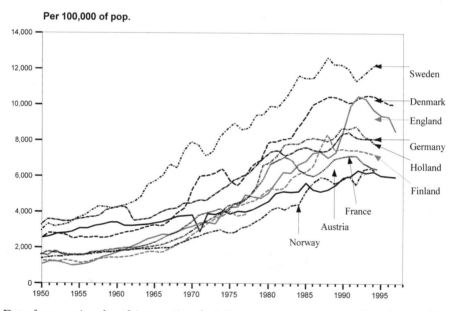

Data from national and international victim surveys are now employed to verify the trends identified on the basis of the official crime statistics. In this context, the objective of carrying out a control of this kind is naturally to come closer to answering the question of the extent to which the levelling off witnessed in the statistics may be the result of a real change in crime trends. If victimological data indicate an increase during the period in question, then this would suggest a reduction in the propensity to report crime rather than a stabilisation in crime levels. The results from the ICVS are not very well suited to a comparison of trends over time. Amongst other things, this is because only three European countries – England and Wales, Holland and Finland – have participated in all four waves of the survey (1988, 1991, 1995 and 1999).[8] Further, there are a number of differences between the four waves that make comparisons across them somewhat uncertain. If incidence data from the three countries that have participated in all four waves are examined, a combined crime indicator shows crime to have increased between 1988 and 1991. Between 1991 and 1999, on the other hand, crime levels appear to have either decreased or to have remained at a more or less stable level (van Kesteren *et al*, 2000, p 49). In combination, these data confirm the levelling off indicated by the official crime statistics.

A large number of countries have conducted *national* surveys, which have included questions on experiences of criminal victimisation. In Europe, however, many countries have not carried out such national surveys over a long period of time. Figure 2 presents crime trends from five European countries as recorded by victim data and official crime statistics. In general, the picture that emerges indicates that the population's reports of exposure to theft/vandalism mirror rather well the trend in levels of crime reported to the police.

Figure 2 A–E: Proportion of victims (%) and the number of reported offences in Sweden (A), Denmark (B), Finland (C), England (D) and Holland (E).

A   Proportion (%) reporting theft/vandalism related victimisation and number of reported theft offences in Sweden, 1970–98

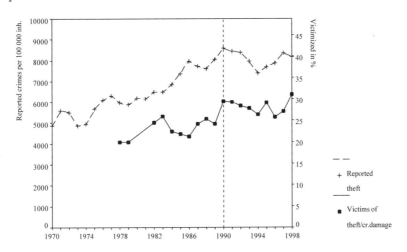

---

8   In total, 22 countries have participated in the four surveys. The European countries that have participated on at least one occasion comprise Belgium, Denmark, Finland, France, England and Wales, Italy, Holland, Northern Ireland, Norway, Poland, Portugal, Switzerland, Scotland, Spain, Sweden, West Germany and Austria. The offence types covered by the surveys are car theft, theft from a car, vandalism of a car, motorcycle theft, bicycle theft, breaking and entering, attempted breaking and entering, robbery, theft from the person, sex offences and assault/threatening behaviour (van Kesteren *et al*, 2000).

B   Proportion (%) reporting theft related victimisation and number of reported theft offences in Denmark, 1970–97

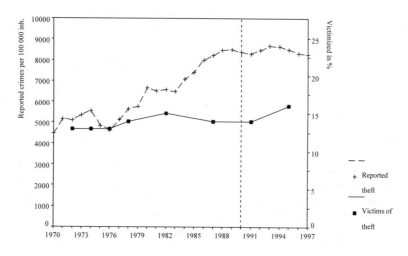

C   Proportion (%) reporting theft related victimisation and number of reported theft offences in Finland, 1970–97

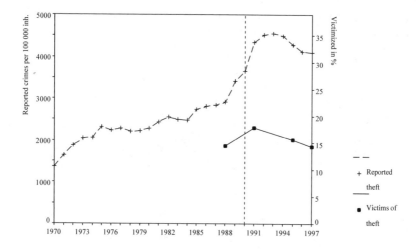

D   Proportion (%) reporting crime related victimisation and number of reported offences in England, 1970–97

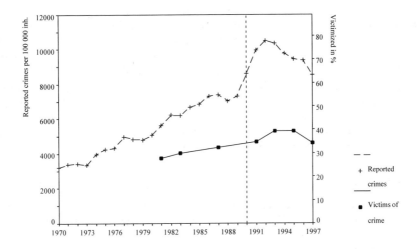

E   Number of theft incidents declared in victim surveys and number of theft offences reported to the police in Holland, 1970–97

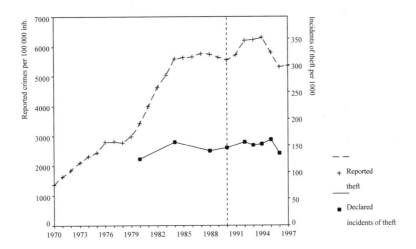

In Sweden, both offences reported to the police and the levels of criminal victimisation reported by the general population increased up until 1990, and stabilised thereafter. Roughly speaking, victim statistics from Denmark remain at a consistent level throughout the period, whereas police statistics increase up until the end of the 1980s and then begin to level off. The victim data from Finland[9] indicate

9   The data for 1997 are the same as those reported to the ICVS.

a reduction in levels of exposure to theft during the 1990s. In England, the data indicate that the 1990s first witnessed something of an increase in levels of victimisation but that these levels then decreased at the end of the period, such that the proportion experiencing victimisation at the end of the period is somewhat smaller than that seen at the beginning of the decade.[10] Thus, there is a correspondence between the victim data and the police statistics, but the fluctuations are greater in the police statistics than they are in the victimological data. In Holland, the situation is relatively stable during the 1990s in relation to theft offences. It should be noted, however, that the victim data collected in Holland differ somewhat from those collected in the other countries; in Holland, these are incidence rather than prevalence data. In Holland, the number of theft offences reported to the police starts to level off as early as the mid-1980s, and the victimological data mirror this trend rather well.

Juvenile crime trends

In order to describe general trends in juvenile crime, we will be using a meta-study based on national surveys from countries with a similar social structure (Estrada, 1999). This study covers the following countries: Austria, Denmark, England and Wales (hereafter referred to simply as 'England') Finland, (West) Germany,[11] Holland, Norway, Scotland, Sweden and Switzerland. The availability of data played an important part in the choice of countries to be included. A search for relevant literature was carried out in a number of databases and there were countries, such as those in southern Europe, for which insufficient material could be found.[12] In addition, contact was established with researchers and research centres in most of the countries covered by the study. Data attained in this way will be referred to below as PI (personal information). Table 2 presents the indicators employed in the studies on which the meta-analysis is based.

In brief (for a more extensive presentation see Estrada, 1999), the results of the meta-study indicate that in several Western European countries – Denmark, Holland, Norway, Scotland and Sweden – juvenile crime trends follow a sharp upward trend during the first decades after the Second World War. This trend is then broken between the mid-1970s and the beginning of the 1980s and thereafter levels off. The pattern is similar in Austria and Switzerland, but here the data are considered weaker. In Finland, England and Germany, the upward trend seems to

---

10 The series relating to all offences has been employed for England. This ought in fact to be comprised of theft offences to a large extent, however, and should therefore reflect trends in these offences relatively well.

11 The description of Germany refers exclusively to that part of the country which was known as West Germany up until 1989.

12 The following electronic databases were used: *Sociofile*, *Criminal Justice Abstracts* and *National Criminal Justice Reference Service*. These databases were trawled using the following keywords: '((Youth or Juvenile) and (trends or crime trends) or (crime rates))' for the years 1980–96. *Abstracts on Criminology and Penology* was available only in book format and here the search was limited to the sections Juvenile Delinquency, Comparative Analysis, Crime Measurement, Crime Pattern and Time Series Research for the years 1980–96.

Table 2: Indicators included in the meta-analysis, by country.

	Sweden	Norway	Denmark	Holland	Finland	Germany	England	Scotland	Switzerland	Austria
Convicted persons	+	+	+	+	+	+	+	+	+	+
All crime types	+	+	+	+	+	+	+	+	+	+
Crimes of violence	+	+	+	+	+	+	+	+	+	-
Juveniles and adults	+	+	+	+	+	+	+	-	+	-
Suspected persons	+	+	+	+	+	+	-	-	-	+
Victim Surveys	+	+	+	+	+	-	+	+	-	-
Theft	+	+	-	+	+	-	+	-	+	-
Domestic debate	+	+	+	-	-	+	+	-	-	-
Self-report studies	+	-	+	+	+	-	-	-	-	-
Detection rate	+	+	-	-	-	+	-	-	-	-

+ = yes   - = no

Explanation of the row headings:

Convicted persons: statistics covering convicted persons.

All crime types: statistics covering juvenile crime trends for all types of crime.

Crimes of violence: statistics covering trends in crimes of violence committed by juveniles.

Juveniles and adults: separate presentation of crime trends for juveniles and adults.

Suspected persons: statistics covering persons suspected of having committed offences.

Victim surveys: victim surveys that allow for comparisons over time.

Theft: statistics covering trends in thefts committed by juveniles.

Domestic debate: a documented domestic debate regarding juvenile crime trends.

Self-report studies: self-report studies that allow for comparisons over time.

Detection rate: a control for possible changes in the detection rate.

have continued into the 1990s. Thus in the majority of countries at least the post-war period does not appear to be characterised by an ever expanding population of young criminals; instead the data are more consistent with Model 2 as presented above.

One central question is the extent to which the trends described are real, or simply the result of, amongst other things, procedural changes in the criminal justice system or variations in reporting behaviour (see above). The most obvious answer is of course that both alternatives are true to a varying extent. In most of the countries studied here, for example, statistics concerning *convicted* juveniles indicate a clear *reduction* over the last 20 years or so. Those indicators which lie 'closer' to the crime event, however, and which are thus less sensitive to changes within the criminal justice system (such as statistics relating to suspects), suggest that the reductions are not real but are rather the result of 'system effects' (see, for example, von Hofer, 1985; Farrington, 1992; Junger-Tas, 1992; Clausen, 1996; Walter, 1996; Estrada, 1999). It is nonetheless important to remember that for most countries these sources do not indicate that the number of juvenile offenders has continued to increase at an undiminished rate during this period. This interpretation is reinforced by alternative statistics. In those countries where self-report studies are available over time, they suggest a stable level of juvenile offenders (Junger-Tas, 1992 and PI; Balvig, 2000; Kivivouri, 2002; Ring, 2003). In addition, as was seen above, the available victim surveys indicate that the underlying crime trends have probably levelled off over the past 15 years. The data from several countries suggest that the rise in crime that remains to be explained once changes in reporting behaviour have been taken into account, ought really to be ascribed to adults (aged 20+) rather than juveniles. Crime trends for adult offenders over the last 20 years are essentially different from those for juveniles in Denmark, Holland, Norway, Sweden and Switzerland (Junger-Tas, 1992; Kyvsgaard, 1993; Clausen, 1996; Niggli and Pfister, 1997; Estrada, 1999).

Trends in violent crime

Violent offending stands out historically as one of, if not the most prominent of the social problems associated with the field of deviant behaviour (Pearson, 1983). As we have entered the new millennium, academics, the media, politicians and the public seem for once to be in agreement that the number of people, and particularly youths, committing violent offences is increasing rapidly in Europe (see, for example, Home Office, 1997; Pfeiffer, 1998; Sunday Times, 1998).[13] Current research into trends in violence in Europe is often based on the various countries' official crime statistics. The reasons for this are reasonably straightforward in that data of this kind are both easily available, and in many countries they constitute the only form of information available. As we have discussed already, however, interpretations of crime statistics are far from self-evident. Since acts of violence may be perceived as a more subjective type of crime than thefts, the recording of acts of violence is also more sensitive to changes in attitudes towards control. In

---

13 At the 51st Annual Meeting of the American Society of Criminology (Toronto, 1999) a seminar was arranged (session 378) for a number of prominent criminologists to discuss the steep increase in violent juvenile offending in Europe.

Sweden, for example, the number of youths convicted of assault increased substantially during the 20th century. This increase is particularly marked from the mid-1980s, from which point the number of convictions tripled up to the end of the 1990s (Estrada, 2001). But does this mean that the level of violence in Sweden has actually increased in such a dramatic fashion? The same statistics show that hardly any youths were convicted of assault during the 1920s. This does not mean that the young people of the time did not commit acts of violence, of course, but rather it suggests that during the 20th century, the means of controlling violence have shifted from the informal to the formal arena (Pearson, 1983; von Hofer, 2000; Estrada, 2001).

On the whole, crime trends are dominated by theft and criminal damage. Since violent crime makes up a very small part of the sum total of offences, changes in the level of violent offending are easily lost in descriptions of underlying crime trends. In Figure 3, we can see that the levelling off witnessed in the overall crime trend is absent from the trend in crimes of violence reported to the police. In the matter of assault offences, the trend is instead characterised by clear increases from around the mid-1960s. As was pointed out earlier, the crime levels in the different countries cannot be interpreted at all. Given this backdrop, it makes sense to look to alternative indicators that may be considered less sensitive to changes in the propensity to report such offences, in order to see whether these data may confirm the increasing trend visible in the crime statistics. The presentation below comprises a description of trends in violence based on alternative data sources, and a special examination of the trends in juvenile violence.

Figure 3: Registered assault offences in eight European countries, 1950–97. Per 100,000 of population.

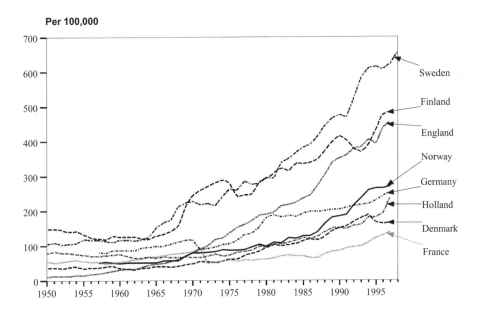

Alternative measures of trends in violence

Figure 4 presents trends in violent crime from six European countries according to victimological data and official crime statistics. The overall picture that emerges is one where the level of violent victimisation reported by the general population is relatively stable over recent decades, whilst levels of violent crime reported to the police increase substantially. In England, Denmark, Norway and Sweden, police statistics on violent offending indicate a dramatic and more or less continuous increase since 1970. At the same time, victim surveys from the different countries present a stable level of victimisation in the population. In Finland and Holland, the main pattern is the same, but here the victim surveys indicate a reduction in levels of victimisation. Thus the different series for violent crime present clearly dissimilar trends.

Figure 4: A–F. Proportion (%) victimised by violence and number of reported assault offences in Sweden (A), Norway (B), Denmark (C), Finland (D), England (E) and Holland (F), 1970–98.

A   Proportion (%) reporting exposure to violent victimisation and number of reported assault offences in Sweden, 1970–98

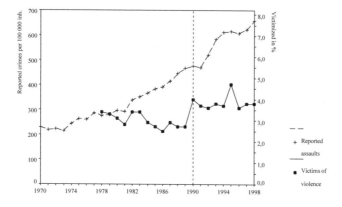

B   Proportion (%) reporting exposure to threatening behaviour/violent victimisation and number of reported assault offences in Norway, 1970–97

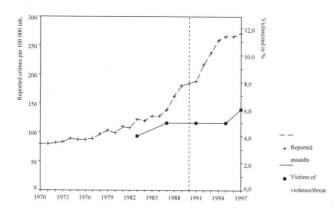

C Proportion (%) reporting exposure to threatening behaviour/violent victimisation and number of reported assault offences in Denmark, 1970–97

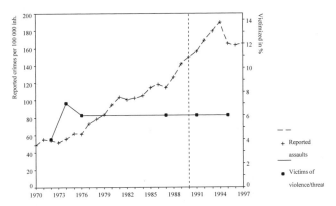

D Proportion (%) reporting exposure to violent victimisation and number of reported assault offences in Finland, 1970–97

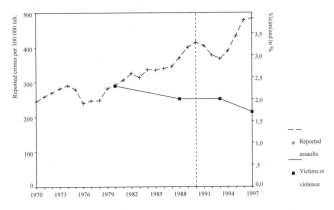

E Proportion (%) reporting exposure to violent victimisation and number of reported assault offences in England, 1970–97

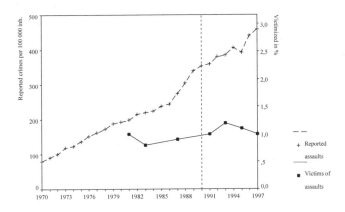

F   Number of violent incidents declared in victim surveys and number of assault offences reported to the police in Holland, 1970–97

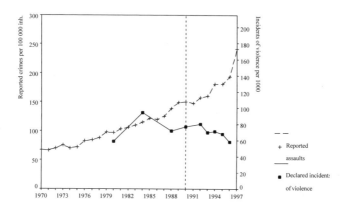

Homicide (murder and manslaughter) constitutes one of the few crime categories where the majority of experts are agreed that not only trends over time, but also crime levels may be compared across different countries – particularly when data are drawn from internationally standardised cause of death statistics. The reason for this is that the dark figure for homicides is assumed to be relatively small. There are also substantial similarities in homicide trends across the different countries examined. For the most part, the post-war period is characterised by increases in Sweden, the remaining Nordic countries and the non-Nordic countries (Figure 5). This increase stands in sharp contrast to the trend witnessed from the second half of the 19th century up until the outbreak of the Second World War. International comparisons have shown that levels of homicide fell substantially during this period in the majority of European countries (Eisner, 1994). During the 1980s, however, the trends underwent something of a stabilisation, particularly by comparison with the statistics relating to assault offences reported to the police. It should be borne in mind that incidents of homicide are very rare, which makes interpretations of trends very difficult over the short term (Ross, 1974; Lenke, 1990; Westfelt, 1998).

Juvenile violence: the Swedish case in a European context

In order to further illustrate the problems associated with drawing conclusions about trends in violent crime on the basis of official crime statistics, this presentation now moves on to a more detailed examination of a single case – namely trends in juvenile violence in Sweden. What makes the Swedish case interesting for an international audience is the fact that Swedish statistics follow the same sharply increasing trend as those found in the crime statistics of other Western European countries (Pfeiffer, 1998; Rutter et al, 1998; Estrada, 1999). Questioning the validity of Swedish crime statistics as an indicator of crime trends thus implies a challenge to interpretations based on official statistics in other countries. It is also our contention that a reasonable interpretation of trends in violence is only possible once alternative indicators have been studied. To the extent that corresponding data are

Figure 5: Homicides in Sweden, the rest of Scandinavia and the remainder of Europe, 1955–95. Standardised values (Y-axis omitted).[14]

Per 100,000

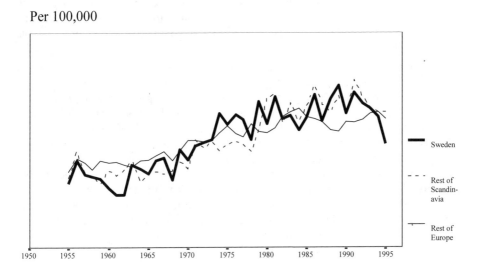

Sweden

Rest of Scandinavia

Rest of Europe

unavailable in other countries, the Swedish material becomes of even greater interest.

A examination of the Swedish victim surveys suggests that the number of juveniles being exposed to violence increased somewhat from the mid-1980s to then slow down again during the 1990s, once again settling at the level witnessed during the late '70s and early '80s. Thus the statistics from victim surveys do not suggest a linear trend in juvenile victimisation (Nilsson and Estrada, 2003). Since 1972, self-report surveys on drug use have been carried out in Stockholm among all students in year nine (that is, 15 year olds). Since 1987, these surveys have also included questions on the students' experiences of violence. These surveys indicate that schoolchildren in Stockholm report neither that more of them have been

---

14 In order to avoid presenting mean-based series which may be misleading as a result of isolated series lying at an appreciably higher level than the others and thus assuming a disproportionately large weight, the series were centred prior to making mean-based series for 'Europe' and 'Scandinavia'. All data is per 100,000 of population. The result is a value on the Y-axis that is standardised and that makes differences of levels between the different territories irrelevant. The relevant comparisons are instead on the directions and movements of the trends. This centring process took the Swedish series as its point of departure, in accordance with the formula:

$$\frac{\text{Mean value of the relevant series in Sweden}}{\text{Mean for country 1}} * \text{Observation in country 1} = \text{Centred observation in country 1}$$

assaulted, nor that more are carrying out assaults, nor even that they have witnessed more acts of violence during the years 1987–98 (Estrada, 2001). Data are available for the years 1995–2001 from a nationally representative self-report study of crime among schoolchildren. These surveys show stable response rates in relation to levels of self-reported violent crime (Ring, 2003). A reasonable summary of the results of victim and self-report surveys is thus: that they do not show a continual increase but rather that violent acts by youths have remained at a more or less stable level since the 1970s.

Since the end of the 1960s, Sweden has maintained a register of patients admitted to public hospitals. This patient register contains, amongst other things, details of the number of persons admitted as a result of assaults. Figure 6 below presents the number of hospital admissions for different age groups.[15] There has been no general increase in the numbers admitted for hospital care as a result of violence. The clear rise in numbers seen during the period 1968–73 is probably most correctly interpreted as indicating the length of the start-up phase for the reporting system. It is interesting to note that the trend is reminiscent of that indicated by the nationwide victim surveys (see Figure 4 above). The higher levels in the 1990s correspond well with those presented during the second half of the 1970s. Here too, the mid-1980s stand out as a low point. A reasonable summary is that the number of hospital admissions resulting from violence has remained at a more or less stable level since 1973 for persons aged 10–25 years.

Figure 6: Absolute number of hospital admissions as a result of violence in different age groups. Sweden, 1968–97.

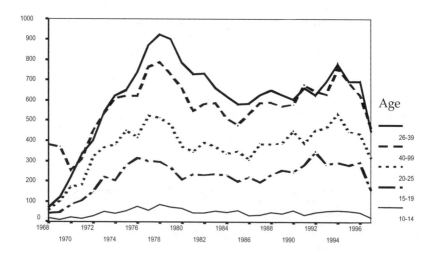

---

15 Hospital admission statistics are presented in such a way that the same person being admitted several times during the same year will be counted once for each admission. The figures for 1997 should be regarded with caution since there has been both a change in the classification system and a drop in the quality of reporting.

Since the 1970s, violence resulting in death has not increased in terms of either the number of youths who are perpetrators or the number who are victims (Estrada, 2001). This suggests at the very least that any increases in juvenile violence that may have occurred have not affected the levels of the most serious forms of violence. Viewed together, these alternative indicators present a completely different picture from that given by the crime statistics. To be blunt, there is very little to indicate a substantial increase in Sweden either in the number of youths falling victim to violence, or in the number perpetrating acts of violence on others, apart from crime statistics which are sensitive to changes in the response to violence.

Comparative research has presented Sweden as a country with similar trends in juvenile violence to those of the rest of Europe (Pfeiffer, 1998; Rutter et al, 1998). What is interesting, of course, is whether this might indeed be the case, but in a rather different way from that described in the literature. This is an empirical question that will not be answered in full here. What can be said, however, is that the example provided by Sweden ought to be interpreted as indicating that analyses of trends in violent offending should not be based exclusively on crime statistics. To the extent that different indicators suggest differences in trends, however, priority ought to be given to those least affected by changes in reporting propensities. As was seen in the presentation of Swedish trends, such indicators comprise various forms of questionnaire survey, hospital data and statistics relating to fatal violence.

Viewed in this way, several of the countries whose data on juvenile violence have been interpreted as indicating an increase present a somewhat less clear picture. In the analyses presented by Pfeiffer (1998) and Rutter et al (1998, p 73), increases in juvenile violence are referred to almost exclusively on the basis of official crime statistics from different countries. This is a consequence of the fact that most European countries lack reliable alternative indicators. In those countries where there are alternative statistics, however, these are more in line with the picture that emerged from the analysis of Swedish data just presented above. Thus, as has been shown, victim surveys from several countries show that the population's experience of violence has not increased over recent years. In addition, there are further alternative indicators from Denmark which show a stable trend as compared with that indicated by police data. Brink et al (1997) present an analysis of hospital data for the years 1982, 1988 and 1994. Their results show that juvenile violence has neither increased nor become more serious. What has increased, however, is the reporting propensity among youths (aged 15–19). Fatal violence presents no increase either (Kyvsgaard, 2000). Danish self-report studies among 14–15 year old students indicate less violence in 1999 than in 1979 (Kyvsgaard, 1992; Balvig, 2000). Finland and Norway show the same pattern as Sweden and Denmark, that is, dramatic increases in juvenile violence as reflected in crime statistics, but a more or less stable level as recorded in victim surveys (Estrada, 1999; Falck, 2000) and self-report studies (Kivivouri, 2002).

Another of the few European countries where alternative indicators of crime trends are available is Holland. Here too, the substantial increase in levels of non-serious violence which are indicated by Dutch crime statistics are not matched by increases in either fatal violence or in the proportion of victim survey respondents saying that they have been threatened (Franke, 1994; Junger-Tas, 1996; Wittebrood and Junger, 2002). The Dutch victim surveys go so far as to indicate that the number of violent crime experiences has diminished during the 1990s for the population aged 15–24 years (personal communication, Central Bureau of Statistics, Netherlands). In Holland, hospital data are also available relating to the number of patients admitted for violent injuries. These data are very reminiscent of those from Sweden, indicating a substantial level of stability over recent decades (Wittebrood and Junger, 2002).

The review presented above thus shows that a number of objections may be raised in relation to the picture of a pan-European increase in violent crime as described by the media, politicians and certain academics. One example of this relates to Pfeiffer's contention that 'when longitudinal data are available from victim surveys, they support the inference from police and judicial data that violent crime among young people has been *rising rapidly*' (1998, p 298, emphasis added); a conclusion that appears quite simply to be mistaken given the data presented in this chapter. Integrating the interpretations of data drawn from alternative sources and crime statistics instead leads to the following hypothesis regarding violence in Europe. Trends in crime do not constitute the primary explanation for the rapid rise in the number of people, and particularly youths, registered by the criminal justice system during the 1990s. This rise is rather the result of a marked shift in the way society reacts to people's actions. We hypothesise that over recent years, the attention focused on violent acts has increased. This increase in attention has occurred in parallel with an ideological shift, from the treatment ideology to a neo-classicist focus on just deserts, which has affected the politics of social control (Tham, 1995; Garland, 2001). Together, these tendencies have lead to an increasing propensity to report acts of violence, which in turn has led to a situation exhibiting all the classic characteristics of a deviancy amplification spiral (Hall *et al*, 1978; von Hofer, 2000; Estrada, 2001).[16]

Conclusion

This chapter has raised a number of the fundamental questions that have to be dealt with in the context of comparative crime studies. In part, these relate to the choice of countries for inclusion in the study, in part, to the choice of data and methods of data collection. The presentation has focused particular attention on the question of the suitability of official crime statistics for analyses of crime trends in different countries. The advantages and disadvantages of different data sources have been discussed. As a result of the shortcomings identified in the various available sources, we draw the conclusion that analyses should not be based on single statistical indicators. A further conclusion drawn in this chapter is that given the data available, it is difficult to make comparisons of crime levels across different countries. One possible way of making such comparisons is instead to focus on trends in crime.

---

16 Estrada (2001) presents two studies testing this hypothesis. The first focuses on the media attention surrounding the issue of juvenile crime during the period 1950–94. The second looks at the concrete effects that changes in reporting propensities may have on the registration of juvenile violence in official crime statistics.

The empirical sections of the chapter illustrate a number of the methodological questions discussed in the introduction. In concrete terms, we have chosen to proceed from the question of how best to describe post-war crime trends in Western Europe. Has the period witnessed a linear and continuous increase in crime? Or is it possible to discern a levelling off in this increase? And if so, is this levelling off a general phenomenon, or is it restricted to one or just a few countries or offence types, for example? In order to answer these questions, the chapter presents a large amount of data from a variety of different sources in 10 or so countries. It is clear that crime levels increased during the post-war period across Western Europe. It is just as clear, however, that this increase has not continued in a linear fashion throughout the entire period. In all of the countries included in the analysis, there is a clear levelling off around the end of the 1980s. Levels of juvenile crime also underwent an increase during the post-war period, followed by a levelling off in this trend. One interesting factor is that the increase in the number of juvenile offenders appears to slow down at the beginning rather than the end of the 1980s. This means that it might be possible to look at the trend in juvenile crime as one possible explanation for the levelling off in the overall crime trend. Further research is required here, however. In addition, the chapter has focused particular attention on an examination of trends in violent crime, which appear on the basis of official crime statistics to have undergone a dramatic increase over recent decades. Using alternative sources of data, such as victim and self-report surveys, hospital data and cause of death statistics, we show that trends in violent crime have also levelled off over recent years. We would contend that the three empirical studies presented in this chapter in themselves show that comparative studies are a practical possibility. What is also clear, however, is that comparative analyses require detailed knowledge of the quality and comparability of the data employed, as well as a healthy scepticism in relation to conclusions drawn on the basis of isolated indicators of crime.

References

Archer, D and Gartner, R (1984) *Violence and Crime in Cross-National Perspective*, New Haven: Yale UP

Aromaa, K (1998) *Accident and Crime Victims in Finland 1997*, Interim report of the 1997 national accident and crime victim survey, No 9, RC 36, Statistics Finland

Balvig, F (2000) *RisikoUngdom. Ungdomsundersogelse 1999* (Youth at Risk), Copenhagen: The National Council for Crime Prevention

Bennett, RR and Lynch, JP (1990) 'Does a difference make a difference? Comparing cross-national crime indicators' 28 *Criminology* 153–82

Brink, O (1999) *Vold i Århus* (Violence in Århus), Dissertation, Aarhus University

Brink, O, Charles, AV, Sabroe, S, Jensen, J and Sorensen, W (1997) 'Mindre Vold og Hyppigere Politianmeldelse' (Less Violence and More Reports to the Police) 84 *Nordisk Tidsskrift for Kriminalvidenskab* 103–14

Cherpitel, CJ (1993) 'Alcohol and violence-related injuries: an emergency room study' 88 *Addiction* 79–88

Chinapah, E (2000) *Tonårsnormer i förändring? En empirisk studie av 15-åringar i en mellanstor svensk stad 1969 och 1995* (Changing teenage norms? An empirical study in a medium-sized Swedish city in 1969 and 1995), Doctoral dissertation, Stockholm: University of Stockholm, Department of Psychology

Clausen, SE (1996) *Barne- og ungdomskriminalitet i Norge 1980–1992.* (Child- and Juvenile Crime in Norway 1980–1992), NIBR-rapport 1996: 4, Oslo: Norsk institutt for by- og regionsforskning

Coleman, C and Moynihan, J (1996) *Understanding Crime Data: Haunted by the Dark Figure,* Buckingham: OU Press

Council of Europe (1982) *Trends in Crime: Comparative Studies and Technical Problems,* Fifth Criminological Colloquium, 23–25 November 1981, Strasbourg

van Dijk, JJM (1997) 'Towards a research-based crime reduction policy – Crime prevention as a cost-effective policy option' 5(3) *European Journal on Criminal Policy and Research* 13–27

van Dijk, JJM and Mayhew, P (1993) 'Criminal victimisation in the industrialised world: key findings of the 1989 and 1992 international crime surveys', in Alvazzi del Frate, A, Zvekic, U and van Dijk J (eds) *Understanding Crime: Experiences of Crime and Crime Control,* UNICRI Publication No 49, pp 1–49, Rome

van Dijk, JJM, Mayhew, P and Killias, M (1990) *Experiences of Crime Across the World: Key Findings of the 1989 International Crime Survey,* Deventer: Kluwer

Doob, AN and Sprott, JB (1998) 'Is the quality of youth violence becoming more serious?' *Canadian Journal of Criminology,* April, 185–94

Eisner, M (1994) *The Effects of Economic Structures and Phases of Development on Crime,* Eleventh Criminological Colloquium, Strasbourg: Council of Europe

Estrada, F (1999) 'Juvenile crime trends in post-war Europe' 7(1) *European Journal on Criminal Policy and Research* 23–42

Estrada, F (2001) 'Juvenile violence as a social problem: trends, media attention and societal response' 41 *British Journal of Criminology* 639–55

Falck, S (2000) 'Barne og Ungdomskriminalitet i Norge på Nittitalet' (Trends in Norwegian juvenile delinquency in the nineties), *Samfunnsspeilet,* No 2/2000, Statistics Norway

Farrington, DP (1992) 'Trends in English juvenile delinquency and their explanation' 16 *International Journal of Comparative and Applied Criminal Justice* 151–63

Farrington, DP and Wikström, P-OH (1993) 'Changes in crime and punishment in England and Sweden in the 1980s' 2 *Studies on Crime and Crime Prevention*

Franke, H (1994) 'Violent crime in the Netherlands: a historical-sociological analysis' 21 *Crime, Law and Social Change* 73–100

Garland, D (2001) *The Culture of Control: Crime and Social order in Contemporary Society,* New York: OUP

Gurr, TR (1978) 'Crime trends in modern democracies since 1945', in *The Cranfield Papers: The Proceedings of the 1978 Cranfield Conference on the Prevention of Crime in Europe*, London: Peel Press

Hall, S, Critcher, C, Jefferson, T, Clarke, J and Roberts, B (1978) *Policing the Crisis: Mugging, the State, and Law and Order*, London: Macmillan

Hanak, G and Pilgram, A (1991) *Der andere Sicherheitsbericht*, Kriminalsoziologische Bibliografie, No 70/71 Spezial, Wien: Verlag für Gesellschaftskritik

von Hofer, H (1985) *Brott och straff i Sverige* (Crime and Punishment in Sweden), Urval No 18, Stockholm: Statistiska centralbyrån

von Hofer, H (ed) (1991) *Nordic Criminal Statistics 1950–1989: Summary of a Report*, Statistical Reports of the Nordic Countries, No 57, Copenhagen: Nordic Statistical Secretariat

von Hofer, H (2000) 'Criminal violence and youth in Sweden: a long-term perspective' 1 *Journal of Scandinavian Studies in Criminology and Crime Prevention* 56–72

Home Office (1997) *No More Excuses – A New Approach to Tackling Youth Crime in England and Wales*, London: Home Office

Huang, WSW (1993) 'Are international murder data valid and reliable? Some evidence to support the use of Interpol data' 17 *International Journal of Comparative and Applied Criminal Justice*

Joutsen, M (1996) *Recent Trends in Crime in Western Europe*, Paper presented at the V European Colloquium on Crime and Criminal Policy, Ljubljana, 25–27 September 1996

Junger-Tas, J (1992) 'Juvenile delinquency in the Netherlands: trends and perspectives' 16 *International Journal of Comparative and Applied Criminal Justice* 207–30

Junger-Tas, J (1994) *Delinquent Behaviour Among Young People in the Western World*, Amsterdam: Kluwer

Junger-Tas, J (1996) 'Youth and violence in Europe' 5 *Studies on Crime and Crime Prevention* 31–58

Kangaspunta, K (1995) *Crime and Criminal Justice in Europe and North America 1986–1990*, HEUNI, No 25, Tampere: HEUNI

van Kesteren, J, Mayhew, P and Nieuwbeerta, P (2000) *Criminal Victimisation in Seventeen Industrialised Countries*, The Hague: WODC

Killias, M (1995) *Crime Policy in the Face of the Development of Crime in the New European Landscape*, Report from the Fifth Conference on Crime Policy, Strasbourg: Council of Europe

Kivivouri, J (2002) *Trends and Patterns of Self-reported Juvenile Delinquency in Finland*, Publ 88, Helsinki: National Research Institute of Legal Policy

Kommer, MM (1995) 'International comparison of crime and criminal justice statistics', in Jehle, JM and Lewis, C (eds), *Improving Criminal Justice Statistics: National and International Perspectives*, Wiesbaden: Kriminologische Zentralstelle EV

Kyvsgaard, B (1991) 'The decline in child and youth criminality: possible explanations of an international trend', in Snare, A (ed), *Youth, Crime and Justice*, 12 *Scandinavian Studies in Criminology* 26–41, Oslo: Universitetsförlaget

Kyvsgaard, B (1992) *Ny ungdom?* (New Youth), Köpenhamn: Jurist-og Okonomforbondets forlag

Kyvsgaard, B (1993) 'Kriminalitetens demografi og forandring' (Demography and change in criminality), in Bay, J (ed), *Kriminalistisk instituts årbog 1993*, Köpenhamn: Kriminalistisk institut, pp 109–23

Kyvsgaard, B (2000) *Vold i 1990'erne* (Violence in the 1990s), Annual Report 1999, Department of Justice, Copenhagen: Denmark

Lenke, L (1990) *Alcohol and Criminal Violence: Time Series Analyses in a Comparative Perspective*, Stockholm: Almqvist and Wiksell International

Lieberson, S (1991) 'Small N's and big conclusions: an examination of the reasoning in comparative studies based on small numbers of cases' 70 *Social Forces* 307–19

Marshall, HI and Marshall, CE (1983) 'Toward a refinement of purpose in comparative criminological research: research site selection in focus' 7 *International Journal of Comparative and Applied Criminal Justice* 89–97

Mayhew, P and van Dijk, J (1997) *Criminal Victimisation in Eleven Industrialised Countries: Key Findings from the 1996 International Crime Victimisation Survey*, prepared for the European Union Conference, Crime Prevention: Towards a European Level, 11–14 May, Noordwijk, the Netherlands

McClintock, FH and Wikström, P-OH (1987) 'Våldsbrottsligheten i Skottland och Sverige. Nivå, struktur och trender' (Violent crime in Scotland and Sweden. Level, structure and trends), in Knutsson, J (ed), *Brottsutvecklingen 1987*, BRÅ-rapport 1987: 5, pp 191–226, Stockholm: Brottsförebyggande rådet

Newman, G (1999) *Global Report on Crime and Justice*, New York: OUP

Niggli, MA and Pfister, F (1997) 'Paradise lost? Paradise ever? On crime development in Switzerland' 6 *Studies on Crime and Crime Prevention* 73–100

Nilsson, A and Estrada, F (2003) 'Victimisation, inequality and welfare during an economic recession: a study of self reported victimisation in Sweden 1988–99', 43 *British Journal of Criminology* 655–72

Pearson, G (1983) *Hooligan: A History of Respectable Fears*, London: Macmillan

Pfeiffer, C (1998) 'Juvenile crime and violence in Europe' 23 *Crime and Justice: A Review of Research* 255–328

Ring, J (2003) *Stöld, våld och droger bland ungdomar i årskurs nio* (Theft, drugs and violence among ninth grade youth), BRÅ-report 2003: 5, Stockholm: The National Council for Crime Prevention

Ross, HL (1974) 'Interrupted time-series methods for the evaluation of traffic law reforms', in Waller, PF (ed), *Highway Safety Programs: How Do We Know They Work?*, papers from North Carolina Symposium on Highway Safety, Raleigh, NC: North Carolina State University, School of Engineering

Rutter, M, Giller, H and Hagell, H (1998) *Antisocial Behaviour by Young People*, Cambridge: CUP

Scott, JE and Al-Thakeb, F (1980) 'Perceptions of deviance cross-culturally', in Newman, GR (ed), *Crime and Deviance: A Comparative Perspective*, Beverly Hills/London: Sage

Shepherd, JP, Ali, M, Hughes, A and Levers, B (1993) 'Trends in urban violence: a comparison of accident department and police records' 86(2) *Journal of the Royal Society of Medicine* 87–88

Skogan,WG (1984) 'Reporting crimes to the police: the status of world research' 21(2) *Journal of Research in Crime and Delinquency* 113–37

Smith, DJ (1995) 'Youth crime and conduct disorders: trends, patterns, and causal explanations', in Rutter, M and Smith, DJ (eds), *Psychosocial Disorders in Young People: Time Trends and Their Causes*, New York: John Wiley and Sons, pp 389–489

Sunday Times (1998) 'Teenage time bomb: juvenile crime is soaring in Britain and across the Continent', 10 November

Sveri, K (1988) *A Comparative Study of the Use of Criminal Measures*, paper presented at the 10th International Criminology Conference in Hamburg

Teune, H (1979) 'A logic of comparative policy analysis', in Ashford, IDE (ed), *Comparing Public Policies*, Beverly Hills: Sage, pp 43–55

Tham, H (1995) 'From treatment to just deserts in a changing welfare state', in Snare, A (ed), *Beware of Punishment*, Oslo: Pax, pp 89–122

Tham, H (1998) 'Crime and the welfare state: the case of the United Kingdom and Sweden', in Ruggiero, V, South, N and Taylor, I (eds), *The New European Criminology. Crime and Social Order in Europe*, Cornwall: Routledge

Tranøy, BS (1993) 'Komparativ metode – mellom ideografiske og nomotetiske idealer' (Comparative method – between ideographical and nomothetical ideals), 23 *Sosiologi idag* 17–40

Walby, S and Myhill, A (2001) 'New survey methodologies in researching violence against women' 41 *British Journal of Criminology* 502–22

Walter, M (1996) 'Kriminalpolitik mit der polizeilichen kriminalstatistik?' 4/96 (Nr 153) *DVVJ-Journal* 209–14

Ward, M (1998) *Barn och Brott av vår tid? Självdeklarerad ungdomsbrottslighet 1971 och 1996* (Youth and crimes of our time? Self-reported delinquency 1971 and 1996), Stockholm: Department of Criminology, University of Stockholm

Westfelt, L (1998) 'Utvecklingen av registrerade brott under efterkrigstiden. Sverige i europeisk belysning' (Trends in registered crime during the post-war period. Sweden viewed in relation to the rest of Europe), in von Hofer, H (ed), *Svensk brottslighet och kriminalpolitik i europeisk belysning*, Stockholm: Studentlitteratur

Westfelt, L (2001) *Brott och straff i Sverige och Europa. En studie i komparativ kriminologi.* (Crime and Punishment in Sweden and Europe – a Study in Comparative Criminology), Doctoral dissertation, Stockholm: Department of Criminology

Wilkins, LT (1980) 'World crime: to measure or not to measure?', in Newman, GR (ed), *Crime and Deviance: A Comparative Perspective*, Beverly Hills/London: Sage

Wilson, JQ and Herrnstein, R (1985) *Crime and Human Nature*, New York: Simon & Schuster

Wittebrood, K and Junger, M (2002) 'Trends in violent crime: a comparison between police statistics and victimisation surveys' 59 *Social Indicators Research* 153–73

Chapter 2
The Use of National Crime Statistics in Comparative Research; Ireland and Scotland Compared

Peter Young

Introduction

The topic of this chapter is the use of national statistics on crime and criminal justice in comparative research. National statistics are produced and published by governments and this is why they are the 'official statistics'. The main aims of the chapter are to describe what these official statistics tell us and to discuss the role they play in comparative research. The argument advanced here is that these statistics are a rich, even indispensable, resource for comparative research but that we must be cautious about their use. As will be seen, the cautions mostly arise from the fact that these statistics were never created as research tools, but evolved in the 19th century as government instruments, intended to measure the characteristics of and ultimately to control populations. This has given rise to a voluminous literature on the problems associated with their use both in a national context and – as the interest in what happens in other countries has become more pronounced – a comparative one as well. The general tone of this literature is highly sceptical. In this view, the national statistics are, at the best, a very imprecise source of information about patterns of crime and criminal justice and, at the worst, so hedged round with problems of interpretation as to make them of very limited use indeed.

This sceptical argument is an important one. It is reviewed below by looking first at the questions raised about the use of these statistics nationally and then considering the additional problems that appear when comparative research is undertaken. Before proceeding to this, however, it is worth stating in bold, general terms the main advantages of the national statistics.

The strength of the official statistics are, first, that they are the most comprehensive sources of data on crime and criminal justice available to the criminologist; secondly, that they are fairly easy to find and access. National crime statistics, through the recorded statistics and crime surveys (where they are done), provide essential information on crime levels and trends in the short and the long-term, and the statistics on criminal justice offer equally privileged information on how a country's criminal justice and penal systems work. Moreover, because most governments regularly publish such information, often these days in a machine-readable form, the statistics are readily available. The national statistics are often embedded in government websites and are also available through the publications of such organisations as the Council of Europe. There is also a third reason why these statistics are central to comparative research. Until an alternative statistical source is created – and it would be difficult to imagine what type of organisation would undertake the task – the national statistics will remain the only one. This is why the statistics are so important to the criminologist. To put it simply, the national statistics provide some of the essential raw materials for both understanding and describing patterns in crime and criminal justice and have therefore a key role to play in the ultimate aim of comparative research – that of theory construction.

This is the positive and optimistic message of the chapter. The chapter will demonstrate the message with the aid of examples drawn from a comparison of the recorded crime statistics of Scotland and the Republic of Ireland, two small countries with distinctive civic cultures and criminal justice systems. The scope of the discussion is restricted to the recorded crime statistics but much of what is said applies also to the criminal justice statistics as well. These two countries are chosen for examination partly because of their distinctive cultures and systems, partly because of their similarity in size and because, as will be seen, they have interestingly different patterns in levels of crime over the period chosen for analysis, 1950 to the late 1990s. There is an additional reason prompting the choice of these countries. Over the last 10 years, I have completed quite extensive research on the crime levels and patterns of each. The results of this research are published as independent, stand-alone studies (Young, 1997; Young, 2001). It is important to state, therefore, that my discussion of the role of national crime statistics does not arise directly from a comparison. Rather, the discussion may be seen as a type of methodological prolegomenon. Examining the crime statistics of the two countries has allowed me to become very familiar with them and has provided an opportunity to reflect on what would be involved in a full-blown comparative exercise using the statistics as the prime source, and this chapter reports upon this.

The sceptical case

This sceptical argument about the use of official statistics is well established in criminology. Indeed, it is the predominant one. For the last two or three decades, criminologists have been highly critical about the value of national criminal statistics, even in the context of their use in providing information about patterns of crime within the country to which they refer. The criminal statistics of a country are composed, in the first place, of the crimes that are reported to the authorities (usually, but not only, the police) and recorded by them. These statistics are known as the recorded crime statistics or the police statistics. The core of the argument focuses upon the problems that the recorded crime statistics are seen to pose. It is said that there exists a 'dark figure of crime', composed of those crimes which are not reported to the police or are not, for various reasons, recorded by them; such crimes are not counted in the national statistics. Criminologists also worry about the impact of changes in these recording practices and, more generally about, the exercise of discretion by individual police officers and by the police as an organisation. The exercise of discretion appears to introduce a degree of instability into the picture, such that the researcher cannot assume that there exist stable patterns in the recording of crimes that are either reported to the police or discovered by them. These concerns are said to make the statistics a poor instrument for measuring the true extent of crime in a country. There are various estimates of the size of this dark figure. It is known to vary significantly with type of crime (burglary and car crime have a high rate of reporting and recording, whereas sexual crime has a much lower rate) but the British Crime Survey 1998, for example, returns a generalised ratio of 4:1, where it is estimated that for every four crimes committed only one is recorded.

To some extent these concerns have been allayed with the development of victim/crime surveys and other instruments such as self-report studies. These are social surveys in which sample populations are asked questions about either their experience of victimisation or about their offending behaviour and the data is then used to measure the extent of the dark figure. Criminologists now recognise that a much fuller (but probably still incomplete) picture can be drawn of the volume of crime in a country by using the recorded statistics and the results of crime surveys together. There are some especially revealing results obtained where it is possible to make a direct comparison between the victim incidents counted in the surveys and the corresponding unit in the national statistics (within the comparable sub-set, as it is known). It is also increasingly accepted that there is a broad similarity in the overall trend in recorded crime and that revealed by crime surveys. When, for example, on a graph, the line for recorded crime rises, so too does the line for victim incidents, although at a less steep rate (see Young, 2001).

National crime surveys are major and expensive undertakings that are normally carried out by governments. Where crime/victim surveys are carried out regularly, the national crime statistics can be said to be composed of them and the recorded crime statistics. Crime/victim surveys are not, however, regularly conducted in all countries. In the case of the two countries being compared here, crime/victim surveys have been carried out in Scotland from the early 1980s but this is not so in Ireland. In Ireland, there have been two national crime surveys but they have been irregularly conducted (1985 and 1998) and are mostly small scale (see Young, 2001). In addition, it must also be recognised that crime surveys, even where they are regularly undertaken, only allow for the fuller picture of the extent of crime to be drawn over a relatively short period. In England and Wales and in Scotland, for instance, crime surveys have only been done for about 25 years. For information about longer-term trends – and this may be of particular importance for comparative research or for research that tries to explore causal questions about, for example, the relationship between social structure and patterns of crime – the only significant source of data is that derived from the recorded crime statistics.

It can be seen that the sceptical attitude toward the use of crime statistics at the national level is well founded. Their problems, however, are compounded when cross-national comparisons – the topic of this chapter – come into focus. At the national level, as has been seen, the crucial issue has been one of measurement, about how much crime the statistics measure and about how to obtain a fuller picture of the volume of crime. At the comparative level, an additional layer of problems is added. These relate to differences in culture and practice and the impact of this on the composition of the national statistics. There is a further issue of the implications of this for the interpretation and use of national statistics in research.

All criminal statistics are products of administrative processes and procedures, including those used in their collection and collation. The statistics reflect the purposes for which they were gathered in the first place and the means of their production. Viewed historically, as has been said, national (recorded) statistics emerged as an aspect of 19th century governmental processes that were primarily aimed at informing those in power so that they may better measure and control populations. They were a part of the 19th century revolution in government growth. This, inevitably, has left its trace upon the statistics. While there are broad similarities in governmental structures in Western Europe, there are also marked differences. Criminological research has shown that within nation-states, local culture is of prime importance in understanding how bureaucracies work. This becomes magnified when comparing the products of the administrative processes of different countries. While most countries now publish criminal statistics, this does not mean that they were collected in the same way – that they necessarily record the same thing. Rather, the statistics reflect the specific administrative, legal and cultural processes within which the criminal justice bureaucracies are embedded. Not only does the criminal law of countries vary in substance and procedure, but so do the structure of the administrative processes used to interpret and enforce it. This has a direct and an indirect impact on the statistics. An example of the direct impact of legal and administrative differences may be found in what are know as 'counting rules'.

The counting rules are, as the name suggests, the specific rules used by the police and other criminal justice agencies to count, and ultimately to record, the crimes and offences reported to them. Different countries and jurisdictions have different counting rules. This is the case with Ireland and Scotland. In Ireland, the most important counting rule used in crimes of dishonesty is called the 'principal offence' counting rule. This states that where there are multiple offences of a similar sort committed by an offender(s) during an incident, only the most serious offence will be counted. This means, in the example given, that only one offence, the most serious, will be counted and end up in the national criminal statistics on crime, although, in court, the offender(s) may have to face more than one charge. The effect of this rule, where it operates, as it does in many European countries, therefore, is to depress the number of crimes recorded. In Scotland, there is no principal offence counting rule. Rather, in the example, each separate offence may be counted and end up in the national criminal statistics with a knock-on effect for the level of recorded crime.

It is not important here to explain why Ireland and Scotland have different counting rules – the answer probably lies in the different social and legal history of the two countries. Rather, the point of this brief example is to show the significance of differences in national practice for how we view and interpret the national statistics in each case and, therefore, how we interpret them comparatively. There are other examples of how variations in administrative procedures affect recorded crime rates. In some countries, for instance, a record of a crime is made when a crime is reported to the police, while in other countries no measure would be made until a suspect is identified and a report forwarded to the prosecutor.

The quality of data can vary quite significantly between one country and another and this can have a direct effect on comparative research. Some countries publish more information about patterns of crime and criminal justice than others and this, clearly, places limits upon what it is possible to discover and investigate. For example, although space precludes a detailed exploration of them here, the data published on the criminal justice system in Ireland is much 'thinner' than that in Scotland. The Scottish Executive publishes a series of statistical bulletins that allow the criminologist to trace in reasonable detail what happens at each stage of the criminal justice system (see Young, 1997). This is not true in Ireland. In Ireland, the data made available by the government is less full – for example, it is not possible to find a continuous series of data on the prison population, even in the 1980s and 1990s – with the result that there are 'gaps' in knowledge. Again, it is not important to investigate in detail why these differences exist but they are probably related, once more, to both differences in administrative procedures and broader cultural traditions of how much information it is seen as normal to reveal.

The reactions to scepticism

So, the sceptical case regarding the use of national statistical sources in comparative research, even in those situations where crime surveys are undertaken, is based upon solid bedrock. How have criminologists reacted to this?

The general response has been to use the national sources in cross-national comparisons of crime rates and criminal justice systems but to hedge the discussion of what they show with a series of warnings. The resulting literature tends to be understandably cautious in tone, highly descriptive, with there being many technical reservations stated about what the data says and about how far interpretations of it can be taken. Some of these traits are evident in what is regarded as one of the more authoritative discussions of the use of national statistics in comparative research:

> … the issue of whether or not it is feasible to use official criminal justice statistics for decision making in crime policy or for conducting scientific studies is one of the classic debates of criminology … In fact, the lack of uniform definitions of offences, of common measuring instruments and of common methodology makes a comparison between countries extremely hazardous (*European Sourcebook of Crime and Criminal Justice Statistics*, 1999).

There have been, however, more specific reactions. First, criminologists have formulated what could be called 'working rules', designed both to recognise the difficulties described and to place limits on the scope of any interpretation. For instance, the Research and Statistics Directorate of the Home Office (United Kingdom) regularly publishes comparative data on crime and criminal justice in the member and accession states of the European Union. This publication prefaces its presentation of data by summarising the difficulties discussed here and, in the light of them, suggests that comparisons between crime levels can never be made in absolute terms but only in terms of trends and patterns (see Barclay and Travares *et al*, 2003). This publication also recognises, however, that some crimes are not affected by the methodological difficulties discussed here, in particular, homicide. The definition of homicide in the criminal law of different countries is similar and therefore it is generally accepted that cross-national comparisons can be made (see, for example, Soothill *et al*, 1999).

Another example of formulating working rules is found in comparative studies of crime rates that respond to the problems described by settling on a common definition of a crime and then applying it in different countries (see, for example, Smith, 1983). This is often painstaking work, involving the close study of how the definitions of crimes differ in the substantive criminal law of the countries to be compared and then reworking the criminal statistics of one of them to fit the definition. The core problem with this approach is that typically it works by taking the definition of the crime given in the law of one jurisdiction and then adjusting the evidence from the comparative country. For example, the Ministry of Justice in New Zealand commissioned a study of the levels of violence in New Zealand compared to that in a number of other countries. The methodology was to note the differences in legal definitions of violence between New Zealand and the comparator but then to adjust the crime figures for New Zealand to agree with the definition of violent offences in the comparator. This meant that violent crimes in New Zealand were measured by the definition of violence used in, for example, England and Wales and the USA (see Ministry of Justice, 2002). This involved the researchers in drawing together violent and sexual assault offences, as defined in the law of New Zealand, so that they fitted with the (apparently) wider definitions of violent crime according to the law of England and Wales and the USA.

The aim here, of course, is to introduce a constant into the analysis and to measure crime levels in different countries by it. The question this raises is whether, in the process of adjustment, the contextual meanings of offences within the criminal law of a country get lost or obscured. The crime of robbery in Scotland, for example, includes offences of a less serious nature than would be included in its definition in England and Wales. To arrive at a constant measure, the less serious offences in Scotland would need, therefore, to be excluded (see Smith, 1983). This would deflate the amount of robbery seen to occur in Scotland. It would also wrench the crime from the cultural context in which it exists. The rules used to count crime are a reflection of a broader cultural context and this requires analysis. Without this contextualised interpretation, the comparison is incomplete and misleading.

The second reaction is extreme in that it consists of abandonment for the national statistics in favour of data derived from the International Crime Victimisation Survey. This is a social survey carried out in participating countries using a standardised telephone questionnaire administered to sample populations. The International Crime Victimisation Survey is the topic of another chapter and, therefore, need not be discussed here in any depth. It is worth remembering, however, that, like national victim and crime surveys, the international one has been conducted for a relatively short period. This limits its use for comparisons of crime rates and levels over the long term. Long-term comparisons are more common and important in comparative research than in research on a particular country. In these circumstances, there is no viable option but to rely on the recorded crime statistics and to accord them a central place in the research.

Even when crime surveys do exist, the position is not fundamentally changed at the practical level. The recorded crime figures are there and remain, potentially, a key source of data. It seems close to defeatism to turn away from them. This would dismiss a source of data that is problematic, but rich. The recorded crime statistics are the most continuous and the fullest record of information about crime that the criminologist possesses. The question, therefore, is what use of these statistics can the criminologist reasonably make? Is the only responsible position that of the deep sceptic? Are there other positions to occupy? This is the challenge that the comparative criminologist has to face: how to come to terms with the problems that these statistics pose, yet make creative use of them.

Coming to terms with and using national statistics in comparative research

The challenge is taken up in this section. The analysis proceeds at two levels. First, a revisionary position regarding the use of national crime statistics is discussed. This revisionary position consists of a re-evaluation of the status of national statistical sources as a reliable indicator of crime trends both nationally and, by implication, comparatively. Secondly, the section will discuss the value of the national statistics within broader interpretative frameworks that widen the type of question we ask of the data. The two levels are connected and this needs to be explained.

Criminological research does not exist in a vacuum. Rather, it is, like all scientific research, an interpretation and a process. Research originates in a sense of curiosity about the social world and how it works; research, in a sense, is about trying to solve puzzles. It differs from common sense puzzle solving, essentially, only in that it does this by methods that are systematic and public. There is a large literature on where these puzzles come from and how they are transposed into more precise research questions and we need not enter into the details of it. Rather, this literature suggests that research questions are generated by a process consisting of a continuous movement between bodies of data, the existing literature on the topic, the type of questions asked by the community of scientists to which the researcher belongs, and the more immediate demands that may arise from practical contingencies, such as patterns of funding. All this involves interpretative movement back and forth between one context and another.

Moving from one context to another can change the questions asked. The questions we ask of a body of data in one context need not be the same as those we pose in a different one. It is this simple, rather obvious, observation that links the levels of analysis in this section of the chapter and informs its argument. I wish to suggest that the imperatives of comparative research lead criminologists to ask a distinctive, if not different, series of questions about the use of national crime statistics than are asked in the sceptical argument described above.

Contexts of interpretation

The central concerns of the sceptical argument reflect a context in which the primary purpose of research is seen to be its relatively close relationship to public policy decision making. Historically, this relationship has transmogrified from optimism to scepticism. The optimism of the 19th century was nurtured by a belief in progress and in the role of science in bringing this about, against the backdrop of the long fall in crime rates that began in about 1850 and lasted until the late 1920s and early 1930s. The scepticism now evident is a product of a more sober environment that emerged in the late 1960s and early 1970s and gathered force throughout the 1980s and 1990s. Now the context was the apparent endless rise in post-war crime combined with the perceived failure of penal policy to halt it.

The scepticism is a response to an awareness that the information available about crime – principally the recorded crime statistics – is at best incomplete and thus a poor basis for informed public policy decision making. It is also, however, a measure of the enduring strength of the belief that research should have a close relationship to decision making – the invention of better measuring tools, above all the crime/victim survey, is testament to this.

Comparative research arises from a different context. Comparative research is more concerned with exploring questions of difference and sameness – whether the crime patterns of the comparative countries are similar or distinctive and what this says about the wider culture and structure of the societies. This poses a different set of puzzles that require to be solved. Their solution, of course, involves questions of measurement – such issues never go away in the social sciences – but these are no longer the central ones. A process starts that results in the criminologist seeing the national crime statistics in a different light. They become a resource to be used for the light they throw on broader issues and questions such as, for example, the causal relationship between different types or attributes of social structure and crime rates and levels. The relevance of the national crime statistics alters as the context of investigation and interpretation shifts. The methodological concerns that are a preoccupation in the sceptical case are still important, but, it is contended, the reaction to them shifts. They move from being always close to the centre of the analysis to become middle range. The problems of measurement and methodology remain to be recognised and discussed, but are they no longer an apparent barrier.

It is tempting to see this shift in interpretative context in terms of a gulf. This would be an exaggeration. Comparative research, it should be observed, is increasingly seen by governments and academic researchers as important in providing information relevant to public policy. The revisionary position, reviewed below, stems in part from public policy concerns. Knowledge about how things are done elsewhere, about the size of the crime problem in other countries, is increasingly seen as important in informing policy choices in the 'home' country. Equally, the internationalisation of both criminology and penal and criminal justice policy has made researchers and practitioners much more sensitive and receptive to comparisons. In these senses, the revisionary position marks a partial retreat from a full-blown scepticism. Its core consists of a re-evaluation of national crime statistics as reliable indicators of crime trends and patterns. This constitutes something of a return to a more optimistic view of their use, even as a tool for measuring the extent of crime.

There is another false exaggeration that requires to be addressed. Some may be tempted to see the shift in interpretative context as one from policy studies to one focused upon the elaboration of theory. It is true that comparative research tends to deal more in generalisations, while public policy research deals more in specifics. It is also true that comparative research very often draws more explicitly on theory than does the public policy literature. This does not, however, make them poles apart. It is too simple to see public policy research as atheoretical or comparative research as irrelevant to policy. The reality is that policy concerns often sharpen up theory and vice versa. Rather, the shift is one in which one set of questions comes to replace another as the dominant, but not exclusive theme. Indeed, one of the challenges of both styles of research is to develop a literature that brings them closer together.

Re-evaluating national crime statistics: the revisionary position

The re-evaluation of the use of national crime statistics has emerged as a consequence of the increased knowledge now available to criminologists about the shape of crime patterns both in their own and other countries. Criminologists have been mapping crime rates for a considerable time now and the intensity of research has increased in the last two decades.

Criminologists, today, know a lot more about patterns of crime over time than was the case, say 20 years ago. There are several (provisional) conclusions, which are as follows.

First, that in the case of the recorded crime statistics, there is a difference in the typical shape of a line measuring crime rates over time. Lines describing recorded property and dishonesty crime over time tend to be more even than lines describing change in recorded violent and sexual crimes. The lines describing change in recorded violent and sexual offences tend to be uneven or staccato in shape. In contrast, a line for recorded property crimes and crimes of dishonesty tends to be smoother, no matter whether the line rises or falls. This is a matter of relativities rather than absolutes. Figure 1 below shows examples that describe changes for some of the recorded property crimes and crimes of dishonesty in Ireland.

Figure 1: Graphs for burglary, larceny from the person and miscellaneous larceny in Ireland, 1950–98.

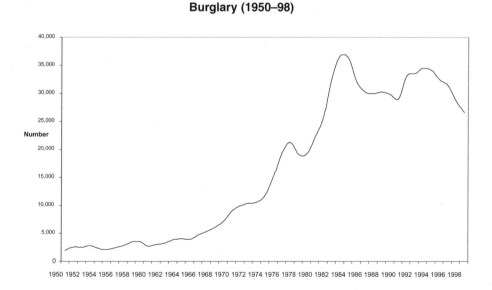

Burglary (1950–98)

Larceny from the person (1950–98)

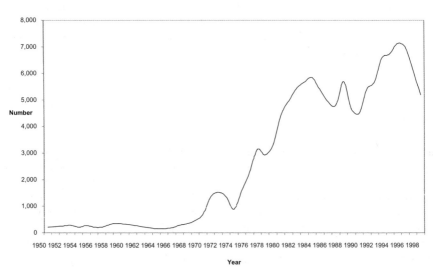

Miscellaneous larceny (1950–98)

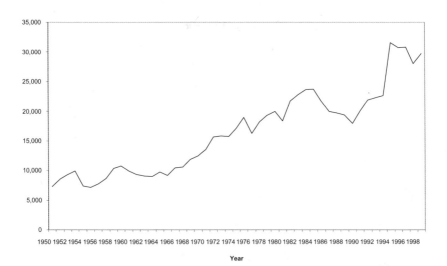

In each case, while there are fluctuations over short periods, the line for each crime for the period as a whole is relatively smooth. Compare these to the lines for recorded lethal violence, robbery and armed crime and for sexual crimes.

Figure 2: Recorded violent crime in Ireland, 1950–98.

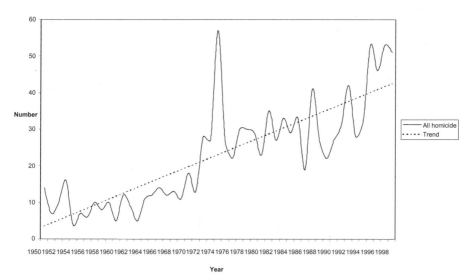

Lethal violence (1950–98)

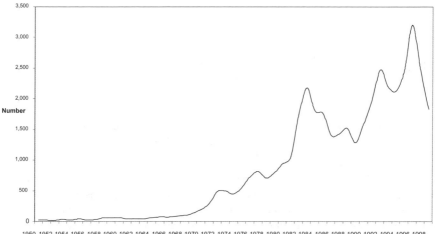

Robbery (1950–98)

Armed crime (1950–98)

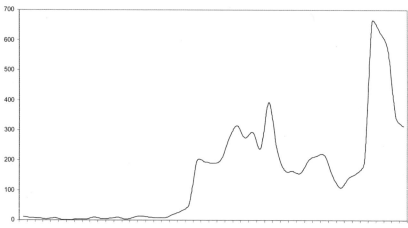

Sexual offences (1950–98)

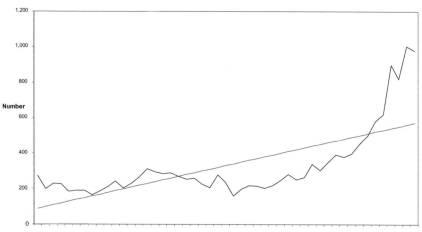

Compared to the lines for crimes against property and crimes of dishonesty, there is a much greater unevenness in the line for each of the violent crimes, particularly for lethal violence. The lines for robbery and for armed crime are similar to one another, but the overall pattern is different from that for lethal violence. While, the line for lethal violence rises throughout the period, the lines for robbery and armed crime are distinct. After a period, 1950–68, when the number of crimes recorded is low and the line flat, there is a sharp increase over a few years, and the pattern then takes on the staccato shape evident in the line for lethal violence.

The line for sexual offences shows a different pattern in some respects. Like the line for robbery and armed crime, there is a period where the line is flat, 1950–79, followed by a smooth but consistent rise thereafter. The case of sexual offences is discussed in more detail below.

There is an important caveat. The unevenness of the lines for recorded violent crimes is, in part, a reflection of the fact that these crimes tend to be small in number. A relatively small yearly increase or decrease, therefore, will have a marked impact – its 'wave' effect will be large. This certainly explains the shape of the lines for violent recorded crime in Figure 2. As recorded crimes against property and crimes of dishonesty together make up the bulk of recorded offending in most countries and are large in number, year on year alterations tend to have less impact – the wave effect is smoothed out to some degree.

What is the significance of the characteristic patterns distinguishing these two groups of recorded crime? There are a number of implications. The relative smoothness of the lines for the numerically larger group of recorded property and dishonesty crimes suggests that there is probably a reasonable degree of consistency in both recording and reporting practice within country overtime. Criminal statistics are a product of reporting and recording practices; this implies that a relatively smooth line is the result of a reasonable consistency in such practices.

It follows that the recorded crime statistics for property and dishonesty offences are a more reliable indicator of underlying trends than was allowed for in the sceptical case. To put this more precisely, it means that the recorded crime statistics for these groups of offences can be seen as the product of a consistent pattern of measurement over time and not as driven by arbitrariness or inconsistency. This removes some of the doubts about the recorded crime statistics as a (relatively) reliable tool for research. We can 'read' these recorded crime statistics with a greater degree of confidence than was once thought. For example, it would allow one to infer that sudden, sharp changes in a line for these offences probably indicates a change in either recording or reporting practice more than a change in the 'real' behaviour of offenders. A change in the real behaviour of offenders is more likely to surface gradually over a longer period, assuming a consistency in recording. The analysis can be pushed further. If there is a sharp increase that results in a step change in the line that thereafter remains around the new high, this suggests that a change in recording practice has occurred. If the line suddenly drops after a few years, then this again is liable to be due to another change in recording practice. It is possible to check this to some extent by seeking for additional internal evidence in the commentaries that accompany the published crime figures. These commentaries often announce when a change in recording practice has occurred. This can then be fed into the analysis and interpretation. (There is a greater openness in the acknowledgment of changes in recording practice these days. This is a beneficial consequence of scepticism.)

How can one read the lines for violent crimes? In the interpretation of the lines for property crimes and crimes of dishonesty, it was argued that it is possible to read their shape in a straightforward manner. This is because the general smoothness of their shape suggests there are only a small number of possibilities. The position with violent crimes and sexual crimes is different. Here, there are a greater number of possibilities to consider. Any one of a range of possibilities affects the lines describing crimes against the person (violent and sexual crime). The staccato shape of the line, combined with their small number (about 2% of recorded crimes), means that changes may be due to alterations in recording and or reporting practice as well as alterations in the underlying real behaviour of offenders.

A reading of these lines is more complex. One way of reading them is to assume that the staccato shape is a product of all of the three variables interacting, sometimes together and sometimes separately. This is very safe but not very discriminating – it does not really tell you very much. A more discriminating reading requires the researcher to widen the context of interpretation by introducing what existing research tells us about these offences. Crime surveys and other research on violent and sexual crime show that both have low rates of reporting, particularly sexual crime. This, however, is slowly changing, with a greater number of victims more willing to report the offence to the police. This helps us to interpret the lines for these offences. It implies, for example, that a continual but gradual increase in the number of sexual crimes recorded is more liable to be the outcome of more victims reporting their offences rather than there being more offending.

This helps explain the line for sexual offences in Ireland described above. The increase in the number of sexual offences recorded in Ireland is most probably due to a change in reporting practice. More victims of sexual offending reported the offence(s) committed against them. This accounts for the gradual upward direction of the line. The question as to why more sexual offences are recorded is a separate one and cannot be answered directly from the evidence in the recorded statistics. The evidence from the statistics does suggest, however, broader questions that can then be investigated. In this instance, for example, the increase in the reporting of sexual offences in Ireland is most probably related to changing attitudes to the Catholic Church and the many cases that have now become known, via a change in reporting practice, of the clergy abusing children in their care.

The reading of the lines for robbery and armed crime changes suggests a different explanation. It was argued above that changes in recording practice tend to cause sharp, step changes in a line – the line 'jumps' to a new high and remains there. The lines for robbery and armed crime certainly show a step change; this takes place in 1968. The shape thereafter, as was observed, is staccato. This implies that the increase is not due to a change in recording practice but that there has been a change in offending behaviour. Again, in this instance, the changes probably reflect the impact of the 'troubles' in Northern Ireland that resulted in increased organised criminal activity in the Republic of Ireland to finance terrorism.

So far, my discussion of the way in which the recorded criminal statistics are reliable has been based upon my own research in Ireland. Other researchers, however, have come to broadly similar conclusions after examining the recorded statistics of other countries.

For example, the same conclusion is reported in a paper by Killias and Abie. Their conclusion is based upon examining the recorded statistics for a shorter period, 1990–95, but their analysis does include more countries (those in the *European Source Book of Crime and Criminal*) (Killias and Abie, 2000). The broader scope of their inquiry also allows them to add to the argument. Killias and Abie accept that there are differences in recording practice between countries, but that the impact of this is, in some sense, neutral with regard to interpretation. The researcher can 'control' for this because it is known. Killias and Abie are not suggesting that the 'bias' introduced by different recording practices can be ignored. Rather, they appear to be suggesting that knowledge of it reduces interpretative noise. Different recording practices may result in distinct patterns of recorded crime but knowing this simplifies the comparison. It allows the researcher to compare patterns that can be regarded as the product of relatively systematic processes.

Additional evidence about the reliability of recorded crime statistics comes from comparing the results of crime surveys with the recorded statistics. This is the second point of the revisionary position. Earlier, in passing, it was stated that there is a similarity in the lines for recorded crime and victim incidents as discovered by crime surveys. So when, for example, a comparison is made between the lines for victim incidents and recorded crimes, there is a broad similarity – when the number of victim incidents reported in a crime survey shows a rise, so too will a line for recorded crime but, typically, at a faster rate (see Young, 2001, pp 86–88). This is an important and revealing comparison. It adds support to the argument above by suggesting that recorded crime statistics pick up on underlying trends much more than was thought. The observation reinforces the case put for the reliability of the recorded crime statistics.

This point must not be overstated. The strength of the relationship between survey crime and recorded crime holds most when comparisons are made for the total of each and then only for certain categories of crime. The crimes in which it is strongest are those, unsurprisingly, which are known to have high rates of reporting and recording. This includes crimes such as burglary and the theft of motor vehicles and from motor vehicles. The relationship holds less in crimes that do not have a high rate of reporting, such as the personal crimes and offences such as vandalism.

There is, therefore, evidence that helps to offset some of the deep and serious doubts raised about the reliability and use of the recorded crime statistics. Recorded crime statistics are reliable indicators but – and this is the important point – in context. The recorded crime statistics need to be placed in the context of their production and interpreted in context. This requires the exercise of judgment and knowledge by the researcher. The knowledge required is a combination of awareness of how the statistics to be compared have been put together and some basic understanding of the typical shape of crime patterns. The implication of work such as that of Killias and Abie is that research has reached a stage where the criminologist can have a greater confidence in the recorded crime statistics so that meaningful comparisons can be undertaken. This confidence is the result of knowledge accumulating by increments and bears out what was said earlier. Research is a process in which there is a constant movement between data, concepts and already existing knowledge. Ironically, it may have been noticed, the prime mover in this has been the sceptical position itself. The legacy of the sceptical argument is that, by making criminologists so cautious about the use of statistics, it has also made them increasingly aware of how and when national statistics can be used. The emerging revisionary literature is a consequence of this; it is increasingly showing how reasoned interpretations can be made of national crime statistics and, in itself, constitutes an advance in knowledge.

Comparative research and benchmarks

One response to the above could be that the argument so far has concentrated mostly on the problems of using national crime statistics in a national context. There has yet to be an equally full discussion that focuses upon their use comparatively.

There is substance in this, but the retort is that the starting point for a discussion of how national statistics can be used in comparative research has to deal with the very telling criticisms made by the sceptical position. The sceptical position makes the use of national statistics highly problematic whatever the context. The point of the argument so far, has not been to deny the validity of the criticisms, but to suggest that their impact may be differentially assessed depending on what has been called the context of interpretation. As the questions we ask change, so too does the use we make of the statistics. The revisionary position is an example of this. As the context shifts more to using national statistics in a comparative context, then different understandings of their strengths and weaknesses emerge.

Notwithstanding this, however, more does need to be said explicitly about the methodology of comparative research. One key stage in comparative research is the formulation of what is called a benchmark concept. A benchmark concept serves the purpose of 'bridging' between culturally specific meanings or expressions of a practice or an institution. For example, as has been said, the criminal law of two countries may give specific meanings, say, to the crime of theft. A benchmark concept bridges the 'gap' created by these differences, so that the researcher can be confident that like is being compared to like.

There is an aspect of the sceptical position that makes it difficult to imagine what a benchmark concept in comparative research on crime rates would look like. The concerns expressed in the quotation taken from the *European Source Book of Crime and Criminal Justice Statistics* and referred to earlier are an example of this. Moreover, even, if the arguments described immediately above are accepted, there is still a fundamental point to be addressed. The point now is one about the comparability of basic criminal law concepts, not about the comparability of the empirical data of different countries. If criminal law is culturally specific, then how can it – or the actions taken upon its basis, such as arrest, prosecution and conviction – be compared?

The call for a benchmark concept in comparative research on crime rates, then, is essentially an argument about bridging between and comparing different conceptual schemes. In order to achieve this, we must have some idea about what type of conceptual scheme criminal law is – about what functions and purposes criminal law serves. The concepts of the criminal law of a country may be conceived of as both constitutive of and a reflection of a system of values by which harm – in this case, law breaking – is assessed and measured. In liberal theories about the nature of criminal law, it is seen as one way in which societies express collective values proscribing harm. The criminal law is also usually seen as hierarchical – the categories in which the criminal law are organised are evaluative in that they establish a scale of harm, normally a simple one from serious to less serious.

The conception of criminal law as a hierarchical system of values is the key to formulating benchmark concepts. In *The Division of Labour in Society*, Durkheim developed a conception of law as an index of social solidarity. By this, Durkheim meant that the values expressed by criminal law reflect the norms and values of the wider society. Durkheim also argued that crime is a normal social fact; that it is regular feature of all societies, precisely because it is, according to him, a necessary feature of group life. These two theses offer mutual support. Durkheim is suggesting that societies exhibit common systems of categories both in their conceptions of harm and by which responses to harm are organised. The concept of crime is a constant feature of societies because it is an expression of a basic ingredient of even the most fundamental form of social life – the group. Social solidarity – the collective conscience or system of values that form a common identity – emerges in a group only as a conception of wrongdoing and of harm are formed. All types of social organisation, from the simplest to the most complex, thus must have conceptual spaces or categories that give expression to concepts of harm, wrongdoing and responses to this.

It was on this basis that Durkheim argued that the criminal law categories of different societies have a marked similarity. Their hierarchical system of values are remarkably similar. At the top of the hierarchy are crimes that offend against what are seen as the basic constituents of social life, including taking human life and the violation of institutions or attributes of institutions that are perceived to be sacred. Lower in the hierarchy will be crimes that offend against facets of social life that are not imbued with a sense of the sacred. Durkheim was perfectly aware that the precise content of crime and, indeed, of what was regarded as sacred, varied with time and place, but, he contended, they are present in all societies, at every stage of their development.

This suggests that the concept of crime itself can be taken as a benchmark concept in research. This is not because the concept of crime is seen to be the same everywhere but because it stands as an index of a common set of values and categories found in all societies. This is a strong thesis. Is there empirical support for it?

The crucial question here concerns the nature of the values expressed in criminal law and the way they are organised hierarchically. If the way in which the categories of the criminal law in Scotland and Ireland are compared, there is a striking similarity. First, both systems are premised upon a distinction between crimes that are seen as serious and less serious and then there are sub-categories within each. In Ireland, the basic distinction was between the serious indictable offences and the less serious non-indictable offences, or, as they are called now, headline and non-headline offences. In Scotland, the distinction is between serious crimes and less serious offences. In each country, within the serious category, there are sub-categories distinguishing between crimes against the person, crimes against property, larcenies and a heterogeneous category of other.

The sub-categories contained in the less serious non-headline offences (Ireland) and offences (Scotland) differ, but the content overall is similar. Here one will find offences connected above all with moving traffic violations, with public order offences and offences against, for example, the relevant telecommunications act(s).

There is not room in this chapter to look at other countries' systems of criminal law in depth. Rather, this is only as an illustration of Durkheim's thesis and its application to the problem discussed here – how to formulate a benchmark concept that enables researchers to undertake comparisons of criminal statistics. The solution is to examine the way in which the categories of a country's criminal law is organised in the light of Durkheim's broader arguments about the functional nature of the categories of knowledge found in different societies. The precise content of the criminal law may differ, but at the categorical or conceptual level there is, typically, a similarity. This enables the researcher to begin the comparison. As the research gets more detailed, it may be that differences begin to appear, but the benchmark will have been established and this will allow variations to be explored.

This argument can be extended. Criminologists tend to ignore the way in which the criminal law is organised as a topic for research. These categories can be explored empirically and add another type of evidence to empirical research. While the broad categories in which modern criminal law is organised remain fairly stable, they are periodically reorganised and also specific offences can move up and down the hierarchy of values from serious to less serious. Criminologists are used to regarding these as changes in recording practice, but these shifts ought to be regarded as worthy of research in their own right for what they tell us about the impact of social change on criminal law. For example, in Scotland at the start of the 20th century, the most common crime of violence was husband and wife assault. This offence was moved down the hierarchy of seriousness over a period of about 30 years, to end up in what were then known as 'miscellaneous offences'. This marks a social change of some significance, as it marks broader changes in social attitude or the response of the authorities to this type of crime.

There is another more general example. Following Durkheim, it has been argued that the categories in which crimes are perceived remain relatively stable. This applies more to the serious categories of crime than the less serious. It is the less serious categories of crime – the non-headline, the offences, the non-notifiable offences, the misdemeanours – that change most. This suggests that it is in this category of crime that the researcher can most easily identify the impact of social change on law. For example, information on recorded crime in Ireland is made available in the yearly reports of the Commissioner of An Garda Siochana (the police force). These reports are available from 1947. It is interesting to examine the specific offences listed in the non-indictable offence category and how they changed overtime. In 1950, the list is small and contains a small number of specific offences such as those against the Noxious Weeds Act, the Agriculture Produce (Eggs) Act and the Offences Game Laws. There are only three rows of offences recording violations of traffic offences. By contrast, in 1998, the list has now extended to 103 separate offences, 46 of which relate to road traffic. This clearly shows the impact of social change on the criminal law and the recorded criminal statistics.

Finally, an alternative view of the use of recorded statistics

This last brief section is concerned with an alternative view of the use of, in particular, the recorded criminal statistics. This view derives from an interactionist perspective on crime and deviance. It differs in several respects from the views discussed so far, but the most significant of these is in the place it allocates to the recorded crime statistics in constructing explanations.

In the view examined so far, the relationship between the data and the explanation is one in which, to simplify matters, the data contains the material that has then to be explained. In an interactionist perspective, this relationship is changed – there is, to use the vocabulary developed here, a shift in interpretative context. An interactionist sees the recorded statistics as fitting into a more general explanation of deviance and crime that stresses the importance of the labelling process. Deviance and crime are said not to be an attribute of an act but of the label applied to it.

In an important but somewhat neglected paper, Kitsuse and Cicourel (1963) apply an interactionist perspective to the use of recorded crime statistics. They introduce the concept of the 'rate producing process'. By this they mean the institutions involved in transferring an act of deviance into a criminal act. The rate producing process consists, in other words, of those powerful institutions able to enforce labels – the criminal justice system, primarily, but also, in certain contexts, probation officers and social workers. Kitsuse and Cicourel suggest that sociologists ought to study the processes by which meaning is ascribed to actions.

The implications of this view are far-reaching. It suggests that far from being a weakness in the recorded crime statistics, the dark figure of crime actually tells you what you want to know. The 'output' of the rate producing process, measured directly by the recorded statistics, provides an insight into the process by which criminal labels are attached to actors. The rate producing process consists of a series of interactions in which a special type of meaning – crime – is ascribed to actions. The recorded statistics are an index of the values, the types of power, involved in the social interactions that produce crime.

Kitsuse and Cicourel never develop this argument systematically and certainly not in the context of comparative research in different countries. Cicourel did, however, apply the logic of the argument in a specific analysis of the rate producing process in his classic study, *The Social Organisation of Juvenile Justice*. Here, Cicourel showed that the reasons why two very similar cities had different rates of juvenile justice were not to do with the attributes of the offenders or differences in the social structure of the two cities. Rather, the rate producing processes differed, in that in one city there was a policy of processing juveniles through the criminal justice system, while in the other, the policy was one of diversion.

This is a comparative analysis within a country. The logic of the argument ought, in principle, to be applicable to international comparisons. This would require the criminologist to view the recorded crime statistics as indicators of differences in the rate producing processes in each (or several) countries. The comparison would thus be between the rate producing processes of different states, not what the recorded crime statistics have to tell us about the extent or volume of crime in each country.

This would constitute a shift in interpretative context that is more profound than that described above. The criminologist, of course, does not have to choose one or the other. As was said, research consists of moving between contexts. It does not mean being fixed in one.

Conclusion

Comparative analysis is difficult work. Yet, as Weber, argued, all sociology is implicitly comparative. Sociology is founded upon the exploration of difference and sameness and in an explanation of these. For Weber, Marx and Durkheim, this was a quest to explore and explain the uniqueness of capitalist or industrial society and ultimately, at least for Weber, the uniqueness of the occident. Using national criminal statistics does not necessitate the taking on of questions that are quite as big as these, but it does involve coming to terms with some of the same issues.

The proposal here is that national criminal statistics are a rich, invaluable, source of data for criminologists. In the last few decades there has been a deep-seated scepticism that has made the realisation of their potential difficult. The solution to this, it is suggested, lies in appreciating that we can ask more than one type of question about, and of, the criminal statistics. There are different contexts of interpretation within which we can place criminal statistics, each of which conditions their use. The realisation of this expands the explanatory agenda and releases the sociological imagination.

References

Barclay G, Travares, C et al (2003) International Comparisons of Criminal Justice Statistics 2001, Home Office Issue 12/03, London: HMSO

Cicourel, AV (1968) The Social Organization of Social Justice, New York: John Wiley

Durkheim, E (1984) The Division of Labour in Society, first published 1893, London: Macmillan

European Sourcebook of Crime and Criminal Justice Statistics (1999), Strasbourg: Council of Europe

Killias, M and Abie, M (2000) 'Comparing crime rates' 8(1) European Journal of Criminal Policy and Research 1

Kitsuse, J and Cicourel, A (1963) 'A note on the uses of official statistics' 11 Social Problems 131–39

Ministry of Justice (2002) International Comparisons of Violence, New Zealand, Wellington: Ministry of Justice

Smith, L (1983) Criminal Justice Comparisons: The Case of Scotland and England and Wales, London: Home Office

Soothill, K et al (1999) Homicide in Britain: A Comparative Study of Rates in Scotland and England and Wales, Scottish Executive, Research Findings, No 36

Young P (1997) Crime and Criminal Justice in Scotland, London: The Stationery Office

Young P (2001) Crime in Ireland, Dublin: The National Crime Council

Chapter 3
Relativism, Transnationalisation and Comparative Criminology

James Sheptycki

Have we now so far lowered our sights as to settle for a relativistic doctrine of truth – rating the statements of each theory as true for that theory, and brooking no higher criticism? Not so. The saving consideration is that we continue to take seriously our own particular aggregate science, our own particular world-theory or loose total fabric of quasi-theories, whatever it may be. Unlike Descartes, we own and use our beliefs of the moment, even in the midst of philosophising, until by what is vaguely called scientific method we change them here and there for the better. Within our total evolving doctrine, we can judge truth as earnestly and absolutely as can be, subject to correction, but that goes without saying (WV Quine, *Word and Object*, 1960).

'Freedom from fear' could be said to sum up the whole philosophy of human rights (Dag Hammarskjöld, Former UN Secretary-General).

Introduction

Herman Mannheim, one of the founders of British academic criminology, was unequivocal on the subject. There can be no immutable standards for 'natural law' and crime is a relative concept:

> There is no single and unchanging concept of natural law. While its underlying idea is the longing of mankind for an absolute yardstick to measure the goodness or badness of human actions and the law of the State and to define their relations and morality, the final lesson is that no such yardstick can be found (1965, p 47).

Writing in defence of the methodology adopted in the International Crime Victimisation Survey (ICVS), Jan van Dijk argued that 'the almost perfect correlations between the ranking of crime types by victims from six regions [of the world] indicates a high degree of consensus about the import of conventional crimes against individuals across the world' (1999, pp 28–29).

These two perspectives reflect on a key problem for comparative criminology. One a relativistic and philosophical view and the other an empirical and positivistic one, both are concerned with the nature of criminology's object. All too often students of criminology are encouraged to range these views along a continuum. This lazy way of thinking holds that on the one hand there is absolute relativism and on the other there is positive science. On this view, the task is to find the right 'balance' between these two viewpoints. The former is easily rubbished as the first step on the slippery slope to solipsism (Leavitt, 1990, p 25). The latter has been strongly criticised for its denial of the role that human consciousness plays in the development of meaning, and consequently, for ignoring the presence of different value systems or ways of looking at things and the conflicts that arise because of those differences. The trick played here is an old one since, having staked out two extreme views, any balance a particular author claims to have struck can be claimed as the Aristotelian 'golden mean'. What makes this balancing act sophistic is that it obscures more than it reveals. In particular, such a balancing act can be used, consciously or unconsciously, to draw a veil over the politics of crime, its definition and control.

These two approaches, the relativistic one and the positive science one, are not at opposing ends of a spectrum at all. They are but two ways among many of looking at the practices of social science generally and criminology in particular. Indeed, if there is a logical opposite to relativism it is absolutism. Where the philosophical relativist says that the truth of the matter depends on one's point of view, the philosophical absolutist says that there can be but one truth. The logical opposite of the scientific point of view is one based on faith or guesswork. Where the scientist painstakingly tries to define and measure phenomena, with more or less due care and attention to methodological shortcomings, the *dilettante* is content with intuitive guesstimates. Both relativism and positive science have their vices; one can conjure up examples of positivist absolutism or relativistic conjecturalism. Simplistic recipes that prescribe an appropriate 'balance' between relativism and science risk producing either a hopeless muddle, or a spurious halo of neutrality.

This problem was probably not quite so urgent in the mid-20th century, when academic criminology was in its period of germination and first great efflorescence. That is because during those years virtually all crimes conventionally defined were understood to be rooted in localities, and criminology was mostly a parochial practice. When Terry Morris published *The Criminal Area* in 1957, or even before that, when Clifford Shaw and colleagues published *Delinquency Areas* in 1929, the ecology and culture of crime in particular local communities is what exercised academic criminologists who, for the most part, confined their attentions relatively close to home. The communities criminologists studied were very often defined as 'inner-city' areas and acolyte students of the discipline were ritually exposed year in and year out to the concentric zone diagram bequeathed to criminology by the Chicago School. In such times, the politics of comparative criminology were safely confined to the academic world. Like collectors of rare butterflies ensconced in museums, comparative criminologists' ideas were rarely discussed outside of the academic setting. Now the butterfly collectors are out of the museum and what they know about butterflies is insightful for what we might do about global warming and air pollution. Similarly, the comparative criminologists have left their seminar rooms to become consultants in global crime control.

It is obvious that the era that confronts us is one that is defined by transnational practices that have changed the nature of localities. Whether it be Croydon in south London, a Parisian suburb like Gennevilliers, or 'world cities' like Toronto, or Mumbai (once called Bombay by the colonial powers), the world according to criminology is no longer composed of neatly defined communities cut off from one another and ready for comparison between their pristine forms. This is not to deny the importance of locality – Paris and Toronto are different from each other, as are London and Mumbai. The city of Chicago is an early exemplification of the transnational city, since the patterns of its zonal development were partly driven by immigration, but it too has its own particularity. Then too, the criminological expertise has become transnational (Chan, Chapter 15, this volume) and crime control solutions are being exported around the globe. Because the world has become transnationalised, crime and criminological expertise are no longer of rarefied interest to a few academic criminologists.

This chapter unfolds in four parts. First I look at the way positivist science has contributed to criminological understanding. Next, there is an examination of relativism as it pertains to comparative criminology. The overview presented in these sections does some disservice to the history of criminological ideas, but I hope it also helps to convey the range of possibilities for transnational criminology. In the section that follows, and by way of illustrative example, I overview some of the available evidence regarding the transnational trajectories of male violence towards women. My intent is to show how the methodological practices of comparative criminology can be reconciled with both its scientific and philosophical roots, even while comparative criminology is challenged by the processes of transnationalisation. I conclude, first by acknowledging the urgency surrounding the contemporary practices of criminology in a globalising world – the pressure to do something about the 'crime problem' – and secondly by urging academic criminologists globally to reach outside the discipline for their moral compass.

The historical currents of positive science and comparative criminology

Positivism was established as a beacon for the human sciences during the time of Auguste Comte (Swingewood, 1984). Historically speaking, positive science has been an attempt to record objectively given relations between observable phenomena, and codify them into generalised or universal laws. The knowledge gained through the practices of positive science forms the basis for the prediction and control of natural and social processes. At its most ambitious, positivism aims to project and sustain a scientific basis for politics, the aim of which is to organise social life on a rational basis. Positivism is the handmaiden of social engineering. 'The essential aim of practical politics,' Comte wrote, is 'to avoid the violent revolutions which spring from obstacles opposed to the progress of civilisation' (Swingewood, 1984, p 42).

The use of positivist methodology in comparative criminology goes back to the earliest days of the discipline. Adolphe Quetelet was one of the first people to apply a sociological positivist approach to the study of crime.[1] Quetelet was the first person to attempt to make generalised comparisons concerning crime rates across different populations using official government statistics because he was practically the first to have such statistics to work with. In 1825, the French Government of the day commissioned the first national statistical tables on crime – the *Compte général* (General account). This account, first published in 1827, included information on the annual number of known and prosecuted crimes against persons and property, whether the accused (if prosecuted) was acquitted or convicted, and details of the punishments meted out. Other information that it recorded included the time of year when the offence took place, as well as the age, sex, occupation and educational status of the accused and the convicted.

1 A distinction between biological positivism and sociological positivism has been drawn. The former has a long history in criminology going back to Cesare Lombroso who introduced the idea of the 'born criminal' to criminology in 1876. This paper has relatively less to say about this variety of positivism, which, in any case, has had less application in the context of comparative criminology.

Using these statistics, Quetelet was able to undertake comparative work on crime rates across France. Using the data from the *Compte* generated between 1826 and 1829 he observed that young males, the poor, those with less education who worked in lowly occupations or were without employment were more likely to be apprehended in, or accused of, committing crime and to be convicted. Moreover, he was also able to show that crime rates differed in different regions of France. One of the conclusions he reached was that poverty in itself did not cause crime. He noted that neither the prevalence of poverty nor the lack of formal education was the key causal factor in predicting crime rates. This was because it was observable that some of the poorest regions, and those with the lowest literacy rates, also had the lowest crime rates. Using statistical methods of considerable sophistication (Quetelet's first calling was as a mathematician and astronomer) he was able to show that a more important factor than poverty itself was the unequal distribution of wealth. It was regions where the poor found themselves 'surrounded by the subjects of temptation' and where they were 'irritated by the continual view of luxury and of an inequality of fortune which disheartens them' that produced higher crime rates (Quetelet, quoted in Beirne and Messerschmidt, 1995, p 346). In other words, by using these statistics and a positivistic comparative method, Quetelet identified the problem of relative deprivation. What is more, using this approach he was able to show that the ebb and flow of relative deprivation helped to explain the rise and fall in crime rates over time. (For a more detailed discussion of the work of Adolphe Quetelet, see Piers Beirne's excellent collection of essays *Inventing Criminology*, 1993.)

In the more recent past, criminologists have been interested to undertake this kind of study on a much bigger scale, comparing rates of officially recorded crime cross-nationally (Wolfgang, 1967; Gurr *et al*, 1977; Kalish, 1988; Bennett and Lynch, 1990; Westfelt and Estrada, Chapter 1, this volume). The immediate problem for this kind of study has been in lack of standardisation in criminal record keeping. The *Compte général* may not have provided a perfect record of all recordable crimes committed in France (a fact that Quetelet clearly recognised), but it had the merit of being reasonably standardised across the country. This has not been true when it comes to making international comparisons. Due to differences in how criminal laws are defined in different national jurisdictions, and different record keeping practices in police and other criminal justice agencies, it has been extremely difficult to make the kind of generalisations that positivist science usually aims at. Observing these difficulties Marvin Wolfgang (1967) advocated a kind of global *Compte général*: 'a team of experts from an international organisation could, like the field representatives of the Department of Justice in the United States, help individual countries to set up and promote reliable reporting systems' (p 66).

Beginning in 1977, the United Nations Centre for International Crime Prevention has undertaken systematic surveys of many countries' official crime statistics. These are the United Nations Surveys of Crime Trends and Operation of Criminal Justice Systems (UNCJS). The first survey compiled information from 72 different countries; by the time of the fifth iteration of this process, data was being received by 103 countries (Newman, 1999, p 5). Criminologists working with officially recorded data of this type have long recognised their shortcomings but have also argued that the 'seemingly insurmountable difficulties in the collection of valid and reliable crime data does not mean that official crime statistics at the international level are totally useless as a measure of crime itself' (Newman, 1999, p 11). One example used to illustrate some of the utility of official records pertaining to criminal victimisation concerns homicide statistics. Noting that data generated by the UNCJS, Interpol and by the World Health Organisation (WHO) are the product of different sets of institutional processes (the former two by police and criminal justice agents, the latter by medical professionals), it becomes possible to compare, and thereby test, the reliability of the different data sets. Such an analysis 'permits the general conclusion that, at least for the case of homicide, the data from the UNCJS are reliable indicators of crime and criminal justice' (Newman, 1999, p 13). These data are thought to be particularly useful in making broad comparisons by grouping countries together according to specific criteria (for example, 'level of development').

Criminologists working in specifically national contexts have long noted the tendency of official crime statistics to undercount instances of crime. Further, generalisations about changes over time in officially reported and recorded crime rates generate considerable discussion as to whether the actual propensity for crime had shifted or whether changes in reporting and recording practice were responsible for the observed changes (Maguire, 1997, 2002). The term the 'dark figure of crime' has been used to describe the tendency to under-reporting, and the strategy of the victimisation survey has been used to provide another measure of crime and victimisation rates independent of governmental bureaucracies. Beginning in the 1970s in the United States and in the 1980s in the United Kingdom, national victim surveys have been conducted at regular intervals. There is not the space here to consider the many methodological aspects of this type of scientific venture, and the kinds of qualifications that need to be made in interpretation of the data, suffice it to say that such surveys do not provide a total picture of crime but can provide pictures that relate selected categories of offences (Maguire, 1997, p 164).

Some participants in these early studies have argued that '... it was inevitable that as more was understood about the value of survey information, and about the effect that methodology can have on how much and what is counted, a case would be made for a standardised survey in different countries' (van Dijk and Mayhew, 1993, p 1). So saying, the data gathered by the first ICVS were presented and discussed. These data were gathered principally by telephone survey and consisted of information about the level of offences, patterns of reporting to the police and fear of crime.[2] They argued that 'the overall annual crime prevalence measure from the two sweeps of the ICVS is a readily understandable indicator of proneness to victimisation in different countries' (van Dijk and Mayhew, 1993, p 35). Further, one of the conclusions that the authors felt justified in arriving at was that victimisation rates were positively related to the degree of urbanisation and that 'due to the

---

2 This chapter draws on findings from two surveys conducted in 1989 and 1992 in 20 countries. Only eight of these countries took part in both sweeps (Australia, Belgium, Canada, England and Wales, Finland, the Netherlands, the United States and Japan). Another seven took part in the 1989 sweep (West Germany, France, Northern Ireland, Norway, Scotland, Spain, and Switzerland) and another five in 1992 (Italy, New Zealand, Sweden, Poland and Czechoslovakia (since separated into the Czech Republic and the Slovak Republic)).

greater supply of suitable targets and perhaps less informal social control, "city air" seems to breed crime in most countries – though Japan is a notable exception to the rule' (van Dijk and Mayhew, 1993, p 35).

I want to return to the issue of Japanese exceptionalism momentarily. But before attending to the relativist case against 'hard' statistical data, I would first like to turn the reader's attention to the aims and purposes of the positivist approach. The goal of the positivistic criminological science reviewed here is to make generalisations about the distribution and causes of anti-social and criminal behaviour. Criminologists working in this vein observe that the evidence they produce suggests generalisable patterns, but also usually recognise that any such patterns are based upon less than complete information from a less than representative sample of societies. The limitations of the data notwithstanding, these criminologists work towards the elaboration of a general understanding about the aetiology of crime (that is, its causes). Most often this will take the form of a theoretical model and not a formal theory. On the basis of the existing empirical data, positivist criminologists attempt to specify the kinds of conditions that produce or exacerbate crime and social disorder and specify connections between broader social conditions (for example, the age profile of the population, or relative rates of deprivation or unemployment) and crime rates. According to Bob Burnham, this science, especially as undertaken under the auspices of the United Nations, has gradually shifted away from a narrow focus on aetiology towards one of assisting participating countries in the management of their respective criminal justice apparatuses (in Newman, 1999, p 2). In either instance, there is a palpable emphasis on engineering lower crime rates, or at least improved standards for their manufacture.

Thus we can see that the focus of much of what can be comfortably described as positivistic comparative criminology holds true to the original aims and purposes set out by Auguste Comte and like-minded thinkers at the dawn of Enlightenment sociology. First, such criminologists aim to develop generalisations and theories based on empirically observable and measurable phenomena. Secondly, on the basis of their evidence and the theories they derive, comparative criminologists working in this tradition aim to contribute to the management of national and, increasingly in the 'global era', international bureaucracies established to control crime. Positivistic science of this sort has placed considerable emphasis on methodological subtlety and its practitioners continually warn about the need to be wary of the shortcomings of the data with which they work. Despite any cautionary note about the shortcomings of available data, criminological positivists remain dedicated to 'knowing the causes of things' and, on the basis of that knowledge, engaging with attempts at social engineering aimed at advancing the 'civilising process'.

Relativist thought and comparative criminology

Relativism, at least in the social scientific and humanistic disciplines, can be viewed as a sceptical counter-weight to the positivist scientific outlook. As such, it may provide the defensive backstop against ill-conceived attempts at social engineering. Sociological relativists claim nothing more than that our view of the world is relative to the concepts with which we order it. Since Karl Mannheim forged the discipline of the sociology of knowledge in the 1920s, relativist thinking in sociology has attempted to understand how systems of thought shape our view of the empirical world. Philosophical debates about the relativity of knowledge and truth have been highly elaborated and it is possible to distinguish a number of different perspectives: Gregory Leavitt observes that the term has diverse meanings, and ones that are not necessarily theoretically or philosophically compatible (Leavitt, 1990, p 7). Terms that he mentions include: contextual, cultural and epistemological relativism, as well as subjectivism. He groups these concepts under the general heading of 'foundational relativism'. Leavitt also discusses 'anti-foundational relativism', which includes ontological relativism, postmodernism (exemplified by the work of Richard Rorty) and hermeneutics. With so many nuances, it is somewhat disingenuous, and perhaps dangerous, to generalise. Nevertheless, all of the people working within a relativist perspective would probably agree that a main problem to tackle is how to understand and appreciate differences in the way that individuals or social groups (be they subcultures, cultures, societies or nations) comprehend and relate to their social world. Further, the sociology of knowledge is very often interested to explain the conditions that allow one view of a particular phenomenon, rather than any other, to rise to prominence.

There are few criminologists who have attempted to articulate a thoroughgoing relativism, and none has done so with more eloquence than Ezzat Fattah who, among other accomplishments, founded the School of Criminology at Simon Fraser University, British Columbia, Canada. After a thorough and scholarly discussion of the many and varied attempts to define the subject of criminology that have been attempted during the history of the discipline, Fattah confidently declared:

> ... definitions of crime are varied. There is no universal or agreed upon definition. Different definitions reflect the multi-disciplinary background of students of crime and suggest that the term 'crime' does not have a single, consistent meaning. It means different things to different people. Each scholar has his/her own conception of what crime is. For this reason, working out a generally satisfactory definition of crime is not as simple as it might appear. One wonders whether it will ever be possible to formulate a definition that integrates the various views and does not place the emphasis on any one aspect of crime to the exclusion or the neglect of others ... [perhaps] all attempts are doomed to fail (Fattah, 1997, p 37).

According to Fattah, the application of the concept of crime to types of human conduct is varied for a number of reasons. Foremost among them is that acts may be defined as criminal for political reasons and so it is possible to argue that:

> Terrorism, like crime, is a relative, pejorative, value-laden, emotionally loaded and ideologically tainted term. With crime, there is at least the criminal code, which singles out certain behaviours and defines them as criminal. There is no equivalent to the criminal codes in the area of terrorism, and people have to rely on their own conceptions and perceptions to designate certain activities as terrorist. In other words, terrorism is in the eye of the beholder. Labelling a certain act as 'terrorist' is a value judgment, a subjective construction of social reality (Fattah, p 58).

Fattah also noted the contested and political nature of other applications of the criminal label, citing euthanasia (which he calls 'mercy killing'), assisted suicide, artificial insemination, homosexuality, pornography, prostitution, gambling, lotteries and abortion as examples. He even argued that the experience of victimisation, abuse and neglect are culturally relative. To a relativist the appropriateness or inappropriateness of criminal labels depends in important ways on perspective. Hence the application of the criminal label is never fixed and, on reflection, always contestable.

What, in practical terms, does this mean for criminology? One thing is immediately evident. Relativism shifts attention away from the so called 'facts of crime' and on to the social processes that define certain facts as criminal. This is in keeping with Durkheim's insistence that 'we do not reprove it because it is a crime, but it is a crime because we reprove it' (1960, p 42). Crime is the product of definition, as Howard Becker famously put it:

> Deviance is not a quality of an act the person commits, but rather a consequence of the application by others of rules and sanctions to an offender. The deviant is one to whom the label has successfully been applied; deviant behaviour is behaviour that people so label (1963, p 9).

This view is incompatible with the notion of born criminals or the existence of a crimogenic gene (biological positivism). If there is not crime, but only acts labelled as such, how could it be said that some individuals are born good and others are born bad? Only after we have been disabused of the Lombrosian fallacy, relativists might argue, does it become possible to study the processes by which some acts become defined as criminal while others, which may entail greater degrees of harm, escape such definition. Studying processes of defining crime yields examples of what the anthropologist Mary Douglas described as 'institutional thinking' (1986). Unmasking the 'social construction' of categories of crime by criminal justice institutions has long been a central plank in the programme of academic criminology. This perspective can be readily applied to the institutions that support the sociological variety of positivist criminology practised by Quetelet and the social scientists following in his wake (for example, see Haggerty, 2001). From this perspective, the *Compte général*, and contemporary equivalents such as the UNCJS (and even innovations such as the ICVS and national crime surveys), attempt to define crime and make it measurable and, in so doing, create and/or reaffirm a socially constructed norm. Seen this way, the task of the comparative criminologist is not merely to compare and contrast the findings (hard data) produced by positivistic social scientists. Rather, it becomes an attempt to compare the social, cultural and institutional context in which certain acts become defined as criminal and measured as crimes. In the context of comparative criminology, and indeed social science more generally, the relativist point of view highlights the abstracted nature of 'positive science', and warns that it is too easily imbued with the quality of objective neutrality.

Relativism in criminology comes in many guises and few, if any, criminologists have attempted to maintain a position of absolute relativism.[3] Fattah, it should be made clear, remained quite grounded by virtue of his abiding interest in the politics

---

3 Most criminological relativists would probably agree that absolute relativism is preposterous. It is a contradiction in terms. If all understanding is relative, that too is a relative statement. A universal claim of the form 'all knowledge is relative' is a logical impossibility and thereby negates itself (Giddens, 1976, pp 63–65).

of victimology. Gregory Leavitt (1990) has argued that philosophical relativism is a highly complex and diverse position, but that in criminology it has tended to be oversimplified, unspecified and contradictory. According to him, 'while relativism in the past and present continues to influence criminological theory, most criminologists are not aware of, or are only superficially aware of, what relativism fully means and how it influences criminology' (p 9). His view is that relativist ideas are a 'bar to science' and it is largely responsible for 'preventing a comparative thesis in American criminology' (Leavitt, 1990, p 25). This is too pessimistic. More often criminological scholars (and certainly European ones) come equipped with an historical sense of the discipline and are apt to think in terms of successive waves of different thought styles.[4] Sociological relativism claims nothing more than that our view of the world is relative to the concepts with which we order it. As such, it is very much in the comparative spirit. It is possible to see how such thought systems change over time as the social conditions that uphold them change and also how different intellectual communities foster and protect specific paradigms. In this sense, criminological relativists tend towards a Kuhnian relativism (Kuhn, 1962) and to a pragmatic and methodological view of the place of relativist thinking in comparative criminology.

To return to the question about how to explain the historically low crime rates in Japan (expressed in both official statistics and the results of victim surveys), comparative criminologists who are sensitive to relativist thinking, should therefore seek to draw on a wide range of sources to enhance understanding and appreciation. Miyazawa (1992) advocates that criminologists combine sources, especially ethnographic studies and quantitative measures of statistical variation, in what he refers to as the 'second best method'. In the Japanese case, he points especially to the need to understand informal social control exercised by families, schools, corporations and traditional religion (on the importance of informal social control and the role of religion for low crime rate societies, see also Wardak, Chapter 4, this volume). According to Miyazawa, these 'are major organisations of informal social control in contemporary Japanese society and they can be characterised by their extremely harsh treatment of members who defy the existing power structure and social arrangements' (1992, p 89). Mechanisms of informal social control are always likely to be important factors in how official crime rates are manufactured and change, but such mechanisms differ between cultures and this can be difficult for criminologists to uncover. In the Japanese case, the way that individuals are located within social groups, and the intensity of social controlling that goes on within them, strongly affects individual propensity towards crime (Komiya, 1999).

There is probably more to the explanation of the Japanese case than differences in informal social controlling by formally legitimate social institutions such as the family and the corporation. Analysis of changing rates of crime in Japan should also try to grapple with the difficult problem of understanding the role of *Yakuza*

---

4 See, for example, David Garland's short history of British criminology (1997). British and European criminology has had a long acquaintance with historical and comparative method. The figure of Sir Leon Radzinowicz looms especially large in this intellectual project (see Hood, 1974).

('organised crime') in the ordering of contemporary Japanese society.[5] It has been observed (Bayley, 1991; Szymkowak and Steinhoff, 1995) that Yakuza perform the socially useful function of disciplining young males (called *chimpera*) through enlistment in underworld activities. These recruits are potential delinquents who might otherwise gravitate towards predatory street crime. However, once enmeshed in the secret social world of Yakuza, criminal violence and criminal activity goes on largely outside of public purview, and as long as it does, Japanese police and criminal justice processes do not make them a public issue. Neither do Yakuza feature prominently in official statistics about the Japanese crime problem. So in Japan, formal and informal social controlling going on within the criminal underworld, and between the criminal underworld and other formal social institutions, affecting officially recorded crime rates.

However, it is not just the organisation of crime, or the organisation of crime control, or the strength of informal social controlling that affects the construction of crime statistics. In the Japanese case, comparativists searching for explanatory clues to the low official rates of crime also need to consider the cultural practices of suicide (*sepuku*) in Japan (Picken, 1979). It is reasonably well established that the 50% increase, over a 10 year period, in the number of suicides (from approximately 21,000 in 1990 to in excess of 32,000 per annum by the end of the century) was the product of economic stagnation and rising rates of unemployment (Takahashi *et al*, 1998). Western criminologists conventionally look at how worsening economic indicators affect crime rates, but they seldom look at the act of suicide (unless suicide is defined as a criminal act, which it is in some jurisdictions). What is striking about the Japanese statistics is that crime rates do not seem particularly sensitive to shifts in the economic statistics (although this too may be changing). Rather, in Japan, where the cultural implications of 'losing face' are more profound, and where losing one's employment amounts to a profound loss of face, the social impact of increasing numbers of men experiencing employment loss seems principally to be expressed in the dramatically rising number of suicides.

Thus, there are a number of cultural variables that contribute to an understanding of the relatively lower crime rates in Japan and, it almost goes without saying, in order to build up a fully rounded appreciation of this complex set of cultural factors, comparativists must strive to understand how these various practices have evolved, and continue to evolve, over time. All of this makes the job of comparative criminology tremendously challenging and, thinking about the global context in which such efforts are now embedded, it is getting more so.

Trajectories

As Miyazawa suggests, with the 'second best method' comparative criminologists can negotiate something like a methodological *rapprochement*. Such a meeting of the minds among academic criminologists has fairly wide currency. Thus, according to Piers Beirne:

---

5 Beirne and Perry (1994) mention only in passing the 'extravagant levels of corporate corruption' in Japan (p 163). See Raz (1992) for a fulsome consideration of the Yakuza in Japanese culture.

... relativism compels us to lay bare the conceptual categories of comparative research, especially where the cultures that we examine have belief systems that differ from the values of western, Judeo-Christendom. But instead of confronting the variable cognitive powers of different belief systems as barriers to comparative research, we should understand them as an additional dimension of research and ask: within the subjective forms of life of other cultures how and why is criminal behaviour defined as it is? ... such an investigation will take us far beyond merely specifying the crime rates of different cultures and the number of infractions. It will tell us why certain actions are regarded as criminal and others are not (1983, *passim*).

Put this way, the project of comparative criminology is an attempt to comprehend similarities and differences in patterns of crime in different cultures and contexts. But it is undertaken by reference to interpretive inquiries which aim to understand the way cultures cohere; and the import that both formal and informal institutions of social control have for such coherence (see also Nelken, 1994a). Such an approach need not discount quantitative measures on epistemological grounds. Indeed, most knowledgeable observers agree that, if anything, the methodological shortcomings of quantitative empirical data render sufficient grounds for caution (Beirne and Perry, 1994). In practice, quantitative data can be pragmatically employed with due regard to their shortcomings, but in order to interpret such data it is necessary to place it in its social, cultural and historical context (Sheptycki, 1999). By such methodological pragmatism, comparative criminologists have attempted to reach out for a better understanding of their object of study.

Such methodological *rapprochement* has become somewhat vexed in the contemporary period, in which it has become difficult to delineate where the boundaries of different cultures lie. The revolution in transportation and communications technologies that took place in the last decades of the 20th century changed the way people, both as individuals and as communities, relate to territory. Geographers called it time-space convergence. Some social scientists came to talk about globalisation, but this term seems overly general and suggests that any culturally blurring or homogenising effects that time-space convergence *might* have are somehow being experienced uniformly (see Sklair, 1991, for a critique of the concept of globalisation). The alternative terminology is that of 'transnationalisation' (Sheptycki, 2000, 2002; Sklair, 1991), which suggests that transnational practices impact on human relationships in diverse ways in different places. Transnational social practices are routine, ongoing and commonplace. Large-scale social institutions, such as transnational corporations (TNCs) and non-governmental organisations (NGOs), engage a variety of such practices. But transnational practices are also something that individual people do. Thus, the more economically fortunate place financial assets in multiple jurisdictions even while they minimise their exposure to taxation. Family relationships – including things like childcare arrangements in divorce settlements and the negotiation of arranged marriages – may take place across national borders. Medical tourism, sex tourism, drug tourism, professional tourism (of academic criminologists) and Disneyfied tourism are all transnational practices. So is the flight of refugees and movement of economic migrants. Transnationalisation is part of everyday life (see Held, 1995, especially his analysis of 'seven sites of [transnational] power', pp 176–89). The prevalence and ordinariness of such practices have made the project of comparative criminology rather more tricky, partly because it has become difficult to find 'pristine cultures' for comparison.

One way to illustrate this is by reference to a specific type of crime: sexual assault and violence towards women by men. This is has been a long-standing issue area for comparative criminologists, not least because, as Peggy Reeves Sanday (1981) explained, there has been a strong assumption in some of the literature on this topic that this kind of violence is an inherent tendency of 'male nature'; as Susan Brownmiller once put it:

> ... 'when men discovered that they could rape, they proceeded to do it' in order to 'keep all women in a constant state of intimidation, forever conscious of the knowledge that the biological tool must be held in awe for it may turn to weapon with sudden swiftness borne of harmful intent' (quoted in Sanday, 1981, p 5).

Were rape and other types of serious male violence towards females to be found across all cultures throughout recorded history, this would be good evidence of the biological basis to patriarchy. As it turns out, comparative anthropologists have been able to show that male violence towards women is not a cultural universal (Sanday, 1981; Levinson, 1989). But it may be becoming one.

Both Sanday (1981) and Levinson (1989) undertook meta-analyses of data contained in the *Human Relations Area Files*. Sanday's study concerned 'rape prone societies', while Levinson's considered family violence in cross-cultural perspective. Sanday showed that rape was not a universal cultural practice and was able to generalise about rape-prone and rape-free societies. In the former, 'men are posed as a social group against women' (Sanday, 1981, p 15). The latter are 'characterised by sexual equality and the notion that the sexes are complimentary' (Sanday, 1981, p 18). Similarly, Levinson examined the available ethnographic data looking at family violence. Among broad conclusions reached were first, that wife beating and physical punishment of children are the two most common types of family violence found throughout the world. Secondly, that wife beating occurs in societies where men have the economic and the ultimate decision making power in the household and where adults resolve conflicts by fighting with one another (p 82).

The strategies for quantification and measurement of the relevant variables are, of course, fraught with difficulty in both of these studies. Both Sanday and Levinson show considerable sophistication and acuity in how they handle the data available to them. Of course, the fact that they produce broadly similar conclusions increases confidence in the reliability of these measures. However, were that all there was to these studies they might not be so interesting. On one level, it is hardly surprising to find that societies that resolve conflict by recourse to violence, and/or enable significant economic inequality between men and women, exhibit a greater propensity to wife battery. Neither is it counter-intuitive to find that societies that accord women high status, or just as high a status as men, are less likely to have large numbers of battered wives or manifest a tendency to 'rape proneness'. Sociological correlation is only part of the comparativist's story and, although such measures do seem to show that the maintenance of patriarchal structures through practices of male violence is not a universal cultural practice, it is not necessarily their most interesting aspect.

What stands out in these studies is the ethnographic detail. For example, Sanday describes the sexual mores of the Gusii people who live in the south-western part of present-day Kenya. For the Gusii, 'normal heterosexual intercourse' is 'conceived of as an act in which a man overcomes the resistance of a woman and causes her pain' (Sanday, 1981, p 10). In this cultural context the married women of a village ceremonially taunt a bridegroom saying:

> You are not strong, you can't do anything to our daughter. When you slept with her you didn't do it like a man. You have a small penis which can do nothing. You should grab our daughter and she should be hurt and scream – then you're a man (quoted in Sanday, 1981, p 10).

To which the groom answers boastfully:

> I am a man! If you were to see my penis you would run away. When I grabbed her she screamed. I am not a man to be joked with. Didn't she tell you? She cried – ask her! (Quoted in Sanday, 1981, p 10.)

Traditional Gusii sexuality is evidently violent. A European or North American ethnocentric view might easily characterise it as one where rape is completely normalised. It is interesting to note, therefore, that Sanday was able to show that women in this culture did define certain specific instances of the sex act as rape, that is: as an illegitimate and illegal act. Even in a cultural context where aspects of sexual violence are ritualised and routine, rape – defined as an abnormal and extortionate transaction – can occur.

The ethnographic data on the Gusii contrasts in interesting ways with other data pertaining to demonstrably less violence societies. Consider Levinson's summary description pertaining to the Buddhist people of central Thailand:

> ... in Thailand both men and women serve equally as midwives and do plowing. They both own and operate farms, inherit property equally, share equally in the property brought to a marriage and divide it equally in the case of divorce. It is not uncommon to find men tending babies while women are off on a business deal; nor is it unusual, as indicated earlier, to see women paddling right along with men as crew members in a boat race (Levinson, 1989, p 105).

The cultural practices described by both Sanday and Levinson are historical and they show that violence is culturally mutable. However, the data to which they refer were mostly gathered in the 1950s and 1960s. At that time, Kenya was not yet an independent state (it gained formal independence in 1963), and Thailand was not yet heavily marred by its proximity to the Cold War conflict in south-east Asia. Much has changed since then in both regions. It is therefore interesting to compare the historical ethnographic snapshots depicted above with pictures from the contemporary scene.

Concerning Kenya, it is interesting to note that, in the run up to presidential elections in 2002 (only the second transfer of power since independence), Amnesty International issued a report calling for the Kenyan Government to address its moral and legal obligations to its female citizens victimised by male violence (at www.amnesty.org). Among many difficult problems identified in the report was the fact that there were no legal provisions pertaining to rape in marriage. Moreover, formal agents of social control such as the police and the military were unresponsive to women's experiences of male violence and were, in many documented instances, complicit in such acts. Amnesty and other human rights NGOs have been documenting quite extreme violence being perpetrated by men against women all across the region in the recent past. But then, as even the most casual observer will know, much of sub-Saharan Africa has fallen into conditions of extreme civil strife. In east Africa the traditional patriarchal-warrior cultures are no longer confined by ritual and tradition, and traditional cultural practices run helter-skelter out of control in conditions that sometimes resemble a Hobbesian state of nature.

Recent writing on familial violence in Thailand also shows that things have changed, and not for the better. For example, a report published by the World Bank entitled *Fighting Domestic Violence In Thailand* (World Bank, 2001) cites statistics which show that violence against women has become a serious and growing problem in the country. Reportedly, 20% of Thai husbands had beaten their wives at least once, and that figure is reckoned to be short of the true figure. The report condemned the attitudes surrounding wife battering among the police, prosecutors, judges, and society that encourage women to suffer in silence. The prevalence of this kind of violence in formerly non-violent Buddhist Thailand has been borne out in other studies. For example, LeeRay Costa (2001) reports on the content of Thai comic books, which, according to him, commonly feature images of marital tension and spousal abuse. The humour of these images derive from assumptions currently held within Thai culture that marriage is an institution that inevitably causes unhappiness for both husband and wife, and that men 'naturally' have the upper hand over women, physically, mentally and politically. What is interesting to Costa is that, while these books do contain images of men beating women, more common are images of wives beating their husbands. In many of these one-frame cartoons, the woman angrily wields her pestle (*sark*) as a symbol of phallic power deriving from her place in the home. In frame after frame she beats her husband into submission (signified by the bumps on her husband's head and his prone position under her feet). These images are funny, Costa tells us, precisely because they are incongruous. Not only are men thought to be more powerful in Thai society, but also violence is seen as their domain, not women's.

There is, by now, a fairly well established interest among academic criminologists concerning male violence against women (Dobash and Dobash, 1979, 1992; Merry, 1999; Sheptycki, 1991, 1993, 1995, 2001). Already there have been quantitative studies concerning trends in prevalence and differences in rates based on original survey research (for example, Heiskanen, 2002 on the ICVS). Even so, criminology is far from being able to provide full answers about the aetiology of male violence against women in a global perspective. At least some of the science is good, but there remains a considerable amount of guesswork. While the available evidence is considerable and our sense of the global trajectory is dour, continuing cultural heterodoxy means that, inevitably, there will be dangers in prescribing global solutions. Transnationalisation is affecting the practice of comparative criminology. Where once we could compare and contrast cultural differences between widely separated communities like the Gusii of south-western Kenya and the Buddhists of central Thailand (and see important differences), we are now confronted with a criminological landscape where such variation is being blurred as we converge, via different paths, on a common future.

The trajectories of transnationalisation are even more varied than this limited example suggests, but clearly the signs are not hopeful. As Manuel Castells (1998) has noted, even while many people and places are being left behind by the processes of transnationalisation, we all ultimately share a common global fate. There is the possibility of a continuing methodological *rapprochement* among comparative criminologists. Miyazawa's 'second best method' and Beirne's call for attention to cultural and historical sensitivity do create the space that allows for a pragmatic synthesis of elements of philosophical relativism and scientific positivism productive of new understandings regarding the object(s) of criminology. While the research imagination may win through in certain circumstances, the whole enterprise may yet founder.

The practice of comparative criminology in the transnational era

Under the circumstances of transnationalisation it is possible to observe that the differences that sustain the project of comparative criminology (and comparative social science more generally) have given way to diffusely intermingled cultural differences. It is not just that migratory pressures blend populations as never before. Even where specific cultural groups remain largely homogenous or geographically static, they are being affected by the trajectories of transnationalisation. It is now difficult for cultures to remain pristine in splendid isolation. This raises new methodological challenges for comparative method. How do we research and compare crime across diasporic cultures? In making comparisons regarding perceptions of crime seriousness, is it important to take account of patterns of cultural and media consumption? In multicultural societies, what are the relationships between intra-group and inter-group criminality? Then too, the traditional problems of comparative criminology, how to synthesise what is known about the 'hard facts' of crime together with what is understood about the nature of their 'relative truths', still remain. All of this is grist for the methodological mill and food for the research imagination.

However, there are dangers because there is pressure to let down the relativistic guard. Where once criminologists of a comparative bent could be somewhat comfortable with the idea that there are no universally accepted definitions of crime, because there is no universal framework of criminal law to apply, this view now looks complacent. Indeed, more than half a century on from the Universal Declaration of Human Rights, and the development of transnational criminal law in areas such as environmental crime[6] (Brack and Hayman, 2002); 'organised crime' (Beare, 2003; Edwards and Gill, 2003); crimes against humanity and war crimes (Gregory, 2000); and 'complex crimes' (Passas, 1995) such as 'white collar and economic crime' (Nelken, 1997, 2002), it also is technically incorrect in certain respects. Still further, the caution that relativism urges upon comparative criminologists seems ill-placed when faced with the brutal reality of violence and crime manifest globally. What seems more important is that we do something. Harking back to Comte, part of the logic of scientific criminology is to know the

---

6 There are at least four: illegal trade in flora and fauna; illegal logging and fishing; illegal transportation and dumping of toxic/hazardous waste; and illegal trade in ozone depleting substances.

causes of things so that we may change them. To rephrase Karl Marx in the context of this discussion: relativists have merely interpreted the world – the point, however, is to change it.

Therefore, conceding to Herman Mannheim and other sociological, cultural or philosophical relativists that there can be no immutable standards of natural law and that crime remains a relative concept seems a luxury that criminologists ought not to indulge in. Yet it is imperative that comparative criminologists remain open to relativist second thoughts. Not all problems defined as crime problems can be solved through judicious global application of the techniques of crime control, even if comparative criminologists are being asked to help do just that (Newman, 1999). The reply to such requests ought to be that, in order to understand crime, and do something about it, we need to understand specific details and how they fit into a broader context. And furthermore, that understanding the broader context and the specific details requires asking political questions about how specific acts come to be counted as crime, or not. Relativism recognises that categories of crime are contestable and seeks to understand the implications of this before making pronouncements about what is to be done. What's good for the Gusii of Kenya might not be good for the Buddhists of central Thailand. Criminalisation may, or may not, be an appropriate strategy for dealing with crimes against the environment, or 'intellectual property theft', just as it may or may not be appropriate in answering any other social problem potentially definable as crime. Relativism seeks to insure against absolutist responses on the basis of scientific truths which, invariably when it comes to human affairs, are only temporary and contingent.

In short, academic criminology needs to stand on two legs if it is to stand at all. By abandoning relativistic thinking and volunteering all efforts to the business (and it has become a business) of positivist empiricism, comparative criminologists risk becoming nothing more than an administrative adjunct to the machinery of global governance. On the other hand, to surrender up the tools of positivist science and sink back into armchair relativism is to risk irrelevance. The comparative criminologist is currently faced with a world that seems much more complicated than it was when the first attempts at international and cross-cultural comparison were undertaken. Globally, criminologists are becoming aware of the difficulties in interpreting the data with regard to 'traditional' criminological foci: murder, assault, theft from dwellings and from the person, and so forth. There is also now an emerging body of empirical knowledge about new forms of transnational crime. However, ultimately, the problem for comparative criminologists is more than solving the methodological puzzles that confront them, or even exposing the complex facets of relative truth that characterise the criminological enterprise. There are many practical questions to answer about the problem of crime and comparative criminologists are being called upon to aid in making judgments about resource allocation. Comparative criminologists struggle to remain standing when faced with the dizzying world of globalisation with its plurality of cultures, interests and conflicts. That they remain upright at all is only because they can stand on two legs: one of positive science and the other the capacity for relativistic reflection. What ultimately guides comparative criminologists in making practical decisions about what they study, how they study it, and how they mould their findings? That is to say, what determines the directions that comparative and transnational criminologists will walk on their two stout legs? I suggest that any moral compass that may provide a way to orient criminology comes from outside the discipline. Mindful of Stanley Cohen's (1982) warnings about 'Western crime control models' I can do no more at this point than allude to the foundational truths of human rights philosophy, expressed in the words of Dag Hammarskjöld at the outset of this chapter, and try to recognise that fear and suffering for one person is fear and suffering for another.

References

Bayley, D (1991) *Forces of Order: Policing Modern Japan*, 2nd edn, Berkeley: California UP

Beare, M (ed) (2003) *Critical Reflections on Transnational Crime, Money Laundering and Corruption*, Toronto: Toronto UP

Becker, H (1963) *Outsiders*, London: The Free Press of Glencoe

Beirne, P (1983) 'Cultural relativism and comparative criminology' 7 *Contemporary Crises* 371–91

Beirne, P (1993) *Inventing Criminology: Essays on the Rise of 'Homo Criminalis'*, Albany: New York State UP

Beirne, P and Messerschmidt, J (1995) *Criminology*, 2nd edn, New York: Harcourt Brace

Beirne, P and Perry, B (1994) 'Criminal victimization in the industrialized world', review essay in 21 *Crime, Law and Social Change* 155–65

Bennett, RR and Lynch, James P (1990) 'Does difference make a difference? Comparing cross-national crime indicators' 28 *Criminology* 153–82

Brack, D and Hayman, G (2002) *International Environmental Crime: The Nature and Control of Environmental Black Markets*, Royal Institute of International Affairs, Sustainable Development Programme

Castells, M (1998) *The Information Age: Economy, Society, Culture, Vol 3: The End of the Millennium*, Oxford: Blackwell

Cohen, S (1982) 'Western crime control models in the Third World: benign or malignant?', in Spitzer, S and Simon, R (eds), *Research in Law, Deviance and Social Control*, Vol 4, Greenwich: JAI Press, pp 85–199

Costa, LeeRay (2001) 'Domestic violence in Thai comic books' 14(2) *Asia Pacific Forum on Women, Law and Development*, August 2001

van Dijk, J (1999) 'The experience of crime and justice', in Newman, G (ed), *The Global Report on Crime and Justice*, New York: OUP together with the United Nations Office for Drug Control and Crime Prevention van Dijk, J and Mayhew, P (1993) *Criminal Victimization in the Industrialized World: Key Findings of the 1989 and 1992 International Crime Surveys*, The Hague: the Netherlands Ministry of Justice

Dobash, RE and Dobash, RP (1979) *Violence Against Wives: The Case Against the Patriarchy*, New York: Free Press

Dobash, RE and Dobash, RP (1992) *Women, Violence and Social Change*, London: Routledge

Douglas, M (1986) *How Institutions Think*, Syracuse, New York: Syracuse UP

Durkheim, E (1960) *The Division of Labour in Society*, Glencoe, Illinois: Free Press

Edwards, A and Gill, P (2003) *Transnational Organised Crime; Perspectives on Global Security*, London: Routledge

Ericson, R and Stehr, N (eds) (2000) *Governing Modern Societies*, Toronto: Toronto UP

Fattah, Ezzat A (1997) *Criminology Past Present and Future: A Critical Overview*, Basingstoke: Macmillan

Garland, D (1997) 'Of crimes and criminals: the development of criminology', in *The Oxford Handbook of Criminology*, Oxford: Clarendon

Geertz, C (1973) *The Interpretation of Cultures*, New York: Basic Books

Giddens, A (1976) *New Rules of Sociological Method: A Positive Critique of Interpretative Sociologies*, London: Hutchinson

Gregory, F (2000) 'Private criminality as a matter of international concern', in Sheptycki, JWE (ed), *Issues in Transnational Policing*, London: Routledge

Gurr, TR, Grobosky PN and Hula, RC (1977) *The Politics of Crime and Conflict: A Comparative History of Four Cities*, Beverley Hills: Sage

Haggerty, KD (2001) *Making Crime Count*, Toronto: Toronto UP

Held, D (1995) *Democracy and the Global Order*, Cambridge: Polity

Heiskanen, M (2002) 'Violence against women and victimization situations according to the ICVS', in Nieuwbeerta, P (ed), *Crime Victimization in Comparative Perspective: Results from the International Crime Victims Survey, 1989–2000*, den Haag: Boom Juridische uitgevers

Hood, R (ed) (1974) *Crime, Criminology and Public Policy: Essays in Honour of Sir Leon Radzinowicz*, London: Heinemann

Jones, T, MacLean, B and Young, J (1986) *The Islington Crime Survey: Crime, Victimisation, and Policing in Inner-city London*, Aldershot : Gower

Kalish, CB (1988) *International Crime Rates*, US Department of Justice, Washington DC: Bureau of Justice Statistics, pp 1–11

Komiya, N (1999) 'A cultural study of the low crime rate in Japan' 39(3) *British Journal of Criminology* 369–90

Kuhn, TS (1962) *The Structure of Scientific Revolutions*, Chicago: Chicago UP

Leavitt, G (1990) 'Relativism and cross-cultural criminology: a critical analysis' 27(1) *Journal of Research in Crime and Delinquency* 5–29

Levinson, D (1989) *Family Violence in Cross-Cultural Perspective*, Newbury Park: Sage

MacLean, BDSP (1989) *The Islington Crime Survey 1985: A Cross-Sectional Study of Crime and Policing in the London Borough of Islington*, unpublished PhD thesis, University of London

Maguire, M (1997) 'Crime statistics, patterns and trends', in Maguire, M, Morgan, R and Reiner, R (eds) *The Oxford Handbook of Criminology*, 2nd edn, Oxford: OUP

Maguire, M (2002) 'Crime statistics, the "data explosion" and its implications', in Maguire, M, Morgan, R and Reiner, R (eds), *The Oxford Handbook of Criminology*, 3rd edn, Oxford: OUP

Mannheim, H (1965) *Comparative Criminology*, London: Routledge and Kegan Paul

Merry, SE (1999) 'Criminalisation and gender: the changing governance of sexuality and gender violence in Hawaii', in Smadych, R (ed), *Governable Places: Readings on Governmentality and Crime Control*, Aldershot: Dartmouth

Milovanovic, D (1996) 'Postmodern Criminology' 13(4) *Justice Quarterly* 567–609

Miyazawa, S (1992) 'The enigma of Japan as a testing ground for cross-cultural criminological studies' 32 *Annales Internationales de Criminologie* 81–102

Morris, T (1957) *The Criminal Area*, London: Routledge and Kegan Paul

Nelken, D (ed) (1994a) *The Futures of Criminology*, London: Sage

Nelken, D (1994b) 'Whom can you trust? The future of comparative criminology', in Nelken, D (ed), *The Futures of Criminology*, London: Sage

Nelken, D (1997) 'White collar crime', in Maguire, M, Morgan, R and Reiner, R (eds), *The Oxford Handbook of Criminology*, 2nd edn, Oxford: Clarendon

Nelken, D (2002) 'White collar crime' in Maguire, M, Morgan, R and Reiner, R (eds), *The Oxford Handbook of Criminology*, 3rd edn, Oxford: Clarendon

Newman, G (ed) (1999) *The Global Report on Crime and Justice*, New York: OUP together with the United Nations Office for Drug Control and Crime Prevention

Passas, N (1995) 'The mirror of global evils: a review essay on the BCCI affair' 12(2) *Justice Quarterly* 801–29

Picken, S (1979) *Suicide: Japan and the West – A Comparative Study*, Tokyo: The Simul Press

Platt, R (1975) 'Prospects for a critical criminology in the USA', in Taylor, I, Walton, P and Young, J (eds), *Critical Criminology*, London: Routledge and Kegan Paul, pp 95–112

Quine, WV (1960) *Word and Object*, Cambridge: MIT Press

Raz, J (1992) *Aspects of Otherness in Japanese Culture*, Tokyo: Institute for the Study of Languages and Cultures of Asia and Africa

Sanday, PR (1981) 'The socio-cultural context of rape: a cross-cultural study' 37(4) *The Journal of Social Issues* 5–27

Shaw, C, Zorbaugh, FM, McKay, HD and Cottrell, LS (1929) *Delinquency Areas: A Study of the Geographic Distribution of School Truants, Juvenile Delinquents and Adult Offenders in Chicago*, Chicago: Chicago UP

Sheptycki, JWE (1991) 'Using the state to change society: the example of domestic violence' 3(1) *The Journal of Human Justice*, Autumn, 47–66

Sheptycki, JWE (1993) *Innovations in Policing Domestic Violence*, Aldershot: Avebury

Sheptycki, JWE (1995) 'Rapacious bluebeards and chivalrous knights: a socio-linguistic view of policing woman battering', *New Waverley Papers*, Politics Series 95/3, June 1995

Sheptycki, JWE (1999) 'Political cultures and structures of social control: police-related scandal in the low countries in comparative perspective' 9(1) *Policing and Society* 1–33

Sheptycki, JWE (ed) (2000) *Issues in Transnational Policing*, London: Routledge

Sheptycki, JWE (2001) 'What causes men's violence against women and violence in intimate relationships?' 12(1) *The Journal of Forensic Psychiatry* 232–39

Sheptycki, JWE (2002) *In Search of Transnational Policing*, Aldershot: Avebury

Sklair, L (1991) *Sociology of the Global System*, New York: Harvester Wheatsheaf

Strauss, M (1999) 'The controversy over domestic violence by women: a methodological, theoretical and sociology of science analysis', in Arriaga, XB and Oskamp, S (eds), *Violence in Intimate Relationships*, Thousand Oaks: Sage

Swingewood, A (1984) *A Short History of Sociological Thought*, London: Macmillan

Szymkowak, K and Steinhoff, PG (1995) 'Wrapping up something long: intimidation and violence by right-wing groups in post-war Japan' 7(1) *Terrorism and Political Violence* 265–98

Takahashi, Y, Hirasawa, H and Koyama, K (1998) 'Suicide in Japan: present state and future directions for prevention' 35(2) *Transcultural Psychiatry* 271–90

Wolfgang, ME (1967) 'International criminal statistics: a proposal' 58 *Journal of Criminal Law, Criminology and Police Science* 65–69

World Bank (2001) *Out of the Silence: Fighting Violence Against Women in Thailand*, published in co-operation with the Office of the National Commission on Women's Affairs (part of the Office of the Permanent Secretary of the Prime Minister's Office of the Thai Government)

Part 2

Area Studies

Chapter 4
Crime and Social Control in Saudi Arabia

Ali Wardak

Introduction

The Kingdom of Saudi Arabia is the largest country in the Arabian Peninsula. It is bounded by Jordan, Iraq, Yemen, Kuwait, Oman, Qatar, UAE, as well as by the Red Sea, the Gulf of Qaba, and the Persian Gulf (Lindsey, 1991; Long, 1997). The Kingdom is divided into four regions – Hijaz, Najd, Asir and the Eastern Province – that are further divided into 13 provinces. The populations of each of these regions have diverse ethnic and tribal origins. To the east is a substantial *Shi'ite* population with cultural links to Iran and Bahrain. Asir has close cultural and historical links to Yemen. The population of Najd mainly consists of indigenous Arab tribal groupings and clans who have lived in the region for generations. Hijaz, Mecca and Medina are home to many descendants of Muslim pilgrims from different parts of the world who stayed on after pilgrimage. And the port city of Jeddah is a vibrant commercial centre with a diverse population, the origins of which are traceable to Persia, Africa, Yemen, and to other parts of the Muslim and Arab world (Helms, 1981; Long, 1997).

Despite the diversity of the population of Saudi Arabia, it is rather homogeneous. The main sources of this homogeneity are the common Arabic language, Arab cultural traditions, adherence to strict Islamic values, and mass participation in collective shared cultural and religious activities (Helms, 1981; Niblock, 1982). The near universal enforcement of these values by Saudi educational, cultural, religious and justice institutions, as well as through the extended family, offers other reasons for this. Critics of the current Saudi rulers see the universal enforcement of these values as state hegemony and as an imposition of a specific religious and cultural identity on the population (Al-Rasheed and Al-Rasheed, 1996; Yamani, 1997). This notwithstanding, there is a palpable consolidation of a common sense of purpose based on Islam and Arab traditions among the population. This sense of collective religio-cultural identity has also been strengthened by the ways the Kingdom and its population are seen by its neighbours and the Muslim world as a whole. The fact that the country is the birth place of Islam, its Prophet, and the location of the two holiest Islamic places in Mecca and Medina, known as *Al-Haramain-al-Sharifain* looms large in the collective conscience of the Saudi people. Pilgrimage to Mecca and Medina is an obligation of every able (physically and financially) Muslim once in his or her lifetime, and therefore, the two cities are visited by hundreds of thousands of Muslims from all parts of the world annually. For many Muslims around the world, Saudi Arabia symbolises Islamic history and the first Islamic community that was led by the Prophet of Islam and his followers. Thus, many Muslims inside and outside the Kingdom expect its rulers to rule the birthplace of Islam and the location of *Al-Haramain-al-Sharifain* in accordance with Islamic teachings. These expectations of millions of Muslims in the Kingdom, and hundreds of millions in the rest of the Islamic world, have played an important role in the cultural and polito-religious organisation of Saudi society.

The total population of Saudi Arabia is estimated at 24.6 million, including 5.6 million resident foreign workers. The latter category mainly come from Egypt, Yemen, Jordan, Syria, Kuwait, Pakistan, India, the Philippines, Sri Lanka and the Republic of Korea (South Korea). Approximately 100,000 of these foreign workers are technical and managerial experts who come from Europe and North America (US State Department, 2003). The Kingdom is one of the world's largest producers of oil and has large oil reserves. The industrial sector includes manufacturing, utilities and construction, and account for around one-fifth of GDP. Moreover, large government investments in the agricultural sector have resulted in self-sufficiency in the production of food grains (US State Department, 2003). The strong Saudi economy has had a huge impact on the expansion of education, public health facilities and on the provision of the general social welfare of the average citizen of Saudi society, and has played an important role in the creation of a conservative, but modern Islamic society.

Saudi Arabia is an absolute monarchy governed in accordance to *Shari'a* (Islamic Law) and the Basic Law of Government that was introduced in March 1992. The King, whose main official title is *Khadem-al-Haramain-al-Sharifain* (the custodian of the holy site of Mecca and Medina), is considered the guardian of Islam. Islam is the state religion and *Shari'a* constitutes the legal system of the country. The King also performs the role of Prime Minister as he appoints and leads the Council of Ministers. The Council is the main organ of the government in executive and legislative matters. The Council of Ministers normally comprises of the King, the Crown Prince, two deputy prime ministers, key royal advisers, key ministers of state, and the heads of the 20 ministries; the overwhelming majority of the members of the current Council of Ministers are non-royals. Although the council makes decisions on the basis of a majority vote, the final decision requires the approval of the King (Niblock, 1982; Aba Namay, 1993; Long, 1997; Salameh, 1989).

The current political organisation of Saudi society does not allow for an elected parliament or political parties. However, the King is advised by *majlis al shura*, or Consultative Council. Members of the Consultative Council mainly include highly educated professionals, religious, and clan leaders who are selected by the King (Aba Namay, 1993; Al-Rasheed, 2002). In order to facilitate a process of political and social reform, the government recently launched the 'National Dialogue' which according to *The Economist* (22 January 2004) includes '... a 70-strong group of worthies, including, unusually for Saudi Arabia, Shias, women and some noted liberals, to debate reform and suggest remedies'. These reforms are seen by supporters of the government as an important step towards the participation of ordinary Saudi citizens in social and political decision making. This indicates that Saudi Arabia is a society at a crossroad. Following the 11 September terrorist attacks in the USA, Saudi Arabia itself has been the target of several terrorist bombings. Pressures from the USA and from Saudi religious radicals have put Saudi rulers under increased strain. While radical religious groups aim for the establishment of an Islamic *khelafa* and the elimination of Western influence by violent means, reformists, international human right organisations and the West call for the political and social liberalisation of Saudi society. Saudi rulers have a complex task in accommodating the contradictory demands from inside and outside the country.

This chapter focuses on an analysis of crime and social control in Saudi Arabia, considered by many to be a 'low crime rate' society (Mourad, 1980; El-Sendiony, 1981; Adler, 1983; Ali, 1985; Souryal, 1987; Interpol, 1988, 2000). Here I will review existing studies and comparative crime figures about Saudi Arabia, and explore various explanations provided by Saudi and Western scholars for the low crime rates. Then, I will examine the main informal, semi-formal and formal social control institutions: the extended family, the school, the mosque, *Ulama* (Islamic legal scholars and theologians) and *Motawwa'in* (religious police) and the formal Saudi judicial system. These social control agencies operate at informal, semi-formal and formal levels and will be analysed in the social and cultural context of Saudi society. It will be argued that it is the complex interplay between the main social control agencies that maintains the 'low crime rate' in Saudi society. However, it is also argued that the high level of social order comes with a price: reduced individual freedoms. That price may be too high for at least some of the people who live there.

Crime in Saudi Arabia

There has been little research on crime and criminal justice in Saudi Arabia. However, the evidence we have consistently indicates that Saudi Arabia is a 'low crime rate' society. Obviously, ranking societies on the basis of official crime rates is not without its difficulties (see Westfelt and Estrada (Chapter 1) and Young (Chapter 2), this volume). But this is further compounded by problems that are specific to Saudi Arabia. First, it is not uncommon for many criminal complaints in Saudi society to be resolved outside the formal justice institutions and therefore remain unrecorded by the police (Souryal, 1987). This even may apply to homicide (Groves *et al*, 1987). Secondly, official crime figures in Saudi Arabia are counted in accordance with the Islamic lunar calendar (*Hijri*), which has 354 days, while the Gregorian calendar (AD) is 365 days. This can have implications for the comparison of cross-national crime figures.

However, most criminologists who have studied crime and criminal justice in Saudi Arabia are aware of these issues. For example, Badr-El-Din Ali (1985), after making adjustment between the Islamic *Hijri* and Gregorian calendars, compared Saudi Arabia's crime figures for 1401 *Hijri* year with 1981 crime figures in the USA and with those of the state of Ohio. Ali (1985, pp 50–51) found that Saudi Arabia's crime rate (per 100,000 population) for all reported crimes was 159 compared to a rate of 5,625.9 on the UCR Index in the USA and 5,284 in Ohio. He further compared figures for specific categories of crimes between the two countries (after taking definitional issues into account) and found that both property and violence offences in Saudi Arabia were significantly lower compared to those in the USA.

Souryal (1987) compared Saudi Arabia's crime figures for 1970–75 with the findings from the United Nations World Survey of Reported Crimes for the same period. Souryal showed Saudi Arabia's murder rate to be 1 per 100,000 population, as compared to the combined world rate of 3.9 per 100,000. The Kingdom's rate for property crime was 1.4 per 100,000 as compared to the combined world rate of 908.5 per 100,000. This study also revealed that the combined world rate for sexual crimes was 24.2 per 100,000, as compared to a rate of 5 per 100,000 in Saudi Arabia. A comparison of crime figures between Saudi Arabia and Kuwait revealed that the Saudi rates for murder, property and sexual offences were significantly lower than those of Kuwait's. A study by El-Sendiony (1981) compared rates relating to violent crime in Saudi Arabia and Egypt for 1978. This study found that the rate of violent crime victimisation in Saudi Arabia was 1 per 38,623 as compared to 1 per 18,587 in Egypt.

Other studies have focused on historical changes in the crime rates for Saudi Arabia. Mourad (1980) examined crime rates in the Kingdom between 1966–75 and found that many categories of crimes declined significantly during the period. The findings revealed that the murder rate declined from 0.3 per 1,000 to 0.1 per 1,000; theft from 0.16 per 1,000 to 0.12 per 1,000; and sexual offences from 0.7 per 1,000 to 0.4 per 1,000 (Mourad, 1980, pp 500–04). Overall, the crime rate per 1,000 population declined from 32 to 18. Also Mourad (1980) reported the findings of another interesting study conducted by Al-Sa'aty, who interviewed 22 elderly people about their memory and experiences of crime and crime control. The study reveals nearly unanimous agreement that prior to 1932, murder, tribal reprisal, robbery, theft and serious assault were commonplace. After the consolidation of the Saudi monarchy in that year (and the implementation of *Shari'a* law throughout the country), crime rates decreased dramatically, while apparent feelings of personal safety and social order improved (Mourad, 1980, pp 505–14). Other studies broadly support these conclusions (Basha, 1979; Basnawi, 1984).

Comparative studies conducted by Western criminologists are largely consistent with the conclusions of the above mentioned studies. Adler (1983) lists Saudi Arabia among her 10 'low crime rate' nations. This general picture is further re-enforced by comparative statistics as reported by Interpol in Table 1, right.

This table shows that Saudi murder and theft rates (1.1 and 70 per 100,000 population respectively) are the second lowest among the 25 countries listed. Saudi Arabia is also shown to be among the low crime rates societies as far as sex offences, assault and drug offences (21, 32 and 35.6 per 100,000 population respectively) are concerned. In addition, the country has the lowest overall crime rate (200.5 per 100,000 population). Although Saudi rates for some categories of crime have slightly increased more recently, they are significantly lower as compared to most of the countries in the world (Interpol, 2000). Furthermore, the low Saudi crime rate is reflected in the country's very low imprisonment rate. Saudi Arabia's imprisonment rate is 110 persons per 100,000 population, but 50.9% of these prisoners are foreign nationals who are in the country as 'guest workers' (International Centre for Prison Studies, 2003; Home Office, 2003).

These studies are in accord with the overall high sense of security and personal safety among Saudi citizens (El-Sendiony, 1981). However, the main question has to do with how we explain the low crime rate in Saudi Arabian society. Most scholars attribute the low Saudi Arabian crime rate mainly to the strong influence of Islam in various spheres of life in Saudi society, particularly to the implementation of *Shari'a*. Mourad (1980), El-Sendiony (1981), Ali (1985) and Souryal (1987) all explain low Saudi crime rates primarily in terms of religiosity and the implementation of *Shari'a* law in Saudi Arabia. Others also express this view. For example, Al-Kattan (1980), a senior Saudi academic and legal scholar, says that:

Table 1: 1988 crime rates (per 100,000 population) in 25 selected countries.

Country	Murder	Sexual	Assault	Theft Offences	Drug	Total
Australia	4.5	55.6	369.6	5,491.2	n/a	6,773.2
Austria	1.8	37.4	1.6	2,505.3	65.3	5,288.2
Canada	5.4	108.2	130.5	5,133.1	232.9	11,414.8
Chile	6.5	32.6	112.5	748.4	15.5	1,309.4
Denmark	5.2	55.4	140.2	8,524.9	253.2	10,500.4
Egypt	1.5	0.4	0.7	39.1	20.7	2,939.0
England & Wales	2.0	52.8	305.4	5,534.1	15.5	7,395.6
France	4.6	37.6	76.3	3,569.1	85.8	5,619.1
Hungary	3.8	13.7	51.9	1,021.9	0.8	1,747.8
Iraq	1.4	9.8	2.6	2,124.2	1.1	2,410.8
Ireland	1.0	11.1	2.9	2,238.0	1.2	2,529.0
Italy	2.2	1.5	33.0	2,085.2	54.1	3,297.9
Japan	1.2	3.8	17.5	1,159.9	1.8	3,297.9
Kenya	4.8	8.1	70.6	86.1	48.1	485.5
Norway	2.0	33.9	36.3	3,936.4	147.6	5,220.4
Philippines	36.9	3.0	51.7	80.7	n/a	316.5
Saudi Arabia	**1.1**	**21.9**	**32.2**	**70.5**	**35.6**	**200.5**
Scotland	10.0	99.3	133.6	6,206.8	102.3	16,796.2
South Korea	1.3	29.5	19.6	229.3	4.4	2,229.3
Spain	2.3	15.0	25.2	1,948.2	61.1	2,519.4
Sweden	7.2	62.3	37.6	7,629.6	362.2	12,836.6
Switzerland	2.3	46.5	48.9	4,336.8	283.2	4,988.0
United States	8.4	37.6	370.2	5,248.0	n/a	5,664.3
Venezuela	9.1	39.3	155.0	867.1	28.9	1,158.3
West Germany	4.2	60.0	102.7	4,382.8	138.8	7,114.0

Source: Interpol (1987/1988), *International Crime Statistics*, Lyons, France: ICPO–Interpol General Secretariat

* This category includes all types of sexual offences except in the Philippines and the United States, where only the 'rape' rate is counted.

> Although positive laws have classified crimes and prescribed punishments for each of them, these laws (which are not divine) lack the force of restraining potential offenders from attempting to commit an offence in the absence of watchmen or those pertaining to judicial authorities. On the other hand the Islamic *Shari'a*, through its influence on human conscience, has the power to eradicate the evil before it prompts the man to commit crime. The power of conscience is much stronger than any other external force … The *Shari'a* through its penetration in the conscience of the believer, purifies him from the roots of evil. The offender, even if not seen by anyone, insists on confessing to get God's judgment in order to be absolved from the offence committed (Al-Kattan, 1980, p 233).

Al-Kattan describes the internalisation of the Islamic belief system and morality as a 'moral vaccination' against criminality. This view is shared by Al-Mutrak (1980, p 408), a high ranking official at the Saudi Ministry of Justice, who says that: 'The Islamic *Shari'a* does not depend only on penalties to combat crime but also strives to prevent crime before its commission. No doubt prevention is better than cure.' He argues that the implementation of Islamic Law in the Kingdom, with its dual emphasis on crime prevention through the internalisation of Islamic belief systems/morality and prompt punishments for those who break his or her contract with God (and the Islamic ruler), has resulted in unprecedented levels of personal safety and security in the country:

> Before the implementation of the *Shari'a*, the Kingdom of Saudi Arabia was a theatre of anarchy, confusion, instability and looting. It was a place where neither life nor property could be safe. When pilgrims came they used to bid their last farewell to their family thinking they might not be able to return home safely. Since the strict implementation of Shari'a and its adoption as the Kingdom's constitution, peace has been fostered everywhere and people's lives and properties are safe. It is rare to hear of a case of assassination or kidnapping (Al-Mutrak, 1980, p 464).

Other Saudi and Arab judicial scholars and educationalists, such as Qutb (1980), attribute the actual and perceived sense of safety and security in Saudi society to Islam and the implementation of Islamic law in the country. This view appears to be shared by ordinary people in the Kingdom. As Adler (1983, p 88) put it: 'Saudis credit the *Shari'a* – in its multi-faceted functions – with their low rate, which persists despite the enormously rapid economic development which the country has been experiencing.' However, Adler also explains low Saudi crime rates in terms of the prevalence of 'informal social controls'. She describes the roles of the family, school and religion, and the ways they operate, as mechanisms of informal social control in Saudi Arabian society. She concludes that countries like Saudi Arabia are characterised by the prevalence of informal social controls that produce '*sinnomie*'. This is a condition of Durkheimian social solidarity that she describes as '… the state of sharing of norms or customs and, beyond that, a system of intact social controls capable of assuring such sharing' (Adler, 1983, p 157). While Adler describes the role of the formal justice system in Saudi Arabia, she does not establish explicit links between the formal and informal control mechanisms in the country.

Arabian and Western criminologists have mainly explained low Saudi crime rates either in terms of: (a) the prevalence of informal social controls; (b) Islam and the application of Islamic *Shari'a*; or (c) a simple combination of the two. The first of these explanations fails to establish links between the formal and informal control mechanisms; it treats formal and informal social controls as if they were independent of one another. The second category is a partial and one-sided explanation reflecting, in the main, the personal opinions of judicial, educational and religious scholars. The third category of explanation is more balanced but is generally lacking in sociological depth and empirical detail. It is the job of this chapter to provide that depth and level of detail. In the next section I will examine the various informal, semi-formal and formal social control agencies that are central to the maintenance of social order in Saudi Arabian society. I will then examine the concurrent and complex interplay between these various social control mechanisms and the ways these impact on crime in Saudi Arabia.

Social control in Saudi Arabia

The concept of social control first entered sociological theory with the publication of Ross's *Social Control* in 1901. Despite certain theoretical advancements since then, problems of definition remain. The overlapping relationship among the forms, kinds, agencies, mechanisms and instruments of social control, and even whether the concept is viewed as an independent or dependent variable (or both), add to the definitional difficulties. Likewise the multi-dimensional and overlapping relationship between social order and social control make it hard to draw a line between the two. Indeed, the concept of social control is defined in a variety of different ways in different academic disciplines (see Gurwich, 1945; Janovitz, 1975; Meire, 1982; Cohen, 1985; Edwards, 1988; Lowman *et al*, 1987; Wardak, 2000; Innes, 2003).

Nevertheless, Ross's highly general description of social control and of its various agencies and mechanisms has been used as a guide by many subsequent theorists and researchers. Ross described social control as 'intended social ascendancy'. 'Social ascendancy' refers to the various processes and a mechanism whereby society attains a super-ordinate position over the individual and moulds him or her in accordance with conventional rules and expectations. Ross (1901, p 320) identified 23 mechanisms of social control that he called 'engines of social control'. The most important of these are: 'Public Opinion', 'Law', 'Belief', 'Social Suggestion', 'Education', 'Custom', 'Social Religion', 'Personality', 'Ideals', 'Ceremony', 'Art', 'Enlightenment', 'Illusion', 'Social Evaluations' and certain 'Ethical' elements.

Using Ross's general description as a guide, I take social control to refer to all those institutions, institutional processes and mechanisms that regulate behaviour and contribute to the maintenance of social order. In the context of the present discussion, five main agencies of social control are identified as central to Saudi society. They are: the extended family, the mosque/*Ulama*, the school, *Motawwa'in*, and the Saudi judicial system. For the purposes for this paper, the extended family and the mosque/*Ulama* are categorised as informal agencies of social control, the school and *Motawwa'in* as semi-formal and the judicial system as a formal agency. Each of these agencies, and the levels that they operate at, are examined below.

The extended family

The family is the most important agency of social control in Saudi Arabia, as it is elsewhere in the Islamic world. The family is an extended social unit where two or more generations of blood relations live together in a traditional cluster of adjacent houses, or in purpose built modern neighbourhoods close to one another (Ghanoubi, 1976; Al-Ghamdi, 1989). Members of the extended family often share property, land and business interests, all of which are heritable. Family business may even mean collective spending from shared income. Shared business is carried out under the auspices of the corporate familial name – a marque of collective *sharaf* (honour) and social status in the society. Thus, the identity of the individual is, in important ways, inseparable from the collective identity of his or her primary social group. As Al-Awaji (1971, p 134) put it: '… the identity of the individual is identical with that of his group. Individual initiative is only encouraged when it serves and enhances the interests of the group.' This inseparability between individual and family has important implications for social control. An individual's behaviour affects his or her family's collective identity and *sharaf*. Consequently, the latter exercises a considerable degree of control over the former.

The Saudi family is a patriarchal social unit where a clear-cut division of labour exists between the males and females. This underpins male domination of Saudi Arabian society as a whole. As Adler put it:

> Division between men and women in Saudi Arabian society is very marked. Until recently, the majority of Saudi women were illiterate (to 1966) although now educational opportunities are available in segregated schools and classes. The activities of women are still very restricted. They are not allowed to work in jobs or frequent areas where they could come into contact with men, to drive automobiles, or to travel independently (Adler, 1983, p 82).

The effect of these restrictions, and the requirement of veiling in public, is the exclusion of women from their full participation in the cultural, economic and political life of the wider society. Hence, while men deal with issues relating to the outside world, women are generally confined to domestic matters, especially to the socialisation of children (Doumato, 1991). Since women play such a central role in the socialisation of children, most aspiring Saudi men prefer to get married to educated women (Adler, 1983). This may explain the expansion of educational opportunities for Saudi women since the early 1970s. It is mainly Saudi mothers who teach their children the fundamentals of the Islamic faith such as belief in one God, the prophethood of Mohammad, the *Qura'n*, angels, the day of judgment, belief in the life after death and the rituals of individual and congregational Islamic worship. Children are also taught the fundamentals of Islamic morality, such as honesty, truthfulness, respect for other people's property, helping the poor, and refracting from verbal and physical violence at home. Thus, Saudi mothers play a hugely important part in the bonding of youngsters to the social and moral order of Saudi society (Doumato, 1991).

Within the Saudi extended family, a strong emphasis is placed on the socialisation of male children into adult roles. Boys are provided opportunities to participate in adult social and religious life and to watch modal behaviour within the wider community. They usually accompany their fathers and other male members of the family to the mosque for collective worship, cultural gatherings and to other social events. In this way, children learn traditional Saudi values such as family loyalty, their obligations to ken and to clan, showing deference to those who are older, generosity, selflessness, hospitality, control over one's emotions, and how to maintain the collective *sharaf* of the family or clan.

The main signifiers of authority in Saudi society are age and gender. Younger people are expected to show deference and obey their elders. Obedience to elders, particularly to parents and grandparents, is central to the stability of the extended family and the clan. Obedience to parental authority is both a cultural and a religious obligation. Rejection of parental authority is considered a sin punishable on the day of judgment. It can also have serious and immediate social and economic consequences for the disobedient son or daughter. Prophet Mohammad says: '*Allah* Almighty may pardon all sins as He pleases, except *auqooq* of parents. He rather hastens (to punish) its doer in his life before death.' (Abu Bakar in Al-Baihaqi). *Auqooq* means continued disobedience and rebellion that is deeply annoying to the parents. The right of parents, usually fathers, to exercise *auqooq* has serious social and economic implications for the 'disobedient' son or daughter throughout his or her life. The *Aaqq* (the person against whom *auqooq* is exercised) cannot, according to Islamic law, inherit his or her father's property; he or she is socially boycotted within the family; and the label becomes a permanent stigma for the 'disobedient' within the community. This control mechanism is further strengthened by parents' crucial role in the arrangement of their young sons and daughters' marriages (Adler, 1983) and by financing their education abroad.

In summary, the Saudi extended family is a powerful agency of social control. As a close knit social group, where members are highly dependent on one another and have a collective identity, the Saudi family is highly conducive to the development of strong attachments between children and parents. Western criminologists have long established that attachment to parents is strongly related to compliance with social and legal norms (Glueck and Glueck, 1950; Nye, 1958; Hirschi, 1969; Farrington, 1973; West, 1982; Sampson and Laub, 1993; Wardak, 2000). Furthermore, religious, social and economic resources enable parents and their surrogates to monitor non-compliance and sanction it consistently, and this may extend into the adult lives of sons and daughters. The values and morality to which children are socialised within the Saudi family are further reinforced in the school.

The school

Although the modern education system was established in Saudi Arabia in the late 1940s and early 1950s, respect for learning has deep roots in Saudi and Islamic history. The Prophet Mohammad is reported to have said that 'gaining knowledge is the [religious] duty of every male and female Muslim'. Traditionally, boys' first educational experience outside the home took place in the *kuttab*. The *kuttab* was a kind of mosque-school where the local *Imam* (Islamic priest) taught boys reading and writing of Arabic script, and memorisation and recitation of the *Qura'n*. Girls were traditionally taught by female teachers in the home (Adler, 1983; Al-Mufadda, 2003). At a higher level, students attended *halaqat*, or informal networks that involved lectures in Islamic jurisprudence, interpretation of the *Qura'n*, *hadith* (tradition of Prophet Mohammad), Arabic literature and rhetoric. Those who wished to specialise in one or more of these areas travelled to Al-Azhar University in Cairo, or to Islamic centres of excellence in Baghdad or Koffa (Iraq).

However, this traditional focus on religious education fell short in meeting the new needs of Saudi Arabian society after the discovery and exploitation of massive oil resources, and the subsequent increased contacts with the outside world during the 1930s and 1940s. In the wake of these developments, the government established a formal education system in 1949–50 (Ain-al-Yaqeen, 1997). The Ministry of Education, responsible for the administration of public education (for male students only), was established in 1954, but public education for females was not established until 1960. Although the Saudi schooling system is organised on modern lines, education, at both school and university levels, remains closely linked to its Islamic roots. Education is segregated by gender and a large part of the curriculum is devoted to religious instruction. Under the influence of *Ulama*, a main concern of the government educational policy has been to 'balance' the impact of secular modern education vis-à-vis Islamic values on which the existing social and political order in Saudi Arabia is based. Modern Saudi education has been designed to promote the idea of nationhood, loyalty to Islam and to the state. According to an official document entitled, *The Educational Policy in the Kingdom of Saudi Arabia* (1978, p 5), education should '... promote a spirit of loyalty to Islamic law and by denouncing any system and theory that conflicts with it and by behaving with honesty and in conformity with Islamic tenets'. This policy is directly reflected in the school curriculum and is justified in the Saudi social and religious context in this way:

> The situation in Saudi Arabia is totally different. Religion at secondary school level is taken seriously, and given a prominent status. Religion is also studied at university level alongside other studies in all years and for all students. Religion and Islamic culture is for all, for the educated and uneducated because it is a programme for life, and because it offers an inner contentment and becalms the soul. True Muslims hold fast to their faith even though they attain the acme of education in their various fields of expertise (Ain-al-Yaqeen, 1997, p 2).

While religious and secular subjects are taught in schools across the Islamic world, in Saudi Arabia, a large part of the curriculum is devoted to Islamic studies. According to Prokop (2003, p 79): '30% of weekly hours in elementary school are dedicated to religious subjects; in intermediate school the proportion is 24% and in secondary school around 35% for those students in the *Shari'a* and Arabic branch and approximately 14% for those in the technical and natural science branch.' Saudi liberal reformists and Westerners have criticised this heavy emphasis on religious education in the school curriculum. Its defenders, however, say that it has been through this marriage between traditional and modern educational concerns that the country has been able to achieve a very high literacy rate and to massively expand higher education in a deeply religious society (Al-Farsy, 1990; Al-Salloum, 1995). Saudi Arabia's literacy rate more than tripled in the past three decades (Sedgwick, 2001) and it has the highest number of university graduates in the region, more than 50% of whom are women (Prokop, 2003).

I will return to the complexities of Saudi education intermittently throughout the remainder of this chapter. What is important to establish at the outset is that the school in Saudi Arabia is not just a transitional bridge between the private world of the family and participation in the wider world of work. It reinforces the religious and cultural values to which children are socialised within the extended family. The school in Saudi Arabia inculcates the same religious and cultural values with which parents socialise their children. These values range from very private to very public: from drinking, eating and dressing to the virtues of cleanliness, honesty, modesty and chastity; and from social manners and greetings, to duties and obligations to parents, kin, neighbours, the needy and to the state, the society, and to the wider Islamic world.

The school plays a very crucial role in the production of social order and in the bonding of youngsters to the conventional world of work and marriage. In the language of criminological control theory, the fact that education is both a religious obligation and a measure of social status, makes the school an agency conducive to the development of strong attachments between young people and society. The consistency between the values of the school, the family and the wider society results in stronger social bonds generally. Western criminologists have consistently shown that attachment to school and family equates with compliance to conventional norms and law-abiding behaviour (Hirschi, 1969; Gottfredson and Hirschi, 1990; Sampson and Laub, 1993; Wardak, 2000). Like the Saudi family, the Saudi school has the cultural and material resources to monitor and sanction non-compliance. However, the concerted focus on religious dogma may also foster intolerance towards other belief systems. The Saudi school curriculum has been criticised and accused of contributing to Islamic radicalism, intolerance and anti-Western sentiments (Wictorowicz, 2001; Stalinsky, 2002; Prokop, 2003). Although Islamic radicalism has, over the past few decades, mainly been associated with secular pro-Western dictatorial regimes (that is, Egypt, Algeria and Iran under the Shah), the existing Saudi educational system may also produce similar effects.

The mosque and Ulama

The mosque is a very important agency of social control in Saudi Arabia. The mosque is an integral part of Islamic religious and cultural life generally. It is central to the social organisation of Islamic cities, towns, villages and neighbourhoods. It even retains its centrality in the social organisation of diasporic Muslim communities in the West (Wardak, 2002). One of the most important reasons for this is because the mosque functions as a place for the five daily prayers, the congregational weekly *jom'a* (Friday) prayer, and the annual congregational *Eid al Fiter* and *Eid al Odha* (the first symbolises the *Ramadan* – fasting – and the second the day of pilgrimage in Mecca). The latter three categories of prayer are of especial importance in Islam as it is obligatory that they are performed in congregation. The various congregational prayers, their related rituals and sermons are not merely occasions in which Muslims perform their religious duties before *Allah* (God). They are constitutive of collective expressions of shared belief, a sense of community and of deeply held feelings of unity, summed up in a passage from the holy *Qura'n* which says: '... You alone we worship; from you alone we seek help; guide us along the straight path ...' (Al-Qura'n, Surah 1). The collective expression of these shared sentiments is conducive to strengthening social cohesion among worshipers. More importantly, it serves as a social occasion for the renewal of their commitment, in public, to Islamic faith and moral principles that are already internalised from childhood. In the mosque, various aspects of Islamic morality are propounded by the *Imam* (Islamic priest) in the contexts of the verses of the *Qura'n* and the traditions and deeds of Prophet Mohammad.

In Saudi Arabia, all businesses and offices are closed for prayer. At such times, the mosque serves as an important platform for religious leaders to discuss various social, political, judicial and other issues from an Islamic point of view. During the annual occasions of *Eid al Fiter* and *Eid al Odha*, reconciliation among disputants in the neighbourhood, village, tribe and city often takes place in the mosque. In addition, despite the fact that, since the 1950s, formal school education has expanded vastly throughout the country and replaced the *Kuttab*, mosque-based learning and teaching continues to exist, particularly in rural areas (see Prokop, 2003). Thus, the mosque in Saudi Arabia not only functions as a place for congregational worship, but also as a place for community-level decision making, a place for the discussion of social, political and judicial issues and as an educational centre.

Central to the performance of these functions is the *Ulama*. *Ulama* is the plural of Alim in Arabic, which means scholar of Islamic theology and law. *Ulama* refers to religious scholars, Islamic judges, lawyers, seminary teachers, and to *Imams*. *Ulama*, play a hugely important role in the social, educational, religious and political life of Saudi society. Other than their role as *Imams* and preachers in mosques, many *Ulama* are involved in the teaching profession. Hundreds of *Ulama*, with formal higher educational qualifications, work as teachers of Islamic education at Saudi state run schools. Other more senior *Ulama* are engaged in teaching and research in the areas of Islamic law and theology at Saudi universities (Al-Farsy, 1990). The Islamic University of Medina and the Islamic University of Imam Mohammad ibn Saud, in Riyadh, are the two main institutions where many Saudi *Ulama* teach and research.

Senior *Ulama* are also involved in the resolution of conflicts. As scholars of Islamic jurisprudence, they understand and interpret Islamic jurisprudence and find rulings for resolving various disputes. Even more importantly, *Ulama* also work as *Qadi* (Islamic judges) in the Saudi justice system, a system based on *Shari'a* law. Thus, *Imams* may function as preachers in the mosque, teachers and educationalists, scholars of Islamic law and as mediators and judges. *Ulama* have a huge social influence in Saudi society and they play a crucial role in providing religious legitimacy for the Saudi monarchy and government policies (Al-Yassini, 1985; Kechichian, 1986).

The influence of the *Ulama* was formalised in 1971 when the Saudi rulers established the Council of Senior *Ulama* – an official body that serves as a forum for regular consultation between the Saudi monarchy and the religious establishment. Thus, in order to 'sell' controversial policies to the Saudi public, the government first needs approval of the *Ulama*. For example, in 1979, when a group of armed Islamic radicals occupied parts of *Al-Hram al-Makki* (a grand mosque which houses one of the two holiest Islamic shrines) the Council of Senior *Ulama* passed a *Fatwa* (religious edict), which approved the use of force to evict the occupiers, despite the fact that, according to Islamic teachings, no use of force or violence is allowed in *Al-*

Hram al-Makki. It is inescapable that Saudi *Ulama* exercise a considerable level of political influence in Saudi society (Al-Rasheed, 2002).

An important characteristic of mainstream Saudi *Ulama* is their adherence to the teaching of *Imam* Mohammad ibn Abd al Wahhab – the 18th century religious scholar – who made a political alliance with *Imam* Mohammad ibn Saud, the political founder of Saudi Arabia. One result of this two century old political alliance is the intermarriages between members of the Saudi royal family and those of *Imam* Mohammad ibn Abd al Wahhab. Many influential members of the establishment *Ulama* today are direct descendants of the *Imam* (Rentz, 1972; Bligh, 1985). Following the jurisprudential school of *Ahmad ibn Hanbal*, *Wahhabi Ulama* rely heavily on the *Qura'n* and *Sunna* (traditions of Prophet Mohammad) as sources of Islamic law. They are more cautious about the use of *Qiyas* (analogical deduction) and *Ijm'a* (consensus of Islamic jurists) by which more reform-minded *Ulama* have attempted to induce social change. The orthodoxy and strong political influence of many of *Imam* Mohammad ibn Abd al Wahhab's descendants (*Al Ashaykh*) appears to have resulted in the alienation of more reform-minded *Ulama*. While some reformist Islamic scholars are critical and call for political reform, others have joined Saudi dissident groups who call for the demise of the Saudi monarchy and its replacement by an even more puritan Islamic *Khelafa* (Dekmejian, 1994).

Despite these frictions and differences, *Ulama* in general are still very influential in Saudi society. In the main, they continue to provide an intellectual and spiritual support and justification of the Islamic values and morality that permeate almost all aspects of life in Saudi society. The convergence of the school, the family and the mosque in promoting an Islamic belief system is highly conducive to the creation of what Stark *et al* (1982) refer to as a 'religious ecology', where religion permeates every aspect of daily life. Although the measurable impact of individual 'religiosity' on proclivities to crime is generally inconclusive (Linden and Currie, 1977; Higgins and Albrecht, 1977; Gannon, 1970), Stark *et al* (1982, p 15) argue that where '... the surrounding community is permeated by religious beliefs and concerns, variation in individuals' religiousness will influence delinquency'. Tittle and Welch (1983) also support this conclusion. Thus, the 'religious ecology' of Saudi society is very likely to have a decisive affect on Saudi crime rates. However, low Saudi crime rates can only be fully explained when the relationships between these influences and the formal justice system are established. But before doing this, it is important to look at how religious morality is enforced by Saudi semi-informal religious police – the *Motawwa'in*.

Motawwa'in

Motawwa'in is the plural of *Motaww'a*, which in Arabic means a person who volunteers, or who obeys. It is based on the general idea of *Al-AMR Bel-Ma'roof Wal-Nahy 'An Al-Monkar* ('ordering what is right and forbidding what is wrong') – a religious duty and social responsibility for every Muslim. The translation of this idea into practice is closely connected with the teaching of *Imam* Mohammad ibn Abd al Wahhab. As such, Saudi Arabia is the only country in the Muslim country in the world (with the exception of Afghanistan under the *Taliban* during 1995–2001) in which this is enforced. The *Motawwa'in* is formally organised under the King, but is autonomous in important ways. Although *Motawwa'in* are paid salaries by government, they are neither part of the Saudi security or police, nor are they trained as law enforcement personnel. There are approximately 20,000 men who perform this role. Typically they are not armed, but they often carry sticks or cudgels that may be used if necessary. They have the authority to detain suspects for 24 hours before turning them over to the formal police. Members of the organisation are usually bearded men who wear the *Thaub* (traditional Arabic white kamees) and look like any other male Saudi citizen.

Motawwa'in have wide-ranging jurisdiction relating to religious and moral issues in Saudi society. Other than working as *Do'at* (missionaries), promoters of public morals, and preachers in mosques, *Motawwa'in* also police male attendance at prayer in the mosques, fasting during the month of *Ramadan*, closure of shops during prayer time, preventing undue mixing of men and women, smoking, drinking alcohol, immodest dressing of women and dancing. A more detailed list of 'ordering what is right and forbidding what is wrong' is provided by the Commission's regulation:

> Prohibited mixing [of sexes] and wanton display [by women, *tabarruj*]; imitation by one sex of the other; proposition by men to women by word or deed; public expressions harmful to modesty or contradictory to morals; operating a radio, television, tape recorders, etc, near to mosques or in a fashion disturbing people at prayer; non-Muslims manifesting their beliefs or the rites of their religion or demonstrating lack of respect for the rites or laws of Islam; offer or sale of pictures, books, or video or audio tapes contradictory to Islamic morals or to the Islamic creed ...; offer for sale of corporeal or depraved pictures or the symbols of a religion not Islam ...; manufacture of intoxicants or their distribution or imbibing them ...; preventing [*sic*] calls to commit scandalous acts such as adultery, sodomy, or gambling, or running houses or sites for committing forbidden or scandalous acts; evident innovations in religion like glorifying specific places or times for which no revealed authority exists, or celebrating feasts or anniversaries or occasions of un-Islamic innovation; practices of witchcraft or magic and attempts to take people's property under false pretences; falsifying weights and measures; [un-Islamic methods of slaughter] at slaughterhouses ...; [improper behaviour at] shops and establishments for making women's clothing (Regulation, Sec 1).

Some of the categories in this long list of 'ordering what is right and forbidding what is wrong' can be read as being in violation of fairly basic principles of human rights (Amnesty International, 2003; Human Rights Watch, 2002), but they are also very vague. For example, in the prohibition of 'public expressions harmful to modesty or contradictory to morals' it is not clear what is 'moral' and what is 'modesty'; do these rules apply to men, women or to both? Similarly, the prohibition of 'proposition by men to women by word or deed' is not only worded in highly vague terms, but it is also highly confusing – does this include proposition by women to men? The discretionary interpretation of such rules is left to *Motawwa'in* who have a reputation of fanaticism and even ignorance (Vogel, 2003). This situation has resulted in the mistreatment and harassment of many Saudi citizens, especially women, young men and overseas workers (Amnesty International, 2003; Human Rights Watch, 2002).

Saudi *Motawwa'in* are modelled on the notion of *Mohtasib* (Islamic market inspector and enforcer of public morality) in classical Islamic jurisprudence. However, *Mohtasib* had the authority to enforce categorical *Shari'a* principles, not issues that are mere matters of *Ijtihad*, or interpretation by individual Islamic jurists or school of thoughts (Mawardi, 1978). For example, veiling of the face, the ban on women's driving and the mixing of the sexes in public are matters of Ijtihad; they are not based on categorical *Shari'a* principles. However, because of the strong social and political influence of the conservative *Ulama* establishment in Saudi society, these practices have not been challenged. As Vogel (2003, p 18) put it: 'The issue of women's driving is an example of how Saudi *Ulama*, acting putatively in a purely private and religious capacity, sometimes assume legislative and administrative functions, functions that properly belong to the ruler and his delegates ...' Indeed, the connection between *Motawwa'in* and the conservative religious establishment indicate that they are more a semi-official police force of the Saudi *Ulama*. Their virtually unquestionable authority confirms this. As Vogel (2003, p 18) further says: 'Perhaps, under these provisions, the Commission considers itself empowered by the King to prevent even acts falling within the realm of *Ijtihad* uncertainty. More likely, however, given the Commission's strong identification with the religious-scholarly establishment, the *Ulama*, it acts under another head.' This raises important questions for the legal and religious legitimacy of *Motawwa'in*, at least in the minds of some Saudis.

As there is no empirical research with regard to the ways the Saudi people are policed by the *Motawwa'in*, it is difficult to assess the latter's role in contributing to the low crime rate in Saudi society. Obviously, *Motawwa'in's* active presence and surveillance practices in city centres, streets and other places can prevent people from engaging in crime and 'immorality'. But the fact that enforcement of moral norms by the *Motawwa'in* is so nearly ubiquitous within Saudi Arabia may have negative consequences; the most notorious being the displacement of immoral behaviour by members of the economic elite to places outside the country. More worrying than the hypocrisy evidenced by this displacement, any differences in points of view between the reform-minded and traditionally-minded Saudis about matters of moral and social order are invariably resolved by re-imposing already established patterns. This drives dissent underground and stores up resentment and trouble for the future. *Motawwa'in* policing practice is legitimated through their influence in the mosque and their close connections with the *Ulama*. In addition, they also appear to be seen favourably by the *Ulama* dominated judicial system – a subject to which I now turn.

The judicial system

The Saudi judicial system strongly reflects the religious and cultural values of Saudi society. *Shari'a* (Islamic law) is considered the sole permissible source of legislation. Legislation is formulated by a resolution of the Council of Ministers, which is then ratified by royal decree, and must be consistent with *Shari'a*. No authoritative acts and regulations are valid unless they are deemed compatible with *Shari'a*. Thus, in order to understand the Saudi judicial system, it is important to understand what *Shari'a* is.

Shari'a in Arabic means 'the path to follow'. *Shari'a* refers to Islamic Law, the primary sources of which are the *Qura'n* and the *Sunna*. The first refers to the holy book of Islam and the second to the record of statements and deeds of the Prophet

Mohammad. However, only a few hundred verses of the *Qura'n* and specific parts of the *Sunna* are legal in nature (Abu Zahra, 1958; Kamali, 1997; Lippman *et al*, 1988). Even taken together, these two sources do not seemingly cover all of the legal issues that arise in a fast changing world. The *Qura'n* and the Sunna do lay down general principles as well as specific rules that can be subject to interpretation and analysis. Thus, after the death of the Prophet Mohammad, the *Caliphs* (leaders of the Muslim community) and the *Sohaba* (the Prophet's associates) appointed prominent Islamic jurists to aid in the correct interpretation of the *Qura'n* and the *Sunna*, and in the extraction of rules (for new situations) that seemingly did not exist in the two primary sources of *Shari'a*.

As a result, *Ijm'á* and *Qiyas* were added as two main secondary sources of *Shari'a*. *Ijm'a*, means the consensus of Islamic jurists on a ruling. When qualified Islamic jurists reach a unanimous agreement on a solution to a specific new problem, their opinion may become binding with absolute authority. *Qiyas*, in the context of Islamic jurisprudence, means anological deduction. That is, that cases and questions not seemingly answered by the primary sources are deduced from similar original cases in the *Qura'n*, *Sunna* or *Ijm'a*, through a process of reasoning by analogy. Only those Islamic jurists who meet strict criteria relating to their knowledge, piety and personal integrity may undertake this process of interpretation. They are also required to fulfil very strict conditions for the kind of cases that may be handled by *Qiyas*. In this way, a bridge is built between divine revelation and the circumstances of modern society. The outcomes of both *Qiyas* and *Ijm'a* are transformed into Islamic law, manifest in the compilation of hundreds of cases and books for use as references in Islamic jurisprudence (Kamali, 1997; Lippman *et al*, 1988). As is reasonably well known, early on, Islamic jurists split into the main two sects – the *Sunni* and *Shi'ite*. The overwhelming majority of Saudis are *Sunnis* and followers of the *Hanbali* school. The finer points of doctrinal difference need not detain us here. What is important to the current discussion is that Islamic jurisprudence in Saudi Arabia has been particularly influenced by the teachings of Muhammad ibn Abd al Wahhab. It is the tenets of this School that are mainly translated into the practice of the formal judicial system. The structure of Saudi judicial system is illustrated in Diagram 1.

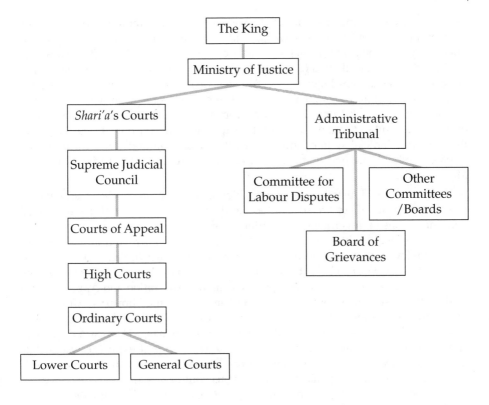

Diagram 1: The judicial system of Saudi Arabia.

As the diagram shows, the Saudi judicial is administered by a system of *Shari'a* courts and specialist administrative tribunals. The Ministry of Justice, which is assisted by the 11 members of the Supreme Judicial Council, is responsible for the overall administration of *Shari'a* courts. Judges are appointed by the King on the recommendation of the Supreme Judicial Council. The independence of the judiciary is protected by law as Article 1 of the Royal Decree 64 (23 July 1975) states: '... judges are independent, and their administration of justice is subject to no authority other than the provisions of Islamic law and regulations in force. No one may interfere with the judiciary.'

The lowest level in the *Shari'a* judicial hierarchy are Ordinary Courts, or courts of first instance. These courts are further sub-divided into Lower Courts and General Courts. Lower Courts mainly deal with minor civil and criminal cases. They also deal with *Ta'zir* (*Shari'a*-based discretionary penalties) and those *Hudud* (fixed *Shari'a*-based offences) that relate to intoxication and defamation. These courts exist in almost all towns in Saudi Arabia and hearings are presided by a single *Qadi* (Islamic judge). However, General Courts have original jurisdiction over all criminal and civil cases, which are heard by a single *Qadi*. Cases relating to the *Hudud* of theft, adultery and capital punishment are heard by panel of three *Qadi* (Karl, 1991; Moore, 1987). Dissatisfied disputants may appeal against decisions reached by the two courts to High *Shari'a* Courts (or the Courts of Appeal). High *Shari'a* Courts may not only hear appeals from Ordinary *Shari'a* Courts, more importantly they have exclusive jurisdiction over *Hudud* and *qisas* (the latter refers to *Shari'a*-based offences against the person). Less serious cases are heard by a single *Qadi*. However, for *Hudud* offences of theft, adultery and capital punishment, a panel of three *Qadis* is required. As Diagram 1 shows, decisions reached in the High Court (as well as in Ordinary Courts) may be appealed to the *Shari'a* Courts of Appeal. The chief justice and a panel of five *Qadis* preside over all appeal cases. Decisions reached at Courts of Appeal are subject to the review of the Supreme Judicial Council. The King is at the top of the judicial system, and has the final review authority and the authority to pardon, should he find that a verdict is not in conformity to *Shari'a* (Karl, 1991; Moore, 1987).

Diagram 1 also illustrates the composition of the Administrative Tribunals. As mentioned earlier, these are specialised courts established by royal decree to deal with infractions of government regulations that are beyond the scope of the *Shari'a* courts; they deal with issues of more secular concern. Each committee operates within a relevant ministry and the scope of its jurisdiction is limited to the activities of that ministry. For example, the Committee for Labour Disputes operates within the Ministry of Labour and Social Affairs, while the Arbitration and Appeals Board deals with the settlement of commercial disputes within the Ministry of Commerce. One of the most important of these committees is the Board of Grievances, which is an independent judicial body directly answerable to the King. The Board deals with complaints about rule breaking by the government and even the *Qadis*. The hierarchical structure of the Administrative Tribunal is similar to those of *Shari'a* Courts. Although most members of the various committees are *Qadis*, one member of each committee must have specialist knowledge about specific regulations and of their relevant technicalities.

This description of the Saudi judicial system clearly indicates that it is based squarely on *Shari'a* and is designed to reinforce the values and morality to which Saudi citizens are socialised in the context of the family, the mosque and the school. The judicial system is, in many important ways, but the formal embodiment of these values and morality. The processes of a complex interplay between the formal, semi-formal and informal agencies of social control and the ways this affects the crime rate is further examined below.

The interplay between informal, semi-formal and formal social controls

The main explanatory accounts for Saudi low crime rates have already been mentioned, and it has been argued here that they provide only a partial and/or simplistic explanation. This chapter discussed in detail the main social control agencies in Saudi Arabia: the extended family, the school, the mosque/*Ulama*, *Motawwa'in*, and the formal Saudi judicial system. A set of distinctions between informal, semi-formal and formal agencies of social control has been made. It has been argued that, at the informal level, each of the extended family and the mosque in Saudi Arabia play an immensely strong role in the socialisation of the Saudi population, especially children, into traditional cultural values and Islamic morality. Parents, *Ulama* and other conventional figures have religious, social and economic resources that enable them to monitor behaviours and to enforce familial and religious values. At the semi-formal level, the Saudi school as a state-sponsored but non-criminal justice agency of social control acts as a bridge between the traditional Saudi family and the world of work and participation in the wider society. In the educational process, the school has its own mechanisms of monitoring behaviour, rewarding compliance and punishing misbehaviour. The effect of *Motawwa'in*, the semi-formal religious police, in maintaining social order may not be easily self-evident to Western readers, but it nevertheless enforces religious values and morality at least at specific places and times and this seems to have more general consequences for social ordering.

The Saudi family, the mosque/*Ulama*, the school, and *Motawwa'in* ensure conformity to core societal values and norms at micro and meso (group) levels. In so doing, each contributes to the maintenance of social order at the macro (societal) level. Thus, the state's aim of reproducing macro level societal order is served by micro and meso level agencies of social control. In fact, the latter are more effective and well placed as compared to the former in producing social order, as they can monitor, reward and punish non-compliance of individuals at almost all times and places. In addition, compliance to group demands at the micro level often takes place voluntarily, spontaneously and without financial or other inducements. There are comparative examples that support this argument. For example Miller and Kanazawa in explaining low crime rate in Japan – a strongly community-oriented society – make this point very lucidly:

> When social control at the group (meso) level is efficient, the result at the societal (macro) level is essentially the same as though the society acted as a single group. If groups are effective as agents of social control and their respective members have higher probability of compliance to group norms as a result, then the society as a whole will consist of individuals who have a higher probability of compliance, *regardless of the actual contents of the norms with which they are complying*. Their higher probabilities of compliance are not owing to their membership in the society, but to their membership in the groups, which function as the actual agents of social control (Miller and Kanazawa, 2000, p 14; original emphasis).

There is much reason to believe that each of the extended family, the school, the mosque/*Ulama* and *Motawwa'in* directly and independently contribute to the low crime rate in Saudi Arabia, as illustrated in Diagram 2. However, this is only part of the explanation for low Saudi crime rates. As discussed earlier, while the micro and meso agencies of social control in Saudi Arabia play a crucial role in the maintenance of social order, they do not operate in isolation from one another. Rather, these micro agencies of social control closely interact among themselves and with the macro level formal social control agencies. There is a hierarchical interplay between all the main agencies of social control which simultaneously reinforce one another. This interplay is illustrated in Diagram 2.

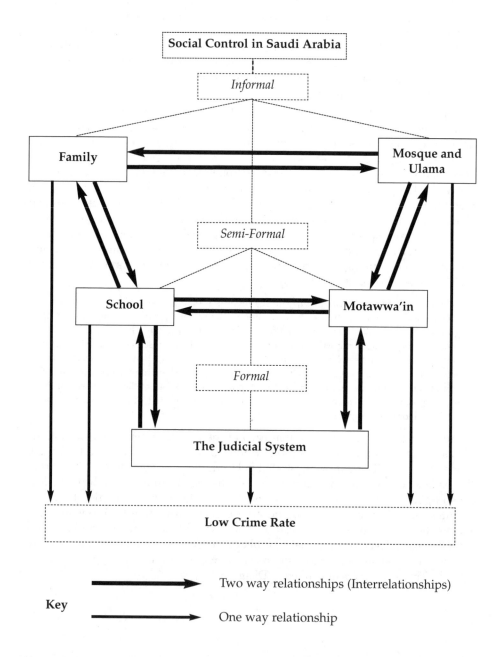

Key

Two way relationships (Interrelationships)

One way relationship

Diagram 2: Interplay between informal, semi-formal and formal social controls in Saudi Arabia.

The family and the mosque/*Ulama* are the most conventional agencies of social control. They strongly and concurrently reinforce one another in instilling an Islamic belief system and in socialising individuals to religious morality. The high level of emotional and social dependence of family members on conventional figures within the extended family, and the strong spiritual and intellectual influence of *Ulama*, have created an 'ecology of religious life', where the individual has little choice but to absorb and comply with the demands of the existing moral order. These two agencies of social control play a particularly strong role in the primary socialisation of Saudi children. But what is special in the case of Saudi Arabia is that the primary socialisation process in the informal settings of the family and mosque is further reinforced by the school, where about 30% of the curriculum is dedicated to Islamic religious education. Hence, the school not only equips individuals with skills necessary for participation in the social institutional life of the wider society, it also helps bridge and extend his or her internalised religious beliefs and values into an understanding and legitimacy of the legal/judicial order at the macro level. These linked processes of socialisation are highly conducive to the diffusion and cohesion of societal values – a situation of 'synnomie' – and therefore to the low Saudi crime rate, as Diagram 2 illustrates.

Furthermore, while these interrelated social control processes within the family, the mosque and the school are mainly concerned with spiritual and moral bonding of the individual to the moral and social order of society at different levels, the *Ulama*, *Motawwa'in*, and the formal judicial system are devoted to the enforcement of moral and legal norms. As Diagram 2 illustrates, these agencies of social control interact and reinforce one another. The fact that the *Motawwa'in* enforce much of what *Ulama* (who also run the formal judicial system) preach clearly shows that these agencies are organically interrelated to one another. More importantly, as Diagram 2 indicates, all the various agencies of social control are further interrelated to one another in a top down direction – the state and its *Ulama*-dominated judicial institutions, by applying Islamic law, and through their influence over school curriculum and over *Motawwa'in*, serve to underpin the enforcement of the Islamic moral and social order that the family and mosque produce at micro and meso levels. It is·this complex and concurrent interplay between micro, meso and macro level social control agencies that re-enforces the social order and maintains it, and it is this complex interplay that explains low crimes rate in Saudi Arabia.

However, it should not escape mention that the price of social order and low crime rates may be too high for those who are socially excluded and politically disenfranchised. As mentioned earlier, many women, some ethnic/religious minorities, some young people, guest workers, and others who do not fully share in or benefit from the existing political and social order, have reasons to resent the mechanisms that produce the high degree of social order in Saudi Arabia. Reports by human rights and other organisations have highlighted the excesses of *Motawwa'in* in enforcing a highly selective version of Islamic morality (Amnesty International, 2003; Human Rights Watch, 2002). In an increasingly modern society, the strong influence of establishment *Ulama* in justifying the existing version of morality has been a main obstacle to social and political reform (Vogel, 2000, 2003).

The Saudi system of social control is under pressure because of its situation in a global context. Certain aspects of the control system clash with new demands as

Saudi society adjusts to the reality of the emerging transnational order. One manifestation of the tension is the emergence of political dissident groups and radical militants. Another is an emerging focus on women's relative unfreedom. A third area of concern is the unequal treatment of foreign guest workers in the country. A fourth is how this Islamic system of social control generally responds to conditions of the global Muslim Diaspora. All of these symptoms point to the need for social, political and legal reform in Saudi society. Many Saudis, including some members of the royal family, seem to be aware of the needs for such reforms. As Prince Al-Waleed bin Talal – a nephew of King Fahd – told the *Washington Post*: 'For a really long time, we have been a closed community. This is a fact you have to acknowledge. To open it up right now is not going to be easy, not going to be swift, not going to be smooth. But it is going to happen' (quoted in *The Economist*, 22 January 2004). Indeed, the social, political and legal transformations that lie ahead for Saudi Arabia are probably going to be very difficult. As of this writing, the country is engaged in a process of 'national dialogue' that includes participation by women, liberals and members of ethnic and religious minorities. It is too early to say what the results might be. Comparative criminologists ought to take a keen interest in future developments, not only because they matter to the evolution of a global order based on justice and human rights. More narrowly, future processes of transformation likely to affect the agencies of social control in Saudi Arabia will have consequences not only for the agencies of social ordering in that country, but also probably in the Middle East generally and perhaps even globally. As such, there are many lessons to be learned about how societies adapt to global conditions and how, or indeed if, distinctive societies with low crime rates can maintain themselves as such. Taking a look at the alternatives, many Saudis may well wish to continue to stress social order rather than individual liberties. Whatever the future holds, it is certain that Islamic culture will continue to provide a fascinating basis for comparative criminology.

References

Aba Namay, R (1993) 'Constitutional reforms: a systemisation of Saudi politics' 16(3) *Journal of South Asian and Middle Eastern Studies* 43–88

Abdullah, A (1990) *al – Bitrol Wa al – Akhlaq* (Oil and Morality), London: Dar al – Duha

Abu Bakar Al-Boihagi, A (1994) *Al-Sunan al-Kubra Lil Baihagi*, Makka: Maktabat Dar Albaz

Abu Zahra, M (1958) *Usul – Alfiqh*, Beirut: Darul Fikr Al-Arabi

Adler, F (1983) *Nations Obsessed with Crime*, Littleton, Co: Rotham

Ain-al-Yaqeen (1997) *Education in the Kingdom of Saudi Arabia*, 15 December, available at www.ain-al-yaqeen.com

al-Awaji, I (1971) *Bureaucracy and Society in Saudi Arabia*, unpublished PhD dissertation, University of Virginia, USA

Albrecht, S, Chadwick, B and Alcorn, D (1977) 'Religiosity and deviance: applications of an attitude-behaviour contingent consistency model' 16 *Journal of the Scientific Study of Religion* 262–74

al-Farsy, F (1990) *Modernity and Tradition: The Saudi Equation*, London: Kegan Paul

al-Ghamdi, S (1989) 'The changing role of rural family: anthropological study in Al-Baha area' 1 *Journal of Arts and Human Sciences* 1–32 (in Arabic)

Ali, Badr-al-Din (1985) 'Islamic law and crime: the case of Saudi Arabia' 9 *International Journal of Comparative and Applied Criminal Justice* 45–57

al-Kattan, MK (1980) 'Effect of religion against crime', in *Effect of Islamic Legislation on Crime Prevention in Saudi Arabia*, Rome: UNSDRI/Saudi Ministry of Interior

al-Mufadda (2003) *The Islamic Education Teacher's Role in Saudi Secondary Schools for Boys*, unpublished PhD dissertation, University of Manchester, UK

al-Mutrak, OI (1980) 'Fixed penalties "Houdoud" and discretionary penalties "Ta'zir"', in *The Effect of Islamic Legislation on Crime Prevention in Saudi Arabia*, Rome: UNSDRI/Saudi Ministry of Interior

Al-Qura'n (1964) Beirut: Dar al-Kutub Al-Islamiyya

al-Rasheed, M and al-Rasheed, L (1996) 'The politics of encapsulation: Saudi policy towards tribal and religious opposition' 32(1) *Middle East Studies* 96–119

al-Rasheed, M (2002) *A History of Saudi Arabia*, Cambridge: CUP

al-Salloum, H (1995) *Education in Saudi Arabia*, Beltsville: Amana Publications

al-Yassini, A (1985) *Religion and State in the Kingdom of Saudi Arabia*, Boulder: Westview

Amnesty International, *Annual Report 2003 – Saudi Arabia*, www.web.amnesty.org

Basha, B (1979) *The Significant Influences of Islamic Law in Decreasing Crime Rate in Saudi Arabian Society*, unpublished PhD dissertation, United States International University, San Diego, USA

Basnawi, I (1984) *Incidence and Control of Crime in Contemporary Saudi Arabia*, unpublished PhD dissertation, United States International University, San Diego, USA

Bligh, A (1985), 'The Saudi religious elite (Ulama) as participants in the political system of the Kingdom' 17(1) *International Journal of Middle East Studies* 37–50

Cohen, S (1985) *Visions of Social Control*, Cambridge: Polity

Dekmejian, H (1994) 'The rise of political Islam in Saudi Arabia' 48(4) *Middle East Journal* 627–43

Doumato, E (1991) *Women and the Stability of Saudi Arabia*, Middle East Report No 171, July–August, 1991, Washington, MERRIP 34–37

Edwards, A (1988) *Regulation and Repression: The Study Of Social Control*, Sydney: Allen & Unwin

El-Sendiony, MF (1981) *The Effect of Islamic Shari'a on Behavioural Disturbances in the Kingdom of Saudi Arabia: A Case Study of Transcultural Psychiatry*, Makkah, Saudi Arabia: Umm Al-Qura University

Farrington, D (1973) 'Self-reports of deviant behaviour: predictive and stable' 64 *Journal of Criminal Law and Criminology* 99–110

Gannon, T (1970) 'Religious control and delinquent behaviour', in Knudten, R (ed), *Crime, Criminology and Contemporary Society*, Homewood, Illinois: Dorsey Press

Ghanoubi, A (1976) *IRQAH: A Village Community in Najd*, unpublished PhD dissertation, University of Manchester, UK

Glueck, S and Gluck, E (1950) *Unravelling Juvenile Delinquency*, Cambridge, Massachussetts: Harvard UP

Gottfredson, M and Hirschi, T (1990) *A General Theory of Crime*, Stanford, California: Stanford UP

Groves, W, Newman, G and Corrado, C (1987) 'Islam, modernisation and crime: a test of the religious ecology thesis' 15 *Journal of Criminal Justice* 495–503

Gurwich, G (1945) 'Social control', in Gurwich, G *et al* (eds), *Twentieth Century Sociology*, New York: Philosophical Library Inc

Helms, C (1981) *The Cohesion of Saudi Arabia*, London: Croom Helm

Higgins, P and Albrecht, G (1977) 'Hellfire and delinquency revisited' 55 *Soc Forces* 952–58

Hirschi, T (1969) *Causes of Delinquency*, California: California UP

Home Office (2003) *World Prison Population List Findings 234*, RDS, London: Home Office

Human Rights Watch (2002) *Saudi Arabia: Religious Police Role in School Fire Criticised*, 15 March, www.hrw.org

Innes, M (2003) *Understanding Social Control*, Berkshire: OU Press

International Centre for Prison Studies (2003) *Prison Brief for Saudi Arabia*, King's College, London, www.kcl.ac.uk/depsta/rel/icps

Interpol (1988) *International Crime Statistics*, Lyons, France: ICPO – Interpol General Secretariat

Interpol (2000) *International Crime Statistics*, Lyons, France: ICPO – Interpol General Secretariat

Janovitz, M (1975) 'Sociological theory and social control' 18 *American Journal Of Sociology* 82–108

Kamali, M (1997) *Principles of Islamic Jurisprudence*, Cambridge: ITS

Karl, D (1991) 'Islamic Law in Saudi Arabia' 25(1) *Washington Journal of International Law and Economics* 131–70

Kechichian, J (1986) 'The role of the *Ulama* in the politics of an Islamic state: the case of Saudi Arabia' 18 *International Journal of Middle East Studies* 53–71

Linden, R and Currie, R (1977) 'Religiosity and drug use: a test of social control theory' 19 *Canadian Journal of Criminology* 346–55

Lindsey, G (1991) *Saudi Arabia*, New York: Hippocrene Books

Lippman, M *et al* (1988) *Islamic Criminal Law and Procedure: An Introduction*, New York: Preager

Long, D (1997) *The Kingdom of Saudi Arabia*, Gainesville: Florida UP

Lowman, J *et al* (1987) *Transcarcerations: Essays in the Sociology of Social Control*, Aldershot: Gower

Mawardi, A (1978) *Al-Ahkam al-Sultaniyya Wal-Wilayat Al-Diniyya*, Beirut: Dar Al-Kutub Al-Ilmiyya

Meire, R (1982) 'Perspectives on the concept of social control' 8 *Annual Review of Sociology* 35–55

Miller, A and Kanazawa, S (2000) *Order by Accident: The Origins and Consequences of Conformity in Contemporary Japan*, Oxford: Westview

Ministry of Education (1978) *Educational Policy in the Kingdom of Saudi Arabia*, Riyadh: Ministry of Education

Moore, R (1987) 'Courts, law justice and criminal trials in Saudi Arabia' 11(1) *International Journal of Comparative and Applied Criminal Justice* 61–67

Mourad, FA (1980) 'Effect of the implementation of the Islamic legislation on crime prevention in the Kingdom of Saudi Arabia: a field research', in *The Effect of Islamic Legislation on Crime Prevention in Saudi Arabia*, Rome: UNSDRI/Saudi Ministry of Interior

Niblock, T (ed) (1982) *State, Society and Economy in Saudi Arabia*, London: Croom Helm

Nye, I (1958) *Family Relationships and Delinquent Behaviour*, New York: John Wiley

Prokop, M (2003) 'Saudi Arabia: the politics of education' 79(1) *International Affairs* 77–89

Qutb, M (1980) 'Influence of Islamic education on crime prevention', in *The Effect of Islamic Legislation on Crime Prevention in Saudi Arabia*, Rome: UNSDRI/Saudi Ministry of Interior

Rentz, G (1972) 'Wahhabism and Saudi Arabia', in Hopwood, D (ed), *The Arabian Peninsula: Society and Politics*, Totowa, New Jersey: Rowman and Littlefield, pp 54–66

Ross, E (1901) *Social Control*, New York: Macmillan

Royal Decree M 64- (23 July 1975) *Nizam al-Qada*, Riyadh: Matabi Al-Hokuma

Salameh, G (1989), 'Political power and the Saudi state' 91 *MERIP Reports* 5–22

Sampson, R and Laub, J (1993) *Crime in the Making: Pathways and Turning Points Through Life*, London: Harvard UP

Sedgwick, R (2001) 'Education in Saudi Arabia' 14(6) *World Education News and Reviews*, available at www.wes.org

Souryal, SS (1987) 'The religionisation of a society: the continuing application of *Shari'a* Law in Saudi Arabia' 26 *Journal for the Scientific Study of Religion* 429–49

Stalinsky, S (2002) *Saudi Arabia Education System*, MEMRI, 30 December

Stark, R *et al* (1983) 'Crime and delinquency in the roaring twenties' 20 *Journal of Research in Crime* 4–23

Stark, R, Kent, L and Doyle, D (1982) 'Religion and delinquency: the ecology of a "lost" relationship' 19(1) *Journal of Research in Crime* 4–24

'The risks of reform' (2004) *The Economist*, 22 January

Tittle, C and Welch, M (1983) 'Religiosity and deviance: towards a contingency theory of constraining effects' 61 *Social Forces* 653–82

US State Department (2003) *Background Note: Saudi Arabia*, www.state.gov

Vogel, F (2000) *Islamic Law and Legal System: Studies in Saudi Arabia*, Boston: Brill

Vogel, F (2003) 'The public and private in Saudi Arabia: restrictions on the powers of committee for ordering the good and forbidding the evil' 70 *Social Research* 749–68

Wardak, A (2000) *Social Control and Deviance: A South Asian Community in Scotland*, Aldershot: Ashgate

Wardak, A (2002) 'The Mosque and social control in Edinburgh's Muslim community' 3(2) *Journal of Culture and Religion* 201–19

Washington Post (2003) 'Saudi blast bares a nation on edge', 22 November, p A12

West, D (1982) *Delinquency: Its Roots, Careers and Prospects*, London: Heinemann

Wictorwicz, Q (2001) 'The new global threat: transnational Salafis and Jihad' 8(4) *Middle East Policy*, Dec, 27

Yamani, M (1997) 'Evading the habits of a life time: the adaptation of Hejazi dress to the new social order', in Lindisfarne-Tapper, N and Ingham, B (eds), *Languages of Dress in the Middle East*, London: Curzon

Chapter 5
Crime, Criminology and Post-Colonial Theory: Criminological Reflections on West Africa

Biko Agozino

Introduction

This chapter will analyse colonial legacies that structure the criminological discourse as it pertains to West Africa. The argument is that the pervasive conflict in West Africa, and the militarisation of social control that accompanies it, is the consequence of imperialism in the colonial and post-colonial eras. I refer to the kind of criminology that grows from this seedbed of conflict as 'gunboat' or 'gunslinger' criminology and suggest that it is not possible to apply the techniques of comparative criminology to this region without an understanding of the long-standing transnational practices of imperialism. I contend that, like the colonial regimes of the past, contemporary post-colonial regimes in West Africa (and much of sub-Saharan Africa generally) have lost the struggle to legitimise themselves through intellectual and moral leadership and have therefore resorted to the well known authoritarian strategies of regimes facing crises of hegemony (Hall, 1996; Gramsci, 1971).

In the struggle to exploit West African people and the territory on which they have lived for millennia, the imperialist power of the advanced capitalist countries actively supports comprador classes in the region (Fanon, 1967). The comprador 'deputy imperialists' of gunslinger capitalism employ weapons of destruction on a mass scale. Meanwhile, the suffering masses of women, students, workers, the unemployed, peasants and bush people have struggled to democratise and humanise their civil societies (Agozino and Idem, 2001). This struggle between the masses on the one hand and the neo-colonial regimes and their imperialist backers on the other is partly played out on the terrain of criminological discourse and similar fronts. In examining criminological discourse as it has been played out in West Africa, we are at the heart of darkness that permeates the global withering away of the boundaries between state and civil society.

Comparative criminologists need to be sensitised to the particular circumstances of West Africa. When I introduce this topic to my students, I like to begin with a reference to Jean Baudrillard's famous assertion that Disneyland is there to conceal the fact that America in its entirety is the *real* Disneyland, just as the penitentiary is there to conceal the fact that the *entire domain* of the social is a prison (1983, p 25). I like this paradoxical reflection because simultaneously it reminds us that, while one does not have to go to Disneyland in order to have fun in America (because the whole country is one elaborate amusement park), all the while, and despite the breathless enthusiasm of consumer capitalism, the society is fast approaching a 'lockdown society' which has made ubiquitous the industrialised delivery of pain in the service of so called 'crime control' (Sudbury, 2003). Pointing out the messy reality that this paradox suggests, where America is neither just a fun place to be nor a land of inmates but at the same time is both, is one way to immunise young criminologists against the good versus evil calculus all too popular among

American politicians. Reminding students of this complexity is important not only when thinking about the politics of contemporary crime control in America (although it certainly is that), but also because most of them do not have direct experience of matters of criminological concern in West Africa – the special concern of this chapter. If American students or students anywhere in the privileged universities of the 'developed world' think about Africa at all (which sadly they are seldom inclined to do), they are apt to conceive of it in simplistic terms as a land of disease, conflict, misery and strife, never realising that there are communities in Africa, communities that harbour real civility, decorousness and humanity. Africa, it is well known, has to contend with horrific violence, for example the genocide perpetrated in Rwanda in 1994 and the organised violence of 'boy soldiers' in Sierra Leone (Shawcross, 2000). However, we should not forget that Africa's complex reality also includes the civility of life represented by the fictional character Ramatoulaye in Mariama Ba's award winning novel *So Long a Letter*, or the heroes and heroines of Wole Soyinka's *Season of Anomy*. Other works of African fiction testify to the fact that life in civil society goes on, despite Africa's travails.

Unequipped with a good grounding in the real historical circumstances of Africa, the criminologist might too easily arrive, by formulaic means, at some banal and uninformative comparative findings. For example, a comparative geographer might begin by noting that Nigeria has a population of about 101,250 million and is roughly 923,700 square kilometres, France has a population of 59,303 million and is roughly 547,000 square kilometres and Texas has a population of about 20,852 million and is roughly 692,405 square kilometres. Thus, these jurisdictions have population-territory ratios of about 108 per square kilometre; 109 per square kilometre and 30 per square kilometre respectively. Comparative criminologists know, because they have counted, that there are about 45,000 people behind bars in Nigeria, 54,000 in France and in excess of 145,000 in Texas (Walmsley, 2000). A particularly dull-witted comparative criminologist might calculate general population to inmate ratios for each territory yielding the following results: Nigeria 44 per 100,000; France 91 per 100,000 and Texas 695 per 100,000 respectively. We can combine these facts to produce the following table.

Table 1: Selected comparative prison population statistics.

Territory	Population	Landmass	Prison population	Imprisonment rate
Nigeria	101,233,000	923,700	45,000	44:100,000
France	59,330,000	547,000	54,000	91:100,000
Texas	20,851,820	692,405	145,000	695:100,000

Such a table would inevitably be read alongside other facts. For example, that the total budget for the American criminal justice system is roughly four times as much as that of the Nigerian state *as a whole*. Or that, while the running costs of the entire government of Nigeria in 2003 were about US$7 billion, the US Department of Homeland Security had a budget of US$40 billion in that year. There is also 'the intolerable racial disproportion in America's prisons and jails' (Stern, 1998, p 50) where at least one out of every three African-American men between the ages of 20 and 29 are either in prison, jail, on probation or on parole. Observing this, one could be forgiven for wondering just what it is the so called advanced countries have to teach West Africans about criminal justice (Agozino, 2000, 2003).

It is tempting to compile statistics of crime and prison populations across West Africa, as is the fashion in most comparative criminal justice textbooks. However, the task in this chapter is different. I want to provide a broad theoretical reading of the history of crime control and criminological discourse in West Africa. The chapter will start with a brief sketch of pre-colonial social control in West Africa before overviewing the transition to modernity ushered in through colonial rule. I will look in some detail at French and British colonial (in)justice policies in West Africa (not forgetting the role of other colonial powers there) and consider some of the more noteworthy consequences of the militarisation of West African civil society. By way of conclusion, I will look at the possibilities of developing more effective humane institutions of governance in the region that would serve the people instead of being against the people.

West African justice and social control from early times to 1800

A fundamental fact of the history of West Africa up to 1500 AD is its geographical isolation. To the north was the vast expanse of the Sahara desert. The great rivers that flow from the centre of the continent descend to the sea via rapids and waterfalls and thus do not provide easy access to the interior. Fringed with mangrove swamp and sandbar with few natural harbours, the coast itself is not very hospitable to the overseas mariner. The earliest states of Africa thus grew up enjoying little or no contact with the outside world. There was a succession of states that ruled over varying degrees of territory in the region – typically ruled over by divine kings upon whose continued personal wellbeing the prosperity of the kingdom depended. Such a ruler was, in theory, despotic (as befitted a near divinity), but in practice his freedom of action was circumscribed by custom and the council of other great men. These early states were in fact loosely organised groupings of tribes and peoples held together by a bureaucracy loyal to the king. But the local chiefs retained much sovereign power (including the power to pass judgment in cases involving criminal wrongdoing) and owed to their ruler not detailed obedience, but tribute as well as men and supplies in time of war. This general pattern is exhibited across the region from very early times (see Ajayi, 1976; Birmingham, 1975; Birmingham and Marks, 1977; Fage, 1977; and Rodney, 1975 for authoritative and comprehensive coverage).

To criminologists and sociologists of social control, the focus of attention is usually quite singular. In the terms of their interest, what cannot be doubted is that social control in traditional West African society was remarkably effective. Witness the observations of the 14th century Muslim traveller and chronicler Ibn Batuta:

> Acts of injustice are rare among them (West Africans); of all the peoples, they are the least inclined to commit any, and the Sultan (Black King) never pardons anyone who is found guilty of them. Over the whole of the country, there reigns perfect security; one can live and travel there without fear of theft or rapine. They do not confiscate the goods of white men who die in their country; even though they may be of immense value, they do not touch them. On the contrary, they find trustees for the legacy among white men and leave it in their hands until the rightful beneficiaries come to claim it (cited in Diop, 1987, pp 127–28).

Across the savannahs and forests of sub-Saharan Africa the process of state formation threw up many rulers. The histories of these political entities is fascinating, although not well known. Unfortunately, they left little in the way of written records and so it is difficult to produce a 'history from below' for West Africa's early times, so there is remarkably little written about processes of dispute resolution or crime control. Diop suggests that the strong sense of morality among West Africans was based on a strict lack of separation between justice and religion, but his account is perhaps too focused on Islamicised African law of a latter period to be of interest here. Traditional West African society was not generally known for severe punishments that later became associated with *Shari'a* Law.

In fact Mokwugo Okoye (1964) gives the most fulsome account of traditional law and custom as it concerns social control, crime and punishment. According to him, African law is 'restitutory rather than retributory in that judges aimed more at suitably compensating the injured party or family rather than at inflicting positive punishment on the offender so familiar in modern European jurisprudence' (p 244). Moreover, 'based on the principle of restitution, even murder, which normally carried the death penalty or banishment, can be compounded in this way, by the payment of blood money ... in satisfaction for the murder of a kinsman' (Okoye, 1964, pp 244–45). African law did temper the primal urge for vengeance by allowing for a *lex talionis* type principle, and the injured party was entitled to take reprisal by 'raiding or burning the house of the offender (not too openly, though) ... or [otherwise] inflicting an equal punishment to the one suffered' (Okoye, 1964, p 245). Trial by ordeal was also practised:

> In which suspected persons were given some dangerous drugs like sasswood juice or esere beans or thrown into a crocodile infested pool or had boiling water or oil poured on them; in each case there were expected to prove their innocence by emerging unhurt (Okoye, 1964, p 245).

Sometimes criminals caught 'in the act' were stoned to death and larceny was seriously punished by beating, maiming, knifing or spearing on the spot. Banishment, a particularly stiff punishment, was also practised and thieves could be nailed on the head or side, or bound with cords and (when not ransomed by their relatives) dragged in the same manner that Achilles did to Hector (Okoye, 1964, p 246). Adultery was punished as a crime, 'for which offenders could be severely beaten or fined in addition to undergoing a purifying ritual' (p 245). However, to focus on instances of punishment would hide the fact that the principle of reconciliation is the crowning point of West African criminal jurisprudence, for 'without it the parties may still feel suspicious of each other or plan further damages' (Okoye, 1964, p 247).

So, traditional social control in Africa was no bed of roses. But neither was it pure barbarism. Its focus on restitution and reconciliation muted the violence of physical punishment, which was, in any case, limited by the principle of 'an eye for and eye'. Ultimately, according to Okoye, under African jurisprudence, 'it is the injured party who "forgives" his offender, not the judge or priest as in the European system, these officials merely witnessing the reconciliation or aiding it while measures were taken communally to prevent future crime' (Okoye, 1964, p 245).

Before the coming of the Europeans, Africa south of the Sahara was in a pre-industrial stage of economic development, but in many parts of West Africa there were sophisticated societies with highly organised networks of long distance trade. Large states and polities were established, grew to domination and fell – some of them greater in terms of population and territorial extent than those which existed at the time in Europe. Of the rest of the world, however, the average African was unaware. It was perhaps mainly for this reason that, at the dawn of pre-modernity, they were about to be overwhelmed by the greatest tragedy in the history of their own, or any other, continent: the 400 year long maritime slave trade.

West Africa's painful introduction to modernity

Long before the arrival of Europeans on the west coast of Africa, the practice of slavery and the trade in slaves existed. But the trade was always limited by geography, certainly insofar as the Europeans were concerned. The indigenous practice of slavery was limited, especially when compared to later when the transatlantic trade was in full swing. The Portuguese were the first to arrive on the coast in the late 15th century, but the slave trade did not increase appreciably at that point. It was the development of the plantation economy in the so called New World that created the enormous market for slaves. Over the succeeding years, decades and centuries, the potential areas of supply increased correspondingly as Europeans established more trading enclaves along the coast. The Portuguese were the first to take a hand in the slave traffic, but as time went on (and as the profits grew), the Dutch, French, English and Americans successively secured what they considered to be their 'fare share of the trade' – let us be clear: a share in the traffic in human beings.

The effect that the transnational traffic in slaves had on African society was nothing short of catastrophic. But then, it must also be stressed that some of the most egregious acts perpetrated by Europeans on the peoples of West Africa happened after the slave trade was ended. Fixing a date for some historic turning point is always somewhat arbitrary. The date we will use here is the decade of the 1880s. The slave trade, it should be noted, was largely finished by then. The final banning of the Atlantic slave trade, agreed to by all but a few European states during the first two decades of the 19th century, signalled a new 'progressive' approach to tropical Africa. Of course, the trade in slaves was not halted at once (see Gregory, 2000, especially pp 108–11, for an account of this process), but the abolitionists hoped at the time that it would gradually be replaced by legitimate trade. Naval patrols (mainly British) harassed illegal slavers and the African hinterland was gradually opened up to exploration. Coastal chiefs were persuaded to accept 'protection' and, in some cases, financial compensation in return for abandoning the slave trade and turning over small trading enclaves to one or another of the European powers.

These developments did not mean that much African territory was being ruled over by Europeans. As the historian JF Ade Ajayi noted, at this time European power was not military, it was naval and their influence could not much extend beyond the coastal enclaves. At that time, the internal politics of the states of the forest zones, and Islamic advance from the north were more significant (Ajayi, 1976, p 221). Even by the 1880s, their territorial presence was not much more than it had been at the beginning of the century. The basis for furious imperial competition and expansion was being laid, however. This was especially true in West Africa, where commercial spheres of influence – areas of 'informal empire' – were already in existence. In this region, the British regarded the lower Niger basin as their own, and the French had begun their drive up the Senegal valley while other continental European powers looked on with greed and envy. It is questionable if Britain and France would have quickly extended their bases of operations in the region were it not for the actions of other European countries. As the 19th century drew to a close, collectively the European powers turned to Africa as a potential source of vast wealth, a prize worth fighting for – *ce magnifique gâteau africain* as Leopold II, King of Belgium called it. The scramble for Africa was on.

Imperial conquest as crime – the case of the Benin Bronzes

Once the scramble for Africa was underway, there was little to stop it, and certainly not any moral compunction. One of the most shocking criminal instances of this period are the exploits of the British Punitive Expeditionary Force into Benin in 1897 (Graham, 1968; Lindqvist, 1997). The campaign against Benin, a small state in what is now southern Nigeria, involved the invasion and destruction of the state, the show trial of its king, the execution of its leading chiefs, the torching of the royal palace and the burning of villages too numerous to count. Ostensibly, the punitive expeditionary force was mounted because human sacrifice and torture was being practised in the kingdom. Consider the account of one RH Bacon, a commander of the force:

> Crucifixions, human sacrifices and every horror the eye could get accustomed to, to a large extent, but the smells no white man's internal economy could stand ... Blood was everywhere; smeared over bronzes, ivory and even the walls (quoted in Graham, 1968, p 366).

It is now generally known that this was largely a pretext. It is not that the killings did not occur. There are eyewitness accounts that show it to be the case. But what is also certainly the case is that this was not everyday practice, nor was it some bizarre ritual of human sacrifice. Rather the killings were an imposition of the criminal sanction. Bloody to be sure, but the intervening centuries during which European slave traffic distorted traditional patterns of political rule and customary practices of social control explain, even if they do not entirely justify, what was happening.

In fact, the expedition against Benin was the culmination of several British assaults on West African kingdoms during the period. This instance of military advance began when a small force of 10 British officers, accompanied by a fife and drum band and 200 African porters, set off for the city state in December of 1896. This force was largely destroyed in an encounter with their enemy on the road to Benin and a punitive expeditionary force of some 1,200 crack British troops was gathered to retaliate. The military advance was bloody for both sides, but in February of 1897 Benin City was captured and put to the torch. The treasures of the city, the Benin Bronzes, were seized and transported back to Europe. Most of the 900 or so statues were sold in Germany, but a handful were acquired by the British Museum where they remain to this day. The military action in the field went on for months afterwards. Villages were sacked and burned, cattle were confiscated to feed the British troops and many, many African people – men, women and children – died.

The British made much of the cruelties of the Benin Kingdom in their justification of military action. Today we might speak of 'humanitarian intervention'. However, it must be emphasised that later investigation has shown that the cruelties practised were not as great as was pictured at the time. The idea of Benin rule as 'blood stained despotism' has not stood up to historical scrutiny. And anyway, any cruel punishment practised in Benin pales into insignificance next to the atrocities of the British military. The punitive expeditionary force advanced into the jungle like Hitler did into the Ukraine (Lindqvist, 1997). To add insult to injury, European museums still refuse to return the Benin treasures – as one curator put it: 'we are not in the business of redressing historic wrongs' (quoted in Gott, 1997).

Comparing French and British colonial criminal injustice policy in West Africa

French colonial policy was characterised by a policy of assimilation. This is not as benign as the term suggests, as the colonised were often persuaded by means of napalm to acquiesce to such (Fanon, 1967). Thus, the French colonial system introduced the civil law tradition into parts of West Africa with codified laws, the inquisitorial system of trials (no jury system) and police courts. The reality, however, is more complex. The French goal in West Africa, as with all other European powers, was primarily resource exploitation. All institutions and especially crime control institutions, were part of this – whether or not it was consistent with the principles of justice found in the civil law tradition.

Virginia Thompson and Richard Adloff (1957) summarise how the policy of assimilation was played out through the criminal justice apparatus. According to them, although French colonial officials often claimed that they were interested in preserving African civilisation, there was always an assumption that French culture was superior, that Africans were ignorant and that African culture was tolerable only insofar as its bearers would be expected to evolve so that they could eventually be ruled according to French law. The few Africans who had 'evolved' (the so called *évolués*) through education were 'assimilated' by being granted French citizenship and they became subject to the jurisdiction of French judges. The majority of West Africans were regarded as 'subjects and proteges' who were ruled by courts that applied 'customary law', although they had the option of litigating in the French courts under the Civil Code. The so called 'customary courts' were chaired by French colonial officials. They would sit in session flanked by two native officials who were formally chosen for their knowledge of the customs of the people, and informally chosen because of their habits of co-operating, in true comprador fashion, with the French authorities. The *indigénat* system allowed the French colonial official to impose arbitrary punishments on Africans for offences that did not exist in the statutes. This was in line with the stereotypical view that the African chief wielded absolute powers, contrary to the picture painted by Diop and others that the power of kings and chiefs was checked by customary law.

After the Second World War, the French began increasing the number (and variety) of courts in West Africa, including *juges de paix* (justices of peace) with wide jurisdiction. Two years later, there was a court of appeal in Dakar that also had jurisdiction over the mandated territories of Equatorial Africa. Later, two more appeal courts were added at Grand Bassam and Bamako. In addition, there were 12 criminal courts, 50 correctionnel courts for minor offences, 56 police courts for summary derelictions and 154 customary courts (Thompson and Adloff, 1957, p 219).

Despite this proliferation of courts, it was reported that there were not enough of them. The major explanation offered for the poor judicial services provided for Africans under the colonial situation was financial. According to Thompson and Adloff (1957, pp 223–25) the scarcity of specialised law schools meant that there were few qualified judges to serve in the colonial territories. French law school graduates were reluctant to choose such locations for their career. Furthermore, law professors interested in studying colonial law were nowhere to be found, forcing a colonial official to attempt the compilation of the customs of French West Africa to serve as a kind of code for the customary courts. This gave rise, in 1939, to the three volumes of *Coutumiers Juridiques de l'AOF* that was widely criticised for trying to solidify the very customs that the French were intent on wiping away as part of the assimilation project. Clearly the so called customary courts were not based on African culture but on rules that the French colonial officials perpetrated for the purpose of facilitating colonial domination.

The direct consequence of the deliberate underdevelopment of the judicial system, under the pretext of scarce financial resources for training and staffing in a system based on extreme exploitation and repression, was that the French relied less on the courts and more on the military to dispense law and order. Walter Rodney (1972) correctly observed that, in the colonial situation, the perceived need was to create and uphold conditions favourable to the efficient exploitation and expropriation of African resources. In quoting none other than François Mitterand, Herbert Ekwe-Ekwe (2003) touched the heart of the long-standing French obsession to control Africa that lingered decades after political independence: 'without Africa France will have no 21st century.'

Gunboat criminology was not a monopoly of the French in West Africa. The British also distinguished themselves in the use of force to win legal arguments against the colonised people of West Africa. Whereas the French pursued supremacy through a policy of assimilation, the British preferred to govern in West Africa by facilitating the rule by the chiefs whom they, in turn, ruled over. The problem was that there were not always chiefs to act as deputy imperialists.

For example, the Igbo of Nigeria are proud to say even today that the Igbo know no king and that all heads are equal. The British colonial officials simply saw this as a sign of backwardness and proceeded to appoint warrant chiefs over the fiercely independent Igbo. The consequence was that Igbo, Ogoni, Andoni and Ibibio women declared war on colonialism in 1929. They attacked the colonial court buildings and the homes of the so called warrant chiefs and destroyed many trading posts of the multinational trading companies. The British made do with gunslinger criminology in turn, and dozens of women were massacred in what the colonial officials condescendingly called the Aba Women's Riot, but which the women themselves still recognise as the Women's War (see Agozino, 1997).

John Arthur (1996) observes that while there are many studies of crime and poverty in Africa, there are few studies focusing on 'how colonial systems of criminal justice affected customary African standards and social control methods' (Arthur, 1996, p 67; but see also Ebbe, 1996). Arthur observes that prior to colonialism, Africans primarily saw crime as a threat to religious morality and responded with rituals for the purification of the community for the benefit of all, including the offenders, instead of being fixated on punitiveness. According to him:

> Punishments took several forms. Deviants were often subjected to informal sanctions such as gossip, ridicule or public humiliation. Property violations, including theft of agricultural produce and livestock, entailed restitutive compensations (Arthur, 1996, p 69).

He observed that death by hanging or stoning was not an uncommon punishment for recidivists, but suggested that this was part of the intrusive traits that came with Islamicisation in parts of Africa. His observation that social control in West Africa is based on restitutive justice is confirmed by Oko Elechi (2003), who highlighted the prominent role that women played in the administration of justice in traditional African settings.

According to Arthur, the advent of European colonisation in West Africa produced 'incarceration and de-Africanisation of social control'. The British colonial officials only supported traditional social control institutions when they facilitated the entrenchment of British control over all aspects of life in West Africa. The dual mandate system that was designed for taxation without representation and control without accountability was resisted strongly by West Africans, forcing the British to set up the West African Frontier Force for the purpose of pacifying resistance to colonialism in the region. It was hardly surprising that the major qualification for becoming a police officer in British West Africa was the experience as a military officer (Ahire, 1991; Anderson and Killingray, 1991 and 1992).

This militarisation of criminal justice administration in West Africa remained after formal de-colonisation, as the neo-colonial regimes continued with the forceful methods of domination that they inherited from colonialism. Moreover, they retained the more repressive penal measures such as the death penalty that the colonial administrations imposed on the hitherto restitutive Africans, in some cases long after the colonial powers had begun the process of abolishing them in their own countries. The communal and healing types of punishments that Africans preferred in the past, for the purpose of preventing the alienation of the offender from the rest of society, have been destroyed by the imperial powers and replaced with repressive fetishes of domination.

Although this section has concentrated on a comparison of British and French crime control and penal policy, it should not be forgotten that there were many other powers that were active in this region. The Kingdom of Belgium gained a very large swathe of territory in the central region, and the Portuguese and Germans were also present. Although the European maps of the day do not show it, the influence of Islamic civilisation was ever encroaching from the desert to the north. The legacy of this diversity of outside forces is a variety of ideological currents. Nor is this variety only due to outside influence. The boundary divisions superimposed on this region during the 'scramble for Africa' were not taken with any regard of the way the local inhabitants related to the territory or governed themselves.[1] Like the military expeditions, courts and other aspects of penal administration, those boundaries were simply asserted. As the colonial regimes were replaced by 'countries' in the latter half of the 20th century, the lines on the map continued in their disregard of ancient traditions and the form of the modern state – replete with its military and penal apparatus – remained superimposed on an impressive array of (in many instances highly complex) traditional societies. Despite the apparent simplicity of forced resource extraction (not to say brutality) under colonial and post-colonial conditions, *everyday* governance and social control in West Africa is nuanced, diverse and complex.

The question as to why the countries of West Africa continued the manifestly unjust policies that were introduced by colonial authorities, despite their varying ideological orientations, is an interesting one. The answer is, in part, that neo-colonialism was never intended to bring freedom to the colonised (Nkrumah, 1968). It is quite naïve to expect an easy transition from the worst authoritarian repression to norms based on, for example human rights law (newly propounded in the aftermath of the so called Second World War – in reality a tribal war between competing imperialist powers). A major part of the reason why the criminal justice system in West African countries remain militarised is because they were specifically designed as militaristic tools for the domination of the people of West Africa and they were retained by the comprador elite to whom the colonial officials merely handed power to. But this simple answer merely disguises the complexities of the situation across West Africa.

Current issues in crime control in West Africa

In 1990 it was reported that: 'Over 90% of Nigeria's prisons are more than 100 years old. Records show that four prisons were built between 1800 and 1850, 11 prisons were built between 1851 and 1900, 83 were built between 1900 and 1950 and 33 prisons between 1951 to date' (African Concord, Vol 5, No 14, August 6, 1990). There was no prison in the place called Nigeria before 1800 – at the very height of the slave trade. If we recall Michel Foucault's vivid descriptions at the beginning of *Discipline and Punish* (1977), Africa was not much out of step with European penalty at that time; there were in fact hardly any prisons in Europe until the late 18th century. One implication of Foucault's analysis is that, if human society could survive for millennia without the need for the prison as a mode of social control, perhaps human society will some day abolish this repressive technology of modernity. It was the European trading companies who first constructed prisons in West Africa and it was primarily for detaining Africans who resisted the banditry of Europeans. The prison emerged in West Africa not as an institution of the criminal

---

1 Nigeria, for example, has three principal ethnic groups (the Hausa-Fulani, Yoruba and Ibo) and a significant number of smaller groups. Furthermore, Nigeria's population is roughly equally divided between Christian, Islamic and Animist religious groupings. The on-again-off-again history of miliary rule, from independence in 1960 until democracy in 1999 (the country was governed by military regimes for all but 11 of its first 39 years), is complex. The coercive power of the military, police and security sectors were forged in these geo-ethnic circumstances and over-determined by the perceived need to keep the territory of the former colony under the roof of one state.

justice system. It was in no way a 'gentling of punishment' (Ignatieff, 1978); it was a tool for organised crimes against humanity. Yet neither did the tide of imprisonment rise as high as it has in the so called 'developed' countries. Perhaps it is in West Africa, and other places on the periphery of what was once all but incontestable European imperial domination, that world penal abolition has its best opportunity.

As hopeful as this sounds, and the world needs hope, unfortunately this is not with the tide of historic development in the region. It was during the period after the scramble for Africa had begun that the number of prisons in Nigeria nearly trebled, reflecting increasing resistance to European penetration of the interior regions. The development of the prison-complex in Nigeria continued during the period of nationalist struggles when imperialist gunboat criminology failed to silence the call for independence. Following independence in 1960, the growth of the prison-complex continued, reflecting the continuing reliance of neo-colonial regimes on gunslinger criminology in order to stifle popular protests in Nigeria. This is not to say that all prisoners are 'freedom fighters' – but the correlation between repression in, and the development of, the so called criminal justice machinery in the region seems clear.

A similar, if far from identical, logic for prison development to that found in Nigeria is common across the whole of West Africa. Where there have been prisons built, they have been built largely as part of an array of techniques for suppressing political resistance to imperialist domination. Furthermore, a similar pattern of development can also be found in the institutions of the police, the military and the mechanisms of adjudication across the region. This is to gloss over important differences, of course. The conditions in Sierra Leone are not the same as Liberia, Gabon or Congo. In all of these places, the degree of violence has risen to such proportions that a new discourse has arisen which emphasises crime as not only a threat to the person but also as a source of instability for the state system across the region. While it is seldom clear to outsiders, behind the scenes there is a continuing hard line of militarised law enforcement implementation without any regard for human rights or environmental degradation in order to preserve that state system and ongoing resource extraction.

It is not too much of an exaggeration to say that the series of criminal acts that culminated in the theft of the Benin Bronzes is being perpetrated every day in the Niger delta. Adeola (2000) and Rodman (2001) have documented how alliances of senior government officials in 'developing countries' and in the countries of the West, together with multinational resource extraction companies (chiefly in mining, petroleum and forestry) have conspired to rob the people and destroy their land. Their analysis is more general than our interests here, taking in the plight of many people around the world. I would like to single out the example of the Ogoni people of southern Nigeria as a paradigm case of the continued subjugation of traditional West African indigenous communities in the present day.

The Ogoni number approximately 500,000 people who traditionally lay claim to a territory of only 650 square kilometres in the southern delta region of present day Nigeria. There they have made a good living through traditional subsistence farming and fishing from time immemorial. The threat to these people really arrived when Shell Petroleum discovered oil in the delta in 1958. With the coming of independence of Nigeria in 1960, this minority group's interests were subjugated to the interests of the multinationals and the new independent state. Almost 14% of Shell's petroleum production – the greatest production outside the USA in fact – comes from Nigeria. Oil accounts for approximately 80% of the Nigerian state's revenue. The Ogoni receive very little monetary benefit from this, but they pay a heavy price for the continuing flow of black gold. Between 1976 and 1991, for example, there were almost 3,000 separate oil spills in the region, each averaging 700 barrels for a total of over two million barrels spilled.[2] There is no reason to suppose that this level of toxic vandalism has abated since 1991. The gas flares from the hundreds of oil wells that scatter the delta-scape burn 24 hours a day.[3] Villagers have to live with the roar of the burning and the area is covered in black soot, which contaminates the water supplies when it rains. There is an Ogoni song that says in part:

The flames of Shell are the flames from Hell

We back below their light

Nought for us to serve the blight

Of cursed neglect and cursed Shell

In spite of their suffering, the vast wealth that is extracted from the earth is not theirs to possess, it is stolen from them without their consent.

To protest against this environmental and humanitarian crime, the Ogoni people formed MOSOP – the Movement for the Survival of Ogoni People. In the early 1990s, these people staged a number of protests, perhaps the most famous of which was the peaceful mass protest in 1993, attended by an estimated 300,000 Ogoni people. In January of 2004, the eight major oil companies operating in the region put their losses down to 'unfavourable conditions in the areas of operation' at approximately US$200 million. This provoked the Nigerian military to retaliate, causing death and injury on an unquantified scale. A leaked memo from a Nigerian government official called for the Nigerian police, army, air force and navy to 'restore and maintain law and order in Ogoni land' in order to ensure 'non-indigenous residents carrying out business ventures' were not molested. The massive violence that ensued killed and maimed untold numbers, but it failed to stop the Ogoni protests. Their most eloquent spokesman, Ken Saro-Wiwa, was arrested and eventually hanged from a hastily built gallows in Port Harcourt on the morning of 10 November 1995. As of this writing, his body lay in an unmarked prison grave until it was quietly exhumed for dignified reburial by his family in mid-2002.

Crimes such as these, crimes against humanity perpetrated in order that 'resource extraction' – with all its environmental devastation – might continue, are still happening. And it is not just the armies of West African states that are involved in the perpetration of the violence. Scott Pegg has documented how oil companies

---

2   To put this figure in perspective, the Exxon Valdez 'accident' in Alaska, the 'most famous oil spill in history' resulted in a spillage of about 257,000 barrels or roughly 10% of the routine spillage in the Ogoni region in a 15 year period. However, whereas the most famous oil spill in history resulted in Herculean clean up efforts (at a cost of US$2.1 billion in 1990), the routine damage experienced on West Africa's coast goes unremarked and its toxic effects are ongoing.

3   In 1995, Shell admitted to flaring 1,100 million standard cubic feet of gas *per day* and the occurrence of acid rain in the delta.

have directly requested assistance from the Nigerian security services, and even that several oil producers have actually transported military troops, all of which resulted in the deaths of unarmed civilians in a number of episodes (1999). Neither are foreign multinationals wholly dependent on the co-operation of comprador 'deputy imperialists'. Consider the actions of Executive Outcomes (EO), a private South African security company run by former members of the South African military and security apparatus – mercenaries in other words. According to Shawcross (2000), the mission of EO is to 'create a climate of peace and stability for foreign investment, focusing on military training, including a particular emphasis on special forces and clandestine warfare' (p 173). In the middle years of the 1990s, EO distinguished itself when, in co-operation with Nigerian and Ghanaian troops, they re-took the Kono diamond mine and the Sierra Rutile titanium dioxide mine in Sierra Leone. The prize for their help in this matter was payment from income *direct from the liberated diamond mine*. Nor are EO the only mercenary group to operate in the area; Sandline International, run by a former British army colonel named Tom Spicer, also play a role in West Africa that can best be described as looting (Shawcross, 2000, pp 180–82).

Rape, plunder, looting and violence. Such events occurred daily in the territorial region encompassed by the state of Congo (the former colonial territory occupied by Belgium) during the early years of the 21st century. In late 2003, when the final version of this chapter was being written, a United Nations panel of experts reported that the illegal extraction of precious minerals from the Democratic Republic of Congo (DCR) was ongoing and adding fuel to the fire of conflict there (Usborne, 2003). This report implicated over 150 companies and individuals, but portions of it remained secret as of this writing, and the names of the guilty corporations are not widely known. The DCR and Sierra Leone may be examples of 'failed states', but these sorts of crimes are not only confined to such territories. Across the territory of West Africa the crimes of neo-colonialism are on the rise.

Conclusion

Not much has changed for the better since political independence for West Africa. The introduction of the new debt slavery, ensuring that in excess of 70% of what West Africans produce is repatriated to 'the West' for servicing of dubious debts, while the lion's share of the remainder is banked in private Swiss accounts by the comprador kleptocrats, has left masses of people to fight and kill one another over crumbs in the intractable civil strife raging across the region. Looking at West Africa as a whole, it is possible to see a partly broken state system that remains only partially in control by virtue of quasi-militarised social control apparatus based in the military, state police and other institutions of organised state violence. This partial control is facilitated on behalf of foreign multinationals that make a profit from the emiseration of local West African people. To this end, the organisation of violence includes what are euphemistically known as 'private security companies' as well as state-based institutions. The control is effective insofar as the foreign multinationals continue to make money, but normal rules and rituals for social ordering are under pressure and life in the villages and traditional communities is difficult. Under these conditions, the rise of vigilante justice and an amplification of civil discord are only to be expected (ICHRP, 2003 and Sheptycki, Chapter 3 of this volume).

But let us not draw to a close on a negative note. To the extent that criminologists in the advanced countries think about matters of criminological concern in West Africa at all, they seem to be inspired by ideas of technology transfer, police and criminal justice system aid, and basically installing democracy along the lines that they know it from their own perspective. Perhaps, it is time to re-invent the project of Frantz Fanon and seek the building of a 'Third Way' in the Third World instead of trying to impose another version of Europe or America in the African tropics. Such could be achieved, as Amilcar Cabral has suggested, by *A Return to Source* (1972) and through *Unity and Struggle* (1979); whereby African culture contributes to the defeat of imperialism, not only for the benefit of Africans, but also for the great mass of Europeans and Americans who also struggle under the weight of a yoke of technological social control at least partly forged in the context of African colonisation.

Adekeye Adebajo (2002), Basil Davidson (1989) and Richard Lobban (1995) provide interesting accounts of Cape Verde, an Atlantic archipelago off the coast of Senegal first encountered by the Portuguese in the 15th century. The complex history of these islands over five centuries, their role in the slave trade, the process of Creoleisation as large numbers of slaves mixed with the few (mainly Portuguese) Europeans living there, the years under Portuguese colonial administration and, later, the protracted armed struggle on the Guinea coast for national independence, is rich and fascinating. The present day descendants (a mixture of Africans, Europeans and Luso-Africans) have charted their own path to achieve economic growth and development, moving from colonial rule to state socialism, and on to a privatised market economy built around tourism, fishing, small scale mining, and agricultural production. Cape Verde distinguishes itself by its peaceful transition from one-party rule to elections and political pluralism.

Cape Verde provides one hopeful answer to the neo-colonial problematic that permeates this chapter. Despite periodic droughts, betrayals and other odds stacked against them, Cape Verdians have pursued a participatory model of development that could serve as a model for the rest of Africa. Davidson thus describes:

> In this island, there are about 45,000 people. There are exactly 11 state police and there are no troops. Whenever a tribunal needs executive power of arrest, incarceration, whatever, it calls on the volunteers of the local militia it has raised. There is no one else to call on (quoted in Davidson, 1989, p 150).

Davidson's ethnography is particularly revealing for comparative criminologists, since one focus of attention concerns the role of the courts in everyday social control. According to him, in 1986, the island had a total of 255 zonal courts staffed with unpaid volunteers from the community.

One case shall have to serve as an illustrative example of how this was working there at that time. Davidson reports the case of a port worker who was habitually drunk and who, under the influence of alcohol, stabbed and badly wounded his neighbour for no reason. He was sentenced to 30 days in prison but the sentence was suspended on the condition that he keep away from alcohol and behave himself. Some days later, he was again the subject of attention arising out of a domestic dispute. It seems that his live-in companion, and the mother of his seven children, had provoked a drunken rage when she neglected to prepare his evening meal. The police arrived and he was charged to court again. This time he was sentenced to serve his 30 days in prison because he failed to meet the conditions previously set. Davidson reported that the magistrates, who were the prisoner's neighbours, went round to the port where he worked to ask for donations in order to pay to feed his children the next day. They informed Davidson that they had no faith in the ability of the prison to reform, but that, in the circumstances, the prisoner left them little choice but to punish. However, their main focus in this case, and in many others observed by Davidson and other ethnographers, was not simply to punish, but to repair and maintain the social fabric of their society after it had been torn asunder by incivility and crime.

It is possible to see in Cape Verde that the community has developed its own capacities, not only for managing everyday matters of social control, but how to manage the political economy as a whole. Some criminologists talk about the 'collective efficacy' of communities (see Bottoms and Wiles, 2002, pp 642–44 for a discussion of the concept). This is the capacity of communities to define collective goals and then organise to achieve them. If we are to think positively about the criminological future of West Africa, if criminologists are to play a positive role in the making of a 'Third Way' for the Third World, then we will need to challenge the alliances between those state parties and private interests that have the most to gain from the present status quo and focus on community capacity building at the most basic level. Any discussion of crime and social control in West Africa that fails to stand up against the ongoing crimes against humanity and environmental degradation must be seen for what it is: gunslinger criminology in the service of continuing imperialist domination.

References

Adebajo, A (2002) *Building Peace in West Africa: Liberia, Sierra Leone, and Guinea-Bissau*, London: Lyne Reinner

Adeola, F (2000) 'Cross-national environmental injustice and human rights issues: a review of evidence in the developing world' 43(4) *American Behavioral Scientist* 686–706

Agozino, B (1997) *Black Women and the Criminal Justice System: Towards the Decolonisation of Victimisation*, Aldershot: Ashgate

Agozino, B (2000) 'Theorising otherness, the war on drugs and incarceration' 4(3) *Theoretical Criminology* 359–76

Agozino, B (2003) *Counter-Colonial Criminology: A Critique of Imperialist Reason*, London: Pluto

Agozino, B and Idem, U (2001) *Nigeria: Democratising a Militarised Civil Society*, London: CDD

Ahire, PT (1991) *Imperial Policing*, Milton Keynes: OU Press

Ajayi, JF Ade (1976) 'West Africa in the anti-slave trade era', in Flint, JE (ed), *The Cambridge History of Africa*, Vol 5, Cambridge: CUP, pp 200–21

Anderson, DM and Killingray, D (1991) *Policing the Empire: Government Authority and Control, 1830–1940*, Manchester: Manchester UP

Anderson, DM and Killingray, D (1992) *Policing and Decolonisation: Nationalism, Politics and the Police, 1917–1965*, Manchester: Manchester UP

Arthur, JA (1996) 'Development of penal policy in former British West Africa: exploring the colonial dimension', in Ebbe, O (ed), *Comparative and International Criminal Justice Systems: Policing, Judiciary and Corrections*, Boston: Butterworth-Heinemann.

Ba, M (1989) *So Long a Letter*, London: Heinemann

Baudrillard, J (1983) *Simulations*, New York: Semiotext(e)

Bauman, Z (1989) *Modernity and the Holocaust*, Cambridge: Polity

Birmingham, D (1975) 'Central Africa from Cameroun to the Zambezi', in Gray, R (ed), *The Cambridge History of Africa*, Vol 4, Cambridge: CUP, pp 325–83

Birmingham, D and Marks, S (1977) 'Central Africa from Cameroon to the Zambezi', in Oliver, R (ed), *Cambridge History of Africa*, Vol 3, 1050 AD–1600 AD, Cambridge: CUP, pp 519–66

Bottoms, AE and Wiles, P (2002) 'Environmental criminology', in Maguire, M, Morgan, R and Reiner, R (eds), *The Oxford Handbook of Criminology*, Oxford: OUP

Cabral, A (1972) *A Return to Source*, New York: Monthly Review Press

Cabral, A (1979) *Unity and Struggle*, New York: Monthly Review Press

Davidson, B (1989) *The Fortunate Isles: A Study in African Transformation*, London: Hutchinson

Diop, CA (1987) *Precolonial Black Africa: A Comparative Study of the Political and Social Systems of Europe and Black Africa, from Antiquity to the Formation of Modern States*, Salemson, H (trans), New York: Lawrence Hill

Durkheim, E (1973) 'Two rules of penal evolution', in Lukes, S and Scull, A, *Durkheim and the Law*, London: Macmillan

Ebbe, O (ed) (1996) *Comparative and International Criminal Justice Systems: Policing, Judiciary and Corrections*, Boston: Butterworth-Heinemann

Ekwe-Ekwe, H (2003) 'The bogey of African-French solidarity', in *USAfrica Online*, www.usafricaonline.com/ekweekwe.africafrench.html

Elechi, OO (2003) 'Women and (African) indigenous justice systems', in Kalunta-Crumpton, A and Agozino, B (eds), *Pan African Issues in Crime and Justice*, Aldershot: Ashgate

Fage, JD (1977) 'Upper and Lower Guinea', in Oliver, R (ed), *The Cambridge History of Africa*, Vol 3, 1050 AD–1600 AD, Cambridge: CUP, pp 463–518

Fanon, F (1967) *The Wretched of the Earth*, with a preface by Jean-Paul Sartre, Farrington, C (trans), Harmondsworth: Penguin

Foucault, M (1977) *Discipline and Punish: The Birth of the Prison*, London: Allen Lane

Garland, D (1990) *Punishment and Modern Society: A Study in Social Theory*, Oxford: Clarendon

Gott, R (1997) 'The looting of Benin' *The Independent*, 22 February

Graham, JD (1968) 'The slave trade, depopulation and human sacrifice in Benin history', in Collins, RO (ed), *Problems in African History*, New Jersey: Prentice Hall

Gramsci, A (1971) *Selections from the Prison Notebooks*, London: Lawrence & Wishart

Gregory, F (2000) 'Private criminality as a matter of international concern', in Sheptycki, J (ed), *Issues in Transnational Policing*, London: Routledge

Habermas, J (1996) *Between Facts and Norms*, Cambridge: Polity

Hall, S (1980) 'Race, articulation and societies structured in dominance', in UNESCO (ed), *Sociological Theories: Race and Colonialism*, Paris: UNESCO

Hall, S (1996) *Hard Road to Renewal*, London: Routledge

ICHRP (2003) *Crime, Public Order and Human Rights*, Versoix, Switzerland: International Council on Human Rights Policy

Ignatieff, M (1978) *A Just Measure of Pain*, London: Macmillan

Lindqvist, S (1997) *Exterminate all the Brutes*, London: Granta

Lobban, R (1995) *Cape Verde – Crioulo Colony to Independent Nation*, Boulder, Colorado: Westview

McCall-Smith, RA (1998) *The No 1 Ladies' Detective Agency*, Edinburgh: Polygon

Nkrumah, K (1968) *Neo-Colonialism: The Last Stage of Imperialism*, London: Heinemann

Okoye, M (1964) *African Responses*, Ilfracombe: Arthur H Stockwell Ltd

Onyeozili, E (2003) 'Gunboat criminology and the colonisation of Africa', in Kalunta-Crumpton, A and Agozino, B (eds), *Pan-African Issues in Crime and Justice*, Aldershot: Ashgate

Pegg, S (1999) 'The cost of doing business: transnational corporations and violence in Nigeria' 30(4) *Security Dialogue* 473–84

Pfohl, S and Gordon, A (1986) 'Criminological displacements: a sociological deconstruction' 33(6) *Social Problems* 94–113

Reiman, J (1979) *The Rich Get Richer and the Poor Get Prison*, New York: Wiley

Rodman, K (2001) *Multinational Corporations and US Economic Statecraft*, New York: Rowman and Littlefield

Rodney, W (1972) *How Europe Underdeveloped Africa*, London: Bogle-L'Ouverture

Rodney, W (1975) The Guinea Coast', in Gray R (ed), *The Cambridge History of Africa*, Vol 4, Cambridge: CUP, pp 223–324

Shawcross, W (2000) *Deliver Us From Evil: Warlords and Peacekeepers in a World of Endless Conflict*, London: Bloomsbury

Soyinka, W (1988) *Season of Anomy*, London: Random House

Stern, V (1998) *A Sin Against the Future: Imprisonment Around the World*, Harmondsworth: Penguin

Sudbury, J (ed) (2003) *Global Lockdown: Imprisoning Women, Engendering Resistance*, New York: Routledge

Thompson, V and Adloff, R (1957) *French West Africa*, Stanford: Stanford UP

Usborne, D (2003) 'Congo: UN says war fuelled by foreign firms', *The Independent*, 31 October

Walmsley, R (2000) *World Prison Population List*, 2nd edn, Home Office Research, Development and Statistics Directorate, Research Findings No 116, London: Home Office

Chapter 6
Some Critical Reflections on the Governance of Crime in Post-Apartheid South Africa

Anne-Marie Singh

Crime prevention and control is mainly the responsibility of government. Indeed, many believe the most important function of the state is the safety and security of its citizens … But the crime problem also needs the attention of government at every level, as well as of business, labour and all other sectors of society (The Nedcor Project, December 1995, p 3).

Introduction

Policing provides the necessary foundation for the operation of a free market. It is the basis for profit, rather than profitable in and of itself. The relation between policing, security and 'foundational orders' generally was articulated by Clifford Shearing when he wrote of the 'significance of peace as a "foundation order" on which other orders – for instance, the order of financial markets – depend and policing as an activity that seeks to maintain this foundation' (Shearing, 1992, p 400). This chapter illustrates this through an analysis of two corporate sponsored business campaigns against crime in South Africa during the middle years of the 1990s. The chapter argues that it was through such campaigns that capital became consciously and collectively involved in restructuring public policing. This was achieved primarily by offering assistance to government for the transformation of the South African Police Service (SAPS) into a 'better trained and equipped police force' (Nedcor, August 1995, p 4). At the same time, these business initiatives in public policing reveal that the corporate sector assumed some degree of responsibility for managing its own security risks: albeit conceived less in terms of rendering assistance to government and more as an activation of a particular kind of citizenship ideal.

The discussion below focuses on four broad areas. First, I describe the 'partnerships' that developed between business and government in South Africa during the period, for managing the 'crime problem', and I outline how industry perceived its role in relation to that of government. Secondly, I question the apparent 'naturalness' of such alliances, suggesting that the interests of both 'partners' are not identical. These associations arose during the period partly because both sides had come to see crime as a threat to the country's shared socio-economic future. The perceived necessity of promoting a properly functioning, legitimate and publicly accountable legal system gained added saliency for the corporate sector in South Africa due to the felt sense of political vulnerability during the post-apartheid transition period. Attempts to persuade government of the utility of partnership with the corporate sector had added urgency because of this. Thirdly, I examine the targets of corporate projects aimed at bolstering public policing, highlighting the reconfiguration of social space in the exercise of surveillance and crime control. I conclude by commenting on the apparent paradox that freedom (of market responses, of individual choice) requires for its guarantee, the existence of a strong sovereign authority armed with considerable coercive powers operating in conjunction with collectively organised corporate power with considerable powers of its own.

Security investments

In the mid-1990s, corporate concerns in South Africa centred on crime, investor relations and government strategies on security and macro-economic development. High profile industry sponsored campaigns on public policing emerged. These aimed at informing and transforming state crime control policies and practices. This section outlines the nature and function of two independent corporate projects on crime, both of which were established in 1995: the Nedcor Project on Crime, Violence and Investment, and Business Against Crime (BAC). These campaigns evinced what O'Malley and Palmer (1996) call 'voluntary collectivism', where the 'business community' is configured in terms of relational ties voluntarily established between individual firms in the context of managing the 'crime problem'. Both projects operated within a framework of a 'partnership' model, wherein government is deemed the primary provider of safety and security. Envisioned as short-term crisis management interventions, the Nedcor Project and BAC sought to 'empower' government to play a more successful leadership role in the 'fight against crime'.

The Nedcor Project

The Nedcor Project on Crime, Violence and Investment was established in April 1995 as a 'public service'.[1] Nedcor Ltd, the holding company of Permanent Bank, Peoples Bank, Nedbank, Syfrets Ltd, Cape of Good Hope Bank, UAL Merchant Bank Ltd, NedEnterprises and NedTravel, sponsors the R3m Project. The Project aimed to inform business about possible contributions to the 'fight against crime', where crime prevention and control rests 'ultimately' and 'exclusively' with government: 'business has a variety of vital roles to play in assisting government in its responsibility to safeguard the security of all South Africans.' These 'vital roles' were expressed in terms of a 'partnership', with business interests centring mainly on the sphere in which crime and violence impact on investment.

Combining research and consultation with over 100 international and domestic organisations, the Project identified both the parameters of the 'crime problem' and possible solutions. This included an overview of the 'actual' situation for 1995–96; the identification of the 'fundamental causes of the crime problem'; an assessment of the impact of crime on foreign investment and the development of strategies to provide investors with a 'better understanding' of the crime situation in order to ensure their ongoing commitment to South African markets; the specification of

---

1 The publication of the *Final Report* in April 1996 and the *Executive Summary of the Main Report* in June 1996 effectively marked the conclusion of the Nedcor Project. However, a subsequent joint venture between Nedcor Ltd, the Institute of Security Studies and BAC resulted in ongoing updates of the Project's results, published as the *Nedcor/ISS Crime Index*. The original database compiled by the Project was later housed at the BAC national office where, as of this writing, it remains.

business initiatives to reduce the impact of crime on society as well as on the business sector; and the identification of large-scale business interventions to address crime at the national level. According to a Project briefing paper, 'Nedcor believes that the information gathered will serve as a databank which will provide the foundation for broadly based initiatives to reduce levels of crime and their impact on our economy' (NEDCOR, August 1995).

A 10 step programme, 'Stop Crime', designed to implement the above objectives, appeared towards the end of 1995. The programme was essentially an enumeration and communications strategy. The Project configured its partnership role in terms of the accumulation and dissemination of knowledge deemed necessary for both the governance of crime and the evaluation of its success. The computerised results of data obtained through survey devices were used to produce statistical information on crime – incidence rate, trends, effects and the like. Nedcor's survey of 500 domestic businesses across service sectors and racial groups – the first of its kind – quantified the cost of crime using such measures as profitability margins, public confidence (in state anti-crime measures) and a 'six-point scale of perceived risk' of personal and corporate victimisation. Another survey of 70 companies in the UK, USA, France, Belgium (and EU), Brazil, Peru and Columbia computed the relative importance, for foreign investment decisions, of 22 factors including crime, violence and corruption. The expressed aim was to situate South Africa's investment favourability globally in comparative terms relating to its political, economic, social and (crucially) security aspects. A third step in the 'Stop Crime' programme, a computerised inventory of 'permanent assets' in the 'fight against crime', amassed an impressive database: a 'name bank' of crime prevention experts with 500 entries and an account of over 700 available national and international 'resource materials' (literature, policy documents, case studies, etc).

Rose (1991) has made the general relationship between statistics and democracy clear. The perceived value of numericised information about crime, just when the new liberal democracy was faced with 'the problem of crime', is made plain in Nedcor documents:

> [S]tatistics are vital. In a modern society all policy makers and implementation relies on statistics. This is also true of policies on crime prevention as well as the identification, detection and conviction of criminals.

But it is not only government that needs this knowledge. The public too must be informed, and the 'Stop Crime' strategy aimed to communicate knowledge about crime to industry and communities, local authorities and central state departments. Provisions for the routine answering of inquiries from community groups and local authorities on the causes, prevention and control of crime were set in place. Workshops were conducted with local authorities. Collaborative projects were undertaken with other corporate bodies and with government. One thousand 'interested people' received the Project's monthly newsletters. Lastly, the publication of the 'Stop Crime' strategy as a newspaper insert distributed through Nedbank branches aimed to reach approximately 900,000 readers. In this way, the Project promoted and participated, shaped and structured a numericised public discourse on security.

Representations of 'crime', interventionist measures and assessments of such measures must all be conducted in the language of numbers. The mapping out of crime's peculiar dimensions – its causes, cycles, victims, perpetrators, frequency, costs, etc – provides the basis for evaluating the state's performance of its 'crime prevention and control function' (that is, the detection and apprehension of criminals through the police, the adjudication of cases through the justice department, and the execution of sentences through correctional services). On the basis of numericised information depicting crime's statistical dynamics, commerce sought to hold government to account and itself undertook various activities against crime. The latter involved industry participation in public policing, effected principally, though not exclusively, through assistance rendered to the SAPS.

Business Against Crime (BAC)

BAC emerged out of a conference, Business Initiative Against Crime and Corruption (BIACC), held at Johannesburg's World Trade Centre in August 1995. Business South Africa (BSA) and the Council of South African Banks (COSAB), with the assistance of the Nedcor Project, organised the conference in response to a state presidential appeal for 'co-operation between public and private sectors in dealing with crime, corruption and violence' (National Business Initiative (NBI) booklet, October 1995).[2] Opened by (then) President Mandela, this high profile event included participants from the corporate and banking sectors, along with six Cabinet Ministers and senior police and defence officials.[3] Conference objectives involved clarifying the crime control roles and responsibilities of business and of government and developing a process of co-ordination.

The official conference summary presented to President Mandela, government ministers and the media, at the end of September 1995, unambiguously identified the state as the principle guarantor of public safety and security. However, the corporate sector sought a significant role for itself, not least in managing its own crime risks, and the document recommended that business 'form a working group on corruption to work towards self-regulation' (BSA circular No 113/95). More than this though, the conference summary highlighted that business was uniquely placed to assist government in the performance of its security functions, because of the special expertise and resources that the corporate sector had to offer. Crime, especially violent crime, was articulated as the single greatest threat to post-apartheid national reconstruction programmes. South Africa was presented as being in the midst of a crime wave of crisis proportions, endangering not only the operation and survival of individual business enterprises, but also the country's economic growth, development and overall wellbeing generally.

Corporate South Africa's contribution to overall levels of security was nothing less than assisting government in setting a national framework and strategic plan for an integrated multi-sectoral attack on crime. The BIACC document proposed a working group of government representatives and other stakeholders (citizens,

---

2 COSAB is a collective business body. BSA is a mandated business organisation focusing on macro-economic growth.

3 Varying accounts put the number of delegates between 400 and 500, with 84 discussion groups.

churches and commerce) to develop a national strategic approach on crime that would co-ordinate efforts among different state departments and between these bodies and individuals, communities and organisations. Industry was to empower criminal justice agencies, a well functioning reactive system in particular being seen to provide the main line of defence against crime and the criminal. Thus, the conference summary envisioned a campaign that would include specific business endorsed projects such as 'Community Police Force Forums, reward schemes for identifying criminals [and] crimewatch phone, TV and radio services', all designed to promote public support of, and confidence in, the police.

The report also offered up some free legal advice, suggesting the introduction of a series of interim legislative changes to achieve practical (lower crime levels) and symbolic ('to demonstrate [political] will' and 'to show that crime doesn't pay') gains in respect of certain offences, mostly involving violence. Crimes such as murder, rape, use of a weapon in the commission of a crime, possession of illegal firearms, vehicle hijacking, dealing in stolen goods, drug trafficking, extortion, witness intimidation and bribery of government officials were listed and characterised as 'detrimental to the national morale'. The repressive interventions proposed to answer these included: search of person and property without a warrant; denial of bail to further the aims of preventive detention; maximum mandatory sentencing; no parole; and no special young offender status.

To facilitate the implementation of the report's recommendations and the co-ordination of private/public partnerships, the conference elected Action Committee was transformed, towards the end of September 1995, into BAC under the auspices of BSA, and managed by the National Business Initiative (NBI).[4] BAC provided a private sector platform imbued with the institutional capacity to assist government in reducing overall levels of crime. A collaborative venture, BAC pooled the substantial resources (financial, technical, human and other) of individual firms. Funded entirely by company contributions (totalling some R40m between inception and 2002), the BAC umbrella covered diverse market sectors – from financial and banking services to travel, tourism and recreation.

How is it that business came to perceive the necessity of having a *collective* body dedicated to fighting crime? How did it come to pass that individual organisations, having initiated independent projects in support of government's efforts against crime, came to endorse BAC? Nedcor Ltd established the R3m Project on Crime, Violence and Investment shortly before donating over R500,000 to BAC and becoming one of its Board members. Why was a collective anti-crime body so appealing to individual companies? Commenting on the creation of BAC, an NBI interviewee put it plainly: 'corporate business felt that crime was a main issue that required a single standing body.'

The issue of crime was self-evidently the greatest threat to national economic growth and success, and it was this threat that united individual companies in a fight against their common enemy. Corporate consciousness about self-protection was a spur to association, and members of the 'business community' seemed to naturally coalesce; responsible corporate citizens standing shoulder to shoulder

---

4   In 1996, BAC became independent of both NBI and BSA. NBI is a collective business body focusing on socio-economic development.

with each other and with the state, in order to help safeguard South Africa's future. Organisations voluntarily participated in BAC because individual and isolated action evidently could be expected to have little impact on the general threat posed by crime. Indeed, ad hoc attempts at high profile interventions by individual companies could conceivably act to amplify problems by raising general levels of fear, while offering little hope of sustainable solutions. Any such bad news could reasonably be expected to further contribute to the loss of skilled employees (through emigration) and dwindling foreign and domestic disinvestment (Fourie and Mhangwana, 1995). The perceived benefits of collective participation in anti-crime campaigns included not only a rise in general levels of security, investment and productivity, but also more high visibility marketing opportunities than would normally be available to individual firms; opportunities for displaying what it is to be a good corporate citizen. We should note here that the government wanted business to make collective representations on the formulation of a national policy and strategy on crime – the absence of which, the BIACC conference concluded, was a major contributing factor to the 'crime crisis'.

Organisational structure

BAC sponsors included a wide range of mid to large size organisations: from those involved in the financial and banking sectors to the chemical industry, mining, professional services, industrial and infrastructural development, motor vehicle manufacturing, the food and beverage sector, travel, tourism and recreation, information technology, advertising and public utilities. The BAC Board of Directors consisted mainly, although not exclusively, of financial sponsors of the body. Meetings were chaired by a Chairperson but day-to-day activities came under the purview of a Managing Director. A number of working groups were struck, concentrating organisational efforts around: the promotion of BAC and the mobilisation of citizen involvement in crime prevention and control measures; white collar crime; legislative and judicial review and criminal justice transformation; the formulation and implementation of strategic policies on crime, especially a national crime prevention strategy; the collation, processing, distribution and management of crime data and information and capacity building and resourcing of the SAPS (that is, management training, satellite communication links and vehicle donations).

Strange alliances?

Industry publications conveyed a certain obviousness about corporate ventures in public policing. In several documents relating to possible contributions to the 'fight against crime', common sense understandings about rising crime and that the need to respond appropriately are invoked. On this view:

> Until the early 1990s, crime was a relatively minor issue for business. Political violence, labour relations, government policy and financial issues were the dominant concerns of business decision makers (Nedcor, December 1995, p 10).

While during this period individual citizens had to protect themselves, corporate South Africa, 'largely ignored the crime situation, or hoped that it would be taken care of by the police' (Nedcor, December 1995, p 14). All this changed. 'Today, studies show that crime is the key factor negatively affecting business confidence in the future' (Nedcor, December 1995, p 10). Industry could ill-afford to ignore the threats posed by crime, nor could it expect government to address them by itself. To be sure, 'the primary responsibility to ensure a crime-free environment rests with the state, and in particular the Ministry of Safety and Security' (Fourie and Mhangwana, 1996, p 8). But truly successful intervention required a multi-agency approach, the establishment of partnerships between government, industry and other parties affected by crime: 'effective and sustainable crime prevention is only possible through coherent and integrated strategies supported by all sectors of society' (BAC, 1996). Business was to assist government, providing expertise as well as financial, technical and other resources for both the development of a national strategic plan to co-ordinate this multi-agency approach and the enhancement of police performance especially.

Undoubtedly, at the beginning of the transition period, many police personnel lacked basic detective and investigative skills. This brand was largely discarded during the apartheid years in favour of techniques of torture and mass detention and relocation. Transition in the SAPS implied deep organisational and cultural reform (Brogden and Shearing, 1993; Cawthra, 1992). However, exclusive concern with attempts to reorient the SAPS towards 'normal' crime work contributes little or nothing to our understanding of how corporate South Africa came to see the solution to problems posed by crime as bound up with transformations of the police. After all, the police are neither the only (Ericson and Haggerty, 1997), nor even the primary (Johnston, 1992; Shearing and Stenning, 1982; South, 1988), agents of policing in modern society. It is not surprising therefore to find, in the Nedcor Project *Final Report and Briefing Paper* to the BIACC, that commerce may confront crime in several ways with varying degrees of police contact and involvement (Singh, 2000). For example, business may retreat into its privatised spaces, employing in-house or contract security and/or providing victim support services to its employees when warranted. Donations may be made, whether financial or material, to local co-operative projects operating within urban and industrial areas, for example, police endorsed Business Watch schemes. Or industry may lend support to the crime prevention initiatives of mandated business organisations like BSA. Alternatively, it may fund a business body such as BAC. None of these options are mutually exclusive (see Johnston, 1992). Take the case of the South African banking group, ABSA, a participant in BIACC, a contributor to BAC and the employer of a huge contingent of in-house private security.

Moreover, it is not at all obvious that government, in developing and implementing its crime control policies, should necessarily come to see this activity as somehow bound up with the economic interests of capital. Or that issues of policing, the administration of justice and imprisonment should occupy an important place within state programmes for macro-economic growth and social development. Nor can one assume that in joining forces to combat crime, business and government are acting in terms of identical interests.

Questioning the self-evidency or 'naturalness' of private/public partnerships in crime control focuses attention on the conditions and factors that enabled the formation of such alliances between business and government. Such partnerships emerged because capital and government came to see their respective needs and interests as in some way commensurate.

In the 'flexible' and 'mobile' alliance established between commerce and government, crime levels came to provide a measure of South Africa's socio-economic progress. But different interpretations existed as to the precise nature of this relationship. For government, the question of safety and security was a question of social justice and equality, of the integration of economic growth and social development, and of the democratisation of state structures (see *Reconstruction and Development Programme*, 1994). For commerce, basic levels of safety and security were seen to provide the foundation for the operation of a free (that is, deregulated) market, for market investment and expansion, and for improved economic performance ('growth of real output per person'), 'leaving no group untouched by the benefits of growth' (South African Foundation, 1996). There is common agreement, though, that crime is a social issue: crime had become 'everyone's problem'. Further, both business and government agreed that their respective interests and objectives could be met by an efficient, effective, professional and legitimate legal system organised around a reactive, crime fighting model. In summary, these developments can be understood in terms of the strategies of persuasion and negotiation, by means of which various state agencies (police, justice, finance) and commerce come to form anti-crime partnerships without relinquishing their formal independence and autonomy (see Miller and Rose, 1990).

Crime, the state and the economy

The 'crime problem' brought into focus a series of macro-economic concerns for corporate South Africa: concerns with the emigration of skilled individuals, with attracting tourism and perhaps most crucially, with securing new client bases and retaining existing ones. Regarding investment decisions, a Nedcor survey of nearly 500 South African businesses – 'white and black owned', across service sectors and of all sizes – found general agreement that rising crime levels inhibit 'fixed investment in new operations, or the expansion of existing operations', with small black owned enterprises facing the most serious threat. Over 55% of interviewees spontaneously identified crime as one obstacle to business expansion and almost 40% regarded it as the most serious factor (Nedcor, December 1995, p 10). High rates of crime, especially violent offences, together with public perceptions of increased risks to personal safety, were therefore understood to undermine the confidence of business owners, executives and investors in the socio-political environment in which they operate. Crime control was always already predominately a state responsibility. This is so because government has an enabling role to play vis-à-vis the economy, since by ensuring a basic level of security, the state provides the necessary condition for the successful functioning of a free market (see Rose 1999, especially Chapter 4). Thus, early Nedcor and BAC proposals called on government to immediately develop a national strategic policy for managing crime (thereby demonstrating state leadership in fighting crime) and to integrate this strategy within the country's *Reconstruction and Development Programme* (thereby signalling state recognition of the crucial link between safety and security and socio-economic restructuring).

In addition to a national plan, commercial groups identified that a well resourced criminal justice system and public police force were key institutional mechanisms by which government could maintain basic levels of public safety and security. The funding and staffing of the justice department and the police became an index of what was termed the 'political will [of government] to seriously tackle the crime problem' (Nedcor, April 1996, p 18). According to Nedcor and BAC, the lack of adequate resourcing undermined the professionalism of criminal justice departments, aggravating an already existing crime situation that accompanied the rapid transition to democratic rule:

> In respect of the SAPS, extremely low salaries, violent working conditions, understaffing, community scepticism and other factors have led to many resignations and, in turn, to low rates of detection and apprehension of criminals ... criminals perceive that with a remote chance of being arrested (combined with low chances of coming to trial and even lower chance of being convicted) they can safely increase the scale of their activities (Nedcor, April 1996, p 5).

Because mere criticism could reasonably be expected to produce negative outcomes – disinvestment, emigration of skilled workers – corporate South Africa offered constructive assistance: committing funds, technological resources and expertise towards improving the efficiency and efficacy of state law enforcement agencies.

Transforming the SAPS

BAC introduced a number of SAPS related 'special projects' that in large part reflected support for a 'professional crime fighting' (Moore, Trojanowicz and Kelling, 1988) model of policing. This can be characterised by reference to its reliance on motorised police patrols, visible police presence, computer aided dispatch, surveillance, investigation, prosecution and the panoply of control technologies typical of modern big city police departments in North America. During the period, the *sine qua non* of 'professional policing' was the imposition of centralised command and control systems, the apotheosis of which was the Compstat system in New York (on the Compstat system, see Chan (Chapter 15), this volume).

Several of these BAC projects focused on rendering the SAPS more responsive to the specific security concerns of corporate South Africa and its investors. For example, proposals for the use of CCTV in metropolitan city centres and for the provision of offices and residential quarters for the SAPS in Johannesburg central business districts, addressed industry's perceptions of inner city decay and rising crime. Both proposals held out the possibility of deterring potential offenders through increased surveillance and of detecting crimes in progress through enhanced police presence.

Consider also the donation of a fleet of 100 BMW automobiles fitted out as police cruisers, the core of a special anti-hijacking highway patrol unit in the Gauteng province. A variety of accounts had previously emerged testifying to the high degree of violence accompanying car hijackings. These also identified upper class business executives and investors as the likely victims of sophisticated syndicates that specifically target 'luxury vehicles' (Wright, 1995; also Nedcor, August 1995). Porous borders to the north were said to make it easy to transport stolen vehicles to nearby territories where they could be altered and resold or stripped for parts; and the absence of *sine qua non* agreement on combating this type of crime ensured low rates of recovery and arrest (AA South Africa, 1995). But not only was Gauteng the 'gateway' for the illegal car export trade, given its proximity to surrounding countries, it is also South Africa's industrial heartland. Hijacking in Gauteng posed particular problems because any '[i]ncrease in personal risk and concerns over safety inevitably leads to a decline in confidence in the operating environment of business' (Nedcor, December 1995, p 10). What the proposal for a highway patrol unit indicated, as did the other two BAC initiatives, was that corporate South Africa actively mobilised to create reassurance in visible and mobile police presence.

Not surprisingly, the view of the police as 'essential for any solution to the current crime crises' seems to have been held by most of the adult population, including those living in South Africa's townships (Nedcor, February 1996, p 4). This was taken to suggest that perceptions of ill-equipped and unprofessional police also inhibit local forms of investment. Thus, a number of other BAC 'special projects' focused on transforming state policing within so-called 'previously disadvantaged communities'. This was, ostensibly, in order to tap into the potential for market growth and development existing at the lower end of the socio-economic spectrum. These initiatives aimed to address the historical imbalance in the distribution of policing resources (Brogden and Shearing, 1993) through the supply of new technology, for example, cellular phones to facilitate police communications in underprivileged areas. Other projects focused on training police management in the more efficient use of existing resources. Consider 'Project Lifeline', which sought to enhance the 'operational performance' of 100 of the most 'needy' police stations through the transfer of management skills (BAC, 1996).

Here, management discourses framed the search for the best use of existing resources at station level (see Crawford, 1994; Garland, 1996; McLaughlin and Murji, 1997; Rose, 1999). The search entailed the creation of a 'fact base' to document the existing situation and to map out areas for improvement. A not untypical example of this, revealed through field observation, concerned one police station just outside Cape Town which had a fleet of four police cars, of which, at any one time, three were out of commission awaiting repairs. Solutions to such resource concerns are not necessarily the prerogative of station management. Therefore, both police personnel and community members (consumers of police services) must need be encouraged to participate in processes for shaping resource use and deployment. However, the authority to evaluate and approve solutions proffered rested with the SAPS Provincial Steering Committee, and so, in the final instance, control over operational matters remained within the centralised authority structures of the police.

Each idea proposed to the Provincial Committees required an 'implementation plan', incorporating performance indicators to 'monitor progress and impact', and those 'essential needs' that could not be met without additional funding from either the public or private sectors were to be the subject of a 'business plan'. Together, these measures indicated that police decision making operated according to a set of managerial practices that provided for the routine and repeated numericised and monetarised evaluation and revision of the decision taken. 'Project Lifeline' and the cellular phone initiative illustrate the belief that, the growth potential of businesses in less privileged communities depended, at least in part, on the local police possessing the capacity to maintain the law and order foundation that underpins the operation of the free market. Such projects do not, however, exhibit much in the way of democratic control of the policy agenda *per se* by these communities.

In different ways, all of the BAC 'special projects' conveyed a particular image of police professionalism. Herein, emphasis is placed on the acquisition of state of the art equipment. Successful policing, it seems, depends heavily on the exploitation of the latest technological innovations. Professional police are well equipped police. The image of police professionalism also incorporated notions of accountability: police management are accountable professionals who invite input from police personnel and community members in the resolution of station resource problems. The station commander 'of the future must emerge as a responsible professional who is self-regulating in his or her personal conduct, who accepts accountability as a personal challenge' (Palmer, 1995, in O'Malley and Palmer, 1996, p 146). Accountability was still channelled upwards, but increasingly it was also channelled outwards, toward private sector sponsors of police service provision such as BAC.

Fighting the crime by numbers

Both the Nedcor Project and BAC agreed that investor concerns could be assuaged by a show of force on the part of the state, but also by other more indirect measures such as the provision of 'accurate' crime data. The implicit view was partly that investors draw conclusions about the security of their investments on the basis of statistical measures of the 'crime rate'. Thus, the availability of appropriate statistics could go a long way toward altering the 'perceptions of existing and potential investors toward the negative phenomena of crime and violence' (Nedcor, August 1995, p 5).

This was to emphasise the importance of numericised information in the management of the crime problem. Statistics were viewed as 'vital' to the development, implementation and evaluation of state anti-crime policies (Nedcor, April 1996). Statistical information is crucial generally to the exercise of socio-political authority (Rose, 1991, 1999) for action. Effective action can only be undertaken where knowledge of the problem exists: 'professionals, planners and politicians can be mobilised to greater effectiveness if they know the size of the challenge facing them as they strive to provide services of all kinds, including safety and security' (Nedcor, August 1995, pp 6–7). In its delivery of security services, government is subjected to assessments conducted in numerical terms: crime rates, number of arrests, conviction rate, security budgets, police remuneration packages, personnel recruitment and so forth.

Numbers also hold special significance for the governance of crime because of the relationship established between practices of quantification and practices of liberal democratic citizenship. Here are highlighted two forms that this relationship may take. First, there is a link between police record keeping and the 'crime reporter' role. The determination of the size of the 'actual crime situation' (Fourie and Mhangwana, 1995) requires citizens to be willing to report criminal activity and 'suspicious' people to police authorities. Business employers and employees, as well as the public more generally, are all understood to have an active part to play in the management of crime through providing the police with information enabling them to calculate the extent of the problem and devise appropriate solutions: 'As long as the public is not prepared to report criminal activities, within and outside the company, it will not be possible to stamp out crime' (Fourie and Mhangwana, 1995, p 11). This notwithstanding that the lack of fit between statistical measures and 'reality' may not so much reflect the failure of citizens to assume the responsibility for reporting crime, but rather the failure of the police to gain public confidence and trust. Secondly, individuals and associations are not only resources for, and objects of, statistical calculation, but themselves are also required to become the kind of calculating citizens that liberal democracy expects (Rose, 1991, 1999). On the one hand, crime statistics proliferate throughout Nedcor and BAC publications, illustrating that public scrutiny of state activity – a key feature of liberalism (Gordon, 1991) – occurs within the technical and seemingly objective framework offered by numbers. Discussions about the complex experiences of criminality and victimisation and about state policies become debates about the 'crime rate'. On the other hand, individuals are guided in their everyday conduct by facts and figures, not by subjective perceptions or anecdotal information on crime. The same applies to business organisations: the computer and electronics industry, for example, began making decisions on how to manage the substantial risk of theft of goods in transit in terms of information co-operatively produced by industry members and stored in a common database (BAC, 1996). Managing crime successfully requires the active participation of a knowledgeable public (see O'Malley and Palmer, 1996).

Numbers do not just provide the basis for action. Rather, statistical calculation itself is a way of acting. Through police recording procedures, victim and household surveys, crime mapping, and other techniques of inscription, 'crime' emerges as an object that is knowable and manageable: as a routine, predictable and systematic phenomenon (Garland, 1997) with identifiable spatial and temporal co-ordinates. Statistics do not simply represent or capture a pre-existing reality; they actually help constitute it. The constitutive role of numbers is well illustrated in Nedcor's call for 'accurate' and 'reliable' crime data to allow for international comparisons in order to both 'judge the severity' of South Africa's crime situation and determine what the *normal crime levels should be* (Nedcor, December 1995, p 1). Standardised calculations of the incidence of crime per 100,000 population enabled comparisons to be drawn between South Africa's crime rate and that of other countries. In this way, Nedcor could establish that, while South Africa's overall crime rate compared favourably with that of the developed West, its murder and assault rates far exceed international averages. In this way, Nedcor projected an ideal norm for levels of violent crime in South Africa.

'Centres of calculation'

In his book *Science in Action* (1987), Bruno Latour advanced the idea of 'centres of calculation', an idea subsequently advanced by Miller and Rose (1990) in the context of their analysis of liberal governance. This idea gains specific purchase in terms of evolving strategies of governance in post-apartheid South Africa: 'Over the past two years the provision of statistics on crime and violence in South Africa has become a growth industry' (Nedcor, April 1996, p 6). Both the Nedcor Project and BAC participated in this development by reworking and synthesising 'official' material and collecting new data. Police recorded crime rates were recalibrated using revised population estimates in order to compare crime trends across the entire South African territory (including the former homelands and self-governing states). In so doing, Nedcor sought to 'add value' (Starr and Corson, 1987) to official statistics.

New efforts were mounted to produce statistical measures of the views and experiences of business operators and investors themselves. An example of this was the Nedcor survey of the impact of crime on domestic business and on foreign investment decisions. Or consider again the previously discussed BAC proposal for the collection and aggregation of data on the theft of computer and electronic goods in transit. Other studies, such as Nedcor's National Crime Survey in 1995, provided new statistical information on the number of South African households affected by property offences and crimes against the person; on the costs of crime at the level of the individual and of society (medical costs, extra insurance); and on public opinion about crime and possible solutions to crime. In effect, Nedcor and BAC operated as little 'centres of calculation', producing statistics that seem to reveal some degree of compatibility between the different concerns, objectives and interests of capital, political authorities and the citizenry.

Such 'private' collection of numbers has commercial value but was not a commercial venture as such. That is to say, Nedcor and BAC were not in the business of 'selling repackaged public data and privately collected statistics, statistical models, and analytical skills' (Starr and Corson, 1987, p 415). Instead, Nedcor and BAC freely offered the statistical information to interested users. Indeed, dissemination and communication of this information was a key strategic objective within these corporate anti-crime campaigns. For example, Nedcor, BAC and the Institute for Security Studies co-operated in the publication of the Nedcor/ISS Crime Index for circulation to 2,000 organisations and individuals in the public and private sectors. The aim was to 'provide a ready reference resource for crime prevention practitioners, policy makers and organisations involved in crime prevention initiatives'. The Index was to 'provide ongoing information about the crime situation in South Africa based on research and information from different organisations', offering 'an overview each month of an area of crime, the current available statistics from the South African Police Services and [an] update [of] these statistics as they are made available' (Nedcor/ISS, 1997, p i).

Consider another example: a national crime prevention programme involving BAC, labour, consumer bodies and various government departments (that is, justice, finance), which proposed the integration of information from private and public sources on the 'incidence', 'trends' and 'developments' pertaining to corruption and commercial crime. Government needs this statistical data generally so that it can make and justify decisions as to the setting of priorities, the allocation of limited resources, the training of police and internal auditors and make legislative changes. Industry likewise needs such information as the basis for self-regulatory mechanisms: codes of conduct, assessment of organisational policies on financial decision making, evaluation of the actions of employees and so forth (Department of Safety and Security, 1996, pp 72–73). To sum up, Nedcor and BAC participated in and helped produce a 'public habitat of numbers' (Rose, 1991, 1999) that became crucial to the liberal democratic governance of crime in South Africa. Within this public habitat, business operators, investors and employees, along with government officials and the citizenry more generally, could calculate the risks posed by crime to the achievement of their specific objectives and decide what to do about it. In so doing they established some common ground – the domain of mutual (in)security.

Responsible corporate citizenship

A Nedcor Project survey in 1995 found that foreign companies were deterred not so much by 'ordinary' crime – even though these rates were high – as by perceptions of political and social instability in South Africa. In fact, crime, violence and corruption, along with interest rates, investor protection, power costs and availability of raw materials, were understood as less of a negative influence on foreign investment decisions than were concerns about the potential for market growth. Such growth was understood to be determined by political and social stability in South Africa and the country's macro-economic policies. High levels of crime and violence were taken to indicate a level of political instability. However, the Nedcor survey determined that what tended to worry foreign investors was not the amount, but the type of crime and violence. It was thought that disinvestment was likely to occur if violence, no matter how occasional or sparse, had a political edge to it (Nedcor, April 1996, p 4).

Corporate involvement in the management of the 'crime problem' had multiple motives. Corporate participation in anti-crime measures was especially motivated by the political vulnerability of industry. Corporate practices during the apartheid years, and the immense powers accrued by corporate bodies in the pre-democratic era, later gave rise to a sense of political vulnerability. Many of the companies involved with BAC and the Nedcor Project provided indirect and direct support to the apartheid regime. Consider the example of Eskom, the national electricity supplier (and a BAC Board member). In a submission to the Truth and Reconciliation Commission (TRC), Eskom acknowledged that it did not always behave like a model corporate citizen, apologising to all black South Africans in general, and black Eskom employees in particular for its actions which, until the late 1980s, entertained and perpetuated apartheid policies (TRC, 1997).

The TRC also received an amnesty application implicating Nedbank, of the Nedcor group, in a security branch operation to divert funds from the National Union of Mineworkers. Not only Nedbank, but also banking institutions more generally, appear to have played an instrumental role in the apprehension of anti-apartheid activists; using banking transactions, particularly withdrawals from automated banking machines, as a way of tracking the movements of 'enemies of the state'.[5] Further, an African National Congress (ANC) discussion document, *The State and Social Transformation*, identified capital as a whole, rather than individual firms or particular market sectors, as an 'important and central factor in the totality of forces responsible for the anti-human misery baptised as apartheid' (ANC, 1996, para 5.1). Thus industry, in the post-apartheid period, needed to demonstrate unequivocal commitment to the new democratic order.

---

5 Charles Small – personal communication, 1998.

Such commitment needed to be more than passing the institutional equivalent of a loyalty oath. It was not that industry might present an ideological challenge to the new state. Rather, immense powers and benefits, accrued by corporate South Africa under the previous apartheid system, were at stake. Consider the example of the mining sector and its veritable 'army' of in-house security personnel amassed to police entire towns and equipped with the same array of weapons as the police, including cannons, shotguns and helicopters (Schärf, 1989). Consider again the public utility, Eskom, commonly referred to as a 'parastatal'. It had operated relatively independently of the apartheid government, having powers normally associated with a state. The loss or blunting of the coercive capacity to order social relations was a distinct possibility in the face of a new post-apartheid government anxious to flex its regulatory muscle.

For example, the Security Officers Act (92 of 1987) created the option of subjecting in-house security to the same controls as the contract sector, and ministerial supervision of parastatals intensified in keeping with the new government's cautious attitude to privatisation (*Reconstruction and Development Programme*, 1994, p 57). Further, the national *Reconstruction and Development Programme* set forth state interventionist strategies to transform the mining, minerals, pulp and paper, tourism and financial industries – precisely those sectors on which the Nedcor Project and BAC drew their support. Measures such as wage determinations, 'black economic empowerment', monetary policies (that is, interest rates), trade policies (that is, tariff reductions on imports), nationalisation and anti-trust legislation aimed to address monopoly practices, corporate insularity, lack of accountability and relative autonomy previously enjoyed by industry under the apartheid system (*Reconstruction and Development Programme*, 1994, especially Chapter 4). In the hope of forestalling, and even preventing the restructuring of its powers and operation, business sought to provide public reassurances that it does not challenge the authority of the state, especially in relation to security issues.

Industry thus engaged in a series of high visibility anti-crime initiatives designed to re-present itself as a 'responsible corporate citizen' (BAC, 1996; but see also Johnston, 1992 on responsible citizenship and corporate sponsorship of police in the UK). These measures aimed not so much to eliminate or reduce crime, but rather, they had high symbolic value, seeking to reassure, persuade and convince government of the good intentions of commerce: 'The objective of Business Against Crime is to empower state agents and to strengthen existing initiatives' (Fourie and Mhangwana, 1996, p 7). Business sought to show itself as providing supportive capacity to government. This can be illustrated through a consideration of two high profile industry projects in the field of public policing: BAC itself and 'Cellwatch', a partnership programme in the Gauteng province involving business, the SAPS and the 'public'.

Marketing sponsorship

Why would private enterprise fund BAC? What is the expected 'return' on such investments? The following answer suggests itself: it is a calculated attempt by organisations to publicly demonstrate that they are good corporate citizens; that they are willing to 'put their money where their mouth is' and contribute financially to the strengthening of governmental capacity to fight crime. In effect, sponsorship is a marketing exercise; something made abundantly clear in the written agreement entered into by BAC and its sponsors. The first paragraph of the document is especially revealing: 'BAC was established in August 1995 by the business sector in order to *materially support* the governmental authorities' anti-crime programs and to *show* public commitment by business to that support' (emphasis added). Nowhere does the agreement outline the manner in which sponsors may participate (if at all) in expenditure decisions. Funders appear concerned less to do good than to be seen to be doing good: 'The value to the sponsor in linking themselves to the aims of BAC is of normal marketing exposure ... These associations are highly desirable at this time and positive association for the Sponsor to his [sic] target consumer is high [sic] probable.'

This agreement provided specific content to the notion of exposure motivation. Three sponsorship tiers were created; each with specific 'rewards' attached to it. Founding sponsors donated R500,000 or more per annum. Their association with BAC would then be publicly communicated in a number of ways. The sponsor's name and logo would be featured in BAC campaigns. Sponsors could expect their brand presence to be 'deliberately and systematically raised on public platforms' including 'speeches and interviews, or TV and radio talk shows and in general PR activities'. Corporate logos subsequently appear on BAC stationery and were included in quarterly newsletters aimed at the corporate sector and governmental sectors. Founding sponsors were also given permission to use the BAC logo and 'other devices' in their marketing programs, at the point of sale or in promotional campaigns; and were permitted use of BAC research. Interestingly, BAC also facilitated direct access to relevant ministries and departments for its sponsors, again illustrating that business sought avenues by which to communicate, reassure, persuade and convince government of its natural place in the new South Africa.

Major sponsors, who contributed between R100,000 to R500,000 per year, obtained similar benefits. The exception was that PR exercises, such as speeches, interviews and TV and radio talk shows, did not so feature the brand presence of the more limited sponsors. Major sponsors were given permission to use, without restriction, any BAC research and could incorporate the BAC logo in their own advertising campaigns. The use of the BAC logo in promotional activities, however, was kept as subject to specific approval.

Finally, donations of under R100,000 per annum earned the sponsor the right to use BAC data and information; to display the BAC logo on corporate stationery; and to use, subject to approval, the BAC association in promotional campaigns. Such sponsors' names and logos would also then be included in BAC printed media campaigns, corporate briefing sessions and in newsletters circulated to the corporate sector. In summary, individual organisations were enticed by the marketing prospects associated with sponsorship of BAC. Investments in state anti-crime measures were to be publicised by contributors themselves. Such publication merged with routine promotional practices – at the point of sale, in promotional programs, on corporate stationery. Moreover, displays of corporate citizenship were undertaken by BAC itself. Indeed, one of BAC's strategic priorities was its communications program. Thus, advertisement strategies pursued under the BAC banner opened up a large public domain in which industry seamlessly linked advertising products to potential consumers, with a demonstration of support for the criminal justice system and the new government generally.

Roving 'eyes': the Cellwatch programme

The Nedcor Project (December 1995, p 11) identified Cellwatch as a successful example of a business supported programme aimed at the prevention and control of crime. A co-operative venture involving the SAPS, Radio 702, Vodacom and cellphone users, Cellwatch aimed to reduce the incidence of car thefts and hijackings in the province of Gauteng and improve recovery rates by creating the 'perception of an increased number of "eyes" watching any attempted vehicle crime'. The scheme worked first by the SAPS providing descriptions and registration numbers pertaining to stolen cars to the radio station (subject to a SAPS assessment of 'chance of recovery' – only those deemed to have a 'high chance of recovery' could expect 'air time'). Radio 702 would then broadcast the details of the stolen car details (and, in the event, news of their recovery) and urge listeners to call a Cellwatch hotline to report sightings. Vodacom would manage the 'hotline' and worked to channel select calls through to the SAPS. A web of seemingly constant surveillance could thus be created; the criminal to be deterred by the perception of increased risk of detection – every cellphone user, whether in a car or on the street, becomes a potential 'watcher'.

A number of comments on the Cellwatch programme are in order. First, whatever the motivation for police and Radio 702 involvement – and one can not assume the interests of all actors in this alliance to be identical (see Miller and Rose, 1990) – Cellwatch was primarily of symbolic value to Vodacom. What was appealing about Cellwatch, as the Nedcor Project noted, is that it shows commerce as willing to make financial and technological investments in public anti-crime measures, and to do so without delay. Certainly, the programme had effects, as it was estimated that half of the stolen cars filtered into the scheme were recovered. But the number of cars recovered is but a proportion of all *officially recorded* car crimes. Further measures of changes in the rate of car crime (the deterrent effect) were noticeably absent in subsequent advertising of programme success.

Secondly, as Davis (1990, especially Chapter 4) observed of 'post-liberal' Los Angeles: electronic technologies are well suited to an exclusionary politics in which surveillance functions to secure the social boundaries of race and class. Note that Radio 702's listener base was primarily (and remains as of this writing) 'upper income adults between the ages of 25 and 49'. Note also the fairly restricted ownership of cellphones, which is relatively closely confined to middle and upper middle class people. Lastly, note that only 'upmarket' cars tended to be included in the programme. It is easy to imagine the 'eyes' focusing on those whose skin colour seems at odd with the make of the car – that is: the marginalised 'Other', particularly black males. Surveillance practically sorts people into categories (the young black male in the BMW as car thief), in order to administer them. However, all individuals, not only marginalised populations, are caught in the web of surveillance (see Ericson and Haggerty, 1997). Surveillance also impinges on the freedoms of the very persons employing such security measures. Consider the cartoon image accompanying some Nedcor Project documentation of the Cellwatch programme. Three cars are in a row, each occupied by two people (six pairs of eyes), all of whom are talking on cellphones. The space between the cars has been erased and it seems the car frames have buckled inwards, trapping the occupants. The car has become a confinement cell – the occupants imprisoned and subjected to the unrelenting gaze of each other.

Conclusions

Corporate sponsorship of the public police became evident in many countries towards the end of the 20th century (Ericson and Haggerty, 1997; Johnston, 1992). But the South African situation appears to display certain unique features: business involvement took a more collective form; the initiatives targeted police operational practices; and the transformation of these practices was linked much more to the imperatives of crime control than to crime prevention. The partnerships between corporate South Africa and government should not be seen simply as responses to rampant crime. Rather, such developments are better understood by reference to a context wherein the roles and functions of governing authorities are being remodulated and revised (see O'Malley, 1992; O'Malley and Palmer, 1996; Stenson, 1993; also Rose, 1999). For the government, as for industry, state action no longer comprises the 'delivery of goods [and social services] to a passive citizenry' (*Reconstruction and Development Programme*, 1994, p 6). An enabling role comes to the fore, one which aims at fostering the exercise of free choice, responsibility, independence and efficiency in all spheres of life. As regards the economic sphere, the state provides the necessary condition for the establishment of rational and efficient market relations by maintaining basic levels of public tranquillity and security. It is thus, through the discursive construction of the state as the primary guarantor of public safety, that commercial investments in public policing become tied to transformations of the SAPS.

The apparent need for a strong sovereign authority – to control crime and thereby enable the operation of a free market – is perhaps better understood not as a vestige of an *ancien régime* for governing (Garland, 1996), nor as a core principle of liberal rule (Stenson, 1993), but in terms of its articulation with specific political programmes, the achievement of particular ends set out in local political agendas (see O'Malley, 1992). It is because crime posed a threat at the macro-economic level, that is to inward foreign investment, that business in South Africa organised collectively to assist government in playing its leadership role in practices of crime control. I have discussed the various kinds of technical expertise offered by business to enable the police to respond directly and forcefully to crime and the threat of crime. This involved the innovative use of existing technology, such as cellular telephony, for crime control purposes (that is, surveillance), uses which were not part of the original product design. Further, the application of legal powers was focused on the poor and the marginalised; on controlling the threats posed by risky populations within urban spaces. Industry also promoted reliance on statistical resources in the 'fight against crime'. Through crime indices and performance audits, political authorities were enabled to 'conduct the conduct' of members of the public and police from a distance. Subsequently, citizens were expected to moderate their behaviour in light of information on 'actual' crime levels, while police performance was measured by matching resources to outputs.

However, all of this might be beside the point, since the business partnerships with government in South Africa were entered into amidst the palpable sense of political vulnerability among the corporate sector. Whatever else, corporate South Africa was anxious to guard and preserve its own power, including its power to marshal coercive force in the maintenance of its own interests. Crime control was a tactical manoeuvre calculated to help forestall attempts to curb corporate influence, monopoly power and access to the organised means of violence. The BAC programme, therefore, projected an image of 'good corporate citizens', and high profile anti-crime initiatives were intended to reassure government that business was not a challenge to state authority. At the same time, in using the crime problem to create an ideological environment that re-affirmed the notion that the business of government is business, we can see the mobilisation of responsibilised corporate citizens for decidedly illiberal ends.

References

AA (Automobile Association) of South Africa (1995) *Car Crime Campaign: A Survey of Motorists' Experiences as Victims of Car Crime*, Johannesburg: AA RSA

African National Congress (ANC) (1996) *The State and Social Transformation*, Discussion Document, November, www.anc.org.za/ancdocs/policy/s&st.html

Brogden, M and Shearing, C (1993) *Policing for a New South Africa*, London: Routledge

Business Against Crime (BAC) (*circa* 1996) *The Time for Action is Now!*, South Africa: Auckland Park

Cawthra, G (1992) *South Africa's Police: From Police State to Democratic Policing?*, London: CIIR

Crawford, A (1994) 'The partnership approach to community crime prevention: corporatism at the local level?' 3 *Social and Legal Studies* 497–519

Davis, M (1990) *City of Quartz: Excavating the Future in Los Angeles*, London: Verso

Department of Safety and Security (May 1996) *National Crime Prevention Strategy (NCPS)*, Pretoria, South Africa: Department of Safety and Security

Ericson, R and Haggerty, K (1997) *Policing the Risk Society*, Oxford: Clarendon

Fourie, A and Mhangwana, V (1995) *The Prevention and Management of the High Levels of Crime and Violence in South Africa*, South Africa: National Business Initiative

Fourie, A and Mhangwana, V (1996) 'Business against crime' 5 *Crime and Conflict* 6–8

Garland, D (1996) 'The limits of the sovereign state' 36(4) *British Journal of Criminology* 445–71

Garland, D (1997) '"Governmentality" and the problem of crime: Foucault, criminology, sociology' 1(2) *Theoretical Criminology* 173–214

Gordon, C (1991) 'Governmental rationality: an introduction', in Burchell, G, Gordon, C and Miller, P (eds), *The Foucault Effect: Studies in Governmentality*, Hemel Hempstead: Harvester Wheatsheaf, pp 1–52

Hudson, B (2001) 'Punishments, rights and difference: defending justice in the risk society', in Stenson, K and Sullivan, R (eds), *Crime, Risk and Justice*, Cullompten: Willan Publishing, pp 144–71

Johnston, L (1992) *The Rebirth of Private Policing*, London: Routledge

Latour, B (1987) *Science in Action: How to Follow Scientists and Engineers Through Society*, Cambridge, Massachusetts: Harvard UP

McLaughlin, E and Murji, K (1997) 'The future lasts a long time: public policework and the managerialist paradox', in Francis, P, Davies, P and Jupp, V (eds), *Policing Futures: The Police, Law Enforcement and the Twenty-First Century*, London: Macmillan

Miller, P and Rose, N (1990) 'Governing economic life' 19(1) *Economy and Society* 1–31

Moore, M, Trojanowicz, R and Kelling, G (1988) 'Crime and policing', in *Perspectives on Policing*, No 2, Washington, DC: National Institute of Justice and Harvard University

Nedcor Project (August 1995) *Briefing Paper*, delivered at the Business Initiative Against Crime And Corruption

Nedcor Project (December 1995) *Stop Crime*, Johannesburg, South Africa: Nedcor

Nedcor Project (February 1996) *Newsletter*, No 7, Johannesburg, South Africa: Nedcor

Nedcor Project (April 1996) *Final Report*, Johannesburg, South Africa: Nedcor

Nedcor/ISS (1997) *Crime Index*, Midrand: Criminal Justice Information Centre

O'Malley, P (1992) 'Risk, power and crime prevention' 21(3) *Economy and Society* 252–75

O'Malley, P (1996) 'Risk and responsibility', in Barry, A, Osborne T and Rose, N (eds), *Foucault and Political Reason*, London: UCL Press, pp 189–208

O'Malley, P and Palmer, D (1996) 'Post-Keynesian policing' 25(2) *Economy and Society* 137–55

Reconstruction and Development Programme (1994), www.polity.org.za/govdocs/rdp/rdpall.html, Pretoria, RSA: Government of South Africa

Rose, N (1991) 'Governing by numbers: figuring out democracy' 16(7) *Accounting, Organizations and Society* 673–92

Rose, N (1999) *Powers of Freedom: Reframing Political Thought*, Cambridge: CUP

Schärf, W (1989) 'Community policing in South Africa', in *Acta Juridica*, Cape Town: Juta & Co, pp 206–33

Shearing, C (1992) 'The relation between public and private policing', in Tonry, M and Morris, N (eds), *Modern Policing*, Chicago: Chicago UP, pp 399–434

Shearing, C and Stenning, P (1982) *Private Security and Private Justice*, Canada: Institute for Research on Public Policy

Simon, J (2001) 'Entitlement to cruelty: neo-liberalism and the punitive mentality in the United States', in Stenson, K and Sullivan, R (eds), *Crime, Risk and Justice*, Cullompten: Willan Publishing, pp 125–43

Singh, A-M (2000) *Governing Crime in Post-Apartheid South Africa, 1990–96*, unpublished PhD thesis, Goldsmiths College, University of London

South, N (1988) *Policing for Profit: The Private Security Sector*, London: Sage

South African Foundation (1996) *Growth For All: An Economic Strategy for South Africa*, Johannesburg: The South African Foundation

Starr, P and Corson, R (1987) 'Who will have the numbers?: the rise of statistical services industry and the politics of public data', in Alonso, W and Starr, P (eds), *The Politics of Numbers*, New York: Russell Sage Foundation, pp 415–48

Stenson, K (1993) 'Community policing as a governmental technology' 22 *Economy and Society* 22: 373–89

TRC (1997) Truth and Reconciliation Commission Human Rights Violations Health Sector Hearings, June 17, 1997, Cape Town, http://shr.aaas.org/trc-med/day1.pdf

Wright, J (1995) 'Crime and its effects on the short term insurance industry', paper presented at the Annual Conference of the Security Association of South Africa, 4 July 1995, Durban

Chapter 7

Critical Realist Reflections on Crime and Social Control in Singapore

Narayanan Ganapathy

The Singapore context: some salient features

Singapore consists of the main island of Singapore and some 63 offshore islands. The main island is about 42 kilometres in length, 23 kilometres in breadth and 584.8 square kilometres in area. It has a coastline of approximately 150.5 kilometres long. The total area, including the offshore islands, is about 647.5 square kilometres (Ministry of Information and the Arts, 1997). As a city-state, Singapore has a negligible rural sector as only 10.8 square kilometres are farm holding areas (licensed farms). The small size of Singapore and its high degree of urbanisation are cited as being advantageous for the police in its enforcement duties, as according to Quah (1994), the limited area of 28.6 square kilometres of forests and relative absence of hilly terrain have reduced considerably the number of hiding places for criminals. This factor, however, has made detection and apprehension of criminals particularly difficult, as the criminals tend to escape to the north to Malaysia by car, or to the south to Indonesia and surrounding islands by boat. The effectiveness of the still maturing Aseanapol, the region's police co-operation body, has not been adequately evaluated.

Singapore has a heterogeneous population of 3,044,300 as at June 1996, and its population density rose from 4,051 residents per square kilometre in 1986 to 4,702 residents in 1996. The population is multiracial and consists of 77% Chinese, 14% Malays, 7% Indians and 1% of people of other races. In terms of religion, 68% of the Chinese are Buddhists or Taoists, and 14% are Christians. Almost all the Malays are Muslims. For the Indians, 53% are Hindus, 26% are Muslims, and 13% are Christians.

The modern police system in Singapore is organised around the British model of law and jurisprudence, as Singapore was a British colony between 1819 and 1959. Many of the functions which the police perform are similar to those of the British criminal justice system: prevention of crime and disorder, preservation of public peace (for community security), and protection of life, property and personal liberty (for individual security). Section 8 of the Police Force Ordinance of 1958 outlines the Singapore Police Force's role as maintaining law and order, preserving public peace, preventing and detecting crime and apprehending offenders. Consequently, from a legislative standpoint, there is nothing particularly conspicuous about the way in which Singapore categorises its major crimes. The nation's criminal code classifies approximately 330 different types of criminal activity in six broad categories (Saw, 1973, pp 1–5). Presently, the SPF has an operationally ready strength of 33,228 officers comprising 9,005 regular officers, 790 civilian officers, 2,829 National Service Full-time (NSF) personnel, 19,374 Operationally-Ready National Servicemen (NS) and 1,230 Volunteer Special Constabulary (VSC) officers (Singapore Police Force, 1998, p 38).

Existing literature (for example, Brodeur, 1995; Reiner, 1995) suggests that two aspects make it possible to identify four ideal types of policing models, which are based upon 'the respective place of societal goals and political aims in the functioning and organisation of a policing system' (Loubet del Bayle, quoted in Monjardet, 1995, p 49). The four models are: (a) a 'minimal' policing model where the societal and political dynamics that influence it are equally weak, (b) an 'arbitrational' model where these two dynamics are equally strong, (c) a 'community' model where a strong societal dynamic dominates a weak political dynamic, and (d) an 'authoritarian' model where a strong political dynamic dominates a weak social dynamic (Monjardet, 1995, p 49). The Singapore model of policing displays certain characteristics that it could well fit into the 'authoritarian' typology: its centralisation under the direct and almost exclusive authority of the executive power makes it a state police. As a consequence of this direct connection with the political, it is characterised, first, by an orientation dominated by an absolute priority to order maintenance in police missions, and secondly – immortalised by the Internal Security Department (ISD) – by a function of political policing, 'high policing' in Brodeur's terms (1983), institutionally and explicitly attributed to maintaining a particular conception of social order, or at least, to euphemise, a police function that does not shy away from intervening in the observation and analysis of the political arena. The Singapore state's concern to prioritise order over justice – as seen in the powers of the Internal Security Act (ISA) which allows for detention of a suspect without trial and the limited transparency that such a process offers – underscores a police role that regards order-maintenance as its primary objective.

This has implications for any attempt at comparative criminology, as such an understanding of the state not only questions the possibility of detaching crime and criminal justice data from their social, economic and political contexts, but also the usefulness of separating issues of 'crime' from 'crime control', particularly in a paternalistic and authoritative regime. Protagonists of comparative criminology have traditionally responded to the latter by specifically drawing attention to what are termed 'cross-cultural crimes', rather than to the processes and institutions of the criminal justice system of local societies (Beirne and Nelken, 1997). In responding to these issues, it might be useful to contextualise any investigation into, and appreciation of, the 'crime problem' in relation to the sources and constructions of knowledge on the nature and extent of crime, as well as the objectives of crime control in a *particular* socio-historical period. This becomes especially important in the Singapore context, as the state police are the only agency that has the resources and legitimate authority to collate and communicate crime data to the populace. In the absence of victimisation and self-reported data, compounded by the paucity of local literature on crime and deviance, our knowledge of the crime problem and processes of crime control remains primarily state-defined and to an extent, ideologically propagated.

Yet, despite the authoritarian character of the Singapore state, it is equally important to acknowledge that its model of formal policing does display elements of the Anglo-Saxon model of 'community' policing based on the idea of 'policing by consent' (Reiner, 1985). This categorisation fundamentally flows from the assumptions that policing in Singapore is high on accountability; undertaken with public consent, which does not mean acquiescence, but a broad tolerance indicating a satisfaction with the helping and enforcement roles of policing; its organisational structure allows the public to express their policing wants and needs; and last but not least, the Singapore Police Force's (SPF) professional culture is epitomised by the officer on the street, close to his community and patrolling his beat with the consent of the general public. The 32.7% of citizen-initiated arrests in the major crimes of outraging of modesty, robbery, housebreaking, motor vehicle theft, rape and murder, for the year 1998 (SPF), and the apparent success of community policing (Quah and Quah, 1987; Bayley, 1989), could be attributed to this model of policing being adopted by the Singapore state.

The ability of the police organisation to amalgamate what appear to be two antagonistic functions of, and demands on, the police, is not a characteristic peculiar to the Singapore state. Classical police studies inspired by critical, revisionist accounts of the history of the 'new' police (Brogden, 1982; Spitzer and Scull, 1977; Storch, 1976) have clearly established that the police function involves both the issuing of 'parking tickets and class repression' (Marenin, 1982, pp 241–66), which Brodeur (1983) describes as 'low' and 'high' policing respectively. Similarly, from a critical viewpoint, the concept of 'community policing', a cornerstone of police and state legitimacy, could simply be a function of an ideology that seeks to 'conceal its iron fist with a velvet glove' and through which the state is able to legitimise its status as monopolists of coercive force. Though not being dismissive about the utility of existing paradigms, discussions regarding models of policing do, nevertheless, tend to suggest that the concrete structures and practices of policing are the realisation of some prior conceptual model. This betrays an over-idealistic and rationalistic account of how policing actually developed and responded to varying demands. They also imply an even more problematic notion (almost an evangelical one), that the Anglo-Saxon model – the 'community' model – is superior to other models of policing, particularly those found in the Third World (Cohen, 1997). Such 'superiority', as Reiner (1985) argues, is part of a professional police ideology that perpetuates the myth of the benevolent bobby (Reiner, 1985, 1995; Brogden, 1982).

From a traumatic past to a 'progressive' present: changing patterns of formal and informal social control

Experience of political and social upheaval in the immediate pre-independence and post-independence years effected major changes on the Singapore state, and on its control apparatus, that were compatible with ensuring an orderly transition to eventual independence. The period particularly marked the intensification in the use of the ISA and the Criminal Law (Temporary Provisions) Act, with the latter primarily empowering the executive to incarcerate the common criminal indefinitely. The chief priority of the criminal justice apparatus then was to address *public order offences*, as the use of these laws was primarily designed to contain the twin problems of communism and communalism, and the violence associated with the Chinese secret societies in Singapore. The Maria Hertogh riots of December 1950, the 1964 communal riots between the Malays and the Chinese in Singapore sparked off during a religious procession on the birthday anniversary of the

Prophet Mohammad, and the 1969 Sino-Malay riots in Kuala Lumpur are sure reminders of the traumatic origins of Singapore, which only underscored the need for robust formal and informal control institutions to ensure social ordering in the newly formed multiracial and multi-religious state.

Towards community policing

The national theme of remaining economically and politically sturdy diffused into the ideology and practice of the criminal justice system in the aftermath of the separation from Malaysia in 1959. The continued use and effectiveness of the Internal Security and Criminal Law Acts, coupled with the 'massive governmental campaigns waged to rid Singapore of urban slums, squalor, and underemployment' (Austin, 1989, p 917) since the mid-1970s, impacted upon the style and character of formal policing to one embracing a more 'communitarian' outlook (Chua, 1995). The adoption of 'community policing' as both an ideological and pragmatic feature of professional policing, which signified the move towards institutionalising the order-maintenance and service roles of the police (Reiner, 1995; Banton, 1964), has to be appreciated in the context of two significant macro-structural developments witnessed in post-independence Singapore.

The first of these is related to the success of the state police in curbing the activities of the secret societies and in minimising the problem of police corruption related to the former since the 1960s, both of which served to enhance its public image. The use of the Criminal Law Act against secret society members, for example, saw a decline of 416 recorded secret society related incidents in 1959 to 241 in 1960, and to 36 in 1973 (Narayanan, 1994, p 47). In 1977, there were only 13 secret societies or secret society related incidents recorded by the Secret Societies Branch (SSB) of the Criminal Investigation Department (CID) ('Police Life 1977', quoted in Narayanan, 1994, p 47). It is estimated that about 90% of secret society members were rendered either moribund or inactive under this ordinance between 1958 and 1993 (personal communication quoted in Narayanan, 1994, p 48). The decline in secret society activities was also the result of rapid social changes occurring in post-independence Singapore society that eroded some of the important traditional functions performed by these societies. As the social system became more differentiated and complex, many functions previously undertaken by secret societies were taken up by modern institutions, of which the Government Civil Service program was the vanguard (Lim, 1971). An important consequence arising from the impersonal processes of recruitment and selection administered by the Civil Service was that it exerted a great impact on the old occupational structure, which was organised along ethno-linguistic lines. For example, job placement through the 'recommendation' of secret societies was not necessary and was replaced by secularised and non-vernacular schools and colleges, with public examination systems embedded in the principles and ideals of meritocracy. In addition, the role of local societies in providing job security for their members had also been partly taken over by trade unions that were largely controlled by the government.

The second factor involved the change in the population distribution on the island. Before the establishment of the Singapore state's public housing agency, the

Housing and Development Board (HDB), in early 1960, and the subsequent proliferation of public housing estates, most Singaporeans lived in small, *atap* or zinc roofed houses. These shanty type houses were piled together in communities known in the vernacular as *kampong*. However, as a result of aggressive government policies to provide public housing for the majority of the population (the proportion increased from 69% in 1981 to 87% in 1990) and the emergence of 'new towns' throughout the island, there was a significant change in the living arrangements of the populace.

These new living arrangements have had a profound effect on the style of law enforcement. With a large proportion of Singaporeans living in high-rise buildings that contain an average of 150 dwelling units or flats, and averages from 10–25 storeys in height, the SPF was forced to abandon, or at least limit, its former method of random motorised patrolling and replace it with 'vertical policing', which involved the movement of patrol officers from floor to floor of high-rise buildings. On 'vertical patrolling', Bayley (1989, p 13) remarks:

> Visiting homes means for the most part calling at apartments in HDB blocks. NPP officers begin at the top floors and work their way down floor by floor, apartment by apartment. They carry clipboards listing the apartments to be visited and briefcases filled with crime prevention pamphlets, stickers with emergency telephone numbers, and business cards printed with the NPP's address and telephone number. The business card contains space for the officer's name, so residents have a personal contact if needed.

Instead of relying on the various police stations, the SPF decentralised its functions and activities through the Neighbourhood Police Post system (NPP). Formed in 1983 as an attempt to replicate the successful Japanese model of community policing based upon the Koban system (thought to be responsible for the high crime clearance rate of about 60% in Japan (Ames, 1981; Bayley, 1991)), the Singapore NPP system is a kind of 'mini-police station situated in the heart of a neighbourhood and catering for the welfare of about 30,000 residents' (Quah and Ong, 1989, pp 275–76). Fundamentally, its main objective is to improve police-community relations and to prevent and suppress crimes by means of public support and co-operation. The formation of NPPs and the reorganisation of police patrols, especially those on foot, bicycles and motor scooters, have been found to enhance the means of surveillance and public security in housing estates. Oscar Newman's (1978) concept of 'defensible space' and Joanna Shapland's notion of 'watching and noticing' (1988, p 117) provides some theoretical grounding for this.

Accompanying the shift in policing methodology in view of the structural shift of population from *kampongs* to HDB apartments, was the need to rejuvenate neighbourhood cohesion and informal social control mechanisms that were associated with the earlier *kampong* way of life. Austin (1989) argues that although the lifestyle in early *kampongs* lacked modem physical comfort and proper hygiene, extended families were able to live in close proximity. Neighbourhoods were held tightly together by bonds of dialect, nationality, race and religion, all ties which provided substantial mutual support. More importantly, they engendered a sense of community identity, mutual assistance among neighbours and local community security (Hassan, 1976, pp 249–68, Chen and Tai, 1977, pp 65–73). Disputes were dealt with at the *kampong* and neighbourhood levels with less reliance on formal law and government intervention. There was a breakdown of neighbourhood cohesion and support patterns associated with the earlier *kampongs* because of the relocation of the population to high-rise HDB flats. This is in accord with Durkheim's perspective, which predicts that societies undergoing rapid economic and social change will experience 'anomie', a condition signifying the breakdown of the moral order and the inability of social control institutions to regulate social conduct. Between the mid-1970s and 1980, Singapore's overall crime increased, causing many to suspect that the ecological changes and perceived absence of informal support structures were responsible (Ong, 1984; Austin, 1989).

The institutionalisation of community policing signified the transition of policing style from a 'watchman' to a legalistic and, eventually, to a service one in the 1980s (see Wilson, 1975a). A local study of the complaints and calls for assistance made to the Jurong Police Station in the western part of Singapore over a one month period revealed that 53% of calls were for non-crime related incidents; slightly higher than calls for crime related cases of (47%). Only one out of four calls to the police for assistance was deemed to be crime related (Ee, 1982, p 73). An SPF study of the '999' calls for assistance to the Police Radio Operations Room (the local police dispatch system) also revealed that, of the 2.2 million calls made to emergency lines in 1997, only 176,586 calls (about 7.9%) were crime related (*Straits Times*, 10 April 1998), the rest being service and nuisance related calls (*Straits Times*, 27 April 1998).

Although the origin of community policing in Singapore is linked to the creation of the Crime Prevention Department (CPD) of the police in 1981, which was later responsible for the implementation of the Neighbourhood Police Post system in Toa Payoh division (Toh, 1988), the concept and philosophy of 'community policing', according to Ong (1989), can in fact be traced to the colonial authority's policy on 'community security'. In his discussion, Ong (1989) demonstrates that even historically during the period of colonial rule, the British had used a device that essentially made the community responsible for a large part of its own security. This was achieved through the appointment or recognition of community headmen who were often linked to the Triad societies. A vivid illustration of this was the technique used by the Governor Cavenagh to quell the riots among the Chinese secret societies in the 1860s:

> The only way in which Cavenagh and his colleagues could hold the societies in check when trouble broke out was to swear in their leaders as special constables and parade them up and down in order, as Cavenagh says with a nice irony, 'to entice them to take a warm personal interest in the preservation of the peace' (Freedman, 1960, p 31).

The Chinese community, to a large extent, had its own institutions and organisations for facilitating social control, and the connection with Triad societies provided much of the resources to achieve social order in the still maturing migrant society. Thus, 'within the early Singapore Chinese community these tightly knit networks of individuals, each fulfilling obligations to and having expectations of the other, defined the meaning of community security' (Ong, 1989, p 940). Whilst assisting the British to bolster their own limited policing resources, this strategy also betrayed a certain dependence on these internal communal controls.

Understanding Singaporean-style 'community policing' historically, especially its relationship with the Triads, serves as a useful reminder: that community policing underpins the crucial role of the informal social control system. The practices of modern community policing embody a wide range of initiatives and activities including: resident patrols, citizen crime reporting systems, neighbourhood watch schemes, home and commercial security surveys, property marking projects, the neighbourhood police post system, neighbourhood police centres, and a variety of programmes for changing the physical environment. Yet, fundamentally, it rests on the idea of a joint partnership between formal agents of social control and the informal social control apparatus of the community in preventing and controlling crime. This understanding of the police-citizenry relationship forms the basis of any definition of 'community policing' (Moore, 1992; Skolnick and Bayley, 1986; Sparrow, Moore and Kennedy, 1990; Hope and Shaw, 1988; Stenson, 1991).

Right realism, crime and social control

The relationship between right realist criminology, crime and agents of social control is succinctly captured in the works of Wilson (1975b) and Wilson and Kelling (1982). The affinity between right realist criminology and social control lies in its emphasis on tackling what it sees as the 'fundamental root causes of crime'. It calls for the socialisation agencies and community institutions to implement broad social measures intended to promote respect for moral values and increase community solidarity, improve police-public relations, reduce criminogenic inequalities and provide diversionary facilities for 'alienated' youth (Heal and Laycock, 1988, p 238). Strengthening socialisation agencies and community institutions is also, to a large extent, about the rejuvenation and development of informal social control networks in the prevention and control of crime. Fundamentally, the basic theoretical assumption which social control addresses is that antisocial behaviour is a product of antisocial conditions.

Here, the Chicago School's legacy of thinking about crime prevention and control is significant in three respects: first, it provides a conceptual link between crime and socially disorganised and socially disadvantaged communities, and suggests that the distribution of both crime and social disorganisation between and within communities can be affected by social policies formulated to alter the urban scene. Secondly, measures against offending should somehow seek to socialise and integrate residents, especially youths, into a shared set of norms and standards of behaviour. And thirdly, it maintains that ordinary members of the community, community institutions and informal social control networks comprising family and kin are effective resources to accomplishing this aim.

The role of the police from a right realist perspective, as Wilson and Kelling (1982) state, lies more in the maintenance of social order than in the direct control of crime. They argue that disorder undermines the processes by which communities ordinarily govern themselves. One popular version, the parable of 'broken windows' (Wilson and Kelling, 1982), suggests that it is important for the police to intervene early in the cycle of social disorganisation to clean up the environment and reduce incivilities – the metaphor being that unrepaired damage encourages further broken windows (Hope and Shaw, 1988, p 16). The parable suggests that if disorderly behaviour such as that of public drunkenness or rowdy youth is not controlled, the affected neighbourhood enters a spiral of decline in which law abiding citizens emigrate from the area, informal social controls weaken, and crime rates begin to rise. Police involvement in 'order-maintenance' facilitates, in the long run, crime control and crime prevention (Young, 1994, p 99). It does so by jump-starting the informal social control system in areas where it has broken down and which are, *ipso facto*, high crime areas (Young, 1994, p 101).

Interestingly, the concept of 'stakeholding' (Chua, 1997), which the cautionary 'broken windows' story recommends, is exemplified in the Singapore Government's provision and conduct of its national public housing programmes. The state's public housing agency, the HDB, which started modestly as an agency entrusted with building 1- and 2-room rental flats for the poor in 1961 (Chua, 1997), had by the mid-1990s constructed more than half a million high-rise flats, housing more than 87% of the resident Singapore population. Furthermore, many of the small rental flats built early on have largely been demolished, making way for larger flats, which are offered as 99 year leasehold properties to the tenants. Importantly, public housing in Singapore is an arena in which every household, as stakeholders in the property market, has been able (up to the present) to make significant financial gains through buying and selling of the leases on the flats. This is a strong incentive to every household to participate actively with the HDB, thereby improving, developing and maintaining basic and ancillary facilities on housing estates with a view to enhancing property values. This, in turn, has promoted the sustenance of informal social mechanisms. Consequently, formal policing emphasises its involvement in the activities of the Residents' Committees (RCs) in public housing estates, police boys' clubs and School Uniformed Groups in an attempt to restore a kampong style neighbourhood. Government policy has been forged on the belief that it has been necessary to support informal social control networks formerly endangered by the dislocation of the population following the shift to HDB public housing projects (Narayanan, 2000).

Residents' Committees and the institutionalisation of neighbourhood watch

The RCs, a form of grassroots organisation, were formed in 1987 for primarily three reasons: first, to ensure a better sense of security and protection from crime, vandalism, drugs and other public order offences and antisocial activities; secondly, to encourage a sense of neighbourliness and racial harmony through sports, social, cultural and other activities; and thirdly, to provide a better channel of communication with the authorities, principally the maintenance section of the HDB and Town Councils. The latter ensures prompt action to problems of lifts, corridor lighting and Public Utilities Board (PUB) facilities (Narayanan, 2000). The police have relied on the RCs to promote awareness of crime prevention among the residents of HDB townships and as a base from which to consolidate police-community relations. The RC members assist the police in spreading the message of crime prevention to other residents by conducting regular visits, organising crime prevention exhibitions, distributing crime prevention literature, giving talks and staging audiovisual shows (Ong, 1984, p 16).

The police assign Neighbourhood Police Post officers to sit in every RC meeting. Their role is to inform RC members about the incidence of crime occurring within the neighbourhood, to encourage appropriate crime prevention measures, and to facilitate community participation in the formulation and implementation of criminal policies. In 'Crime prevention: Singapore style', Quah (1994) outlines the Singapore police's philosophy as one primarily concerned with the 'anticipation, recognition and appraisal of crime risk, and the initiation of action to remove or reduce those risks'. In short, the RCs provide the 'vital social infrastructure' responsible for the police management of crime prevention and control (Ong, 1984).

One of the most important developments in the course of this partnership was the establishment of the Neighbourhood Watch Scheme (NWS) in 1981. This was described in its official brochure as 'an informal arrangement among a few immediate neighbours to help each other protect themselves against robbers, thieves and molesters by looking after each other's home and wellbeing'. This state-orchestrated project engineers a collective 'public minded' strategy as opposed to the individual focused, 'private minded' responses to crime that are typical of most citizens (see Rosenbaum, 1988, p 126). Essentially, Neighbourhood or Block Watch involves citizens in a constituency coming together in relatively small groups (usually at a precinct level) to share information about the local crime problems, exchange crime prevention tips, and make plans for engaging in informal surveillance ('watching and noticing') (Shapland, 1988, p 117).

The most controversial aspect of the right realist approach lies in its emphasis on the criminalisation of even minor *public order offences* and *incivilities* that purportedly escalate the tendencies of *real crime* (Narayanan, 2000). Critics might invoke the Durkheimian perspective and suggest that what will follow from this premise is a continuing need to further escalate and expand the definition of crime (possibly even inventing new crimes) in order to continue to preserve the collective conscience by constantly enforcing its moral contours and boundaries. Criminal categories in Singapore, consonant with the 'disorder equals crime' equation, have thus ranged from major crimes like murder, robbery, theft and rape to those minor crimes and regulations affecting individual lifestyles and personal etiquette such as personal grooming (for example acceptable length of hair for males), flushing of public toilets, and even chewing of gum. The description provided by Austin (1989, p 916) is illustrative:

> Other regulations, which were necessarily imposed due to the extreme size and density of the populations, pertain to littering behaviour. Trash dropped on the sidewalk may bring a $500 fine. Spitting on the street or walkway is likewise seen as littering as well as a health hazard nuisance. The mobility of the citizen, whether on foot or in a vehicle, is highly regulated. Jaywalking may result in a $50 penalty ... Queuing for taxis is highly organised, and in parts of the city a taxi driver can be fined for picking up passengers at any point along the road other than at a queuing station. Further examples of community regulations are prohibitions against fruit or flower picking on any public land on the island, and a curfew against noise, generally in effect after 10 pm ... All citizens on reaching the age of 12 years are required to be fingerprinted and to carry official identification. Any change of address must be reported to the authorities within two weeks or the violator is subject to a $5000 fine, two years imprisonment, or both ...

It is this feature of Singapore society, the image of a highly regulated and disciplined society, which is usually cited in the local and international literature as contributing to a low crime rate in the city-state. Official statistics relating to crime must always be interpreted with caution before being used as assumed 'reliable' indicators for comparative purposes (Jupp, 1989, pp 92–101). This is the case with

Singapore, where official criminal statistics are a product of the Police Intelligence Department (PID). Independent studies do, however, indicate that the crime rate in Singapore is far lower than in most countries in the West and elsewhere in Asia (Buendia, 1989; Clutterbuck, 1985; Ong, 1984; Austin, 1989; Quah, 1994).

Recent crime statistics released by the PID for the year 2002 showed that the crime rate was the second lowest in 15 years after 2001, despite a 9.95% increase in total seizable offences (cases where the police could effect arrest without a warrant according to Schedule Criminal Procedure Code). Total recorded crime rose to 31,971 from 29,077 cases in 2001. Theft and related offences constituted more than half (52.9%) of the total seizable offences, with offences in this category witnessing an 8.6% increase from 15,573 to 16,920 cases in 2002. Juvenile crime – which has always been an area of concern for the police – saw a 55.8% increase in the number of juveniles arrested for the year 2002 (PID Statistics).

Unpacking the academic discourse on crime in Singapore

Academic debate has both an interior and exterior history. The interior history is the interchange between scholars buttressed by the material strength of departmental hierarchies and the underpinning of publishing outlets, together with access to external funding. But however autonomous this academic debate is considered to be by many of its participants, the interior dialogue is propelled by the exterior world. The dominant ideas of a period, whether establishment or radical; the social problems of a particular society; the government in power and the political possibilities existing in a society – all shape the interior discourse of the academic. Nowhere is this more evident than in criminology and the sociology of law. Exterior problems of crime, of lawmaking, of political options and current ideas, all profoundly shape the theories emanating from the interior world of academic criminology and legal scholarship ... (Young, 1994, p 71).

In Singapore, criminological research undertaken in the Sociology Department of the National University of Singapore (NUS), and contained in journal articles, consultancy works commissioned by the Ministry of Home Affairs, and other publications has clustered around three main areas. These relatively distinct areas consist largely of research done on *Chinese secret societies* (Wynne, 1941; Comber, 1959; Buckley, 1965; Blythe, 1969; Mak, 1973, 1981; Trocki, 1990; Long and Chiew, 1981; Chiew, 1983; Narayanan, 1994), *drug abuse* (Hanam, 1973, 1976; Wan and Yong, 1973; Ong, 1975a, 1975b; Lee, 1973, 1976; Teo, 1989; Ong, 1989; Mak, 1990; Yahya, 1991) and *crime prevention* (Ong, 1976; Mak, 1987; Pakiam and Lim, 1983; Quah and Quah, 1987; Austin, 1989; Ong, 1989; Quah, 1994). The re-emergence of the problem of secret societies after the Second World War (Narayanan, 1994), and an increase in drug abuse and criminal activities among the youth in the 1970s due to a perceived influence of a decadent Western culture (Goh, 1979) are identifiable factors which have directed research interests to these areas.

It is important to recognise that specific theories emanating from such research and from the interior world of academic criminology were also influenced by the kind of exterior history indicated by Young (1994). None of this is to suggest a relativism of theory but rather it is to point to its reflexivity, to the fact that theory emerges out of certain social and political conditions, and that each theory maintains a certain understanding of the criminal or the crime event. Further, as

Downes and Rock (1985) pointed out, criminology is not one coherent discipline but a collection of independent, sometimes conflicting theories.

Academics in Singapore have not as yet produced any particularly distinctive Singapore-oriented criminological theory. The theoretical framework used to conceptualise the crime phenomenon in Singapore does not differ in any marked degree from those in Western democracies. Nonetheless, evidence suggests that most empirical research and theoretical debate on crime and deviance in Singapore has relied extensively on social control theory of deviancy (Narayanan, 2002). The appeal of social control theory lies in its supposed greater explanatory power, and also in its alignment with the political and social persuasion of the Singapore state in emphasising macro-sociological (formal control systems) and more importantly, micro-sociological (informal control system) factors in promoting conformity in society (Narayanan, 2002).

Notable here is the Singaporean political elite's overwhelmingly Hobbesian world view, which assumes that human beings by nature are both asocial and antisocial. This provides the fundamental justification for the need to strengthen formal laws and to 'widen the net'. This Hobbesian view of the citizens has been the baseline for justifying the legislative powers of the ISA and the Criminal Law (Temporary Provisions) Act of 1955, Chapter 67 (revised 1985 edition) which allow the police to detain a person without trial for a maximum of two years. Political discourses on the possibility of another September 1964 race riot (that killed 13 and injured more than 100), the 1969 race riots, the 'Marxist conspiracy' of May 1987 and recently, the arrest of the local Jehamaah Islamiah (JI) cell members (linked to the Al-Qaeda terrorist organisation) have all been cited to justify the importance and relevance of these laws, and their draconian powers. These laws are thought to exemplify the ability of the state to preserve social order and provide the opportunity for its citizens to take pleasure in the safety and security which has come to characterise modern Singapore.

Both empirical research and theoretical debate on crime in Singapore have relied extensively on social control theory. Its common sense appeal and greater explanatory power readily aligns itself with the political and social persuasion of the state in emphasising the family being a key source of moral values (Hill and Lian, 1995, p 156). The family is understood to promote conformity in society. For this reason, it has assumed a central role in criminological research in Singapore. 'The family has been called upon to preserve the traditional cultural values and bear the responsibility for socialising the children in the virtues of the "rugged society"' (Kuo and Wong, 1979, p 11). The state aims to ensure the preservation of the family unit, whose role is clearly defined in the *White Paper on Shared Values* (1991, p 3). The family is seen as the 'fundamental building block out of which larger social structures can be stably constructed'. Abdullah Tarmugi, Minister of Community Development and Minister in charge of Muslim Affairs, outlined the importance of maintaining the family as a tool for inculcating good moral values in children (1995, p 99):

> Our families' strength and cohesiveness draw much from the traditional values that the various communities in Singapore hold and cherish. These values served us well over the past decades. We are therefore mindful that our traditional values and institutions should not be eroded by external influences and lifestyles which diminish the

importance of the traditional family and encourage nonchalance towards sexual morality ...

Alternative lifestyles (largely understood to be a Western cultural product), deficiency in 'Asian' values, inadequate socialisation, ineffective child rearing, lack of parental supervision, absence of good role models, casual sexual relationships and single parenthood are all seen to undermine the stability and structure of the traditional family unit, which is in turn perceived to be the cause of delinquency. These factors relate to what Harriet Wilson calls aspects of 'chaperonage' – relating to 'strict' rather than 'permissive' standards of morality (Wilson, 1980; Wilson and Herbert, 1978, p 176).

As early as in 1958, Benjamin Williams, in his investigation into the profile of a habitual offender, found that the single most important factor contributing to a present recidivist re-offending was the quality of relationships that an offender experienced in the home and wider informal community. Evidence that the family is as an important variable in explaining juvenile and adult criminal offending is also evident in a range of other research from the region: 'Social aspects of drug abuse amongst young people' (Vasoo, 1973); 'The drug scene in Singapore' (Hanam, 1973); 'Profiles of delinquents in Singapore' (Ngien, 1977); 'Vandals and vandalism in Singapore' (Fatt, 1978); 'A study on the psychosocial characteristics of male inhalant abusers in Singapore' (Teo, 1989); 'Crimes against property' (Wong, 1985); and 'Academic achievement, school adjustment and delinquency process' (Miao and Kong, 1971). It is interesting to note that the first few studies on female delinquency, Woon's 'Drug abuse among female addicts' (1976); Cheow's 'The delinquent girl in Singapore' (1959); and Kwa and Purushotam's (1974) 'Female delinquency in the light of the quality of the adolescent's home background' used similar variables to in explain the aetiology of female crime. For example, Kwa and Purushotam used variables like size of the family, controls in the home, parent-child relationship, and level of disorganisation in the family (that is, 'broken' home) to outline a causal theory of delinquency production. They conclude, in part, that 'more non-delinquents than delinquents came from homes characterised by a quality of family life that is better' (1974, pp 67–68).

A number of studies on the phenomena of gangs and youth drug use in Singapore (Mak, 1981; Wee, 1985; Man, 1991; Yahya, 1991; Noordin, 1992) employed subcultural and/or strain theoretical frameworks. Yahya (1991), for example, detailed the social process of how Malay youths become drug abusers, and identified some of the motives and rationalisations that were commonly used by the participants to sustain their drug activities. A notable aspect of this study is the recognition of how otherwise positive cultural features of the Malay community – the emphasis on a closely knit familial network and in-group solidarity – act as catalysts in the formation of a delinquent subculture since the essential group structure needed for the formation of a subculture has already been laid. In-group solidarity also tends to facilitate the learning process of becoming a member of a deviant subculture, for example, learning to smoke from the self-made pipe, to use the syringe, or even to achieve the desired level of being 'high'. Similar indications about the role of culture in the formation of delinquent subculture were also evident in Murphy's now classic study in which he investigated the problem of juvenile delinquency in the Chinese, Malay and Indian communities in Singapore (1963).

An interesting feature of these subcultural studies, with the exception of Mak's (1973, 1981) study on secret societies, were the attempts of the researchers to locate the origin of criminality within the family – an apparent reliance on the anchor point of social control theory. Research on Marina Kids, Malay drug subcultures and 'Mat Rokers' contains some very rich and intriguing data on the phenomena of criminal subcultures in Singapore. These studies have tended to turn to the family and informal social networks for individualised explanations as to why members join subcultures. Factors like poor parenting skills, poor parent-child relationships, lack of supervision over children, an inadequate or negative socialisation process, and transmission of an incompatible value and moral system to that of mainstream society are frequently cited in these studies as possible causes of criminal behaviour. The origin of criminality is once again rooted within the apparent 'dysfunctionality' of lower working class families.

Social policy in Singapore has been designed to curb the growth of the lower classes by restricting the size of working class families. This is achieved through the management of the Small Families Improvement Scheme – which was introduced primarily to 'help low income couples improve and upgrade themselves by keeping their families *small*' (Ng, 2003). This provides cash grants for women who agree to undergo sterilisation. Parents who agree to have no more than two children also qualify for assistance under the scheme (Hill and Lian, 1995, pp 153–54). In addition to these eligibility clauses, eligible participants should not possess any 'O' level passes in the GCE state examination, and have a combined monthly income of not more than (Singapore) \$750. This policy reflects the concerns of the political elite, who believe that every society has approximately 5% of its population who are more than ordinarily endowed, physically and mentally and that every care must be taken to ensure that this 'elitist group' receive the best nurturing that the state can offer (Rodan, 1996). Concomitantly, an equal effort must be expended to reduce the size of the physically, intellectually and culturally anaemic population – that is the lower working classes (Ng, 2003). The Small Families Improvement Scheme received further legitimisation through concerns expressed by Prime Minister, Goh Chok Tong, in 1993, that most dropouts from the educational system – about 1.7% of the total cohort (*Straits Times*, 16 August 1993) – are from large families living in a one or two room HDB flat, and having parents who have not attended secondary school (Hill and Lian, 1995, p 153). Policies to limit the size of working class families reflects a policy assumption on the part of the Singapore state that it is the middle class or the bourgeoisie, rather than the working class family, that plays the more effective role is social development (Berger and Berger, 1983, p 189; quoted in Hill and Lian, 1995, p 157).

When it comes to both sociological explanations and political discourses on the relationship between *crime* and *class*, a radical Marxist analysis is markedly absent in the Singaporean consciousness. This could be due to the prevalent perception amongst politicians, criminal justice professionals and the wider public that there are no distinct *class* differences in Singapore (Noordin, 1992). In Singapore, crime tends to be defined in terms of the variables of *ethnicity* and/or *race* (Benjamin, 1976). The 'ethnicisation' of crime is evidenced by the existence of formally mandated ethnicity-based self-help organisations, namely the *Chinese* Development Assistance Council (CDAC), MENDAKI (for *Malays*) and the Singapore *Indians* Development Association (SINDA) (emphasis added). The concentration on the relationship between ethnicity and crime depoliticises the crime problem by projecting it as constituting a peculiar 'community' character. This deflects attention from the wider structural, economic and social inequalities generated by state institutions and policies, particularly those associated with the capitalist mode of production. The state both maintains its legitimacy and protects the capitalist mode of production by appearing to take targeted action against the 'lumpen proletariats' of particular *ethnic* communities on behalf of all 'respectable' members of that community and of the wider citizenry. Kelsey's excellent work on gangs, for example, illustrates how the potential spread of dissatisfaction, which occurs when a capitalist economy is in crisis, is prevented by the criminalisation of that dissatisfaction, by presenting it as a 'law and order' issue to a frightened and receptive public (1980, p 5, quoted in Gidlow, 1982), hence concealing the crisis of legitimacy it embodies.

Conclusion

The chapter began with a discussion of, first, the possibility of detaching crime and criminal justice data from their social, economic and political contexts, and secondly, the usefulness of separating issues of 'crime' from 'crime control', particularly in a paternalistic and authoritative regime. These issues have important implications for the intellectual concerns of comparative criminology. It is argued here that any investigation into, and appreciation of, the crime problem must necessarily evaluate the sources and constructions of knowledge on the nature and extent of crimes as well as the objectives of crime control in *particular* socio-historical periods. This becomes especially important in the Singapore context, as the state police are the only agency that has the resources and legitimate authority to collate and communicate crime data to the populace. In the absence of victimisation and self-reported data (compounded by the relative paucity of local scholarly literature on crime and deviance), our knowledge on the crime problem and processes of crime control in Singapore is primarily state-defined and ideologically propagated.

In such a political and intellectual climate, an analysis of the policing system in relation to the authoritarian state offers an important starting point to conceptualising the phenomena of crime and the representations of it in Singapore society. While there are theoretical and methodological reasons to avoid simplistic talk of 'police models', the analysis pursued here does show that, in Singapore, policing tends to be readily aligned with the 'authoritarian' model of policing, where a strong political dynamic dominates a weak social dynamic. At the same time, the chapter also shows that Singaporean policing also displays features of the Anglo-Saxon model of 'community' policing based on the idea of 'policing by consent'.

Theoretically, the examination of the academic and political discourses on crime control reveals the distinct prominence of the social control perspective of a right realist variety. This could be explained, first, by its appeal to the political and social persuasion of the Singapore state in emphasising formal and informal control systems, particularly the family, in promoting conformity in society. Secondly, the popularity of the social control perspective is attributed to the political elite's overwhelmingly Hobbesian view of its citizens, which provides the fundamental justification for the need to expand the criminalisation process. That Singapore is an orderly, regulated and disciplined society (especially compared to Western liberal democracies), has often provided the justification for essentially repressive laws and an attitude of 'zero tolerance' towards perceived acts of non-conformity: the Singapore solution.

High levels of conformity and social discipline, however, are achieved at the expense of individual freedom of expression, which tends to arrest any development of an 'alternative discourse'. Further, the idea of working through consensus, as prescribed by the *White Paper on Shared Values* in Singapore, means that strategies undertaken by reformers and academics have to focus on accord rather than conflict. This is particularly telling given the authoritative nature of the Singapore state and its successful use of co-optative strategies to neutralise opposing voices (Chua, 1995). For example, the activities of pressure groups, interest groups and non-governmental organisations are restricted by the Societies Act which limits the kind of statements that such organisations may make, especially those defined by the state as 'political'. These may range from commenting on government policies to criticising methods of governance. Indeed, the government has clearly indicated that 'political commentary' may legitimately be made only by those who have explicitly joined a political forum, either through their membership of a political party or through a mandate given by the government, usually through state-sanctioned feedback units.

Given Singapore's political and social climate, the arrest of the intellectual development of criminology is palpable. In Singapore, the state has been very successful in ideologically propagating a criminology that seeks to individualise the problem of criminality as a predicament intrinsic to particular ethnic families. A consequence of this is the neutralisation of alternative explanations of crime that seek to focus on macro-level social and economic institutions. Whatever potential the explanatory power of social control theory has, the reduction of criminological theory in this way has forced a general abdication of intellectual responsibility to look at equally important structural factors such as those of class, race and gender. It is not that the informal social control exerted by strong and healthy families is unimportant, but rather, as Wilson writes:

> ... the essential point of our findings is the very close association of lax parenting methods with severe social handicap ... if these factors are ignored, and parental laxness is seen instead as an 'attitude' which by education or by punitive measures can be shifted, then our findings are being misinterpreted. It is the position of the most disadvantaged groups in society, and not the individual, which needs improvement in the first place (1980, pp 23–34).

Methodologically too, the narrowness of focus in Singaporean criminology is even more marked, with most researchers choosing to work with published official data on crime. Attempts to develop and test hypotheses from official data ignore (and thereby obscure) the social processes involved in the construction of those statistics. Fortunately, a few local researchers have been successful in punctuating the methodological monotony by injecting the qualitative sociologies of phenomenology, constructionism and interactionism. The state of criminology in Singapore is in dire need of researchers who are able to step outside imposed theoretical and methodological boundaries to capture and practise the criminological imagination.

References

Abdullah, T (1995) 'Singapore's approach to social development' 19(2) *Speeches* 88–92

Ames, W (1981) *Police and Community in Japan*, Berkeley: California UP

Austin, T (1989) 'Crime and its control', in Sandhu, KS and Wheatley, P (eds), *Management of Success*, Singapore: Institute of Southeast Asian Studies

Banton, M (1964) *The Policeman in the Community*, London: Tavistock

Bayley, DH (1989) *A Model of Community Policing: The Singapore Story*, US Department of Justice, National Institute of Justice

Bayley, DH (1991) *Forces of Order: Policing Modern Japan*, Berkeley: California UP

Beirne, P and Nelken, D (1997) *Issues in Comparative Criminology*, Aldershot: Dartmouth

Benjamin, G (1976) 'The cultural logic of Singapore's "multiculturalism"', in Riaz, H (ed), *Singapore: A Society in Transition*, Kuala Lumpur: OUP

Berger, P and Berger, B (1983) *The War Over the Family: Capturing the Middle Ground*, London: Hutchinson

Blythe, W (1969) *The Impact of Chinese Secret Societies in Malaya*, London: OUP

Brodeur, JP (1983) 'High policing and low policing: remarks about the policing of political activities' 30 *Social Problems* 507–20

Brodeur JP (1995) *Comparisons in Policing: An International Perspective*, Aldershot: Avebury

Brogden, M (1982) *The Police: Autonomy and Consent*, London: Academic

Buckley, CB (1965) *An Anecdotal History of Old Times in Singapore 1819–1867*, Kuala Lumpur: OUP

Buendia, HG (1989) *Urban Crime: Global Trends and Policies*, Tokyo: United Nations

Chen, PS and Tai, CL (1977) *Social Ecology of Singapore*, Singapore: Federal Publications

Cheow, LY (1959) 'The delinquent girl in Singapore', unpublished academic exercise, University of Malaya

Chiew, SK (1983) 'A profile of secret society gangsters in Singapore', in *Proceedings of the Second Asian-Pacific Conference of Juvenile Delinquency*, Seoul: Cultural and Social Centre for the Asian and Pacific Region

Chua, BH (1995) *Communitarian Ideology and Democracy in Singapore*, London: Routledge

Chua, BH (1997) *Political Legitimacy and Housing: Stakeholding in Singapore*, London: Routledge

Clutterbuck, R (1985) *Conflict and Violence in Singapore and Malaysia 1945–1983*, Singapore: Graham Brash

Cohen, S (1997) 'Western crime control models in the Third World: benign or malignant?', in Beirne, P and Nelken, D (eds), *Issues in Comparative Criminology*, Aldershot: Dartmouth

Comber, W (1959) *Chinese Secret Societies in Malaya*, London: Augustin

Downes, D and Rock, P (1985) *Understanding Deviance: A Guide to the Sociology of Crime and Rule-Breaking*, Oxford: OUP

Ee, GW (1982) 'The functions of the Singapore Police Force: a case study of the Jurong Police Station', unpublished academic exercise, National University of Singapore

Fatt, YT (1978) 'Vandals and vandalism in Singapore', unpublished academic exercise, University of Singapore

Freedman, M (1960) 'Immigrants and associations: Chinese in 19th century Singapore' 3(1) *Comparative Studies in Society and History* 25–48

Gidlow, B (1982) 'Deviance', in Spooney, P, Pearson, D and Shirley, I (eds), *New Zealand Perspectives*, Auckland: Dunmore Press

Goh, KS and The Educational Team (1979) *Report on the Ministry of Education 1978*, Singapore: Government of Singapore

Hanam, J (1976) 'Our problem', in Singapore Anti-Narcotics Association (ed), *Conquer Drug Abuse Now*, Singapore: Singapore Anti-Narcotics Association, pp 4–6

Hanam, J (1973) 'The drug scene in Singapore', in Lee, SK and Choa, TC (eds), *Drug Misuse in Singapore*, Singapore: Singapore Medical Association

Hassan, R (1976) *Singapore: Society in Transition*, Kuala Lumpur: OUP

Heal, K and Laycock, G (1988) 'The development of crime prevention: issues and limitations', in Hope, T and Shaw, M (eds), *Communities and Crime Reduction*, London: HMSO

Hill, M and Lian KF (1995) *The Politics of Nation-building and Citizenship in Singapore*, London: Routledge

Hope, T and Shaw, M (1988) 'Community approaches to reducing crime', in Hope, T and Shaw, M (eds), *Communities and Crime Reduction*, London: HMSO

Jupp, V (1989) *Methods of Criminological Research*, London: Routledge

Kuo, ECY and Wong, AK (1979) *The Family in Contemporary Singapore*, Singapore: Singapore UP

Kwa, KH and Purushotam, S (1974) 'Female delinquents in the light of the quality of the adolescent's home background: a comparison between delinquents and non-delinquents', unpublished academic exercise, University of Singapore

Lee, SH (1973) 'Some aspects of student drug abuse', unpublished academic exercise, University of Singapore

Lee, SW (1976) 'Recidivism among drug users: a case study', unpublished academic exercise, National University of Singapore

Lim, HT (1971) 'The origin of the Malayan civil service' 26 *Journal of the South Seas Society* 46–60

Long, FY and Chiew, SK (1981) *A Study on the Profile of Chinese Secret Society Members*, report submitted to the Ministry of Home Affairs, Singapore

Low, KH (1995) 'Recognising strangers: gay cruising in the city', unpublished academic exercise, National University of Singapore

Low, S (1993) 'Lesbianism in Singapore', unpublished academic exercise, National University of Singapore

Mak, LF (1973) 'The forgotten and rejected community – a sociological study of Chinese secret societies in Singapore and western Malaysia', unpublished working papers, University of Singapore

Mak, LF (1981) *The Sociology of Chinese Secret Societies: A Study of Chinese Secret Societies in Singapore and Peninsular Malaysia*, Oxford: OUP

Mak, LF (1987) 'Private and public high rise housing and fear of victimisation' 1 *Chinese Journal of Sociology* 133–48

Mak, LF (1990) *Report on Drug Addiction in Singapore*, report submitted to the Ministry of Home Affairs, Singapore

Man, YC (1991) 'A sociological study of the Marina Kids', unpublished academic exercise, National University of Singapore

Marenin, O (1982) 'Parking tickets and class repression: the concept of policing in critical theories of criminal justice' 6 *Contemporary Crises* 241–66

Miao, SM and Kong, GL (1971) 'Academic achievement, school adjustment and delinquency process in a housing estate school', unpublished academic exercise, University of Singapore

Ministry of Information and the Arts (1997) *Singapore Facts and Figures*, Singapore: Ministry of Information and the Arts

Monjardet, D (1995) 'The French model of policing', in Brodeur, JP (ed), *Comparisons in Policing: An International Perspective*, Aldershot: Avebury

Moore, MH (1992) 'Problem-solving and community policing', in Michael, T and Morris, N (eds), *Modern Policing*, Chicago: Chicago UP

Murphy, HBM (1963) 'Juvenile delinquency in Singapore' 61 *Journal of Social Psychology* 201–31

Narayanan, G (1994) 'The development of criminal policies in the suppression of Chinese secret societies in Singapore', unpublished Masters thesis, Brunel University

Narayanan G (2000) 'Conceptualising community policing, crime prevention and criminology: a Singapore perspective' 33(3) *Australian and New Zealand Journal of Criminology* 266–86

Narayanan, G (2002) 'Crime and deviance', in Tong, CK and Lian, KF (eds), *The Making of Singapore Sociology: Society and State*, Singapore: Brill and Times Academic Press

Narayanan, G and Somo, V (1993) 'Indian gangs in Singapore', paper presented at the Biennial Seminar/Conference, 15 August 1993, Tamil Language Society of the National University of Singapore

Newman, O (1978) *Defensible Space: Crime Prevention Through Urban Design*, London: Architectural Press

Ng, E (2003) 'Social escorts in Singapore', unpublished academic exercise, National University of Singapore

Ngien, S (1977) 'Profiles of delinquents in Singapore', unpublished academic exercise, University of Singapore

Noordin, S (1992) 'Mat Rokers: an insight into a Malay youth subculture', unpublished academic exercise, National University of Singapore

Office of the Prime Minister of Singapore (1991), *White Paper on Shared Values*, Singapore: Government Press

Ong, JH (1975a) *The Problem of Drug Abuse Among Singapore Youths*, report submitted to the Ministry of Home Affairs, Singapore

Ong, JH (1975b) *A Profile of the Criminal in Singapore*, report submitted to the CIU/CID, Ministry of Home Affairs, Singapore

Ong, JH (1976) *Criminal Patterns of Housebreaking and Thefts and Robberies with Special Emphasis on Crimes in HDB Estates*, report submitted to CIU/CID, Ministry of Home Affairs, Singapore

Ong, JH (1989) 'Community security', in Sandhu, KS and Wheatley, P (eds), *Management of Success*, Singapore: Institute of Southeast Asian Studies

Ong, SC (1984) *Crime trends and Crime Prevention Strategies in Singapore*, paper presented at UNU-UNAFET International Expert Meeting in Tokyo, 29–31 May

Ong, TH (1989) *Drug Abuse in Singapore*, Singapore: Hillview Press

Pakiam, JE and Lim, M (1983) 'Temporal patterns of crime in Singapore' 7(2) *International Journal of Comparative and Applied Criminal Justice* 159–94

Quah, JST (1994) 'Crime prevention: Singapore style' 14 *Asian Journal of Public Administration* 149–85

Quah, JST and Ong, SC (1989) 'Singapore', in Buendia, HG (ed), *Urban Crime: Global Trends and Policies*, Tokyo: The United Nations University

Quah, S and Quah, JST (1987) *Friends in Blue: The Police and Public in Singapore*, Singapore: OUP

Reiner, R (1985) *Politics of the Police*, London: Harvester Wheatsheaf

Reiner, R (1995) 'Myth vs modernity: reality and unreality in the English model of policing', in Brodeur JP (ed), *Comparisons in Policing: An International Perspective*, Aldershot: Avebury

Rodan, G (1996) 'Class transformations and political tensions in Singapore's development', in Robison, R and Goodman, D (eds), *The New Rich in Asia: Mobile Phones, McDonalds and Middle-Class Revolution*, London: Routledge

Rosenbaum, DP (1988) 'A critical eye on neighbourhood watch; does it reduce crime and fear?', in Hope, T and Shaw, M (eds), *Communities and Crime Reduction*, London: HMSO

Saw, SH (1973) *Singapore Standard Crime Classification*, Singapore: National Statistical Commission

Shapland, J (1988) *Policing with the Public?*, London: HMSO

Shapland, J and Hobbs, D (1987) *Policing on the Ground in Highland*, Oxford: Centre for Criminological Research

Singapore Police Force (1977) *Police Life*, Singapore: Singapore Police Force

Singapore Police Force (1998) *Annual Report 1997/98*, Singapore: Singapore Police Force

Skolnick, JH and Bayley, DH (1986) *The New Blue-line: Police Innovation in Six American Cities*, New York: Free Press

Sparrow, MK, Moore, MH and Kennedy DM (1990) *Beyond 911: A New Era For Policing*, New York: Basic Press

Spitzer, S and Scull, A (1977) 'Social control in historical perspective', in Greenberg (ed), *Corrections and Punishment*, Beverly Hills: Sage

Stenson, K (1991) 'Making sense of crime control', in Stenson, K and Cowell, D (eds), *The Politics of Crime Control*, London: Sage

Storch, R (1976) 'The policeman as domestic missionary' 30 *Journal of Social History Today*

Straits Times, 16 August 1993; 10 April 1998; 27 April 1998

Teo, PH (1989) 'A study on the psychosocial characteristics of male inhalant abusers in Singapore', unpublished academic exercise, National University of Singapore

Toh, SM (1988) 'Community policing in Singapore: a case study of the Toa Payoh Neighbourhood Police Post', unpublished academic exercise, National University of Singapore

Trocki, CA (1990) *Opium and Empire: Chinese Society in Colonial Singapore 1800–1910*, Ithaca: Cornell UP

Vasoo, J (1973) 'Social aspects of drug abuse amongst young people', in Lee, SK and Chao, TC (eds), *Drug Misuse in Singapore*, Singapore: Singapore Medical Association

Wan, PY and Yong, HK (1973) 'Drug addiction amongst youths in Singapore', unpublished academic exercise, University of Singapore

Wee, YG (1985) 'Breakdancers: an exploratory study', unpublished academic exercise, National University of Singapore

Williams, B (1958) 'The habitual offender', unpublished academic exercise, University of Malaya

Wilson, H (1980) 'Parental supervision: a neglected aspect of delinquency', *British Journal of Criminology* 20

Wilson, H and Herbert, G (1978) *Parents and Children in the Inner-City*, London: Routledge & Kegan Paul

Wilson, JQ (1975a) *Varieties of Police Behavior*, Cambridge, Massachusetts: Harvard UP

Wilson, JQ (1975b) *Thinking About Crime*, New York: Vintage

Wilson, JQ and Kelling, G (1982) 'Broken windows', *The Atlantic Monthly*, pp 29–38

Wong, KSC (1985) *Crimes Against Property: A Study of Violent and Non-violent Offenders*, unpublished PhD thesis, National University of Singapore

Woon, CM (1976) 'Drug abuse among female addicts', unpublished academic exercise, National University of Singapore

Wynne, WL (1941) *Triad and Tabut*, Singapore: Government Printing Office

Yahya, SC (1991) 'Drug abuse: a sociological study of Malay drug addicts in Singapore', unpublished academic exercise, National University of Singapore

Young, J (1994) 'Incessant chatter: recent paradigms in criminology', in Maguire, M, Morgan, R and Reiner, R (eds), *The Oxford Handbook of Criminology*, Oxford: OUP

Chapter 8
Crime and Criminal Justice in China 1949–99
Carol Jones

The past and the present

Talk about crime in China cannot be understood outside its political context. During the Maoist period (1949–76), for example, Cold War propaganda demanded that China be depicted as tranquil, socially unified, harmonious and crime-free, the opposite of the decadent, crime-ridden, capitalist, 'West'. Since 1979, however, it is said that China has experienced a 'crime wave' and is becoming more like the 'West'. In 1979, Deng Xiaoping returned China to capitalism and to law. Symptomatic of this was the re-establishment of the Chinese criminal justice system in the 1979 Criminal Law (CL) and Criminal Procedure Law (CPL).

Those in favour of this shift (Rightists or Reformers) argued that China's 1949 peasant revolution had accidentally leapfrogged a necessary stage on the road to socialism. China must experience capitalism since, according to Marx, only when all stages of the evolutionary process had been properly completed could true communism occur. Since capitalism was historically necessary, its by-products (crime, inequality) were also inevitable. As with modernisation theory, crime was a product of material forces outwith political control, impossible to eliminate without reverting to Maoism, the command economy and international isolation.

However, those who clung to the ideals of Maoism (Remnant Maoists or Leftists) did not see crime as inevitable but as a consequence of Deng Xiaoping 'Opening the door to the West'. On their view, foreign investment had flown in but so had the 'flies' of 'Western' decadence. Crime was thus something contagious China 'caught' from the West.

The one point of agreement between these two factions was that crime was something endemic to capitalism. For those who favoured going down the 'capitalist road' it was something which simply had to be borne: their opponents disagreed. Some of the oscillations in what was said and done about crime in post-Mao China have their origin in struggles between these factions of the ruling elite. Even post-Mao, then, talk about crime was highly politicised.

At the grass roots level, the public also talked about crime. Surveys indicated a Chinese public worried about the deterioration of public order since 1979, with almost 50% saying they did not dare go out on the streets at night (Tan Shen and Li Dun, 1993, p 353). Official statistics also showed massive rises in 'public security offences' as well as rises in serious crime.

The dominant view which emerges from this discourse is that Chinese crime and criminal justice fall into two distinct periods:

(i) the Maoist Era (1949–76) when crime was virtually non-existent; and

(ii) the post-Mao period (1976–) marked by successive 'crime waves'.

The Maoist Period (1949–76)

The mid-1950s to mid-1960s in China is remembered as a 'Golden Age' of social cohesion, stability and order, of a virtuous people working for the common good, living frugally but honestly, 'when doors were left unlocked at night and no one pocketed anything found on the road'. It was also a time of successive campaigns aimed at building socialism (increasing production, grain output, etc) as well as eliminating negative or 'bad elements' (beliefs and practices which undercut socialism).

Cohen's account of Chinese criminal justice at this time describes large numbers of unpublished regulations, instructions, orders, policies, reports and judicial interpretations continuously revised in the light of China's experience and needs (Cohen, 1968, p 23; Tanner, 1999, p 21). Those who persistently resisted communism were imprisoned, exiled or executed. Certain offenders, such as landlords, simply had to be coerced or killed for land reform to succeed (Chen, 1960, p 73), since the exploiting classes would never voluntarily relinquish their power – it had to be taken from them by force. As Mao famously said, revolution is not a dinner party.

When offenders were 'struggled against' depended on what was seen as harmful behaviour at the time; *how* they were handled depended on their class background – someone from a bad class background (for example, a landlord family) received harsher punishment than someone from a proletarian or peasant background. Offences which reflected a 'contradiction between the state and the people' were dealt with more severely than 'contradictions amongst the people', which reflected not so much opposition to socialism as an erroneous understanding of it. Such 'errors' could be corrected through 'thought reform'. This 'remoulded' offenders so that they shed their old ideas and 'adopted a proletarian outlook'. 'Struggle sessions' (sometimes large-scale, public affairs) helped offenders acknowledge their errors, make 'self-criticism' and become good socialist citizens.

Re-Education Through Labour (RETL) and Reform Through Labour (RTL)

During these early years, a division arose between judicial punishments handed down for 'serious offences' by the courts after trial, and administrative punishments handed out by the police for other offences, without trial. Imprisonment and execution were sentences of the court. The death penalty could be suspended for two years whilst imprisoned offenders demonstrated whether they were capable of reform; if they did not, the sentence was carried out. Offenders sent to prison were deemed to have caused 'serious harm' to society. They were sent for Reform Through Labour (RTL or *laogai*). Prisons doubled as production units and were overseen by the Ministry of Justice.

The 'seriousness' of RTL offences was not defined by law but by the authorities and changed as the priorities and policies of the CCP changed. However, opposition to the CCP always merited RTL or execution. This explains why, at the end of the Maoist period in 1976, China's prisons were full of 'counter-revolutionaries'. Estimates as to how many people were incarcerated during the Maoist period vary widely. The Chinese authorities always insisted that the prison population was very low, but overseas critics put the numbers held in the *laogai* system between 1949 and 1979 as somewhere between 6–8 million, 16 million, and 50 million (see Seymour and Anderson, 1998, p 18; Wu, 1996). Tanner estimates that of those imprisoned in the 1950s, about 90% were classed as 'counter-revolutionaries' (Tanner, 1994, cited in Seymour and Anderson, 1998, p 16).

In 1957, the CCP ordered that counter-revolutionaries and other 'bad elements' be subjected to a period of re-education if their behaviour was not serious enough to deserve a long prison sentence (Tanner, 1999, p 39). They were to be sent to Re-Education Through Labour (RETL) centres (*laojiao*) for up to five years. Offenders were those whose behaviour was deemed to have fallen 'somewhere between crime and error' (Seymour and Anderson, 1998, p 19). RETL institutions were 'to reform into self-supporting new persons those persons with the capacity to labour who loaf, who violate law and discipline, or who do not engage in proper employment, and in order to preserve public order and to benefit socialist reconstruction' (Fu, 1997, p 134). Schools, parents, enterprises or any other organisation to which an individual belonged could ask for the sanction to be applied (Fu, 1997, p 134). The main targets were city dwellers and those who:

(i) did not engage in proper employment, behaved like hooligans, and who, though 'they steal, swindle, or engage in other such acts, are not pursued for criminal responsibility' but who violated security administration and whom repeated education failed to change;

(ii) counter-revolutionaries and anti-socialist reactionaries whose crimes were minor, had been expelled from their work unit or school and had no way of making a living;

(iii) persons who had the capacity to labour but for long periods refused to work, or 'destroy discipline and interfere with public order', had been expelled from their work unit or school and had no means of livelihood; and

(iv) those who did not obey work assignments, arrangements for getting them a job or warnings to get a job, and who 'ceaselessly and unreasonably make trouble and interfere with public affairs and whom repeated education fails to change' (Tanner, 1999, p 40).

RETL was applied by local committees, 'grassroots organs of social control', consisting of representatives from the local organs of civil administration but in practice dominated by the police. The same committee which applied the sanction could extend or remit the period of detention at its discretion, so that some people found themselves detained indefinitely. RETL was overseen by the Ministry of Public Security (PSB, China's police force), and the power to detain offenders for RETL was purely an administrative (that is, non-judicial) power. It was always intended to be an *informalised* system of state control.

Many of those sent to RETL were classed as petty offenders, 'loafers' and 'idlers' who were failing to contribute to the building of a new China. Others, such as prostitutes, adulterers and gamblers offended against socialist puritanism, or displayed 'feudal thinking', 'greed, acquisitiveness and selfishness'. Some were political dissidents but the 1957 RETL Regulations placed this second – most of the behaviour targeted was not overtly political (Tanner, 1999, p 40).

Forced job placement

On completion of their RTL sentences, prisoners could also be sent to Forced Job Placement (FJP), established in 1954. Rebuilding China required a large, compliant and cheap workforce, particularly in heavy industries and agriculture. Labour camps could request permission from the PSB to transfer prisoners who had completed their sentence to FJP. Thus, prisoners who should have been released were kept within the confines of the camp to undertake productive work. The absence of any time limit on FJP effectively meant that a detainee could face a lifetime of internal exile in forced labour.

Campaign justice

Many 'offenders' sent to RETL, RTL and FJP in the 1950s were rounded up during one of Mao's many mass campaigns. In 1951, for example, the 'Three-Anti' and 'Five-Anti' campaigns targeted 'three enemies of the economy' (bureaucratism, waste and corruption). Chen characterises this as a period of:

> public trials, mass arrests and executions, and a horrible system of mutual spying and informing which penetrated into the intimate circles of the family ... Accusations and confessions filled the air; public trials and swift punishment in the form of dismissal or fines or imprisonment or even summary execution were given wide publicity; and all 'patriotic citizens' were urged to take up 'tiger hunting', that is, expose specific cases ... (Chen, 1960, p 52).

Esther Cheo Ying[1] recalls that such campaigns:

> swept the country like a dose of salts, and officials, writers, artists, people in the public eye were purged and flushed out in a tidal wave of hysteria. Then the criticism meetings and self-examinations were intensified among the mass of government workers to pinpoint anyone who had the same ideas and sympathies as the people in trouble ... (Ying, 1980, p 85).

Fear of becoming a target of criticism meant that everyone needed to be seen to participate in the campaigns. Listening to and mobilising the masses around social problems was a style of governance ('the mass line'). There were campaigns against flies (in which everyone had to kill a quota of 10 flies per day) and sparrows (blamed for eating grain). Crime was simply another kind of target. Thousands of offenders were rounded up and placed in detention centres and labour camps; some were executed, others endured 'struggle sessions'.

New campaigns started every time the CCP identified a new 'evil'. In 1956, Mao initiated a campaign to 'Let 100 Flowers Bloom' (that is, allow alternative ideas to be aired). The unexpectedly bitter attacks on the Party which were voiced led to another campaign in 1957 to root out 'Rightists'. The anti-Rightist campaign bore all the hallmarks of the Maoist regime's conception of crime as a political act. 1957 saw the end of what Cohen calls the 'Golden Age' of Chinese law. A draft Criminal Code circulated within the National People's Congress (NPC) in 1956 was abandoned and

---

1 I am indebted to Robert Turner and Lindsay Ward for alerting me to Cheo's little-known book about her experiences in China during this period.

a 1963 criminal code was also mothballed following the onset of the Socialist Education Campaign. Nothing was heard of either until the drafting of 1979 Criminal Law (Tanner, 1999; Bonavia, 1981).

In Maoist China, therefore, a 'crime' was not an act of breaking the law, since there was no law to break. There were regulations on the penalties for murder, rape and other 'ordinary crimes', and the measures to be taken against 'counter-revolutionaries', but all these were unpublished (Shao-chuan Leng and Hungdah Chiu, 1985, p 123). Moreover, as Bonavia writes, a political activist who caused the death of someone seen as a 'bad element' might escape prosecution, whilst a former landlord who accidentally killed a party activist would almost certainly be sentenced to death (Bonavia, 1981, pp 134, 136).

'Wrong thinking' could also be an offence. It is impossible to estimate how many people were sanctioned for erroneous thoughts, since many were dealt with by 'struggle sessions' in their work unit (*danwei*) or neighbourhood committees. In China, this web of informalised state controls were likened to the KGB, a secret 'police'. The 'nosy old ladies' of the Neighbourhood Committees *were* mediators but they were *also* spies in the community. One Chinese critic accused the CCP of subjecting the masses to 'surveillance by plain-clothes police, whose main job was to make all kinds of intelligence reports to the Party organisation' (cited in Chen, 1960, p 164). Another criticised the all-pervasive system of Party control whereby 'through the length and breadth of the nation, in every unit, big or small, down to the smallest government department or bureau, there is always a Party man ...' (Chen, 1960, p 165).

These were not institutions of civil society outwith the state, but informalised institutions *of* the state. They were led by political activists; group pressure was always manipulated from behind the scenes; 'public confessions were demanded and given wide publicity' (Chen, 1960, p 30). Non-government organisations, such as the Young Communist League, the Women's Federation and the All China Federation of Trade Unions, were central to enlisting participation in the control of 'counter-revolutionaries' and criminals (Lubman, 1999, p 42). Using these *informalised* mechanisms of state control, the CCP penetrated deep into the social fabric and personal life, extending what Shue (1988) calls 'the reach of the state'. They created a gaze far more 'panoptical' than anything designed by Bentham.

The Security and Punishment Act (and Regulations) or SAPA

The local committees were what Fu calls the 'first line of defence' in China's armoury of social order measures, creating and maintaining 'socialist morality' (Fu, 1997, p 133). The 'second line of defence' against disorder was a swathe of administrative regulations, and the third (the 'reserve army') the criminal law.

The 'second line of defence' included RETL and the Security and Punishment Administration regulations (SAPA). SAPA was introduced in 1957. It aimed to control the population of the cities and operated as a 'sort of shadow criminal law' administered exclusively by the police (Tanner, 1999, p 37). It allowed them to impose a warning, a fine, and/or administrative detention.

SAPA was intended as an intermediate sanction, to be imposed where criminal sanctions would be too severe but where informal warnings, social censure and persuasion had failed (Cohen, 1968, p 200). SAPA offences ('public security offences') included anything which detracted from a 'healthy cultural environment' (Tanner, 1999, p 38). Early regulations covered over 60 offences, including prostitution, gambling, disturbing public order, harassing women, illegal possession of guns and knives, gang fighting, selling reactionary books, spreading rumours and making trouble, forging documents, wilfully making loud noises that disturbed city residents, throwing lumps of mud at trains, using obscene language, beating up others, damaging agricultural crops and livestock, dumping rubbish or filth in the streets, urinating or defecating in the street, drying things in the sun, or cooking articles with a foul odour, dirtying well water, cursing others, intentionally damaging grass, flowers or trees in city parks, taking the lead in an uproar, and wilfully pasting advertisements or items of propaganda in places other than those assigned (Cohen, 1968, pp 214–18; Tanner, 1999, p 38).

It was not always clear where the line was to be drawn between offences which required SAPA punishment and those which demanded RETL or RTL. The police determined the 'seriousness' of the harm and hence which came next. Those detained under SAPA could be held for not less than half a day and not more than 10 days. However, since there was no judicial oversight of this system (and no rule prohibiting them from not doing so), the police could play a cat and mouse game with offenders, detaining them for 15 days, releasing them, and re-detaining them for another 15 days. Offenders might also be asked to pay compensation and make a statement of repentance (Cohen, 1968).

Shelter and Repatriation (S and R or *shourong qiansong*)

'Shelter and Repatriation' was another administrative measure applied by the police. It was first used to send former Guomingdang troops, 'refugees' and the unemployed out of the cities into the countryside. In the early 1950s, over 1.2 million ex-Guomingdang servicemen were rounded up, together with over 750,000 refugees in the coastal areas and around 1.1 million jobless people in seven main cities. 1.12 million 'vagrant beggars' were also put into custody and 'educated' (HRW/HRIC, 1999).

S and R was used repeatedly to control the flow of migrant workers from the countryside into the cities. China's *hukou* is a system of household registration dividing the population into rural and city dwellers. By prohibiting movement between the two it has 'decisively shaped' China's social system by creating a hierarchy in which city dwellers and state sector workers gained privileged access to income, healthcare, housing, grain rations, education, employment, and retirement (Fei Guo, 1996). Those who lived in the countryside were bottom of the hierarchy (Fei Guo, 1996). When, in the 1950s, the CCP encouraged them to take jobs in China's industries, the numbers who rushed into the cities exceeded demand. Famine also drew peasants to the cities in search of food. Cities became crowded with unemployed, homeless, and poverty stricken migrants. Thus, in 1953, the CCP ordered that peasants who were not employed in the cities, as well as vagrants, to return home. In 1956, under 'repatriation', over 420,000 vagrants were taken into custody and educated, and 90 'vagrant education farms' were established to which more than 26,000 people were sent (HRW/HRIC, 1999). During the 1959–61 famine which followed the Great Leap Forward, S and R was also deployed against peasants seeking to enter the cities in search of food. Many were detained and sent home, where they died of hunger (HRW/HRIC, 1999). In 1959, three million people were subject to S and R, in 1960, six million and in 1961, two million (HRW/HRIC, 1999). Those detained were peasants 'who enter the cities and become homeless and have no food', and city dwellers who 'have no means of livelihood and are homeless' (HRW/HRIC, 1999). By 1963, there were 101 Resettlement Farms (*anzhi nongchang*) holding 36,000 persons who could not be 'repatriated'.

S and R remained 'on the books' throughout the Maoist period. In the 1980s, it was revived to control the flow of population set into motion by Deng's economic reforms.

Shelter and Investigation (S and I or *shourong shencha*)

'Shelter and Investigation' (sometimes called 'Shelter for Examination') was yet another administrative measure introduced in the 1950s. Like S and R, its roots lie in the famine caused by the Great Leap Forward, when starving people flocked from the countryside to the cities searching for food (Tanner, 1999, p 35). However, it was specifically aimed at 'roving criminal suspects' (that is, persons thought to be committing crimes whilst wandering from place to place, or who had committed criminal acts but refused to give their name and address. See Clarke and Feinerman, 1995, p 143; Hsia and Zeldin, 1993, p 8).

In 1963, the Ministry of Public Security decided to build S and I centres modelled on centres for S and R, established in 1961 in the major cities (Tanner, 1999, p 36). Detainees were held whilst the police investigated their backgrounds and activities. Importantly, however, S and I was not to be used against:

(i)   persons suspected of committing crimes in their *local* area;

(ii) persons whose backgrounds were clearly *known*; or

(iii) persons against whom there was *evidence* to prove that they had committed a crime (Hsia and Zeldin, 1993, p 8).

However, when S and I was revamped by the police in the 1980s, it was extended to detain precisely these groups of people.

The Cultural Revolution

The Cultural Revolution (1966–76) is usually spoken of in China as a period of extraordinary lawlessness, 'the 10 years of turmoil', 'hooliganism', 'smashing and looting'. The organisations of the state were dismantled; public order collapsed. Youth across China left their homes and families to participate, some joining the Red Guards. (Later, China's rise in juvenile crime would be linked to this.) The rank and file in every institution were called upon to expose Party officials who had become 'capitalist roaders', adopted an authoritarian manner in their work, a superior attitude towards the workers, or had taken advantage of their position

(Robinson, 1969, p 14). Those who were not executed or imprisoned were 'sent down to the countryside to learn from the peasants'. Street processions, public denigration and execution of suspects were common. At the height of the Cultural Revolution:

> it was enough to make a slip of the tongue or the pen and refer to a political leader – particularly Mao – without the required degree of reverence, or accidentally break a bust of him, or smear his picture in a newspaper or magazine, to be accused of being a 'counter-revolutionary' and suffer vicious harassment by teenage Red Guards or be sent to prison or a labour camp … (Bonavia, 1981, p 136).

There are no reliable figures for crime and disorder in this period. It is generally agreed that thousands of people were punished in violent, highly arbitrary and capricious ways. The People's Liberation Army eventually brought the Cultural Revolution to a halt, but with no formal judicial systems, it fell to the police to restore and maintain public order. This placed them in powerful position when, on the death of Mao in 1976, the CCP sought a return to law and order.

The post-Mao period: 1979 and the 'Turn to Law' and the free market

China's 'Turn to Law' in 1979 is usually seen as a reaction to the arbitrariness of the Cultural Revolution. The 1979 CL and CPL were the first in China since 1949. Thoughts would no longer be crimes; there was to be a written criminal code and only specified officials would have the power to invoke it. Deng's 1979 economic reforms were also welcomed in the 'West' as signalling China's return to the 'capitalist road'. In terms of law and economy, therefore, 1979 was widely seen as a clear break with the past. However, certain continuities in policing can be detected.

Under the 1979 CPL, the police fell under the authority of the Ministry of Public Security; the procuratorate (prosecution) under the Supreme People's Procuracy; and the Ministry of Justice, and the courts under the Supreme People's Court. The police were responsible for detection, investigation and arrest, the procuratorate for approval of arrests, formal accusation and prosecution, and the courts for trials. Suspects were granted the right to be defended either by a lawyer or another person of their choice (Lubman, 1999, p 162). However, as in many other Civil Law systems, the procuratorate and judiciary retained the power to investigate. The result, Fu argues, was a system of overlapping jurisdictions and conflicts of institutional interest (Fu, 1997, p 130).

The new CL specified eight types of crime: counter-revolutionary offences; endangering public security; undermining the socialist economic order; infringing a citizen's personal or democratic rights; encroachment upon property; disrupting the governing of social order; malfeasance; and offences against marriage and family. A 'counter-revolutionary' offence was 'any act committed with the aim of overthrowing the political order of the dictatorship of the proletariat and the socialist system and endangers the People's Republic of China' (Leng and Chiu, 1985, p 124ff). Such acts included sabotage and criticisms of state and Party policy. They carried a lengthy prison sentence and/or the death penalty. 'Undermining the socialist economic order' included offences such as profiteering, speculation, tax evasion, and smuggling. Offences such as fraud, theft, robbery and embezzlement fell into the category of 'encroachment upon property'. 'Endangering public security' included arson, harming the security of the person, public property or public safety. 'Disrupting the governing of social order' included drug trafficking, selling pornography, prostitution, gambling, mob disturbances, 'hooligan' activities, harbouring criminals and so forth. 'Infringing the personal or democratic rights of persons' included forcing women into prostitution, rape, kidnapping, homicide, gathering together to smash, beat or loot, the use of torture to extract confessions, and tampering with elections (Leng and Chiu, 1985).

Articles 179–84 dealt with offences against marriage and family, which included bigamy, the abandonment of a family member, abandonment of the old, young, or an invalid, the abduction of minors under 14, breaking up a military marriage, and interference with the freedom of marriage. Malfeasance included acts by state officials such as dereliction of duty, bribery, and divulging state secrets. What constituted a 'state secret' or a 'counter-revolutionary' offence was very vague. The definition of 'socially dangerous' was also determined 'not only by the sum total of all the components of the crime ... but also by current, extraneous conditions' (Leng and Chiu, 1985, p 133). Thus, the law was still an instrument to protect socialism and advance the dictatorship of the proletariat. Legality was not an end in itself.

With regard to criminal procedure, under the CPL, proceedings could be initiated by the police, citizens, non-government agencies, victims, procuratorate or courts. Usually, it fell to the police to decide whether or not an offence constituted a 'crime'. Only when a case was formally filed, and the investigation began, was the crime recorded. China's crime statistics therefore depended totally upon whether or not cases were filed by the investigatory agencies (Fu, 1997, p 132). Once a case had been established by the procuratorate, the file was sent for trial. A trial was heard by a judge and two 'people's assessors' or three judges.

However, no trial could begin until the verdict had been decided by the police, prosecution and judges. The practice of 'verdict first, trial second' (*xian pan hou shen*) reflected the fact that Chinese courts were supervised by, and integrated into, the political structure. 'Important or sensitive' cases were not handled by the court at all, but by an Adjudication Committee. Every court had such a committee. Consisting of the vice-president of the court as well as members of the local people's congress and Party officials, its role was to ensure that certain cases were decided in keeping with Party policy.

Though the 1979 law introduced trials, these still resembled Maoist courts. There was no presumption of innocence or right to silence – the person on trial was presumed guilty. The trial itself was not about establishing guilt or innocence but a morality play and a display of state power. In theory, defendants were entitled to call and cross-examine witnesses, argue the facts of the case and be defended by a lawyer. In practice, proceedings were inquisitorial rather than adversarial, witnesses were almost never called, and lawyers permitted a very limited role. Trials were (and are) basically 'paper procedures'.

The CPL left the police as the 'gatekeepers' of the new system. Moreover, it did nothing to limit their vast array of extra-judicial sanctions. These could be used without recourse to the criminal courts at all, allowing the police to circumvent the suspect's new due process rights. Since 1979, the police have in fact processed offenders using these administrative powers two or three times more than they have used their criminal powers. Up to six times as many offenders are 'sentenced' by the police for public security offences as by the courts. Crime figures derived from the official legal system thus give a highly misleading picture of crime in China.

The 1980s: 'Strike Hard' anti-crime campaigns (*yandas*)

China's economic reforms were accompanied in the 1980s by a 'crime wave', giving rise to heightened fear of crime amongst the public. There was also something of a moral panic about crime amongst the CCP leadership. The 1950s – 'when China had its lowest ever annual crime rate' – was seen as the 'norm' (Leng and Chiu, 1985, p 131). Set against this ideal, the current trends were an aberration. The contrast with the 1950s was explicitly made by Vice Justice Minister, Xie Bangzhi, who stated that, between 1950 and 1960, crime in China averaged about 570,800 per year. In a report to the NPC in 1980, China's chief prosecutor, Huang Huoqing, stated that more than 84,000 offenders had been prosecuted in the first half of 1980 alone, and that more than 50% were suspected of serious crimes (Leng and Chiu, 1985, p 131). However, as Pearson has argued in the UK, claims that the past was more peaceful and orderly are suspect (Pearson, 1983). In a China undergoing rapid change, nostalgia for the past is understandable but not necessarily accurate. Many offenders in the 1950s had been dealt with by extra-judicial means. They never appeared in the crime figures. Thus the 'crime rate' for the 1950s and 1960s may have been artificially low. Bakken estimates that between 1949 and 1966 there were about 956,000 criminals (about 8–9 per year per 100,000), most of whom were classed as 'political offenders' or counter-revolutionaries. Rises in 'crime' in 1957 and 1958 were also mainly due to arrests during the anti-Rightist campaign, when 90% of all those detained were 'counter-revolutionaries' (Bakken, 1993, pp 29, 33). By 1980, the number of counter-revolutionaries had fallen to 10%, and by 1981 there were only 577 left in the total prison population (2.5%). The types of crimes and criminals were now 'different'. 'The nature of the crime has degenerated from hooliganism and street fighting in the late 1970s to murder, rape, armed robbery and hijacking in the 1980s' (Fu, 1994, p 12).

The Chinese authorities apparently thought that the official crime figures grossly underrepresented the 'true' extent of crime, internal research suggesting a figure three to four times higher (Dutton and Lee, 1993, p 318). Reform had brought many strangers into the cities, weakened informalised disciplinary mechanisms, increased people's anxieties, weakened trust, and heightened fears of crime. Research indicated that a majority of the public felt that the public order situation was deteriorating; almost 59% thought current punishments were too light and wanted quicker and heavier punishments for criminals (Li Tianfu, 1991).

Rises in serious crime, crimes of violence and juvenile crime were regarded as especially worrying, heralding 'new forms of criminality' (Fu, 1994). Juvenile crime was explained in terms of: (i) youth violence during the Cultural Revolution; (ii) youths sent down to the countryside returning to the cities without jobs or homes; and (iii) the 'decadent' and 'immoral' practices ushered in by reform. According to

Fu, juvenile delinquency was a novel form of crime, crime amongst rural youth being 'an unknown phenomenon' in Mao's China. Between 1950–59, juveniles accounted for only about 20% of the total criminal population; this rose to 30% between 1960–65 and rose again to 60% between 1978–80. By 1984 it stood at 63% and from 1985–89 it rose to 71.1% (Fu, 1994, p 10). Bakken differs slightly, arguing that in 1956, juvenile crime accounted for 18% of all crime, rising to 32.3% in 1957 and again to between 40% and 50% during the Cultural Revolution, peaking around 1973. Having fallen in 1975, juvenile crime began to rise again in the late 1970s. In 1979, youth delinquency accounted for 47.6% of total crime, rising sharply in 1988 to 75.7% (Bakken, 1993, p 37).

Most of this crime was committed by under 18 year olds (Bakken, 1993, pp 37–38). Indeed, youths were said to be committing their first offence at a younger age – 13 in the 1980s compared to 17 in the 1960s (Bakken, 1993, pp 37–38). Of those convicted of murder, 35% were under 18 at the time of the offence; 48% of those convicted of robbery; and 47% of those convicted of rape were also under 18.

Thus, whilst China's overall official crime rate was low compared to other countries included in the UN crime statistics, its rates for juvenile delinquency were two to three times higher (Bakken, 1993, p 34). Alarmingly, this suggested that young people were becoming more delinquent, more dangerous, and at a younger age than ever before. There is evidence of a panic as early as 1979, when a joint report was sent to the Central Committee of the CCP about juvenile delinquency (Fu, 1994, p 8). At this time, the solution was thought to lie in rescuing and educating youth. The first campaign against crime in 1981–83 therefore used old methods of 'education and persuasion', setting up juvenile tribunals and sending 'wayward women' to centres for re-education.

At the same time, however, the NPC modified the 1979 CL and CPL to grant (for the period 1981–83) the right to approve the death sentence to the higher peoples' courts in cases of murder, rape, robbery, bombings, arson and sabotage.

The 1981–83 campaign had some success. Whilst 890,281 criminal cases were filed by the PSB in 1981 (a rate of 8.9 per 10,000), only 748,476 were filed in 1982 (7.4 per 10,000). A *People's Daily* report of September 1982 put the crime rate for the first half of 1982 at 16.7% lower than for the first half of 1981 (Tanner, 1999, p 84). Absolute numbers for robbery, theft, fraud and counterfeiting fell. Official statistics indicate that the total number of serious crimes committed in China in 1980 were 50,000, rising to 67,000 in 1981 before falling again to 64,000 in 1982 (Tanner, 1994).

By 1982, the police were claiming an improvement in social order in the cities, where crime was said to have dropped by about 25% (Leng and Chiu, 1985, p 131; Fu, 1994). Within a month of the 1981 NPC resolutions, over 4,000 offenders had surrendered, over 820 escapees had returned to reformatories, and over 1,600 prisoners from labour camps had been caught (Fu, 1994). More than 168,000 criminal cases were reported and some 68,000 offenders apprehended.

However, this disguised a rise in serious crime – the number of murders placed on file in 1982 (9,324) was not much lower than in 1981 (9,576), and reported rape cases increased from 30,808 in 1981 to 35,631 in 1982 (Tanner, 1999, p 86). The crime figures also indicated an apparent rise in female criminality. Female offenders who, in the 1960s, committed their first offence at 24 were now committing more crime and at an earlier age (17). In the 1950s and 1960s, women had comprised between 1–3% of all criminal offenders. This rose to between 5–7% in the 1970s and to 9–10% in the early 1980s (Tanner, 1994, p 243; Kang Shuhua, 1992, cited in Tanner, 1994, p 213). The proportion of female juvenile offenders in the convicted female population noticeably increased. Their offences were mainly vice-related and theft. The most common offence for which women were sentenced to RTL was homicide, often of husbands involved in extramarital affairs (Tanner, 1994, p 206).

60–70% of women serving time in RTL and RETL centres in the late 1980s were detained for 'sex crimes'. 'Sex crime' was a category not included in the 1979 CL. However, it was subsumed into the category of 'hooliganism', which could be dealt with by criminal and non-criminal sanctions (see Tanner, 1994). 'Hooliganism' covered anything which offended public decency, 'poisoned the social atmosphere', 'destroyed socialist relationships', 'sexual hooliganism', and 'sexual promiscuity' – all very broadly defined (Tanner, 1994, p 206). Women charged with 'sexual hooliganism' under SAPA were punished with 15 days' detention or a fine, or sent for RETL. 'Sex offenders' also accounted for about 95% of women undergoing RETL (Bakken, 1993; Tanner, 1994). 90% of all crimes amongst young girls were defined as 'sexual transgressions' (Bakken, 1993, p 18).

Did this mean that Chinese women were becoming more 'criminal'? Bakken argues that the Chinese state regarded the expression of female sexuality as dangerous and degenerate, marking a 'slippery slope' to crime and the breakdown of society's moral order (Bakken, 1993). The suppression of 'sexual licence' was also important because one of the CCP's early successes had been the eradication of prostitution and vice. That such offences should re-emerge so rapidly after 40 years of communism cast doubt on this achievement.

Bakken argues that some of these themes of degeneracy and the breakdown of the moral and social order were also evident in the state's response to juvenile delinquency. Certainly, the crackdown on juveniles came during a wider political campaign against 'spiritual pollution'. Embracing Deng's call to get rich, people were pursuing hedonistic, extravagant and ostentatious lifestyles, discarding older, Maoist, morality. Juveniles once dealt with by local committees now came to the attention of the police and courts, raising their profile in the recorded crime figures.

Reform had also attracted large numbers of young, unmarried male and female migrants into China's cities, many of whom were unemployed and living outside the net of state control. Tapping into more generalised anxieties about change, the breakdown of social order and moral decay, these 'drifters' sparked a panic about delinquency, crime and disorder (*dongluan*), at the heart of which was the figure of the Chinese 'hooligan' (*liumang*) (Bakken, 1993).

The 1983–85 yanda

At the end of the first campaign in 1983, recidivism rates for youth remained extremely high; fear of crime continued to grow. By the spring of 1983, a more severe policy towards all crime was being advocated, heralding the onset of the first *yanda*, the 'strike hard blows against crime' campaign. Severe and 'dictatorial' methods were called for (Tanner, 1999). The Central Committee of the CCP Decision, 'Regarding Striking Heavy Blows Against Criminal Activities' argued that:

The experience of the past few years fully proves that only if we resolutely organise a number of major battles in the spirit of 'severe and rapid punishment, one fell swoop' and show absolutely no mercy in striking determined blows against criminal elements will we be able to strike fear into the hearts of criminal elements, to instruct and save the many young people who have been led astray, better implement the guiding principle of comprehensive management of public security and reverse the present abnormal situation (cited in Tanner, 1999, p 83).

Instructions for the 1983 campaign were relayed directly from the Party centre to the provincial and local levels. A strengthening of 'comprehensive management' and 'stronger coercive measures against crime was called for, including more police patrols, inspection points and strengthened ideological indoctrination of the public security forces' (Tanner, 1999, p 87). In July, a major crackdown was announced.

Fu explains how the *yanda* worked. Public fears and complaints were brought to the attention of the Party Committee in the cities, which then mobilised the mass media to 'create a mood' in society:

... the general public are encouraged to report any criminal activities to the police, and criminals are advised to surrender themselves. At the same time, meetings are held by the police to set the strategy of the war. Preparations are then made: cars and trucks are borrowed for the mass arrest; detention rooms are set up and targets are specified. Then, one night, all the police are sent out simultaneously to raid the targets ... A mass arrest is often followed by public trials and humiliating parades. Finally, the alleged criminals meet their punishment and the police claim victory (Fu, 1994, p 282).

In 1983, the Standing Committee of the NPC again amended the 1979 laws 'to facilitate the campaign and legalise the measures already taken by the authorities'. The criminal law was revised to allow punishment, up to and including the death penalty, for offences of leading a 'hooligan group'; causing intentional injury; injuring state personnel or civilians who expose or arrest criminals; leading a group engaged in the abduction and sale of people; illegal manufacture, trade, transport or theft of weapons or explosives; organisation of sects or secret societies; the use of superstition to carry out counter-revolutionary activities; and luring, forcing or sheltering women in prostitution (Tanner, 1999, p 92).

'Strong measures' to deal with the pressing problem of crime also meant removing 1979 procedural guarantees for certain offenders and introducing 'swift' and 'severe' penalties (Leng and Chiu, 1985, pp 129, 133). 'Swiftness' meant that the police, procuratorate and courts were to speed up the process by co-ordinating their anti-crime measures under the leadership of the Party. 'Severity' meant imposing the maximum penalty within the scope of the law. In serious criminal cases, courts were not to be bound by Art 110 of the 1979 CPL, which provided that defendants should be notified of the charges against them seven days before the trial (Tanner, 1999, p 93). Time for appeal against a verdict was shortened from 10 days to three, and it was no longer incumbent on the authorities to inform defendants of their right to a lawyer.

In their fight against crime, the authorities now had a range of legal and administrative measures at their disposal. S and I remained part of the police repertoire, together with S and R, RETL, SAPA and the CL. Of these, the administrative measures, such as S and I, perhaps proved the most useful. By estimating how many known 'troublemakers' lived in each area, 'each precinct station made a sweep of its own area, bringing in the requisite number of persons for "shelter and investigation"' (Tanner, 1999, p 87). There were mass arrests, hurried investigations and trials; sentence (including execution) followed promptly upon conviction. Amongst those rounded up were rapists, drug traffickers, sellers of pornography, 'hooligans', 'counter-revolutionaries' and other 'troublemakers'. Those accused of 'sexual promiscuity' included unmarried people who had engaged in consensual sexual relations (including homosexuals) and anyone violating principles of order and morality (Tanner, 1999, p 94). Record numbers were punished. By January 1984, the campaign had led to 100,000 arrests and 5,000 executions. The RTL and RETL systems took in an extra 563,000 inmates in the first six months of the campaign, pushing the total to approximately 1,260,000. By October, it was reported that 1,027,000 criminals had been arrested in the 'first battle', mainly for robbery, arson, rape, murder, and hooliganism. 975,000 had been prosecuted, 687,000 sent to RTL, another 169,000 to RETL, and 24,000 sentenced to death (Tanner, 1994, p 276).

Estimates as to how many were executed during the crackdown are difficult to verify. One source puts the figure at over 40,000 cadres and civilians (see Leng and Chiu, 1985). Revised figures estimated that from 1983 to 1985, 861,000 were sentenced to death with a two year reprieve; 687,000 entered the RTL system, and 169,000 the RETL system (Tanner, 1999, p 98). Photographs of executions were exhibited in public display cases. Though mass public executions did occur, the principal means of publicity were mass sentencing rallies, followed by a parade of prisoners through the streets on open trucks, with cards indicating their name and crime hung about their necks.

The figures did not necessarily reflect a real increase in crime as, during the *yanda*, offenders already convicted, sentenced (and, in some cases, released) were sentenced again if their original sentence was considered 'too lenient'. Some of the increase was also due to the willingness of the authorities to prosecute as crimes offences previously handled by administrative measures – Tanner says that the heightened atmosphere of the campaign led to young men who accidentally brushed up against women in the street being accused of attempted rape or 'hooliganism' (Tanner, 1999).

Re-working old tools in the war against crime

By early 1984, the most aggressive phase of the campaign was over (Tanner, 1999). The *yanda* continued into 1985 but at a 'lower velocity' (Tanner, 1999, p 93). During it, however, the message had been conveyed to the police that legal rules and due process need not be followed if they hampered crime control. Moreover, it was their long-standing administrative powers, used in new ways against new targets, which seemed to be the most effective in the 'war against crime'.

The revamping of these administrative powers to deal with China's 'new criminal classes' had begun in 1978, when the Ministry of Public Security extended S and I to 'criminal elements' suspected of committing serious crimes roaming from place to place (Hsia and Zeldon, 1993, p 11). By the mid-1980s, administrative and criminal powers were being treated as coterminous. In 1980, the State Council merged S and I with RETL and RTL (Tanner, 1999, p 36). In 1984, the Ministry of Public Security stipulated that suspects were to be interrogated only for 24 hours, and that their families and work units were to be informed of their whereabouts and the reasons for their detention. Even the Supreme People's Court apparently discussed whether time detained for S and I could be retrospectively offset against imprisonment under criminal law (Tanner, 1999).

Statistics for S and I showed that 55% of detainees were not 'roaming criminal elements' but local persons whose names, addresses and backgrounds were known. A 1989 study found that only 60% of those detained for S and I met the criteria of being roaming criminal suspects who refused to give their name, address and background (Yang Lianfeng and Wei Huaming, 1993; Zhao Shiming, 1990; Epstein and Wong, 1996, p 6). About 80–90% of persons eventually convicted by the criminal courts were initially detained under S and I (Epstein and Wong, 1996).

Since those detained were being held because they were suspected of committing a crime, they should in theory have been dealt with according to criminal procedure, with its time limits and protections. However, S and I did not require evidence; it could be used to hold people for one month in the first instance, two to three months in complex cases, and indefinitely for those 'who refused to divulge their real names or place or origin' (Tanner, 1999, p 37; see also Epstein and Wong, 1996; HRW/HRIC, 1997). The police could use it to detain people for far longer periods than those envisaged by the law (Epstein and Wong, 1996; Fu, 1997; Tanner, 1999).

S and I thus epitomised the large penumbra of administrative powers available to the police. These gave them enormously flexible 'crime fighting' tools in a virtually unregulated environment. Instead of being displaced by the 1979 CPL, their 'sub-legal' powers simply continued to run in parallel with it.

Even where new legal rules were announced to curb police practice, the message that 'results came first' made them ineffective. Detaining a person under 'supervised residence' had, for example, been officially abolished in 1980 but was still in use years later (Clarke and Feinerman, 1995, p 147). Similarly, though the Supreme People's Court outlawed police use of torture to obtain confessions, it remained (and remains) widespread, encouraged by the fact that judges allow such evidence to be admitted at trial. This lack of regard for law is unsurprising given the sub-text of the *yandas* and the low regard for law during the previous 40 years of CCP rule. The police, used to carrying out Party policy, understood that procedural regularity came second to results.

The initial results of the *yanda* appeared to endorse their 'ends justifies the means' approach. Crime had dropped dramatically. In 1982, 748,476 cases had been filed; this fell to 610,478 in 1983 and 514,369 in 1984 (Tanner, 1999, p 98). The very sharp decrease (36%) between the autumn of 1983 and spring of 1984 occurred when the campaign was at its most aggressive (Tanner, 1999, p 107). The *yanda* also led to a decrease in gang offences, harassment of women and street fighting (Tanner, 1999, p 101). Figures for 1983 are uncertain, but PSB statistics show 610,478 crimes and an overall crime rate of 59.81 per 10,000.

This effect, however, was short-lived. Although serious offences had declined by 40.4% in Beijing in 1984 as compared with 1983, by March 1985 they had risen again by 15.2% (Tanner, 1994, p 276). The figure for April 1985 was 57.1% higher than it had been in April 1984 (Tanner, 1994, p 276). Nationwide, crime began to rise again in 1984 and by 1985, the number of serious crimes filed stood at 84,000. In 1986, this figure shot up to 98,000, by 1987 it was 122,000, and in 1988 it reached 128,000 (Dutton and Lee, 1993, p 319). Homicide rose by 11% between 1987 and 1988; robbery by almost 60%; serious theft by over 75% and rape by 14%. In some provinces, such as Jiangsu, serious theft more than trebled between 1980 and 1990.

As Dutton and Lee point out, this meant that by 1988, the total number of cases registered had doubled since 1984 and was still rising as the 1980s came to an end. Between January and May 1990, the total number of serious criminal cases on file stood at 171,000, a 23.2% increase over the figures for 1989 (Dutton and Lee, 1993, p 319; see also Wang Fang, 1991). Other figures indicate a steady increase in the crime rate (5–5.2 per 10,000 population) from 1984 to 1986, rising from 5.4 in 1987 to 20.1 in 1990. Theft, robbery and swindling all showed rapid and dramatic increases, though rape fell from second place in 1981 to fourth place by 1990. Serious crime (serious theft, homicide, robbery, assault, rape) had begun their rise in 1984, when the *yanda* was still in full swing.

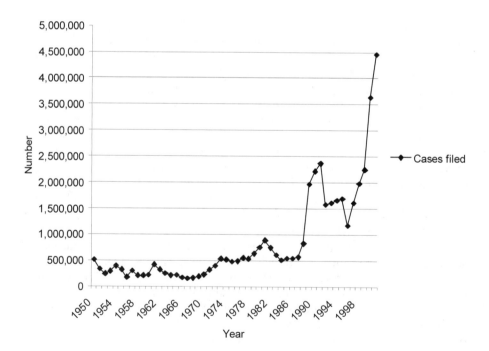

Figure 1: Criminal cases filed, 1950–2001.

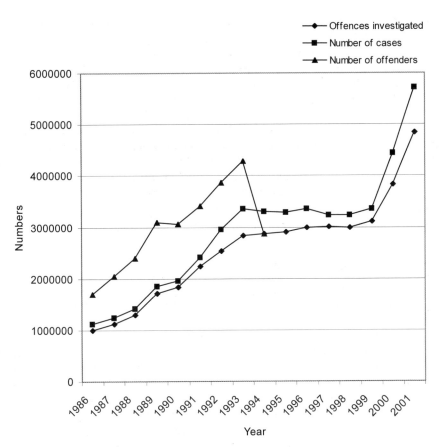

Figure 2: SAPA offences, 1986–2001.

As crime rates started to rise again at the end of 1984, doubts about the *yanda's* effectiveness began to set in (Tanner, 1999, p 101). The decreases achieved were 'unstable'. Apart from the dramatic increase in certain types of crime, there were also other, unintended, consequences. Many of those incarcerated resented 'campaign-style justice'. Minor offenders, who would normally have been dealt with leniently, had received unusually severe punishments. The pre-emptory nature of the trial process led to many doubtful convictions. The vast numbers incarcerated fuelled prison overcrowding and unrest amongst aggrieved inmates (Tanner, 1999). Images of public executions negated the message to foreign investors that China was a land of law, leading a sensitive Party leadership to ban public parades of criminals and public executions (Tanner, 1999, p 103). RETL was a useful alternative. It drew less criticism from the 'West' since it operated in the shadows. Like other administrative sanctions, there was no trial and therefore no publicity.

The sense of 'crisis management' permeating these times seems to have spurred the Ministry of Public Security to issue its 'Regulations for the Management of Shelter and Investigation' in 1984, and the NPC Legal Work Committee to regularise the legal basis for S and I. In 1987, the SAPA of 1957 was replaced by a new Security Administration Punishment Act. Although this introduced the right to sue the police, it also extended the period of administrative detention by the police to 15 days (Epstein, 1992). The Supplementary Re-Education Through Labour Regulations of November 1979 had already amended the 1957 RETL Regulations (Wu, 1992, p 1) reducing the term of RETL detention from five to three years, with one year's extension. However, since the CPL still allowed the police to detain people 'without having to go to the trouble of arrest, prosecution and trial' and use RETL as a means of preventative detention, 'a great variety of offenders ... received RETL sanctions, including parents who hide their fugitive children, lawyers who are suspected of conducting illegal activities in defending their clients, pickpockets, and ... political dissidents' (Tanner, 1994, p 105; Amnesty International, 1991, p 36).

Despite all this activity, crime continued to rise. The 1983–85 *yanda* ended in 'total failure' (Fu, 1994, p 7). Bakken calls it a 'useless and bloody affair' (Bakken, 1993, p 50).

1985–89: more campaigns

The end of the first *yanda* in 1985 saw the start of a different type of campaign. The 'Spiritual Civilisation' campaign attacked the degenerating conduct of Chinese life. The pureness and selflessness of spirit of Maoist times seemed (particularly to remnant Maoists) to have been deluged by materialism, hedonism and selfishness. The masses were to mobilise around the 'Five Talks' (politeness, civil behaviour, morality, attention to social relations and attention to hygiene) and the 'Four Beauties' (beautiful language, beautiful behaviour, beautiful heart and beautiful environment). Criminality was placed in the context of wider incivility. In almost Foucauldian terms, 'Spiritual Civilisation' made self-governance the key to order.

Like the *yanda*, 'Spiritual Civilisation' did not work. Crime continued to rise. Though some petty crime fell, homicide and rape rose; serious theft tripled between 1982 and 1986, and a record level of violent crime was recorded in 1986, with 65.1% of homicides, rapes, assaults and armed robberies being committed by youths. This rose to almost 74% in 1989 (Tanner, 1999; Bakken, 1993). Between 1986 and 1987, homicide rose by 11%, robbery by almost 60%, and serious theft by almost 76%. By 1988, cases of robbery and serious theft had risen by almost 60% and 76% compared with 1987, whilst homicide rose by 11% and assault by almost 9%.

The late 1980s saw the figures for all 'public security offences' rise by 31%, with steep rises for crimes of violence and offences such as counterfeiting, gun and knife control violations, disrupting public order, assaults, frauds, snatchings, group snatchings and gambling (Cheng Yang, 1994, p 62). That the police were using SAPA rather than invoking the criminal justice process seems to be borne out by the fact that between 1986 and 1989, the number of people handled under SAPA was between 3.75 and 4.67 times the number dealt with under the criminal law (Cheng Yang, 1994, p 63). About six times as many people were 'sentenced' for SAPA offences. 1986 also saw the deployment of all forms of criminal and administrative measures against demonstrators as protests took place in cities across China, provoked partly by politics and partly by the impact of economic reform.

At the end of the 1980s the crime figures were far worse than at the start. Overall, between 1986 and 1990, crime increased from 11.7 to 17.8 per 10,000 population, but even this was outstripped by the 75% rise in SAPA offences (Tanner, 1999, p 111). Theft and other property crimes accounted for the greatest number of offences. The absolute volume of theft cases dealt with as 'public security offences' increased by 26.4% during 1988–89. SAPA cases of assault also rose by 74% between 1989 and 1990, and offences of disrupting public order by over 80%. Offences such as grabbing of money and goods, looting, gambling, destruction of goods and violations of household registration all showed massive increases of between 100% and 200% (Cheng Yang, 1994; Tanner, 1994).

By the late 1980s, the CCP was faced with the fact that crime had increased exponentially and that its attempts to reduce crime had failed. Arguably, the campaigns had amplified public anxiety about the 'crime problem'. In the absence of any better remedies, an anti-'Six Evils' campaign began in 1989, aimed at eliminating the favourite 'remnant Maoist' targets – drug trafficking, prostitution, gambling, pornography, the selling and trafficking in women and children, and feudal superstition. Gangs were rounded up, books and magazines confiscated and burnt, tapes seized and gambling money confiscated. By December 1989, the Ministry of Public Security was claiming that it had netted some 350,000 offenders and generated 140,000 cases.

In early May 1990, another campaign against serious crime was launched under the planning of the Central Political Science and Law Commission. In May and June, over 37,000 criminal gangs were said have been caught and over 350,000 cases detected. By 1991, the number of major crimes was eight times higher than it had been in 1981 (Bakken, 1994) and still rising.

Yet another campaign, against theft, began in 1991 and, in the same year, a high-powered committee, headed by Qiao Shi, was set up with a view to improving social order 'by legal, administrative, economic and educational means' (Foreign Broadcast Information Service (FBIS), 22 March 1991). Calls were once again made for a hard crackdown on crime and criminals.

The CCP was not winning the war against crime. The *yanda* had confirmed public perceptions that more and more violent crimes were being committed, that the 'new' criminals were more 'dangerous', and that more people than ever were re-offending (Epstein and Wong, 1996, p 497). Recidivism was, of course, also a sign of political failure. It suggested that 'thought reform', so central to communism since the 1950s, did not work. Though attempts were made to reinvent Maoist-style community mechanisms for the reintegration of offenders, a new 'criminology' emerged. Offenders were no longer victims of incorrect class consciousness, but selfish, greedy people, calculating the profits and losses of crime. As elsewhere, this 'rational actor' theory led to a more punitive approach to crime.

The police, exhausted by their continuous wars on crime, were criticised by Party and public alike for their failure (Fu, 1994). Their record for solving cases had declined quite markedly after the 1983–85 *yanda*, though prosecuting offences under SAPA kept many offences out of the official crime figures. The police wished to shed their unpopular image as Party enforcers of everything from grain quotas to the one child policy and reinvent themselves as 'professional crime fighters'. Part of this meant remodelling themselves as law abiding. However, they had received 'double messages' from the leadership throughout the 1980s. Law was said to be important but they had learnt that where law hindered results, it could be ignored.

1989: crime, disorder and 'turmoil'

The end of the first decade of economic reform saw heightened public concerns about crime and corruption. The conspicuous failure to prosecute corrupt Party officials and their children did nothing to increase public confidence in the leadership. In 1989, such concerns coalesced with other social, economic and political discontents to produce mass protests in Beijing and other Chinese cities. The pro-democracy demonstrations in Tiananmen Square were widely interpreted abroad as student protest. In China, the fact that they involved thousands of ordinary Chinese, including many from the working classes, raised hard questions about the legitimacy of a Party said to rule China in the name of 'the people'. Tiananmen was the biggest challenge to the CCP in its history.

The leadership responded by declaring martial law and mobilising the PLA against the demonstrators. Thousands were sentenced by the courts to RTL or death, and thousands more were detained by the police for several years without trial under their RETL powers (Amnesty International, 1991). The images of state violence, which flashed around the world during this crackdown, damaged China's international profile. Possibly in an attempt to repair this damage, in 1990 the CCP announced a new law, the Administrative Litigation Law (ALL), to make abuse of power by the police and other public officials subject to legal redress. Complaints about public officials had been processed through the *xin fang* offices attached to provincial and national government offices (Lai, 1996, p 10). About a million complaints per year were being received (Biddulph, 1993, p 15). The ALL provided a legal remedy. Statistics indicate that complaints surged and that the police were one of the two most complained about departments.

Success, however, was infrequent. Of the cases brought in the early 1990s, the original administrative decision was upheld or withdrawn by the complainant in 70% (Epstein, 1994a, p 39). Even so, Epstein argues, in at least *some* cases the courts managed to call the police to account (Epstein, 1994a, pp 16, 17). These cases provided useful propaganda. The 1979 CPL had promised a government accountable to law and equality of citizens before the law. As EP Thompson (1975) has argued, rulers relying on such laws for public support must on occasion live up to their rhetoric. The 'little man' has to win against powerful state officials (some of the time). The powerful themselves must also to be brought to justice (some of the time). Such measures help persuade the public that the country is being governed by wise leaders in a fair, equitable and just manner.

More law followed. In 1992 new rules on RETL were also issued (Clarke and Feinerman, 1995, p 142). There followed a Police Law (1995), a Prisons Law (1994) an Administrative Punishments Law (1996), a Lawyer's Law (1997) and new Criminal and Criminal Procedure Laws (1997). However, China was still in the midst of a war on crime and a crackdown on dissidents. More law did not necessarily mean more due process and fewer administrative powers. As one Chinese commentator put it when describing changes in the 1997 Criminal Law, the name of the legal weapon was being altered but not its basic nature, its tasks or its effectiveness (Guo Qun, 1997, p 80).

In the aftermath of 1989, Deng's critics used concerns about crime as a vehicle for attacking reform more generally. On a tour of the south in 1992, Deng accommodated them by reaffirming reform but attacking the re-emergence of 'old evils'. The 'Anti-Six Evils' campaign was revived. By 1993, however, the rate for serious crimes stood at seven times that of 1983 (Tanner, 1999, p 107). The main types of crime highlighted in the press were 'hooligan' gangs, vandalism, vice, loan sharking, banditry, railway robbery, armed robbery by mobile organised crime gangs, the kidnapping of women and children, triad-related crime, and smuggling. Sensational media reporting fuelled people's sense that China was now a far more dangerous place than in the past. The rise in SAPA offences confirmed that it was not just 'serious' crime but all kinds of offending which were on the increase.

The 1990s: 'stability and reform'

By the mid-1990s, the tools to fight crime had become more legalised and policing more professional. Tiananmen seems to have provoked a shaken CCP leadership into a sustained crackdown on all forms of disorder. RETL, S and I, S and R, and SAPA continued to be used, and used more frequently than the criminal law. Their targets included not only criminals but those wishing to 'split the country' (advocates of independence for Tibet and Xinjiang), those contesting the CCP's monopoly on power (pro-democracy groups) and groups loyal to leaders outside China (notably the Falun Gong and the Roman Catholic Church). Measures introduced to deal with political dissent and social instability included the 1993 State Security Law, which consolidated a 1988 Law on the Preservation of State Secrets. The definition of a 'state secret' was extremely vague. The laws 'created a web in which any person expressing views contrary to those promoted by the Chinese state, or associating with others for a purpose not sanctioned by the government, may be caught'. There was also 'a striking trend' towards prosecutions for 'counter-revolutionary propaganda and incitement', with around 80% of all counter-revolutionary cases falling into this category by 1991. Order – if not law – had become central to the CCP. Law was one way of achieving it.

Administrative power provided another. Apart from the use of RETL in the aftermath of Tiananmen, the leadership also called for the use of administrative measures to strengthen the management of the migrant population, 'beggars who roam around on the streets' being identified as the some of the culprits in the 1989 'turmoil and counter-revolutionary rebellion' (HRW/HRIC, 1999).

A Comprehensive Management of Social Order programme was launched in 1991. This revived control measures used in the late 1970s against young offenders (HRW/HRIC, 2002, p 40). Party organisations at grass roots level were mobilised to 'block opportunities for criminals and ... build an excellent and orderly society' (HRW/HRIC, 2002, p 40). S and R was employed to 'rectify social order ... in concert with the war on criminals being waged by the politico-legal system' (HRW/HRIC, 2002, p 40). As during the *yandas*, post-1989, the police were effectively permitted to detain anyone perceived as disturbing the social order and 'obstructing reform'. Migrant workers became a target. 'Blindly flowing' into China's cities, they were seen as 'deviant', causing 'instability' and crime and thus requiring control and 'management'. A mass of new regulations was introduced to regulate migrant workers and continuous offensives were launched against them under the rubric of making China's cities 'civilised and safe neighbourhoods' (HRW/HRIC, 2002, p 43). In 1995, the Beijing authorities employed 5,000 armed police during the bulldozing down of 'Zhejiang city', a shantytown in the city (Dutton, 1998, p 112ff). Similar campaigns were reported in China's southern coastal cities where new factories attracted migrant workers.

By the end of the 1990s, the number of people detained in this way had more than doubled. So many ordinary migrant workers were detained that by the end of the decade they made up the vast majority of those detained in S and R centres. Some provincial regulations explicitly allowed S and R to be employed as a punishment (HRW/HRIC, 2002). Detention centres were said to be often 'little more than holding pens' for all those whose presence on the streets was deemed unseemly or inconvenient, as well as 'anyone police officers decide to send there ... those attempting to make a living ... or those ... the authorities do not wish to have in a particular city' (HRW/HRIC, 2002). City 'clean ups' became routine in the lead up to major events, such as the Asian Games, National People's Congress meetings, major festivals and, in 1999, the 50th anniversary of the founding of the People's Republic. Thousands of people considered undesirable by urban authorities were detained, including beggars, street children, garbage collectors, prostitutes and the homeless, people in low status occupations who lacked a city *hukou, and* people exercising their constitutional right to complain to the authorities about official misbehaviour (HRW/HRIC, 1999). Most were detained under S and R, and by the late 1990s, upwards of two million people were detained this way every year. Between 5% and 20% were children. Most detainees came from marginalised social groups, generally referred to by the city authorities as 'three nos personnel' (*sanwu renyuan*), having 'no papers, no job and no fixed abode ...' (HRW/HRIC, 1999).

Dutton argues that the most serious and frequent human rights abuses in China lie not with persecution of political dissidents but rather with the routine harassment of these *mangliu*, that is, those who 'blindly travel' into China's cities to make a living and follow the Chinese equivalent of the American Dream. A new 'subaltern' class, they live on the margins and are identifiable as 'outsiders' by the way they speak, dress, walk and address others (Dutton, 1998, p 8). They are far more numerous than their 1950s counterparts for whom the regulations were developed. Dutton estimates that about 3% of the total city population in the early 1950s came from the countryside, rising to about 6% in the early 1960s. After 1978, however, the flow outstripped anything that went before – Dutton suggests that a conservative estimate of the daily flow would be over 40 million people or about 15% of the total urban population (Dutton, 1998, p 12). This phenomenon, he argues, has induced 'something of a social panic', resulting in harsh, ad hoc policing methods (Dutton, 1998, p 13).

Such policing became the routine means by which the Chinese authorities dealt with this 'dangerous class'. Echoing the 'Great Incarceration' of Victorian England, old powers were extended and new means developed to detain a mixture of the indigent and the homeless; street children; runaways; the mentally ill; victims of trafficking; unemployed migrants; people suspected of crimes; petitioners; the marginal, 'undesirable' and 'dangerous'; beggars; itinerant persons; those lacking identification papers; and 'others whom the police regarded as aimlessly wandering around the country, being in the wrong place' (HRW/HRIC, 2002; Cohen and Scull, 1985). Mass roundups were normalised, especially in the lead up to Anti-Drugs Day, Chinese New Year, and China National Day. Large bonfires of confiscated drugs were burnt and offenders executed en masse. China acquired the reputation for executing more people than all the other countries of the world added together. As a deterrent, however, this had no effect on crime. It did, however, convey a message about the power of the state and went some way to persuade the public that the authorities were serious about tackling crime. By the mid-1990s, such crackdowns had become a normal part of policing, broadly conceived. *Yandas*, once sporadic, became routine. Annual, biennial and even triennial campaigns were launched targeting local as well as national 'crime problems'. In 1996, another major *yanda* began and a third arm was added to the public order effort in the form of a revived 'Spiritual Civilisation Campaign', backed by the leader-in-waiting, Jiang Zemin. In the same year, major revisions of China's criminal laws were undertaken.

The 1997 Criminal Law and Criminal Procedure Law: due process or crime control?

To many foreign observers, the 1997 CL and CPL signified that, post-Tiananmen, China was returning to the rule of law. In China itself, however, the President of the Supreme People's Court called upon courts at all levels to apply it as part of the latest 'Strike Hard' campaign. Thus, whilst some saw the laws as embodying a new commitment to due process, others saw them as part of a reinvigorated attack on crime to safeguard unity and stability.

The 1997 CPL did introduce a number of improved due process rights and made the trial system more adversarial. It abolished 'verdict first, trial second' (a person could only be convicted *after* a trial). It also enabled legal representation at an earlier stage in the criminal process, gave lawyers a bigger role at trial and made the initial stages of the process (where the suspect was in police custody) more transparent and accountable to law. However, since 1997, the number of defendants being represented by a lawyer has declined, mainly because of the harassment lawyers experience when they try to use their new powers.

Whilst the CPL curbed the 'shadowy administrative detention practices' of the police prior to arrest by abolishing S and I, the compromise was a strengthening of the police's *legal* powers to detain (Fu, 1997, p 137). Article 69 applied to people who were 'strongly suspected' of having roamed from place to place committing crimes, committing repeated crimes, or forming gangs to commit crimes. This category of person could formerly be detained for seven days prior to arrest. The CPL now gave the police the power to detain them for 30 days. Moreover, the period which the prosecution was given to authorise an arrest was extended from three to seven days. Once added to the 30 days before the police had to seek such authorisation, this effectively meant that a person could be detained for 37 days without charge. Moreover, the time held in custody only began once a suspect's identity had been established; previous time in custody did not count. In addition, if, part way through the 30 day period of detention, the police suspected that the detainee might have been involved in another crime, they could restart the clock so that the 30 days began again from the new date. Extensions beyond 30 days could also be sought in 'serious' or 'complex' cases, or where investigations required the police to travel to far-off places to collect evidence.

In summary, the new CPL took S and I powers away from the police but it compensated by giving them the formal legal means of dragging out detention almost indefinitely. As McBarnet has observed of UK criminal procedure, China's 1997 due process provisions were *for* crime control – the police did not have to *abuse* the law to detain suspects – all they had to do was *use* it (McBarnet, 1981).

Moreover, only about a third of all offenders were ever processed by the formal legal system; the remaining two-thirds were dealt by police administrative powers. The rights introduced by the 1997 CPL may have improved the lot of criminal suspects but they made no difference at all to the vast majority of offenders coming into contact with the police. Nor did the CPL specifically prohibit the authorities from using different types of extra-judicial detention in succession. Where elsewhere suspects against whom a criminal case proved weak before or after trial might be freed, in China they could still be detained administratively.

Another 'progressive' change in the 1997 CL was the fact that the term 'counter-revolutionary' was dropped. Reports in the Chinese press continued to talk of 'counter-revolutionaries', but lawmakers wished to delete the term from the 1997 Criminal Law. In its place, they favoured the offence of 'endangering state security'. This new category 'broadened the capacity of the state to suppress dissent' (HRW/HRIC, 1997). The legal protections available to suspects under the old 1979 CPL had never applied to those detained by the State Security Police for security offences. Security and stability were, by the mid-1990s key concerns. 'Splittists' and secessionists now became specific targets, whilst the definition of sedition and subversion was also widened (HRW/HRIC, 1997). Moreover, RETL remained available for use against dissidents. A 1982 document had moved them up to first place on the list of RETL targets (Tanner, 1999, p 40) and by the 1990s RETL was being widely used against political dissidents, as well as ordinary criminals (Epstein, 1994a, p 10).

Within China itself, Jiang Zemin presented the 1997 CPL and CL as part of the state's continued offensive against crime. The new laws were intended to make China's anti-crime measures more rational and effective. Public disorder, provoked principally by the unrelenting push for deeper economic reform, required more effective 'comprehensive management'. There were numerous reports of mass demonstrations by discontented workers and peasants across the country, as well as ongoing attacks by separatists in Xinjiang. The policy of 'Stability and Reform' summed up the CCP's position on such issues. Several lessons had been learnt in 1989. One was the need to address the public's concerns about rising crime and corruption more effectively, and the strengthening of China's legal institutions and complaints mechanisms in the early to mid-1990s went some way towards this. Another lesson, however, was the need to strengthen the forces of order and ensure that the Party (rather than 'the people') had first call on the loyalty of the army and the police. A strong state was deemed imperative. The police and the army were 'rectified' to ensure 'correct thinking' and named as the 'vanguard' of reform. If social dislocations and discontent 'obstructed' reform, the state would have the means to manage them. The People's Armed Police were strengthened. Police resources and equipment were upgraded. The 1997 legalisation of police powers dovetailed with their ambition to professionalise but also made repression a more intense, sophisticated and legal affair.

Conclusion

In Maoist China, crime and the state's response to crime were highly politicised affairs. The post-Mao period has seen attempts to gradually 'de-politicise' them, and the swathe of laws enacted in the 1990s did go some way to distance politics from crime. However, this shift may have been more apparent than real. Law has become politics by other means.

Domestically, legality became increasingly important in China as a means of renegotiating the relationship between the rulers and the ruled. Internationally, legality was also required to plug into the global economy and re-join the international community. But adopting neo-liberal economics and refashioning the criminal law does not necessarily make a country less authoritarian. Many capitalist societies are politically neo-conservative and many of their criminal justice systems were fashioned to accommodate the dislocations and inequities of their own 'Great Transformations'. The rule of law and due process have often played an important symbolic role in this process – one reason why Mao regarded them as 'Rightist'.

In all societies, crime and law are partly shaped by history, tradition and culture. But they are also shaped by how regimes harness these to alter or preserve the status quo. China is often spoken of as 'different' from the 'West', its relatively low crime rates usually attributed to its Confucian heritage, said to emphasise harmony, stability, social solidarity and consensus. In their search for the recipe for the crime-free society, criminologists may become mesmerised by such talk. When they hear it in China, they should be doubly cautious. In 1990s China, Confucianism was rehabilitated by the CCP. Harnessed to 'Spiritual Civilisation', it assisted the 'ordering' of society, its reverence for hierarchy, strong leadership, and authoritarian rule legitimising the use of strong measures against anyone and anything which challenged the regime.

In China, tradition and culture are resources which, like old Maoist methods of policing, can be dusted down and put to new use in the reordering of China. Politics and economics have indelibly shaped the definition of crime and the response to crime since reform. In the post-Mao period, the argument about whether China should take the 'capitalist road' has been won. The days of pursuing the 'old evils' and 'decadent behaviour' have given way to the policing of anything which threatens China's economy, be this economic crimes like embezzlement, protests, demonstrations and strikes, or opposition to the development of a business district on the site of residents' housing. As reform deepens, more sections of society will be adversely affected, and more are likely to be criminalised. We can therefore expect 'crime' in China to continue rising for some time.

Rising crime places the CCP in a political double bind. In the absence of democracy, its mandate to rule depends heavily on persuading the public that it is doing a good job of running China. Rising crime calls this into question. The *yandas* (in some form or other) must therefore continue if the Party is to be seen to be listening to public concerns and fighting the war against crime. But *yandas* tend to put results before legality, have short lived results, amplify people's awareness of the 'crime problem' and lead to calls for ever harsher anti-crime measures. It seems, therefore, that like many 'Western' societies, China is caught in a spiral from which escape will prove extremely difficult.

References

Amnesty International (1991) *Two Years After Tiananmen*, New York: Human Rights Watch

Bakken, B (1993) 'Never for the first time: "premature love" and social control in today's China' 7(3) *China Information*, Winter 1992–93, 9–27

Bakken, B (1994) 'Crime, juvenile delinquency and deterrence policy in China' 30 *Australian Journal of Chinese Affairs* 29–58

Berman, HJ (1972) *Soviet Criminal Law and Procedure*, Cambridge, Massachusetts: Harvard UP

Biddulph, S (1993) 'Review of police powers of administrative detention in the People's Republic of China' 39(3) *Crime and Delinquency* 337–54

Bonavia, D (1981) *The Chinese*, London: Allen Lane

Bonavia, D (1984) *Verdict in Peking: The Trial of the Gang of Four*, New York: Putnam

Chen, THE (1960) *Thought Reform*, Hong Kong: Hong Kong UP and OUP

Clarke, DC and Feinerman, JV (1995) 'Antagonistic contradictions: criminal law and human rights in China' 141 *China Law Quarterly* 135–54

Cohen, JA (1968) *The Criminal Process in the People's Republic of China 1949–1963*, Cambridge, Massachusetts: Harvard UP

Cohen, S and Scull, AC (1985) *Social Control and the State*, Oxford: Blackwell

Dikotter, F (2002) *Crime, Punishment and the Prison in Modern China*, London: Hurst

Dutton, M (1992) *Policing and Punishment in China*, Cambridge: CUP

Dutton, M (1998) *StreetLife China*, Melbourne: CUP

Dutton, M (2000) 'The end of the (mass) line?' 27(1) *Social Justice* 30–74

Dutton, M and Tianfu, L (1993) 'Missing the target? Policing strategies in the period of economic reform' 39(3) *Crime and Delinquency* 316–36

Epstein, EJ (1989) 'Administrative litigation law', *China News Analysis*, No 1368, 1 June

Epstein, EJ (1992) 'A matter of justice', in Kuan Hsin-chi and Brosseau, M (eds), *China Review*, 5.1–5.37

Epstein, EJ (1994a) 'Legal documents and materials on administrative litigation in the People's Republic of China' 27(5) *Chinese Law and Government*, Sept–Oct

Epstein, EJ (1994b) 'Law and legitimation in post-Mao China', in Potter, PB (ed), *Domestic Law Reforms in Post-Mao China*, Armonk, New York: ME Sharpe, pp 19–56

Epstein, EJ, Byrnes, AC and Gaer, FD (1994) 'The People's Republic of China', in Dunkel, F and Vagg, J (eds), *Waiting For Trial*, Freiburg: Max Planck Institute, pp 793–836

Epstein, JE and Wong, SHY (1996) 'The concept of "dangerousness" in the People's Republic of China and its impact on the treatment of prisoners' 36(4) *British Journal of Criminology* 472–97

FBIS (Foreign Broadcast Information Service, now known as World News Connection) www.newsbank.com/public/fbis.html

Fei Guo (1996) 'China's internal population migration since the 1980s: origins, processes and impacts', unpublished PhD thesis, University of Hawaii

Finder, S (1989) 'Like throwing an egg against a stone? Administrative litigation in the PRC' 3(1) *Journal of Chinese Law*, Summer

Fu, HL (1998) 'Criminal defence in China: the possible impact of the 1996 criminal procedure reform' 153 *The China Quarterly*

Fu, HL (1997) 'Criminal Procedure Law', in Wang Chengguang and Zhang Xianchu (eds), *Introduction to Chinese Law*, Hong Kong: Sweet & Maxwell

Fu, HL (1994) 'Bird in a cage: police and political leadership in post-Mao China' 4 *Policing and Society* 277–91

Fu, HL (1994a) 'A case for abolishing shelter for examination: judicial review and police powers in China' 17(4) *Police Studies* 41–60

Guo Qun (1997) 'Guanyu Fan'geming Zuihang de Tiaozheng' I Cui Qingsen (ed), Zhongguo Danda Xingfa Gaige. Shehui Kexue' ('Whose security?': "state security" in China's new Criminal Code'), Wenxian Press cited in HRIC, New York, p 8

HRW/HRIC (Human Rights Watch/Human Rights in China) (1997) 'Whose security? "State security" in China's new Criminal Code' 9(4) *HRW/HRIC Reports* New York: HRW/HRIC

HRW/HRIC (1999) 'Not welcome at the party: behind the "clean up" of China's cities – a report on administrative detention under custody and repatriation', New York: HRW/HRIC

HRW/HRIC (2001) 'Empty promises: human rights protections and China's criminal procedure law in practice', New York: HRW/HRIC

HRW/HRIC (2002) 'Institutionalized exclusion: the tenuous legal status of internal migrants in China's major cities', New York: HRW/HRIC

Hsia, Tao T and Zeldin, WI (1993) 'Sheltering for examination in the legal system of the PRC' 7 *China Law Reporter*

Kang Shuhua (ed) (1992) *Fanziuxue Tonglun (General Criminology)*, Beijing: Beijing daxue chubanshe

Lai Pui-fong, Fonna (1996) 'Comparative study of the redress of administrative detention: Hong Kong and the People's Republic of China', unpublished Masters dissertation, University of Leicester

Law Yearbook of China, Beijing: Law Publishing House

Lawyers Committee for Human Rights (1993) *Criminal Justice with Chinese Characteristics*, New York: Lawyers Committee for Human Rights

Lawyers Committee for Human Rights (1996) *Open to Reform? An Analysis of China's Revised Criminal Procedure Law*, New York: Lawyers Committee for Human Rights

Leng, Shao-Chuan and Chiu Hungdah (1985) *Criminal Justice in Post-Mao China: Analysis and Documents*, Albany: New York State UP

Li Tianfu, (1991) 'Research and assessment of public perceptions of social order in contemporary China', paper presented to 7th Annual Australian and New Zealand Society of Criminology Conference, October 1991, University of Melbourne

Li Xiancui (1998) 'Crime and policing in China', paper presented to Australian Institute of Criminology, 7 September 1998

Lubman, SB (1999) *Bird in a Cage: Legal Reform in China After Mao*, Stanford: Stanford UP

McBarnet, D (1981) *Conviction: Law, State and the Construction of Justice*, London: Macmillan

Pearson, G (1983) *Hooligan: A History of Respectable Fears*, London: Macmillan

Polanyi, K (1957) *The Great Transformation*, Boston: Beacon Press

Robinson, J (1969) *The Cultural Revolution in China*, Harmondsworth: Penguin

Rothman, D (1971) *The Discovery of the Asylum: Social Order and Disorder in the New Republic*, Toronto: Little, Brown

Scull, A (1979) *Museums of Madness: Social Organisation of Insanity in 19th Century England*, Harmondsworth: Penguin

Seymour JD and Anderson, R (1998) *New Ghosts, Old Ghosts: Prisons and Labour Reform Camps in China*, Armonk, New York: ME Sharpe

Shue, V (1988) *The Reach of the State*, Stanford: Stanford UP

Tanner, HM (1994) 'The theoretical bases of labour reform' 9 *China Information*, Winter

Tanner, HM (1995) 'Policing, punishment and the individual: criminal justice in China' 20(1) *Law and Social Inquiry*, Winter, 277–303

Tanner, HM (1999) *Strike Hard! Anti-crime Campaigns and Chinese Criminal Justice 1979–1989*, Ithaca, New York: East Asian Program, Cornell University East Asia Series

Tanner, MS (2000) 'State coercion and the balance of awe: the 1983–86 "Stern Blows" anti-crime campaign' *The China Journal*, July, 93–125

Tan Shen and Li Dun (1993) 'Urban development and crime in China', in Guldin, G and Southall, A (eds), *Urban Anthropology*, Leiden: EJ Brill

Thompson, EP (1975) *Whigs and Hunters: The Origin of the Black Act*, Harmondsworth: Penguin

Wang Fang (1990; 1991) 'Report on current conditions of public security work and social order', paper presented to 7th session of the NPC Standing Committee, FBIS (trans)

Wang, YF (1992) 'Urban juvenile crime in urban China', MA thesis, Burnaby: Simon Fraser University

Wu, H (1992) *Laogai: The Chinese Gulag*, Boulder: Westview

Wu, H (1996) *Troublemaker: One Man's Crusade Against China's Cruelty*, New York: Times Books

Wu, Z (1990) *Tens of Millions of People Locked Up in Prisons Outside the Legal System*, 153 Chenming 89–92, 1 July 1990, Joint Publications Research Service, JPRS Report: China, 31 October 1990

Yang, Cheng (1994) 'Public security offences and their impact on crime rates in China' 34(1) *British Journal of Criminology*, Winter, 54–68

Yang Lianfeng and Wei Huaming (1993) 'Research on incorporating holding for investigation into the criminal enforcement measures', 5 *faxue inglun* 29–33, 52, Wuhan Law School, 29 (September–October) 1989

Ying, Esther Cheo (1980) *Black Country Girl in Red China*, London: Hutchinson

Zhao Shiming (1990) 'The sheltering for examination system must be perfected', 8 Faxue 28–30, 10 August

Part 3

Transnational Crime Issues

Chapter 9
Transnational Organised Crime
Adam Edwards

Introduction

The perceived threat of transnational organised crime (TOC) exemplifies dilemmas posed when we speak of crime in a global context. The debates that have accompanied its increasing prominence on the agendas of key international organisations, such as the United Nations, Group of 8 leading industrialised nations and the Council of Europe, are evidence of official concern over the illicit consequences of globalisation. On the other hand, they also signal scepticism over the scope, dynamics and impact of this threat. Advocates of TOC as a legitimate object of global governance cite the *prima facie* increase in opportunities for cross-border crimes generated by developments in transport, information and telecommunications technology, accompanied by the decreasing regulation of international trade and the abolition of internal borders between nation-states participating in continental trading blocs, such as the Association of South East Asian Nations (ASEAN), the European Union (EU) and the North American Free Trade Agreement (NAFTA). Sceptics have questioned the extent and even the existence of this threat, observing that much official discourse on TOC is characterised by unsubstantiated assertion. Some such sceptics have denied ontological status to TOC altogether (Sheptycki, 2003a). Sceptics of TOC talk have used a variety of data to illustrate the point that the organisation of serious crime remains predominantly contained within local markets.

This chapter examines the case made by advocates and sceptics of TOC and considers the broader lessons of this dispute for an emergent 'transnational criminology'.[1] A distinction is made between three discrete translations of TOC: as a real problem characterised by the external threat that ethnically defined outsiders pose to legitimate social orders; as a real problem generated by the increased opportunities for the commission of serious crimes that have accompanied processes of globalisation; and as an ideological obfuscation of the internal challenge to, and product of, polarised social formations, especially market societies. It is argued that each of these translations embodies different kinds of criminological knowledge which, in turn, presuppose certain policy responses. This emphasises the actual and potential role of criminological knowledge as 'governmental *savoir*', that is, as intellectual instruments that render populations thinkable for the purposes of their government (Foucault, 1991; Smandych, 1999).

1 This chapter develops arguments initially made in articles co-authored with Pete Gill (Edwards and Gill, 2002a, 2002b; Edwards and Gill, 2003b) and informed by findings from a two year programme of research seminars on the subject of 'Policy Responses to Transnational Organised Crime', funded by the UK Economic and Social Research Council (Grant No: R45126479698). The various contributions to this seminar programme are available in an edited volume (Edwards and Gill, 2003a). The author would also like to thank Professor Vincenzo Ruggiero and Professor Ernesto Savona for their critical discussion of this volume at the third meeting of the European Society of Criminology, University of Helsinki, 27–30 August 2003, which has also influenced the argument of this chapter.

As governmental *savoir-faire*, translations that advocate TOC exemplify some of the pitfalls of transnational criminology. The very concept of transnational reproduces the social-legal presumption of the nation-state as the basic denominator for comparative research. If the specific effect of different criminal legal codes is in question, then this focus is clearly cogent given that most are organised in terms of national jurisdiction. If, however, the purpose of comparative criminology is to question the actual practices of crime and governmental responses that go beyond law enforcement, then alternative foci are needed. The broader sociological literature argues that processes of globalisation accentuate *localities*, rather than nations, as the new 'nodal' points for understanding social and political change. It is, therefore, proposed that transnational criminology be de-limited to comparative social-legal studies, whilst more sociological comparisons of crime control take 'glocality', rather than transnationality, as their referent. The concept of glocality has been coined to capture the iterative relationship between local social relations that are adapting to the global market place and processes of globalisation whose effects are filtered by diverse local political, economic and cultural histories. It is suggested this iterative relationship provides fertile ground for comparative criminological research as it is better placed to inform an understanding of the plural contexts of crime control policy change, transfer and learning.

The rise of transnational organised crime

The social-legal bias in thinking about organised crime can be traced in both 'archaic' and 'limited' conceptions of TOC (Woodiwiss, 2003). The archaic conception has a long historical provenance in attempts by sovereign authorities to consolidate their rule of law over national territories and thereby secure jurisdiction against smuggling and consequent loss of customs and excise duties. Relative to this archaic concern, however, the rise of TOC as a specific object of governmental concern in the 1990s can be attributed to the increasing preoccupation of Western governments with the perceived threat of ethnically-based, 'Mafia type' organisations to the security of their political economies. This historically limited conception manifested itself in the immediate aftermath of the Cold War, first in a conference hosted by the Centre for Strategic and International Studies in Washington DC in September 1994 and addressed by the heads of the United States' Federal Bureau of Investigation, Central Intelligence Agency and Financial Crimes Enforcement Network which, it is argued, gave birth to a new 'global pluralist understanding of organised crime' (Woodiwiss, 2003, p 20). The summary of this conference, provocatively entitled 'Global Organised Crime: The New Empire of Evil', defined this novel security threat in terms of 'Worldwide alliances ... forged in every criminal field from money laundering and currency counterfeiting to trafficking in drugs and nuclear materials' that, 'present a greater international security challenge than anything Western democracies had to cope with during the Cold War' (Raine and Cilluffo, 1994, p ix).

Later, in December of that year, the United Nations convened the World Ministerial Conference on Organised Transnational Crime in Naples, in which the imprimatur of this new global pluralist understanding and its implications for the greater co-ordination of international law enforcement was made clear (Woodiwiss, 2003, pp 21–22). The generalisation of US inspired thinking about the causes, dynamics and appropriate policy responses to organised crime around the international relations circuit culminated in the launch of the United Nation's Convention against Transnational Organised Crime in Palermo in December 2000. This launch was attended by upwards of 100 countries, demonstrating a remarkable degree of consensus in official circles on the existence and character of TOC. Central to this consensus is a belief in the ethnic basis to organised crime. This idea has its origins in the Mafia conspiracy theories espoused in various official policy making fora of the United States Federal Government throughout the post-Second World War era, from the Senate investigating committee headed by Estes Kefauver in 1950–51 through President Johnson's Commission of Law Enforcement and the Administration of Justice in 1967, to Nixon's Organised Crime Control Act 1970 to Reagan's Commission on Organised Crime in 1983 (Woodiwiss, 2003, pp 15–17).

Diagnosing transnational organised crime

The meaning and possible consequences of TOC as an official discourse can be clarified through diagnosing its governmentality. How do particular narratives translate into 'problems of government' as thinkable for the purposes of control? Governmentality has been defined as, 'the intellectual, linguistic and technical ways in which phenomena are constituted by government as governable problems' (O'Malley, 2001, p 134). From the perspective of governmentality studies, 'policy strategies are not just responses to external social problems. Rather, the 'problems' they address are given shape and recognition by the emerging policy discourses, in which academic theories and research can play a critical role' (Stenson, 2000, p 36).

Diagnosing the models of social explanation and criminological knowledge entailed in official discourse on TOC also provides a foundation for thinking beyond this discourse, for imagining how other forms of criminological understanding can be brought to bear in thinking, 'how not to be governed thus' (O'Malley, 2001, p 134) and to act, therefore, as sources of policy innovation. Such diagnosis also reveals the self-referential character of official and critical narratives insofar as particular translations of a problem presuppose certain policy responses whilst obviating others (Edwards and Gill, 2003b, p 267ff). It is in this proscription of problems and policy responses that translations of transnational crime and control are relevant for broader debates over the direction of comparative criminological research. I want to argue that a focus on transnationality obscures the interplay between processes of globalisation and their instantiation in specific localities and, as a consequence, promotes a weak understanding of the varied contexts for crime control.

Transnational organised crime as an external threat

The emphasis in official discourse on the ethnic base of organised crime implies a focus upon *actors* rather than *activities* or *contexts*, and so the connecting threat in post-1945 US Federal Administrations has been a focus on various outsider groups such as the 'Colombian Cartels', 'Chinese Triads' and, more recently, the 'Russian Mafia', which have been added to the longer-standing suspicion of the 'Italian Mafia'. Consensus on the UN Convention reflects the evolution of policy responses to organised crime in the European Union, which had, simultaneously, been developing policies for international co-operation in law enforcement, security and intelligence since the early 1970s in response to fears over political violence, immigration and, subsequently, over the criminogenic consequences of the 'freedom of movement' across national borders entailed in the Single European Market (Bigo, 2000).

Recent policy initiatives in the EU have begun to challenge this ethnic outsider conception of organised crime; it is recognised in the *New Millennium Strategy for the Prevention and Control of Organised Crime* that whilst there is an increasing threat from organised criminal groups outside the territory of the EU, nationals and residents of Member States pose 'a significantly greater risk' (Elvins, 2003, p 29). Even though organised crime can be portrayed more as an 'enemy within' rather than as an alien conspiracy, however, the New Millennium Strategy still perpetuates the preoccupation of official discourse with a 'pyramidal' conception of organised crime. Official discourse remains preoccupied with the activity of hierarchically structured, ethnically-defined, groups who collaborate for prolonged periods of time and whose pursuit of profit and political power threatens an otherwise satisfactory political economy whether from within or without (Levi, 2003).

At a more profound level of understanding, this official discourse embodies a 'criminology of the other' (Garland, 1996, pp 461–63), in that it produces an exogenous understanding of the causes of organised crime. This is explicitly the case in the very etymology of trans*national* organised crime, where security is defined in relation to the external threats encountered by nation-states. Organised crime is still portrayed as an attack upon political economies that are assumed to be satisfactory, or at least non-criminogenic, and should, *ipso facto*, be secured in their existing format. In the long-standing tradition of criminologies of the other, criminality is assumed to be a consequence of pathological actors who are essentially different from 'us', the normal, law abiding, consensual majority. In this 'essentialising of difference' lies the tacit political uses of threat to affirm the righteousness of a particular social order and displace responsibility for its problems onto 'deviant' others (Young, 1999).

To problematise crime in terms of the demonising of others presupposes certain strategies of control, whilst negating others. For, having defined certain ethnic and social groups as the TOC problem, any responsibility that specific political-economic arrangements may have for generating criminality and other social harms is erased. Security becomes, instead, the business of enforcing, punishing, containing, disturbing and dismantling these outsider groups (Adamoli *et al*, 1998, p 131ff). The denial of the responsibility that such arrangements may have for crime and social harm reaches its apogee in the strategy of 'securitisation' (Bigo, 1994; Buzan *et al*, 1998). Problems of government can be located along a spectrum from non-politicised (there is no public debate and public authorities disavow their involvement) through politicised (where the issue is subject to ongoing democratic debate) to securitised where, 'the issue is presented as an existential threat, requiring emergency measures and justifying actions outside the normal bounds of political procedure' (Buzan *et al*, 1998, pp 23–24).

It has been argued that the securitisation of organised crime has undermined debate over the nature of the threat and the appropriate policy response. The consequent deployment of control technologies, such as the extension of intelligence and surveillance operations to cover all financial transactions, electronic and mobile telephonic communications and the confiscation of purportedly criminal assets, formulated by policy making bodies such as the Financial Action Task Force (FATF) and the EU's Multi-Disciplinary Group on Organised Crime (MDG), are not subject to any democratic oversight, and the evidential basis for these policies remains insulated from public scrutiny (Elvins, 2003; Sheptycki, 2003b).

The problematisation of TOC in terms of pyramidal groups and their 'kingpins' or 'core nominals' not only presupposes control strategies of enforcement, punishment, containment, disturbance and dismantling, it also constrains the interpretation and appraisal of these strategies. Intelligence led policing, for example, has been criticised for its 'self-replicating and self-guiding' character in focusing upon measures of activity, such as arrest rates, seizures of illicit goods and the confiscation of proceeds (Sheptycki, 2003b, pp 51–52). Whereas measures of the outcomes of such strategies, for example, reductions in the consumption of illicit narcotics and associated harms, question the very *raison d'être* of law enforcement and open up the political space for devising alternative strategies of control (Ekblom, 2003), measures of activity are self-serving in that they imply the need for more enforcement, the further extension of surveillance and greater investment in intelligence gathering (Sheptycki, 2003b).

Increased opportunities for transnational organised crime

Disenchantment with criminal justice alone as a crime control strategy has been a key factor in the rise of an alternative paradigm, which switches the focus away from the punishment of pathological offenders toward the prevention, or at least reduction, of opportunities for the commission of particular types of crime, in specific situations, at certain moments, by 'rational' actors (Graham and Bennett, 1995, pp 47–70; Clarke, 1997). Counterpoised to the 'criminology of the other', this 'criminology of the self' regards offenders as essentially the same as their victims and certain implications for defining the objects of control follow from this (Garland, 1996, pp 461–63).

Instead of investigating the attributes of 'core nominals' or criminal organisations and deducing problems of crime from these attributes, this narrative is concerned with those factors that make certain organised crime events possible (Stelfox, 2003). It assumes there will be a 'supply of motivated offenders' and argues that it is less important to understand the dispositional qualities of their motivation than to identify how this supply coincides with the availability of 'suitable targets' and the absence of 'capable guardians' in particular places at certain moments to produce crime (Felson, 1994). As such, patterns in the incidence, prevalence and concentration of organised crime are interpreted in terms of social trends that generate increased opportunities. For example, technological innovations in communication and intelligence sharing amongst 'criminal fraternities' (Dorn, 2003) and the abolition of border controls create suitable targets for crime, such as electronic commerce and the evasion of customs and excise duties, whilst negating, or enabling the circumvention of, capable guardians.

This problematisation has also influenced the redefinition of criminal organisations in terms of protean social networks rather than immutable, pyramidal, hierarchies (Coles, 2001). From this perspective, organised crime is enabled through the episodic co-operation of actors with a diversity of skills and resources and this, in turn, is facilitated by intermediaries, or 'criminal contact brokers', who supply criminal entrepreneurs for the purposes of accomplishing particular jobs (Klerks, 2003). These intermediaries have been central to replenishing the capacity of criminal co-operatives after particular actors have been removed by law enforcement operations. They are key targets for control hitherto obscured by the pyramidal conception of organised crime and the consequent focus on 'bosses'. In this narrative, a further distinction is made between the 'molecular' and 'strategic' objects of opportunity reduction (Ekblom, 2003). Molecular objects of control include those specific social networks and proximal circumstances involved in the commissioning of particular crimes. Strategic objects refer to the broader social contexts, such as markets for the production, exchange and consumption of illicit goods and services, which generate the supply of motivated offenders, presence of suitable targets and absence of capable guardians.

This emphasis upon the need to understand the contexts of certain crime events marks a key difference with the narrative of organised crime as an external threat. To emphasise contexts that generate increased opportunities for crime is to recognise that crime events are embedded in particular places and experienced at specific moments; they are woven into the everyday routines of social relations (Felson, 1994). Whereas the external threat narrative invariably proceeds by enumerating checklists of abstract features that provide a content definition of organised crime and then deduces organised crime from these features (Adamoli *et al*, 1998, pp 4–10), the increased opportunities narrative 'reproduces' the causes of crime from an examination of specific events. It then seeks to tailor various technologies of crime prevention to the diverse local contexts and thus routines in which they occur (Pawson and Tilley, 1997; Ekblom, 2003).

Again, certain strategies of control are presupposed in this problematisation, an exemplar of which is the strategy of 'market reduction' (Sutton, 1998). Once overly homogeneous concepts such as TOC are disaggregated into more concrete objects of control, such as illicit trafficking of narcotics, the different dynamics of production, exchange and consumption entailed in the markets for such goods and services can be realised. From this perspective it is argued that control strategies have been preoccupied with curtailing the supply of illicit goods and services through operations against 'core nominals' and organised crime groups (OCGs), whereas a more effective focus for control is the exchange and consumption of such goods and services. Reducing the opportunities for exchange and consumption will, it is presumed, reduce the motivation to provide illicit goods and services on behalf of offenders. From this axiomatic principle, the market reduction approach (MRA) argues that the basic aims of control should be to instil in offenders an appreciation that dealing in illicit goods and services is at least as risky as offending in the first place, and to make the purchase, exchange and consumption of illicit goods and services more risky for all concerned (Sutton *et al*, 2001, p vii). Increasing the risks associated with the exchange and consumption of illicit goods and services can be accomplished by disabling key intermediary actors in illicit markets, especially 'fences' – those who knowingly purchase illicit goods and services with the intention of selling them on to end consumers – such as commercial enterprises (jewellers, pawnbrokers, second-hand dealers, etc), residents (who organise local illicit markets), and hawkers (often the offenders themselves who sell directly to consumers). Although the MRA was initially developed, as with other opportunity reducing technologies, to control volume crimes such as domestic burglary and automobile theft, it is argued its principles can be generalised to other kinds of illicit markets, especially those in narcotics, so long as the particular dynamics and contexts of the markets in question are appreciated (Sutton *et al*, 2001, p 4) and has, subsequently, been identified as a potentially important innovation in the control of organised crime (Stelfox, 2003; Ekblom, 2003).

Although this narrative can be credited with pinpointing the need for 'multi-agency' initiatives against crime, it has been criticised for the limits to its introspection of the causes and control of crime and other social harms. It is argued that criminologies of the self are adaptive to, rather than critical of, the social orders within which they are deployed (Garland, 1996, p 463ff, *passim*). The strategy of opportunity reduction and its attendant technologies of control are defined through a critique of criminal law enforcement as a partial and blunt instrument of control, but not through a critique of the ends of control *per se*, which are 'provisionally accepted' as a reduction in those behaviours proscribed by the criminal law (Pease, 2002, p 970). It is acknowledged, however, that without an ethical foundation, the deployment of opportunity reducing technologies can undermine social relations of trust and tolerance whilst exacerbating inequalities in the provision of security and the experience of victimisation (Pease, 2002, pp 970–72).

For all the rhetorical insistence in the 'increased opportunities' narrative on the need to contextualise crime and its control, the image of offending that is produced by criminologies of the self is one of ahistorical rational actors abstracted from the particular social context and cultural milieu in which they *acquire* an understanding of who they are, what is in their 'rational' interests and how these can be advanced (Edwards and Gill, 2002b, p 248; Hobbs, 1998b, 2001). The retort of advocates of opportunity reduction is that such 'dispositional' questions are impossible to answer and are, in any case, irrelevant to an understanding of how crime events can be prevented (Clarke, 1997). Yet it is precisely for this eschewal of dispositional analysis that the increased opportunities narrative can be criticised as contradictory: policy makers are simultaneously encouraged to tailor control to the specific contexts in which crime events occur but are asked to do so using models of offending behaviour that negate contextual understanding (see Taylor, 1999).

The internal challenge of organised crime

Counterpoised to both narratives of crime as an external threat and as a product of increased opportunities for its commission is a more sociological understanding that regards interactions between crime and control as the products of certain kinds of social, economic and political arrangements. From this perspective crime is endogenous to particular social orders and it is in this sense that problems of crime are regarded as an 'internal challenge', rather than as an alien threat. The internal challenge narrative is also distinct from the idea of crime as a consequence of increased opportunities in that it replaces a focus upon the rational choices of atomised individuals, abstracted from their actual social contexts, with a focus upon the differential cultural, political and economic *associations* between individual and collective actors in historically specific contexts.

Reference to the differential associations entailed in criminal activity reflects the influence of Edwin Sutherland's thinking upon this narration of transnational organised crime (Ruggiero, 2002). Sutherland's proposition that 'white collar crime' belies the deterministic correlation between disadvantage and offending and suggests that criminal behaviour, *per se*, 'is learned in association with those who define it favourably and in isolation from those who define it unfavourably' (1949, p 234) has provided a conceptual foundation for an alternative problematisation of TOC. Criminal activity is regarded as the outcome of interactions infused with a subcultural valorisation of offending as legitimate conduct. However, beyond Sutherland's social psychology of how certain individuals or small groups of actors become criminal, it is argued that criminal associations embody the cultural values of, and are enabled by, entire social formations, especially free market societies (Taylor, 1999, pp 156–63). Further, the dissemination of the 'entrepreneurial spirit' throughout civil society and into the routine, everyday, activities of commerce, coupled with the relentless competitive pressures of the global marketplace generates greater incentives for corruption and the contravention of regulations on trade, for example, in the armaments industry (Taylor, 1999; Ruggiero, 2000a, pp 99–105).

Inspired by Sutherland's work, this narrative has raised questions regarding interdependencies between nominally licit and illicit entrepreneurs in market societies. It is argued that criminal associations are not contained within an 'underworld' or 'dirty' marketplace that parallels the 'upperworld' of 'clean' business. Rather, they segue into 'grey' markets of exchange between licit and illicit actors, as in, for example, the role of certain financial institutions in laundering the proceeds of criminal organisations and the employment of criminal organisations by licit business to circumvent environmental protection laws and dump toxic industrial waste (Block, 1991; Ruggiero, 1998). The idea of grey markets also suggests a broadening of the entrepreneurial activities beyond those formally proscribed in criminal legal codes. The cue for governmental response is 'social harm' rather than the narrower signifier of 'crime'. Critics of existing policy responses to TOC, that depict organised criminal activity as external to the operation of licit markets, often point to the activities of multinational business and note that the consequences of licit market exchange, whilst perhaps not illegal, can, nonetheless, be sometimes considered harmful to civil society (Rawlinson, 2002, 2003; Slapper and Tombs, 1999, pp 131–62; Croall, Chapter 10 this volume).

Interdependencies between 'dirty' and 'clean' markets have also been examined in terms of the stretching of criminal associations across different spatial scales. In these terms there is a certain ambiguity over the status of TOC in the internal challenge narrative. Some acknowledge its utility insofar as it updates Sutherland's ideas for the era of globalisation. Opportunities for licit wealth creation enabled by the growth of transnational commerce, the deregulation of international markets and the construction of continental trading blocs (ASEAN, EU, NAFTA) also establish abundant opportunities for illicit transnational commerce, not least in the trafficking of narcotics (Ruggiero, 2002, pp 180–81). Even so, the over-homogenised imagery of TOC is deconstructed to reveal that globalisation is selective in its distribution of licit, illicit and grey market opportunities for accumulation. With regard to licit business, the multinational corporations that are successfully exploiting the opportunities of deregulated markets are, emphatically, Western. The converse of Western corporate capital's mobility is the immobility of entrepreneurs and the wider citizenry in the developing world. It is, therefore, a moot point as to whether the demons of TOC, the Colombians, Chinese, Russians, Turks, etc, are as mobile as their licit Western counterparts in transnational commerce (Ruggiero, 2002, pp 180–81).

The selectivity and unevenness of globalisation has, in the broader sociological literature, been argued to accentuate the importance of localities, rather than nations, as the new 'nodal' points and basic units of analysis in social and political change (Lash and Urry, 1994, pp 279–313; Hirst and Thompson, 1996, p 170ff). Thinking from within this tradition, some commentators have eschewed the very idea of TOC as a contentless abstraction that is 'devoid of [actual] relations', rather, 'Unlike previous eras, contemporary organised crime with its emphasis upon drugs, fraud and counterfeiting, simultaneously occupies both the local and the global. It is ... "local at all points"' (Hobbs, 1998a, p 143). As a consequence the overlapping of licit and illicit enterprise occurs within 'glocalities' whose diverse cultural, political and economic histories shape the possibilities for criminal enterprise (Hobbs, 1998a, 1998b).

This focus on 'glocal' rather than 'transnational' organised crime implies a further revision to the concept of human agency deployed in the narratives of 'external threat' and 'increased opportunities'. In place of the 'ethnic other' or the 'rational self' models of agency, it is argued that criminal associations entail not just instrumental-rational but also affective and habitual dispositions. These embody routines, prejudice, amorous attachments etc, on the basis of which entrepreneurs decide who to trust and do business with. If this is the case with licit enterprises, which may collapse precisely because they *fail* to adopt rational, utility maximising, approaches to the calculation of the risks, efforts and rewards associated with particular ventures, then such cultural qualities of interaction are accentuated for illicit entrepreneurs operating in hostile, law enforcement environments where trust is at a premium (Hobbs, 2001; Hall, 1997; Klerks, 2003).

The narrative of organised crime as an internal challenge to certain social formations has not accomplished the same degree of influence over official discourse as have narratives of external threat or, as is increasingly the case, of increased opportunities (NCIS, 2000). Nonetheless, it can still be understood as a governmentality insofar as its problematisation presupposes certain governable places and actors and technologies for their control. This narrative presupposes interventions against the social preconditions for the formation and reproduction of criminal associations. Ethnographic research into the dynamics of criminal networks in English localities has, for example, identified the operation of local housing and labour markets as central to an understanding of how networks are formed and reproduced or disabled (Hobbs, 1998b; Hobbs and Dunningham, 1998). The implication of this is that social policy interventions should be prioritised in official discourse on crime and control. In addition, it is argued that policing and criminal justice interventions can have perverse, unintended consequences in generating lucrative markets for organised crime, as in, for example, the regulation of narcotics (Rawlinson, 2003; Stelfox, 2003). Another policy implication of this narrative is the need for action research into the structures of different markets; how they unevenly distribute cultural, political and economic capital amongst competing entrepreneurs; and the contribution of policing and regulation to the creation, stagnation or collapse of such markets (Edwards and Gill, 2002a).

A more profound implication of the internal challenge narrative, however, is that such technologies of control should be deployed towards the end of social, not just criminal, justice. This is, arguably, the key quality distinguishing this from the other two narratives discussed in this chapter. For, in their domination of official discourse, criminologies of the other and self have disassociated strategies of control from political debate over the ends of government; instead they promulgate 'policies for managing the danger and policing the divisions created by a certain kind of [neo-liberal] social organisation' (Garland, 1996, p 463–66). So, whereas others have noted the dangers inherent in a 'criminalisation' of social policy (Crawford, 1998), the implication of this narrative is that crime control policy is 'socialised'.

Conclusion: actors, activities and contexts

It is possible to draw broader lessons from these alternative diagnoses of TOC for comparative criminological research. They suggest three basic predicates for comparison: actors, activities and contexts. Ethnicity clearly provides a key resource for the organisation of serious crimes in hostile environments; where trust is at a premium, familial and broader kinship networks provide insulation against policing and intelligence operations (Werdmolder, 1998). A problem, however, with the external threat narrative in official discourse on TOC is that it reifies ethnicity, mistaking this as the necessary organising feature of serious crime when the other research reviewed above suggests it is but one, contingent, determinant of organised criminality. This is not to suggest that criminal organisations cannot employ ethnicity as a resource in the trafficking of illicit goods and services, but even here such organisations are unlikely to control the entire operation from production through to distribution to end consumers. Rather, they may become involved in a narrow section of a particular market, for example, the role of Albanian organisations in trafficking narcotics into Italy, but after importation the actual control of local markets for the distribution of these drugs is likely to be captured by 'domestic' networks of dealers (Ruggiero, 2000b). Indeed it is precisely when external organisations seek to overreach their control of illicit markets that violent turf wars ensue and are invariably won by local actors who possess greater resources, especially knowledge of local markets and dealers. As such, and notwithstanding the potential for such reification to fuel bigoted constructions of criminality (see Keith, 1993), this focus on ethnicity obscures the importance of other kinds of actor, such as the intermediary 'criminal contact brokers' and episodic associations revealed in social network analyses of criminal activity. Criminal organisations often atrophy precisely because networks premised on ethnicity limit the scope for expansion and diversification into multiple sectors for the production, exchange and consumption of illicit goods and services. At a certain point these networks have to recruit beyond familiar contacts in order to reproduce themselves, and it is at this point that co-operatives are vulnerable to disruption and intelligence operations; an argument that has been used to explain the 'paradoxes of organised crime' (Paoli, 2002).

Switching the focus of comparative research from actors to activities promises a more determinant insight into the actual dynamics of organised crime. Questioning not who is involved and why they are involved, but *how* organised crimes are accomplished, enables a deconstruction of the over-homogenised imagery of TOC into very different concrete activities such as trafficking narcotics, armaments and people. This has been the principal insight of the application of theories of opportunity reduction to organised crime. Comparative research into how serious crimes are organised can also inform an understanding of those relations that are necessary for serious crime to occur. Here, Felson's (1994) abstract discussion of routine activities provides a repertoire of analytical devices for conceptualising the conduct of organised crime. The crucial limitation of the increased opportunities narrative, however, is its understanding of human agency. In place of reified ethnicity it proposes the equally reified 'rational actor', mechanically calculating the risks, effort and rewards irrespective of the contingent social contexts in which these actors acquire an understanding of how to organise.

Conceptualisation of, and research into, the diverse social contexts of organised crime and its interrelationship with control is still at an early stage (Dorn, 2003) but ethnographic research into the differential associations that enable or preclude the formation and reproduction of criminal co-operatives has identified important avenues for comparative research. It is suggested that key shifts in local housing and labour markets have a major effect upon the development and sustainability of criminal networks, with the implication that such social policy 'levers' as housing, employment and transport policies can be manipulated to control the preconditions for organised criminality (Hobbs, 1998b). This insight is especially important given, certainly in Western Europe, the increasing fear and consequent persecution of migrant populations. The simplistic association of migrants with the import of crime, especially organised crime, is accentuated by the ethnic actor model of criminality, with the potential for provoking serious civil unrest as vigilante assaults upon these latest folk devils are amplified by vindictive media coverage.

Avoiding the potentially regressive consequences of crime control strategies that are informed by the ethnic actor model and other crude, voluntaristic conceptions of human conduct, entails a research programme that takes the contexts of crime seriously (Taylor, 1999). In advancing this programme, however, there must be reservations about the utility of the concept of transnationality, as it applies to crime. The strong criticism of this concept argues that it is a contentless abstraction, a figment of policy discourse, that bears no relation to the actual experience of social relations thought to be, 'local at all points' (Hobbs, 1998a). Thus there are clearly processes of globalisation, such as the intercontinental trafficking of narcotics, armaments and people, but their impact is not uniformly experienced. Rather, such processes are uneven in their impact as they are filtered by local social conditions, and these conditions are as much a product of decisions about social policy as they are of criminal justice and crime reduction policies. The weaker criticism of the transnationality perspective is that it remains a pertinent focus for research into the conduct of cross-border activities and of organised criminality in cyberspace but cannot differentiate between other kinds of social context. To this end, the concept of 'glocality' may prove a more fruitful organising framework for comparative criminology.

Adopting the focus upon glocality suggests further revisions to the predominant conception of TOC and the research programmes that are driven by both the external threat and increased opportunities narratives. Both share a preoccupation with what, in contemporary criminological thought, has been called the 'aetiology of deficit', which is preoccupied with explaining organised crime in terms of some inadequacy, such as, 'absence of the state, pathology and lack of control, relative poverty, and delinquent subcultures', as opposed to 'affluence, development and the control of resources' (Ruggiero, 1996, p 33). Shifting the paradigm of causal explanation from that of deficit to affluence entails a reversal of the lens through which TOC has been viewed. In place of a concern over the opportunities that globalisation presents to criminal organisations in the developing world, to threaten the security of western political economies, and notwithstanding the victimisation they cause within the developing world (Goodey, 2003), there are crucial questions for transnational criminological research into the export of illicit goods and services from the West, such as the role of corporations in the armaments, energy and pharmaceutical industries. In a globalised world, the asymmetrical control of resources pertains to illicit as well as licit trade; the more opportunities that actors have in the context of deregulated, licit markets, the more opportunities these same actors have for illicit activities and for the legitimation of these activities.

References

Adamoli, S, Di Nicola, A, Savona, EU and Zoffi, P (1998) *Organised Crime Around the World*, Helsinki: HEUNI

Bigo, D (1994) 'The European internal security field: stakes in a newly developing area of police intervention', in Anderson, M and den Boer, M (eds), *Policing Across National Boundaries*, London: Pinter, pp 161–73

Bigo, D (2000) 'Liaison officers in Europe: new officers in the European security field', in Sheptycki, J (ed), *Issues in Transnational Policing*, London: Routledge

Block, A (1991) 'Organized crime, garbage and toxic waste: an overview', in Block, A, *Perspectives on Organized Crime: Essays in Opposition*, Dordrecht: Kluwer

Burchell, G, Gordon, C and Miller, P (eds) (1991) *The Foucault Effect: Studies in Governmentality*, Brighton: Harvester Wheatsheaf

Buzan, B, Wæver, O and de Wilde, J (1998) *Security: A New Framework for Analysis*, London: Lynne Rienner

Clarke, RV (1997) 'Introduction', in Clarke, RV (ed), *Situational Crime Prevention: Successful Case Studies*, 2nd edn, Guilderland, New York: Harrow and Heston

Coles, N (2001) 'It's not what you know – it's who you know that counts: analysing serious crime groups as social networks' 41(4) *British Journal of Criminology* 580–94

Crawford, A (1998) *Crime Prevention and Community Safety: Politics, Policies and Practices*, London: Longman

Dorn, N (2003) 'Proteiform criminalities: the formation of organised crime as organisers' responses to developments in four fields of control', in Edwards, A and Gill, P (eds), *Transnational Organised Crime: Perspectives on Global Security*, London: Routledge

Edwards, A and Gill, P (2002a) 'Crime as enterprise? The case of "transnational organised crime"' 37(3) *Crime, Law and Social Change* 203–23

Edwards, A and Gill, P (2002b) 'The politics of "transnational organised crime": discourse, reflexivity and the narration of "threat"' 4(2) *British Journal of Politics and International Relations* 245–70.

Edwards, A and Gill, P (eds) (2003a) *Transnational Organised Crime: Perspectives on Global Security*, London: Routledge

Edwards, A and Gill, P (2003b) 'After transnational organised crime? The politics of public safety', in Edwards, A and Gill, P (eds), *Transnational Organised Crime: Perspectives on Global Security*, London: Routledge

Ekblom, P (2003) 'Organised crime and the conjunction of criminal opportunity framework', in Edwards, A and Gill, P (eds), *Transnational Organised Crime: Perspectives on Global Security*, London: Routledge

Elvins, M (2003) 'Europe's response to transnational organised crime', in Edwards, A and Gill, P (eds), *Transnational Organised Crime: Perspectives on Global Security*, London: Routledge

Felson, M (1994) *Crime and Everyday Life*, Thousand Oaks, California: Pine Forge Press

Foucault, M (1991) 'Governmentality', in Burchell, G, Gordon, C and Miller, P (eds), *The Foucault Effect: Studies in Governmentality*, London: Harvester Wheatsheaf

Garland, D (1996) 'The limits of the sovereign state: strategies of crime control in contemporary society' 36(4) *British Journal of Criminology* 445–71

Goodey, J (2003) 'Recognising organised crime's victims: the case of sex trafficking in the EU', in Edwards, A and Gill, P (eds), *Transnational Organised Crime: Perspectives on Global Security*, London: Routledge

Graham, J and Bennett, T (1995) *Crime Prevention Strategies in Europe and North America*, Helsinki: HEUNI

Hall, S (1997) 'Visceral cultures and criminal practices' 1(4) *Theoretical Criminology* 453–78

Hirst, P and Thompson, G (1996) *Globalisation in Question: The International Economy and the Possibilities of Governance*, Cambridge: Polity

Hobbs, D (1998a) 'The case against: there is not a global crime problem' 3(2) *International Journal of Risk, Security and Crime Prevention* 139–43

Hobbs, D (1998b) 'Going down the glocal: the local context of organised crime' 37(4) *The Howard Journal* 407–22

Hobbs, D (2001) 'The firm: organisational logic and criminal culture on a shifting terrain' 41(4) *British Journal of Criminology* 549–60

Hobbs, D and Dunningham, C (1998) 'Glocal organised crime: context and pretext', in Ruggiero, V, South, N and Taylor, I (eds), *The New European Criminology: Crime and Social Order in Europe*, London: Routledge

Keith, M (1993) *Race, Riots and Policing: Lore and Disorder in a Multi-Racist Society*, London: UCL Press

Klerks, P (2003) 'The network paradigm applied to criminal organisations: theoretical nitpicking or a relevant doctrine for investigators? Recent developments in the Netherlands', in Edwards, A and Gill, P (eds), *Transnational Organised Crime: Perspectives on Global Security*, London: Routledge

Lash, S and Urry, J (1994) *Economies of Signs and Space*, London: Sage

Levi, M (2003) 'Criminal asset-stripping: confiscating the proceeds of crime in England and Wales', in Edwards, A and Gill, P (eds), *Transnational Organised Crime: Perspectives on Global Security*, London: Routledge

NCIS (National Criminal Intelligence Service) (2000) *The National Intelligence Model*, London: NCIS

O'Malley, P (2001) 'Governmentality', in McLaughlin, E and Muncie, J (eds), *The Sage Dictionary of Criminology*, London: Sage

Paoli, L (2002) 'The paradoxes of organised crime' 37 *Crime, Law and Social Change* 51–97

Pawson, R and Tilley, N (1997) *Realistic Evaluation*, London: Sage

Pease, K (2002) 'Crime reduction', in Maguire, M, Morgan, R and Reiner, R (eds), *The Oxford Handbook of Criminology*, 3rd edn, Oxford: OUP

Raine, LP and Cilluffo, EJ (1994) *Global Organized Crime: The New Empire of Evil*, Washington, DC: Centre for Strategic and International Studies

Rawlinson, P (2003) 'Bad boys in the Baltics', in Edwards, A and Gill, P (eds), *Transnational Organised Crime: Perspectives on Global Security*, London: Routledge

Rawlinson, P (2002) 'Capitalists, criminals and oligarchs – Sutherland and the new "robber barons"' 37(3) *Crime, Law and Social Change* 293–307

Ruggiero, V (1996) *Organised and Corporate Crime in Europe*, Dartmouth: Ashgate

Ruggiero, V (1998) 'Transnational criminal activities: the provision of services in the dirty economies' 3(2) *International Journal of Risk, Security and Crime Prevention* 121–29

Ruggiero, V (2000a) *Crime and Markets: Essays in Anti-Criminology*, Oxford: OUP

Ruggiero, V (2000b) 'Criminal franchising: Albanians and illicit drugs in Italy', in Natarajan, M and Hough, M (eds), *Illegal Drug Markets: From Research to Prevention Policy*, New York: Criminal Justice Press

Ruggiero, V (2002) 'Introduction – fuzzy criminal actors' 37(3) *Crime Law and Social Change* 177–90

Sheptycki, J (2003a) 'Against transnational organized crime', in Beare, M (ed), *Critical Reflections on Transnational Organized Crime, Money Laundering and Corruption*, Toronto: Toronto UP, pp 120–44

Sheptycki, J (2003b) 'Global law enforcement as a protection racket: some sceptical notes on transnational organised crime as an object of global governance', in Edwards, A and Gill, P (eds), *Transnational Organised Crime: Perspectives on Global Security*, London: Routledge

Slapper, G and Tombs, S (1999) *Corporate Crime*, Harlow: Longman

Smandych, R (ed) (1999) *Governable Places: Readings on Governmentality and Crime Control*, Dartmouth: Ashgate

Stelfox, P (2003) 'Transnational organised crime: a police perspective', in Edwards, A and Gill, P (eds), *Transnational Organised Crime: Perspectives on Global Security*, London: Routledge

Stenson, K (2000) 'Crime control, social policy and liberalism', in Lewis, G, Gewirtz, S and Clarke, J (eds), *Rethinking Social Policy*, London: Sage

Sutherland, E (1949) *White-Collar Crime*, New York: Holt, Rinehart and Winston

Sutton, M (1998) *Handling Stolen Goods and Theft: A Market Reduction Approach*, Home Office Research Study 178, London: Home Office

Sutton, M, Schneider, J and Hetherington, S (2001) *Tackling Theft with the Market Reduction Approach*, Home Office Crime Reduction Series Paper 8, London: Home Office

Taylor, I (1999) *Crime in Context: A Critical Criminology of Market Societies*, Cambridge: Polity

Werdmolder, H (1998) 'Moroccan organised crime in the Netherlands' 3(2) *International Journal of Risk, Security and Crime Prevention* 111–20

Woodiwiss, M (2003) 'Transnational organised crime: the global reach of an American concept', in Edwards, A and Gill, P (eds), *Transnational Organised Crime: Perspectives on Global Security*, London: Routledge

Young, J (1999) *The Exclusive Society: Social Exclusion, Crime and Difference in Late Modernity*, London: Sage

Chapter 10
Transnational White Collar Crime
Hazel Croall

Introduction

The collapse of major banks and corporations amid revelations of false accounting and fraud have been felt around the globe and alert attention to the worldwide impact of white collar and corporate crime. Despite this, much political, popular and academic focus on transnational crime has been concerned with organised crime. Yet legitimate and illegitimate industries alike exploit the opportunities provided by globalisation to move capital and production outside the reach of regulators, and both are involved in illegal forms of cross-border trading. The global activities of corporations and financial institutions, often the focus of anti-globalisation protests, often involve far greater harm than many conventional crimes, even transnational ones. The study of white collar crime has always involved unmasking the activities of seemingly respectable occupational groups and organisations. At the same time, the study of crimes of the powerful has always posed fundamental questions about how crime is popularly and legally defined and about the role of criminalisation. Such issues remain pertinent in an era of globalisation, indeed they may be more so.

Many questions can be asked about the relationship between globalisation and white collar crime, including whether globalisation has produced greater opportunities for such criminals. How is white collar crime to be defined in a global context? How is it related to other forms of transnational crime (some of which are outlined in other chapters of this book)? As will be seen below, many harmful business activities are not, in any technical legal sense, crimes. So, what issues does transnational white collar crime raise for global criminalisation, regulation and control? This chapter will start by looking at the definition and nature of white collar crime in a comparative criminological and global context. It will look at some examples of transnational white collar crime before considering its global and local impact. Finally, it will explore some of the issues which this raises about the analysis and control of white collar crime.

White collar crime in a global context

Since Sutherland (1949) introduced the concept of white collar crime as 'crime committed by a person of high social status and respectability in the course of his occupation', it has been an awkward category to define and incorporate within criminology (Croall, 2001a; Nelken, 2002). Is it to be defined by the social status and respectability of actors, or by the occupational location of activities? It is characterised by an ambiguous criminal status, low rates of prosecution and relatively lenient punishment – is it therefore really 'crime'? This, taken along with its location in formal, professional and legitimate occupational roles makes it less visible than other forms of crime and exposing it has been a major theme of research. This raises quotidian questions about the ability of high status individuals and powerful organisations to avoid the full force of the criminal law (Sheptycki, 2003a).

The issues often centre on the definition and categorisation of the many different forms of crime deriving from occupational roles. Most criminologists now accept a broad distinction between occupational white collar crime, in which perpetrators seek to gain personally at the expense of clients or employers, and corporate or organisational crime, in which the crime benefits the organisation by prioritising profitability or survival at the expense of safety, quality, environmental and social considerations. The category, 'white collar crime', has also generally been restricted to 'legitimate' occupations and organisations to distinguish it from the illegal businesses associated with organised crime, although this distinction is arguably quite blurred in reality (Ruggiero, 2002). Some criminologists argue that the relationship between the legal and illegal businesses involved in crime should be seen as being ranged along a continuum between legitimacy and illegitimacy, rather than consisting in artificially watertight conceptual boxes of crime types (Edwards and Gill, 2002; Croall, 2001a).

White collar crime raises vexing ideological and political considerations (Slapper and Tombs, 1999). Should the category be restricted to 'criminal' offences or should harmful business activities, irrespective of formal status in relation to criminal law, be included? On the one hand, including all harmful business activities immediately attracts criticisms of subjectivity and political bias. On the other, excluding activities widely regarded as causing avoidable harm precludes exploring broader questions of how and why only some business activities are criminalised. Why, for example, is it illegal to produce, distribute and sell heroin yet legal to do the same (subject to some restrictions) for alcohol and tobacco? Such questions are unlikely to produce consensus. Some critical criminologists have argued that the category should encompass the widest possible range of harmful corporate and governmental activities, but most restrict the category to activities which are subject to some form of administrative or civil law procedures, if not the criminal law itself.

These issues are particularly pertinent in a transnational and comparative criminological context, not least because of terminological confusion. While 'white collar crime' is academically and popularly recognised in many English speaking and some European countries, in others, such those in Scandinavia, the term is scarcely used (Korsell, 2002). The term 'economic crime' is sometimes preferred, although this, along with terms such as 'business crime' can be criticised as somewhat vague (Naylor, 2003) and as not distinguishing between legitimate or illegitimate businesses, or between crimes committed by businesses and those, analogous to burglary or theft which victimise businesses. Different cultural and legal definitions about what constitutes criminal business activities must be into taken account at every turn. For example, what is seen as corruption or bribery in many Western countries may be culturally accepted in others (Nelken, 2002), and the distinction between fraudulent and acceptable sales practices varies within and between nations. Many Western countries have criminally enforceable regulations to protect workers, consumers and the general public from the hazards associated with industry, regulations which, very often, are not as advanced in developing countries. Moreover, tax law and other aspects of financial regulation also differ considerably between jurisdictions. These variations are important – not only because they make comparative research difficult, but also because they enable individuals and companies to avoid the law in one country by placing their business in another.

This is in turn related to the phenomenon of globalisation which, while its characteristics and effects are much debated, is widely acknowledged to have been accompanied by financial deregulation which has enabled the free movement of finance capital and business enterprise. Improved transport, communications and the internet have led to the de-territorialisation of many businesses. Money and production can be moved around the world, companies can operate in several countries simultaneously and, indeed, some no longer require a national base but rather can exist in some, almost metaphysical, world 'offshore' (Sheptycki, 2000). Laws and regulations on the other hand are jurisdictionally based most often within defined national boundaries, creating regulatory 'voids' (Tillman, 2002), 'spaces between laws' (Michalowski and Kramer, 1987) and the problem of 'jurisdiction shopping' (Sheptycki, 2000). The developing wave of global capitalism, and the white collar criminals who ride it, can easily avoid the letter of the law in one or another country even while their activities clearly breach its spirit in all of them.

Globalisation therefore provides the context for what can comfortably be described as transnational crime. Unfortunately, although this term encompasses the activities of legitimate and illegitimate businesses, it has become more narrowly identified with organised crime (Block, 1999; Passas, 2000; Sheptycki, 2003b, 2003c). Many criminologists argue, however, that the definitions should not be so exclusive. Passas (2000, p 17), for example, defines transnational crime as:

> cross-border misconduct that entails avoidable and unnecessary harm to society, is serious enough to warrant state intervention and is similar to other kinds of acts criminalised in the countries concerned or by international law.

Crime is transnational, Passas argues, when offences or victims are located in, or operate through, more than one country. In a similar vein, Gilbert and Russell (2002, p 214) define transnational corporate crime as 'conduct by corporate entities ... doing business in two or more nations that creates avoidable harms in at least one nation, which may or may not be the site of corporate activity'. These corporate actions either 'violate existing criminal, civil or regulatory law' or are 'manifestly harmful to persons, property, indigenous cultures or the environment'. These definitions take account of many of the points raised above – they enable the inclusion of activities which are not, legally speaking, criminal, while restricting the category to activities which are criminalised or subject to legal intervention in some of the jurisdictions concerned. As well as highlighting the proper place of international human rights conventions and those relating to crimes against the environment, they also raise the important issue of international law enforcement capacity.

This chapter will focus on the transnational activities of largely legitimate businesses while recognising that sometimes legitimacy may be difficult to determine. Following on from the definitional discussion above, it will also include activities that, while possibly legal in some technical sense, cause avoidable harms that may be regulated by law in at least one concerned jurisdiction. But before discussing broader issues in relation to globalisation, criminalisation and regulation, the chapter will explore selected forms of what can be described as transnational white collar and corporate crime. Many of these examples are what Passas (2000) describes as 'crimes without law violations', including financial frauds and tax evasion. Others derive from the 'forum shopping' activities of corporations who choose to operate in countries offering low rates of taxation, lower labour costs and less stringent financial and worker health and safety regulations – described by some critics of globalisation as the corporate 'race to the bottom'. Other regulatory issues arise in the context of the great variety of cross-border trading, often involving both legal and illegal enterprises in which both legal and illegal goods may be transported between countries.

Offshore havens

A major feature of many forms of transnational crime is the use of offshore financial centres, which, while most often associated with the money laundering activities of organised crime and terrorism, were originally developed as a means of avoiding tax and other financial regulations (Blum, 1999). The numbered Swiss bank account is legendary. While the services provided by offshore banking centres vary, they generally provide very low rates of taxation, loose financial supervision and confidentiality (since they do not always co-operate with regulators in other jurisdictions, see: Beare, 2002a; Johnson and Holub, 2003; Sheptycki, 2000). Companies can use these centres without having much of a physical presence in the jurisdiction in question, often through the use of 'shell companies' (corporate vehicles that mask ownership details and provide anonymity). The use of offshore facilities has expanded with globalisation. Indeed many major financial centres, including the City of London, now offer 'offshore' facilities. The term can be misleading since it has traditionally had a limited association with banking systems in such places as the Grand Cayman Islands or the Bahamas (Johnson and Holub, 2003). The term is a source of confusion in another way, since by focusing on their use by organised crime and terrorism, this has diverted attention from the extent to which individuals and legitimate companies use them to evade or avoid taxes (Nelken, 2002; Beare, 2002a). Criminologists have estimated that a mere 10% of so called 'hot money' circulating offshore is attributable to organised crime (Ruggiero, 2000b). It is difficult to underestimate their importance to global capitalism since they harbour enormous sums of money: according to one estimate up to one-third of all global wealth (Boyle, 1998).

'Global pirates'

An example of how these shelters can be used by financial fraudsters is provided in Tillman (2002). He studied 'global pirates' involved in insurance and investment frauds whose operations involved numerous individuals and companies operating in dozens of countries. Insurance, argues Tillman, is particularly criminogenic as it involves taking premiums with promises to pay in the future. Risks are passed on by selling policies to other companies – in many cases located offshore. The frauds explored in this study were assisted by other factors – in California a proposition requiring all insurance providers to cut rates led to the withdrawal of major insurance companies from 'high risk' markets which included smaller companies seeking health insurance. This provided space for the sale of low cost policies which were then passed on to a variety of offshore companies, many of which had few assets to meet claims, and premiums were diverted for the personal benefits of fraudsters. As regulators caught up with one company, assets were moved to a different company in a different location.

Eventually, the loopholes in the regulatory structure were tightened, but the perpetrators diversified into different types of fraud. One example involved the sale of 'promissory notes' in which investors were offered apparently low risk/high yield investments backed up by 'guarantees' to pay by seemingly respectable insurance companies. These were again located offshore with few assets. This particular fraud was estimated by the US Securities and Exchange Commission to have amounted to $300 million and involved both 'white collar' fraudsters and organised criminals moving into new markets. Even the offshore bases themselves could be fictitious. There were examples of 'fantasy islands' or 'virtual nations' based on tiny areas of land or sea that offered 'economic citizenship' and even passports that could permit otherwise excluded people to enter Western countries.

Tax evasion and avoidance

Offshore financial centres are also widely used to minimise tax liability. This may be either illegal (tax evasion) or legal (tax avoidance) – although a very difficult to define boundary separates the two. Tax avoidance schemes are often extremely complex and are based on the advice of professional legal and financial advisers and, while legal, may be quite clearly against the spirit of the law and can lead to 'legal leapfrogging' in which legislators and regulators close one loophole, only for experts to discover another (McBarnet, 1988). Avoiding taxes has been described in the United States as 'unpatriotic', although an entire industry has grown up around corporate tax evasion with the biggest five accounting firms charging corporations a proportion of the savings gained from the use of tax shelters (Beare, 2002a).

Considerable sums are saved, as revealed in Johnson and Holub's (2003) exploration of 'corporate flight'. Enron, which collapsed following a bankruptcy petition in 2001, was revealed to have avoided $409 million in US taxes over five years through the use of shelters, and was under investigation for tax evasion in Bolivia (Tombs and Whyte, 2003). Many multinational corporations avoid tax by locating subsidiaries offshore. According to Tombs and Whyte, by doing so, major US corporations can expect to reduce tax liability by between 10 and 25%. Some companies are now relocating head offices or reincorporating offshore because of the huge tax savings. Sheptycki (2000, p 143) reported that, through judicious use of offshore banking havens, Rupert Murdoch's News Corporation limited its tax exposure in the last years of the 1990s to a mere 6% annually. In contrast, Disney paid about 31% in corporate tax during the same period. Tombs and Whyte liken offshore incorporation through shell companies to the use of 'flags of convenience' in international shipping. The benefits due to tax avoidance alone are palpable, but just as a Panamanian registered vessel is, actuarially speaking, a risk and a danger on the high seas, so too is a shell company registered in Aruba a risky investment vehicle.

These kinds of activities, described by the OECD as 'harmful tax competition', have considerable impact on rich and poor countries alike. By facilitating capital flight, offshore banking practices reduce the tax base and deprive governments of revenue, shifting the tax burden onto the less mobile – chiefly small businesses and middle class wage earners. It is not for nothing that the US Treasury Department describes this as the nation's biggest tax enforcement problem (Beare, 2002a). Despite this, regulatory efforts have focused on the problems of organised crime and money laundering, with the presidential administration of George W Bush in particular being reluctant to take substantial action against tax evasion. This provides further evidence, if any was needed, of the relative leniency concerning aspects of white collar crime in comparison with organised crime.[1]

Jurisdiction shopping

Another example of corporate 'crimes without law violation' is 'forum shopping' or 'jurisdiction shopping'. In this context we are concerned with corporations which choose to locate production in developing countries in order to take advantage of low wages and lenient health and safety regulations as well as minimise exposure to taxation. Jurisdiction shopping may also prove advantageous because corporations may be less exposed to the possibility of private legal actions that attempt to hold them liable for their conduct (Gilbert and Russell, 2002). Developing countries often compete to host multinational corporations and do not find it easy to resist their advances since they provide the financial means to service external debts and much needed employment (Passas, 2000). Some such countries may sign deals without taking full account of the hazards involved. This 'race to the bottom' has been associated with a range of harmful activities including the 'dumping' of toxic wastes and unsafe products; the use of child labour; the failure to pay a living wage; the production of defective products; and the exposure of uninformed and unprotected workers to dangerous working conditions (Gilbert and Russell, 2002). While these may not, legally, be criminal in the jurisdiction concerned, they are examples of just the kinds of activities that would be subject to criminalisation 'at home', and therefore ought to be included in our definition of transnational crime as discussed previously.

The best known example of the catastrophic effects of such activities was the death of 3,000–5,000 people, and the harm to at least 200,000 more, following the release of methyl isocynate from a chemical plant run by Union Carbide in the Indian town of Bhopal in 1984 – its effects are still being felt today (Sarangi, 2002). While no successful criminal prosecution ensued, it was established that the plant was poorly designed and located, and had less adequate systems of safety than equivalent plants in the United States (Punch, 1996; Pearce and Tombs, 1993). Less stringent health and safety standards have also been associated with high numbers of deaths at work, noted in countries such as China and Mexico (Brown, 2002). Moreover, workers can be doubly exposed to hazards at work and environmental

---

1 This may be loaded with irony, since at least some American citizens hiding their wealth offshore may object to the huge amount of government spending on the 'military industrial complex' or the 'apparatus of the penal state'.

damage in their community. European companies operating abroad, encouraged by the fiscal benefits from local governments, have also been linked to 'labour intensive or slave type exploitation' (Ruggiero, 2000a), including the use of cheap and forced labour in south-east Asia, the employment of local labour in unregistered workshops in rural areas and the use of prison labour in Malaysia and Burma. Crimes against the environment have also been facilitated through forum shopping.

Another aspect of transnational corporate crime is the sale of dangerous goods in less developed countries after they have been banned in the West. The drug Thalidomide, associated with a variety of deformities in children, was sold in the third world after being banned in the West (Braithwaite, 1984). Another notorious example of this concerned an intra-uterine contraceptive device called the Dalkon Shield, which caused infections and infertility in thousands of US women (and killed at least 17). After it was withdrawn from the market in the United States, half a million units were sold overseas mostly in Africa (see Finlay, 1996). Another well known and, as is so often the case with white collar crime, ambiguous example concerns the marketing of infant formula in developing nations by the Nestlé Corporation. Mothers in these nations lack the necessary access to clean water or sterilisation and often cannot read the instructions on the bottles – facts apparently known to decision makers in the corporation. As a result of the successful marketing of these products, it is estimated that millions of children suffered dysentery and severe health problems, while thousands actually died of dehydration or malnutrition from contaminated or diluted formula (Gilbert and Russell, 2002).

The 'race to the bottom' is associated with other forms of crime. Locating abroad has for long been linked to the bribery of officials and governments (Braithwaite, 1979). This is often justified as necessary to secure contracts and as accepted practice in some countries. Indeed until as recently as 1997, companies could claim tax relief on bribes offered to public officials abroad (Elliott, 1997; Pallister, 2001). Environmental offences such as the disposal of toxic waste may involve organised criminal groups providing a service to legitimate industries (Ruggiero, 1996).

The criminogenic effects of world financial institutions

Amongst the 'avoidable harms' discussed by critics of globalisation is the impact of the policies of financial institutions such as the World Bank. Entire economies, the environment and local communities can be damaged as a result of the way in which these global financial institutions lend money to or fund projects in developing countries. It is worth emphasising that lending decisions are usually based on economic rather than strictly humanitarian considerations. While stretching the concept of 'crime' to include these activities might seem inappropriate, it is possible to make a strong argument that the activities of the World Bank can indeed be described as 'transnational state finance crime'. According to Friedrichs and Friedrichs (2002), this involves co-operative endeavours between international financial institutions, transnational corporations and political elites in developing countries which lead to demonstrably harmful activities in violation of international law or international human rights conventions. The damage inflicted on local communities by dam building projects, often initiated to support foreign industries, is widely recognised. In a case study of one such project, Friedrichs and Friedrichs (2002) found that it led to the flooding of a forest, the destruction of subsistence crops, the destruction of the way of life of fisherman following a decline in the fish population and the spread of water borne diseases. Protests were brutally repressed although eventually the dam gates were reopened.

The structure of the World Bank is criminogenic, or at least it causes great social harm. Its formulae for decision making forefront the economic aspects of its operations. The priorities reflected in its incentive structure rewards officials for making large loans that encourage large costly projects. While the resulting harms are not intended as such, international financial institutions are arguably subject to international conventions requiring them not to exacerbate conditions impinging on human rights. It follows that the World Bank is therefore at minimum criminally negligent through its failure to take account of the impact of its loans on indigenous peoples and the environment. The UN Universal Declaration of Human Rights states that in no case should a people be deprived of their means of subsistence. Hence, the Friedrichs argue that, when the policies and practices of international financial institutions result in avoidable harm and lead to a violation of widely recognised human rights, these actions should be considered to be crimes, whether or not specific violations of international or state law are involved.

Illicit trade

While white collar crime is often associated with high status perpetrators or large multinational corporations, and organised crime with highly organised criminal cartels, both forms of crime (at both the local and international level) have been associated with smaller enterprises and with loosely organised networks which include businesses operating at the margins of legitimacy and whose activities may involve both legal and illegal trading (Croall, 2001a; Ruggiero, 2000a). These may involve trading in goods which, while otherwise legitimate, are being illegally produced, distributed or sold. The 'smuggling' of cigarettes in order to evade revenue is perhaps one of the best documented examples of this (Beare, 2002a; Van Duyne, 2003). There are other areas of concern such as the transnational distribution and marketing of food products which breach labelling or quality regulations, trade in 'counterfeit' goods, or the facilitation of illegal immigration (which often has the result of providing a large pool of cheap labour for legitimate organisations). The Common Agricultural Policy of the European Union has produced a large number of subsidy frauds involving trade across international barriers (Passas and Nelken, 1993). Customs and other officials have been bribed to enable such trading and otherwise legitimate transportation companies have been, knowingly or unknowingly, used to assist transportation. While often associated with organised crime, these trades more often involve a range of legitimate, illegitimate and semi-legitimate enterprises whose members often have few prior links with 'organised crime' (Ruggiero, 2000a). These matters need to be briefly considered here in order to demonstrate the involvement of legitimate industries and the blurred analytical distinctions between the categories of 'white collar', 'organised' or 'enterprise' crime.

One example is that of people trafficking. While this is often attributed to organised crime, a wide range of personnel are involved and, of particular interest for the current discussion, traffickers can provide a service to legitimate industry (Ruggiero, 1996). Illegal immigrants are widely found in low paid casual employment on farms, building sites, restaurants and care homes. Indeed, one report suggests that parts of the food and fish packing industries are dependent on migrant casual labour recruited by 'gangsters' – practices which have led to prosecutions for tax and VAT fraud (Lawrence and Evans, 2003). In other examples, immigrants have been recruited by unregulated or informal employment 'agencies' (Ruggiero, 2000a). In one case in the UK, women were recruited from India, Africa and the Philippines to work in the National Health Service. They were then told that there were no vacancies and forced to work in private nursing homes, their passports were confiscated and they were forced to sign illegal contracts and to work over 60 hours per week for a mere £4 per hour (Browne, 2001). Other 'agencies' require immigrant labour to hand over passports and to only work for one employer, and have been implicated in the recruitment of domestic workers and Asian women destined to be 'exotic wives' (Ruggiero, 2000a).

Another example is provided by the growing international trade in contraband cigarettes created by the different excise duties imposed on cigarettes by different countries (Beare, 2002b; Van Duyne, 2003). This trade has been found to involve a variety of personnel including ex-miners (Taylor, 1999) lorry drivers and a range of loosely organised criminal networks – some with little prior criminal involvement (Van Duyne, 2003). Large tobacco companies have been found to be complicit with regard to the smuggling of tobacco. Indeed, Margaret Beare refers to 'organised criminals with white collars' and to 'white collar organised crime' in her discussion of how major tobacco companies were directly involved with the cigarette smuggling across the US-Canadian border (Beare, 2002b). In the UK, one tobacco company, Imperial, was criticised for selling large numbers of cigarettes into markets where demand was low – enabling them to be smuggled back into Britain by so called 'gangs'. Richard Bacon, Conservative MP for South Norfolk was reported in *The Guardian* (20 June 2002) as stating in the UK House of Commons, that over the recent past Imperial Tobacco had been exporting 1.7 billion cigarettes a year to Latvia – 'enough for every man, woman and child to consume 722 cigarettes a year' (Hencke, 2002). The trade in both counterfeit and contraband cigarettes has become so large that UK customs officials estimate that one in five cigarettes smoked in Britain is either smuggled or counterfeit.

Food is also subject to cross-border frauds, and adulterating food with water and other cheap substitutes is one of the oldest forms of food fraud. Meat is particularly vulnerable as, particularly when frozen, it is difficult to trace its origin or contents, which enables a variety of frauds and other offences. During the BSE crisis in Britain, for example, farmers and meat exporters breached the export ban on beef. In one case, British beef was found by Dutch customs officers as it was being transported in a consignment of frozen beef destined for Russia and Egypt after being re-labelled as Belgian meat. Not only was the meat illegally sold internationally, those involved also claimed subsidies worth more than £700,000 (Brown, 1997). Dutch manufacturers have been alleged to have 'dumped' frozen chickens with artificially increased weight through the addition of chemicals and water and also to have deliberately added cow and pig meat to chicken imported into Britain (Uhlig, 2003; Lawrence and Evans, 2003). Imported sausage products have also been found to contain horsemeat which, while not 'criminal', if not declared, could be expected to highly offend British consumers who are culturally unaccustomed to eating it. Crises concerning the British beef industry in the latter years of the 1990s revealed both the extent of illegal meat smuggling into the UK, and across Europe as a whole, as well as long-standing ill-preparedness of governmental authorities, regulators and enforcement officials in the face of it. Nor was meat fraud a peculiarly European problem. *The Daily Telegraph* newspaper reported that polo ponies had been stolen and sold for dog meat in Argentina (Froggatt, 2003) and the processing of 'deadstock' (that is, animals that are already dead on arrival at the abattoir) has been reported in Ontario, Canada in the *Toronto Star* (Cribb, 2003). While meat has been particularly fertile in terms of criminal opportunity, the same is also true for the different ways in which the label 'organic' and 'non-GMO' are applied to food and this is also readily subject to fraud.

The growth of telemarketing and e-commerce means that many goods can be sold without any face-to-face contact between buyer and seller or any opportunity for the seller to inspect goods – situations providing opportunities for fraud. In a survey reported by the UK Financial Services Authority, for example, 28 British and 35 overseas sites were found offering unauthorised investment advice or illegally advertising investment products (Bachelor, 2001). Contemporary readers will be familiar with SPAM e-mail offering a variety of 'business propositions', so called 'wonder drugs' and cheap cigarettes and counterfeit products. Drugs which are only available by prescription in some countries but freely available elsewhere can be sold and the UK Office of Fair Trading (OFT) has raised concerns about 'bogus health claims', reporting that enforcement agencies in 19 countries have found over 1,000 sites offering health products such as 'miracle cures', slimming and weight loss products, treatments for cancer, arthritis, sexual performance and hair loss (including a tablet to be taken with alcohol to prevent a beer belly!) (OFT, 2002; Cozens, 2002). Many of these drugs may be adulterated or counterfeit – consumers hoping to buy Viagra, Zyban or Prozac may find themselves in receipt of dummy tablets or heavily diluted fakes.[2] More bizarre are sites offering 'weird foods' such 'chocolate-coated insects' and 'cricket lick-it' lollipops which contain a complete insect inside the sweet (ITSA, 2001). It is however less clear how many consumers avail themselves of these offers and more research is needed to establish the extent of victimisation – some offers are so clearly bogus that few would be taken in (Wall, 2003). Nonetheless the growth of e-commerce raises enormous opportunities for fraud.

The global impact of white collar crime

Assessing the impact of white collar crime on a national let alone global scale is far from easy. Victimisation is not as directly felt as is the case for other crimes – victims are often unaware or suffer little individually although the gains may be large.

---

2 Viagra, a male anti-impotence treatment, was identified as being in use as a recreational drug within weeks of its being licensed in the UK. The drug quickly gained popularity on the 'rave dance scene' with both males and females (Hall, 1999).

Indeed, many offences are seen as victimless or as having impersonal victims such as 'business' or, in the case of tax evasion, the 'government'. In others the willing participation of a 'victim' in a transaction can lead to perceptions of 'gullibility' as is often the case, for example, with fraud. In some cases victimisation is indeed problematic – particularly in illicit trading which involves market relations of supply and demand. For example, illegal immigrants willingly purchase clandestine passage and may go on to accept low paid work. Another example is work in the sex industry, which may be 'a price worth paying' to many who are escaping conditions of extreme hardship in poor, underdeveloped or conflict ridden regions (Ruggiero, 2000a). Consumers willingly buy counterfeit and contraband goods – for example, the 'fake Rolex' travel memento, or faux designer clothing – and even 'smuggle' these goods across borders. Counterfeiting may also benefit legitimate manufacturers by promoting their brand image – although it may also threaten employment to those in legitimate industries (Ruggiero, 1996).

The global effects of transnational white collar crime are considerable. As seen above, entire countries and third world communities are adversely affected by the corporate 'race to the bottom', as are the communities they abandon in the search for more favourable environments (Bauman, 1998). The effects of major corporate frauds can be felt worldwide. The collapse of BCCI, for example, affected individuals, businesses and countries across the globe, from small investors in third world countries to nations who had invested in the bank. In the UK, the Western Isles council had to considerably reduce expenditure on welfare projects as a result of their losses (Croall, 2001a). So called 'victimless' tax evasion reduces, as seen above, the amount of revenue which governments have at their disposal.

Moreover, and despite its diffuse effects, white collar crime affects the most vulnerable since victimisation so often reflects wider structures of inequality (Croall, 1999; Croall, 2001b). The reduction of the tax base is most likely to affect the poorest in any nation and places, as seen above, a higher tax burden on smaller businesses and lower income groups. It is the economically weak states that are most unlikely to resist the effects of corporate crime (Gilbert and Russell, 2002) and within those it is the poorest and most vulnerable people, especially women and children, who are most affected (Brown, 2002; Sarangi, 2002). While many financial frauds target the wealthy, others affect more vulnerable victims. For example, the insurance frauds discussed by Tillman (2002) left many small businesses, some adversely affected by the Los Angeles riots, without compensation along with low paid employees who could not pay medical bills. Many investment frauds deliberately target older people, who have a great interest in maximising and sustaining their income through old age (Croall, 2001b). Women have been disproportionately affected by the development of unsafe contraceptive devices and pharmaceutical products which were also 'dumped' in the Third World (Peppin, 1995)

Globalisation, white collar crime and regulation

The enormous, although immeasurable, extent and impact of what can be described, if only provisionally, as transnational white collar and corporate crime illustrates that the biggest threat of transnational crime emanates 'not from stereotyped ethnics but from legitimate corporations and other organisations'

(Passas, 2000). As has always been the case with white collar crime, however, it remains almost hidden and less likely to be legally or socially constructed as 'crime'. Indeed, as seen here, much of what has been described as 'crime' consists of law evasion rather than law breaking. The involvement of legitimate industries in clandestine trading is shrouded because of the focus on criminal gangs and illegitimate enterprises. Seen in a global context, white collar crime continues to raise fundamental questions not only about the relationship between globalisation and crime, but also about the role played by criminalisation and the differential regulation of harmful business activities in an international context.

While a full discussion of the multi-faceted relationships between globalisation and crime, in themselves both contested categories (Nelken, 2002; Findlay, 2000), lies beyond the scope of this chapter, a number of issues are raised in relation to white collar crime. Many have suggested that globalisation has led to an increase in, and the development of, new forms of crime (Sparks and Loader, 2002). But has it? This is not easy to answer. It has always been difficult to estimate the amount of white collar crime let alone whether it has increased (Nelken, 2002) and, in any event, much of it is not, legally, crime. Many of the activities described above are not 'new' – smuggling goods across borders, avoiding taxes and maximising profit at the expense of social considerations have a long history. Nonetheless, crime is related to social and economic change, and criminal and legitimate businesses alike exploit changing opportunities and create their own (Ruggiero, 2000a). Globalisation has enabled businesses to be less constrained by geography and national boundaries providing space to exploit 'regulatory voids'. As Tillman (2002) points out, offshore insurance frauds display classic elements of deception, such as clever salesmanship and gullible victims, while at the same time possessing features of the 'new economies'. Rather than looking at the quantity of crime, it is more interesting to explore the wider relationships between globalisation and white collar crime along with issues of criminalisation and regulation.

While the relationships between crime and globalisation are much debated (Nelken, 2002; Findlay, 2000), most agree that crime is a significant aspect of globalisation and some indeed argue that globalisation is 'criminogenic' (Passas, 2000). Advocates of globalisation promote it as means of securing greater prosperity for all nations whereas its critics point to the economic polarisation, between and within nations, which it has created (Bauman, 1998). Cultural homogenisation has also heightened material expectations across the globe (Nelken, 2002). To Passas (2000), this, along with the greater asymmetries of power, has produced anomie on a global scale as many groups experience victimisation and relative deprivation. Globalisation has therefore been linked to crimes of 'resistance' among the dispossessed, including terrorism and fundamentalism, the acquisitive crimes of those in the communities abandoned as a result of the corporate race to the bottom and so called 'crimes of domination', such as those of corporations (Barak, 2001).

Of particular relevance to white collar crime is the neo-liberal ideology promoting market freedom and deregulation and prioritising profit maximisation which has accompanied globalisation. To many commentators this provides the ideological and legal space for crime to flourish. As Findlay (2000, p 223) argues, criminal enterprises are consistent with global economic cultural values as 'common themes for crime and globalisation are commodification and profit'. For Passas

(2000, p 41) 'global neo-liberalism and serious crime go hand in hand'. The ability of transnational corporations to freely engage 'abroad' in activities which would be criminalised 'at home' results from their power over national laws and macro-economic policies within the cultural hegemony of neo-liberalism (Passas, 2000). One critical criminologist has gone so far as to pronounce the disappearance of corporate crime (Snider, 2000). These activities would, argue Gilbert and Russell (2002, p 215) be 'transnational corporate crime' if victims or governments had the power to 'ascribe the harms to criminal activity rather than mere aggressive competition'. Similar points could be made about the activities of global financial institutions which, as Friedrichs and Friedrichs (2002) illustrate, could be held to be in breach of Human Rights Conventions and are sanctioned within neo-liberal values.

While globalisation provides a context for the transnational crimes of both legitimate and illegitimate businesses, the activities of the former are, seemingly by definition, less likely to be subject to criminalisation. In other respects their activities are closely related to the extent that they can become virtually indistinguishable – are the 'global pirates' described by Tillman (2002), for example, to be categorised as organised criminals or, as he argues, the 'white collar criminals of the future'? Their businesses were, in many respects, illegal, as they had no means or intention to pay clients. Offshore centres host the 'flight capital' of both legitimate business and the money laundering of illegitimate businesses – indeed the latter can only take place with the co-operation of the former. As Rosalind Wright, a former director of the Serious Fraud Office in the UK commented, criminals cannot put money through the legitimate banking system 'without the help of other criminals who have, all too frequently, qualifications as lawyers, accountants or bankers' (Wright, 2002, p 241). These professional experts also advise legitimate businesses how to legally avoid taxes (McBarnet, 1988). Moreover as seen above, a host of illegitimate cross-border trades involve a variety of relationships between legitimate and illegitimate enterprises. Legitimate businesses provide employment for illegal immigrants, illegal businesses smuggle the products of legitimate businesses, sometimes with their collusion, and many depend on the bribery of state employees and involve otherwise legitimate transportation and retail businesses.

To describe many of these activities as either organised or white collar crime may be difficult and may also divert attention from the issue, so long central to analysis, of why some forms of business activity are criminalised while others are not. While money laundering, drugs and people trafficking are encompassed by the 'war' on organised crime, there are few signs of a 'war' on tax avoidance or corporate forum shopping. Fears of the corrosive influence of organised crime, which as many commentators point out are exaggerated, may reflect the characteristics of the perpetrators rather than the activities. Criminalisation has long been associated with a fear of the 'other', and the perpetrators of organised crime have for long been seen as 'others', from the Italian Mafia to Colombian drug cartels and the many 'organised' crime groups associated with the end of the Cold War, such as the so called Russian Mafia (Block, 1999; Ruggiero, 2000b; Sheptycki, 2003b, 2003c). As Nelken (2002) points out, the deregulation of financial markets saw the criminalisation of 'insider trading' – as more 'outsiders' were allowed to trade. Ruggiero (2000b, p 188) points to an 'alien conspiracy theory' within which 'official concerns about transnational crime appear to be centred on the feeling of vulnerability that developed countries harbour towards criminal activity originating in other countries'. In this way, legitimate businesses can influence the 'criminalisation' of competitors leaving its own harmful activities relatively free from regulation – thereby potentially reducing the effectiveness of the law in relation to all forms of transnational crime.

This raises important issues about the regulation of business in an international context. Should more of these harmful activities be criminalised? How can they be regulated? Is criminalisation important? Apart from the political and ideological difficulties of 'criminalising' the activities of powerful business groups, many also object on legal and technical grounds (Croall, 2003; Slapper and Tombs, 1999). It is difficult to hold corporations liable for their actions as the criminal law deals primarily with individual guilt. Regulators and prosecutors face enormous difficulties in attributing criminal blame and punishment is limited as corporations cannot be sent to prison and fines may be trivial in comparison to either the harm done or corporate financial turnover. On the other hand, it can also be argued that the criminal law has a symbolic and moral function – it remains the strongest means of expressing the unacceptability of activities and of imposing state punishment as opposed to private sanctions (Pearce and Tombs, 1997; Croall, 2003). Applying the criminal label does therefore count, an argument that can also be applied to the human rights implications of the activities of corporations and financial institutions (Friedrichs and Friedrichs, 2002). Some have suggested that new laws should be created to take account of the transnational nature of many of these activities (Sarangi, 2002).

How would such transnational crimes be regulated? At present laws and regulations are generally tied to nation-states – which enables their evasion through jurisdiction shopping. 'Home' states lack jurisdiction and 'host' states may be unable or unwilling to take action for economic and political reasons (Gobert and Punch, 2003). To many commentators, this suggests the need for a transnational capacity to investigate and prosecute these forms of crime (Gilbert and Russell, 2002; Gobert and Punch, 2003). An international court with broad competence and universal jurisdiction would also possess sufficient authority and weight to impose sanctions on entities which may be 'economically more robust than the nation-state in which the criminal harm occurred' (Gilbert and Russell, 2002, p 226).

Gobert and Punch (2003) discuss some of the issues raised when considering such an international forum. Existing international organisations dealing with crime have tended to focus on organised and conventional crime through agencies such as Interpol and the recently instituted International Criminal Court (ICC), which is not recognised by the United States and other nations, has a limited competence focused primarily on 'war crimes' and on prosecuting individuals rather than companies. A proposal by France to include 'legal persons' within the scope of the ICC treaty (which would have made it possible to try corporate entities as such) was rejected. Abuses of human rights conventions may be subject to international proceedings but generally only states and state actors can be prosecuted (although in South Africa companies can be prosecuted in domestic courts for human rights violations). Echoing the points made above by Friedrichs and Friedrichs (2002), Gobert and Punch (2003) cite a growing consensus that corporations, as well as states, should be held to account for human rights violations. They outline a number of initiatives on the part of international organisations such as the OECD and the EU in relation to corporate responsibility for human rights. Some progress has been made, but it should not escape criminological notice that such progress has been achieved by recourse to 'soft law', where compliance is voluntary and there are no legal means to compel adherence or to hold violators to account. Despite the lack of enforcement powers, these advances may nonetheless signal something of a normative shift towards new (and higher) standards of human rights.

Some international organisations have taken action. In particular, the OECD has attempted to secure tougher regulations for offshore tax havens, including greater accountability and more sharing of information and co-operation with government regulators. It is interesting to note, however, that such initiatives have been stoutly resisted, for example by the Republican right in the United States who wish to protect the use of tax havens (Johnson and Holub, 2003). It is perhaps not surprising to see that developments in enforcement capacity against white collar crime and related forms of criminality are uneven, especially in comparison with organised crime as it has traditionally been portrayed. Thus, the EU has moved quite quickly to the establishment of a 'Euro CIA', with broad powers to investigate organised crime and terrorism cases across the territory of the Union (Evans-Pritchard, 2002). At the same time, the EU's efforts to police fraud against its own institutions – notorious for their leaky accounting practices – continuously falter (Tupman, 1999). Looking broadly at institutional development over the recent past, as welcome as an ICC has been, it is not likely that it will accrue either broader competence (for example, over human rights violations by private corporate entities) or universal jurisdiction in the near future. The reasons for this are partly to do with the politics of sovereignty, but it is also partly due to pure problems of conflict of laws. As Gobert and Punch (2003) observe, many states simply do not have laws enabling the prosecution of companies under the guise of 'legal persons'. One possibility is that international conventions might be passed which require, or at least places responsibility on, nation-states to prosecute in home countries (Gilbert and Russell, 2002).

In conclusion then, the issues which white collar crime has always raised for criminology are particularly relevant in a global context. Despite its similarity to many forms of organised crime, it is less visible and less likely to be regarded as 'crime'. Many economically and socially harmful activities find space to flourish in the climate of deregulation and are morally justifiable in the context of neo-liberalism. A large number of these activities are not legally crimes although clearly in breach of the spirit of much national and international legislation. Bringing transnational white collar and corporate crimes into view is suggestive of the potential of international law and regulatory strategies while it draws into question the traditional focus on narrowly defined areas of transnational organised crime. Above all, criminologists interested in drawing attention to white collar and corporate crime show that, transnationally, issues of criminal law and justice are inextricably linked to issues of human rights and social justice.

References

Bachelor, L (2001) 'Watchdogs net 28 UK web scams', *Guardian Unlimited*, 29 June, accessed 21 February 2005

Barak, G (2001) 'Crime and crime control in an age of globalisation: a theoretical dissection' 10 *Critical Criminology* 57–72

Bauman, Z (1998) *Globalisation: The Human Consequences*, Cambridge: Polity

Beare, ME (2002a) 'Searching for wayward dollars: money laundering or tax evasion – which dollars are we really after?' *Journal of Financial Crime*, February, 259–67

Beare, ME (2002b) 'Organised corporate criminality – tobacco smuggling between Canada and the US' 37(3) *Crime, Law and Social Change* 277–91

Block, A (1999) 'Bad business: a commentary on the criminology of organized crime in the United States', in Farer, T (ed), *Transnational Crime in the Americas*, New York: Routledge

Blum, J (1999) 'Offshore money', in Farer, T (ed), *Transnational Crime in the Americas*, New York: Routledge

Boyle, D (1998) 'The scandal of the tax havens', *New Statesman*, 13 November, pp 23–24

Braithwaite, J (1979) 'Transnational corporations and corruption: towards some international solutions' 7 *International Journal of the Sociology of Law* 143–67

Braithwaite, J (1984) *Corporate Crime in the Pharmaceutical Industry*, London: Routledge and Kegan Paul

Brown, D (1997) 'Meat plants closed for breaching export ban', *The Daily Telegraph*, 15 July

Brown, G (2002) 'The global threats to workers' health and safety on the job' 29(3) *Social Justice* 12–25

Browne, A (2001) 'Abused, threatened and trapped – Britain's foreign "slave nurses"', *The Observer*, 27 May

Cozens, C (2002) 'Beware "miracle cure" ads, government warns', *The Guardian*, 20 November

Cribb, R (2003) 'Sick cattle sent to Aylmer plant; ill animals were slaughtered', *The Toronto Star*, 22 September

Croall, H (1999) 'Corporate victims' 36 *Criminal Justice Matters* 4–5

Croall, H (2001a) *Understanding White Collar Crime*, Buckingham: OU Press

Croall, H (2001b) 'The victims of white collar crime', in Lindgren, S-A (ed), *White-Collar Crime Research. Old Views and Future Potentials: Lectures and Papers from a Scandinavian Seminar*, National Council for Crime Prevention, Sweden Bra-Report 2001, p 1

Croall, H (2003) 'Combating financial crime: regulatory versus crime control approaches' 11(1) *Journal of Financial Crime*, July, 45–55

Edwards A and Gill, P (2002) 'Crime as enterprise? The case of transnational organised crime' 37(3) *Crime, Law and Social Change* 203–23

Elliott, L (1997) 'Britain takes lead against corruption', *The Guardian*, 23 September

Evans-Pritchard, A (2002) 'Eurofile: £33m budget passed for Euro-CIA', *The Daily Telegraph*, 27 April

Findlay, M (2000) *The Globalisation of Crime: Understanding Transitional Relationships in Context*, Cambridge: CUP

Finlay, L (1996) 'The pharmaceutical industry and women's reproductive health', in Szockyj, E and Fox, JG (eds), *Corporate Victimization of Women*, Boston: Northeastern UP

Friedrichs D and Friedrichs J (2002) 'The World Bank and crimes of globalisation: a case study' 29(1–2) *Social Justice* 13–36

Froggatt, C (2003) '£60,000 polo ponies are stolen for dog meat', *The Daily Telegraph*, 5 March

Gilbert, M and Russell, S (2002) 'Globalisation of criminal justice in the corporate context' 38 *Crime Law and Social Change* 211–38

Gobert, M and Punch, M (2003) *Rethinking Corporate Crime*, London: Butterworths

Hall, C (1999) 'Club-goers are putting their lives at risk by taking Viagra for fun', *The Daily Telegraph*, 25 February

Hencke, R (2002) 'Tobacco giant in illicit sales query', *The Guardian*, 20 June

ITSA (2001) 'Buying on the internet: the gateway for future food scares', Institute of Trading Standards Administration Press Release, 20 June

Johnson, J and Holub, M (2003) 'Corporate flight: "moving" offshore to avoid US taxes' 10(3) *Journal of Financial Crime*, January, 246–54

Korsell, L (2002) 'Economic crime', in *Crime Trends in Sweden 1998–2000*, Stockholm: National Council for Crime Prevention

Lawrence, F and Evans, R (2003) 'Letters expose chicken scandal complacency', *Guardian Unlimited*, 24 May, accessed 30 August 2003

McBarnet, D (1988) 'Law, policy and legal avoidance: can law effectively implement egalitarian strategies?' 15(1) *Journal of Law and Society* 113–21

Michalowski, R and Kramer, R (1987) 'The space between laws: the problem of corporate crime in a transnational context' 34(1) *Social Problems* 34–54

Naylor, R (2003) 'Towards a general theory of profit driven crimes' 43(1) *British Journal of Criminology* 81–101

Nelken, D (2002) 'White collar crime', in Maguire, M, Morgan, R and Reiner, R (eds), *The Oxford Handbook of Criminology*, 3rd edn, Oxford: OUP

OFT (2002) 'Sweeping up bogus health claims', press release, 19 March, available at www.oft.gov.uk/News/Press+releases/2002/PN+14-02.htm

Pallister, D (2001) 'Ban demanded on overseas bribes', *The Guardian*, 4 April

Passas, N (2000) 'Global anomie, dysnomie and economic crime: hidden consequences of neo- liberalism and globalisation in Russia and around the world', *Social Justice*, Summer, 16–44

Passas, N and Nelken, D (1993) 'The thin line between legitimate and criminal enterprises: subsidy frauds in the European Community' 19 *Crime, Law and Social Change* 223–43

Pearce, F and Tombs, S (1993) 'US capital versus the Third World: Union Carbide and Bhopal', in Pearce, F and Woodiwiss, M (eds), *Global Crime Connections: Dynamics and Control*, London: Macmillan

Pearce, F and Tombs, S (1997) 'Hazards, law and class: contextualising the regulation of corporate crime' 6(1) *Social and Legal Studies* 79–107

Peppin, J (1995) 'Feminism, law and the pharmaceutical industry', in Pearce, F and Snider, L (eds), *Corporate Crime: Contemporary Debates*, Toronto: Toronto UP

Punch, M (1996) *Dirty Business: Exploring Corporate Misconduct*, London: Sage

Ruggiero, V (1996) *Organised and Corporate Crime in Europe: Offers That Can't Be Refused*, Aldershot: Dartmouth

Ruggiero V (2000a) *Crime and Markets: Essays in Anti-Criminology*, Oxford: OUP

Ruggiero V (2000b) 'Transnational crime: official and alternative fears' 28 *International Journal of the Sociology of Law* 187–99

Ruggiero V (2002) 'Introduction – fuzzy criminal actors' 37(3) *Crime, Law and Social Change* 177–90

Sarangi, S (2002) 'Crimes of Bhopal and the global campaign for justice' 29(3) *Social Justice* 47–52

Sheptycki, JWE (2000) 'Policing the virtual launderette', in Sheptycki, JWE (ed), *Issues in Transnational Policing*, London: Routledge

Sheptycki, JWE (2003a) 'The governance of organised crime in Canada' 28(4) *The Canadian Journal of Sociology*

Sheptycki, JWE (2003b) 'Global law enforcement as a protection racket; some sceptical notes on transnational organised crime as an object of global governance', in Edwards, A and Gill, P (eds), *Transnational Organised Crime: Perspectives on Global Security*, London: Routledge

Sheptycki, JWE (2003c) 'Against transnational organised crime', in Beare, M (ed), *Critical Reflections on Transnational Organised Crime, Money Laundering and Corruption*, Toronto: Toronto UP

Slapper, G and Tombs, S (1999) *Corporate Crime*, London: Addison Wesley Longman

Snider L (2000) 'The sociology of corporate crime: an obituary' 4(2) *Theoretical Criminology* 169–206

Sparks, R and Loader, I (2002) 'Contemporary landscapes of crime, order and control: governance, risk and globalisation', in Maguire, M, Morgan, R and Reiner, R (eds), *Oxford Handbook of Criminology*, Oxford: OUP

Sutherland, EH (1949) *White Collar Crime*, New York: Holt, Reinhart & Winston

Taylor, I (1999) *Crime in Context*, Cambridge: Polity

Tillman, R (2002) *Global Pirates: Fraud in the Offshore Insurance Industry*, Boston: Northeastern UP

Tombs, S and Whyte, D (2003) 'Enron and on ... and on ... and on', available from Centre for Corporate Accountability, www.corporateaccountability.org

Tupman, B (1999) 'The sovereignty of fraud and the fraud of sovereignty; OLAF and the three wise men' 7(3) *Journal of Financial Crime* 1–18

Uhlig, R (2003) 'Chicken is being contaminated with pig protein', *The Daily Telegraph*, 21 May, p 6

Van Duyne, P (2003) 'Organising cigarette smuggling and policy making, ending up in smoke' 39 *Crime, Law and Social Change* 285–317

Wall, D (2003) 'Cybercrimes: media myths or stark reality', unpublished paper delivered at Glasgow Caledonian University, April

Wright, R (2002) 'The hiding of wealth: the implications for the prevention and control of crime and the protection of economic stability' *Journal of Financial Crime*, February, 239–43

Chapter 11
Transnationalisation and Corruption; Some Theoretical and Practical Implications
Bill Tupman

... corruption threatens the rule of law, democracy and human rights, undermines good governance, fairness and social justice, distorts competition, hinders economic development and endangers the stability of democratic institutions and the moral foundations of society (Council of Europe, Criminal Law Convention on Corruption, 27 January 1999).

Introduction

This chapter examines how conventions and policy documents originating from transnational organisations in recent years define corruption and their proposals for dealing with it. First it presents a brief overview of problems the academic literature has found in defining and operationalising the concept of corruption. In doing so, the chapter takes a deliberately interdisciplinary approach, drawing primarily on political science and economic theory and, to a lesser extent, other social science approaches. The aim of this interdisciplinary approach is to show how recent developments in political and economic thought may help in understanding corruption in a global context. Work focusing on the role of the state, development, game theory and trust, and economic models of criminality may help in the consideration of policy and its probable effectiveness, but these separate concepts cannot deal adequately with 'transnational corruption'. The chapter also examines the definitions and assumptions built into a number of efforts at transnational policy development and argues that there is some way to go before policy reflects the state of academic analysis.

Academic approaches to corruption

Some of the problems of studying corruption are similar to those of studying fraud and white collar crime. The people involved may be powerful, the offences they commit are poorly defined in law, they do not consider what they are doing to be illegal and their 'crimes' are often considered 'victimless'. When they are brought to court, prosecution frequently fails because of the complexity of the cases and the judicial process. The offenders may have good financial resources and so can retain effective defence lawyers. Criminologists frequently contrast this adversely with 'blue collar' crime, where imprisonment is the common outcome. It is sometimes argued that civil, rather than criminal, proceedings would be more appropriate because such proceedings are more likely to have some positive outcome and, hence, a modicum of general deterrence might be achieved through that avenue.

A complicating issue is that some see corruption as an element of many crimes rather than as a separate phenomenon in itself. Corruption may be subsumed under fraud, nepotism and bribery, or indeed white collar crime itself, or organised and political crime. This can widen the field of study to, for example, crime groups and terrorists operating within the EU today who seek fraudulent documentation to help them move people about freely. So, is corruption an identifiable phenomenon that can be studied as a thing in itself? Is it an inevitable aspect of human behaviour or something that is avoidable? Another way of putting this is to ask if corruption is a precursor for other specific crimes? The opposite may well be true and some political scientists argue that the *absence* of corruption is a necessary precursor for democracy.

The concept of corruption is based on the idea of 'some "naturally sound condition" from which corrupt acts deviate' (Philp, 1997, p 446). Sociologists and anthropologists debate whether corruption is simply a matter of cultural differences: 'Your corruption is my normal business practice; your bribe is my mark of respect.' It can be difficult to draw a clear line between nepotism or insider dealing, on the one hand, and networking on the other. Career building in both West and East has long been characterised by patron-client relations. Some individuals join freemasons' lodges, the Rotarians or golf clubs in order to make contacts that will help them in their businesses or careers rather than to engage in the primary activities of these organisations. In China, without *guanxi*, nothing could be achieved. *Guanxi* is a concept that describes the Chinese practice of networking. It is understood as the network of relationships among various parties that co-operate together and support one another on the basis of 'you scratch my back, I'll scratch yours'. In essence, this boils down to exchanging favours, which are expected to be done regularly and voluntarily. Foreign (that is, Western) business ventures in China may find the institutions of *guanxi* difficult to embed within. The charges of cultural relativity that may arise from these kinds of experiences therefore present problems for the study of corruption in a transnational context. The question, 'Does corruption exist as an identifiable phenomenon that can be studied as a thing in itself?' is relevant, for the definition of what is 'really' corrupt varies from culture to culture (on cultural relativism, see also Sheptycki, Chapter 3 this volume).

Corruption has been operationalised in many ways. It may be seen as a structural problem or one of individual and cultural morality. It may be studied through individual examples or through theoretical modelling. As Andvig *et al* say, in an excellent review of the literature, '... the study of corruption has been "multidisciplinary" and dispersed ... [i]t has been studied as a problem of political, economic, cultural or moral underdevelopment, and as mostly as something in between' (Andvig *et al*, 2000). Because the focus of this chapter is the relationship between academic literature and policy against corruption, the following review of academic literature will focus on several approaches to understanding corruption. As Hutchcroft says in the context of studying the relations between rents, corruption and clientelism: 'It is valuable to draw insights from three literatures, with distinct lineages, that overlap but all too rarely interact' (Hutchcroft, 1997, p 639).

Democracy, development and corruption

The central issue for political scientists has long been whether corruption is a positive or negative force in the economic and political development of a particular country (Nye, 1967; Huntington, 1968; Scott, 1972). There is also a long-standing argument that corruption is simply a method of exercising political influence (Huntington, 1968; Scott, 1969). Several decades ago, Scott argued that there would be no corruption if governments simply sold jobs and services to the highest bidder (Scott, 1972), a point of view that plays out rather differently in the current era where neo-liberal ideology (which advocates the privatisation of government) prevails.

A consistent concern since the rise of neo-liberal thinking in the 1980s has been the degree to which the state should be involved in the economy. A variety of stances can be taken. On the one hand, there is the view that the free market should be allowed to operate without regulation, as this will provide greater efficiency and ultimately greater social justice. On the other hand, there is also the point that the market, being operated by fallible and frequently venal human beings, requires regulation in order to provide some measure of ethical and redistributive justice. According to the former view, opportunities for corruption follow in the wake of state intervention in the operation of the marketplace. Whether such corruption adds to efficiency or detracts from it again is debated. Conversely, both the removal of state bureaucracies from oversight of production in ex-communist states and the insertion of quasi-governmental bodies into regulatory positions in Western democracies can be argued to have opened up possibilities for political corruption (Heywood, 1997, p 430).

One theme in the political corruption literature takes a 'structural' approach that looks at the nature of state development. If Britain historically has been relatively free of political corruption because of the separation of the government and the administration, does this mean that corruption is inevitable where there is no such separation? Médard would argue that the basis for entrenched corruption in Africa is the lack of distinction between the public and private spheres, in which other cultural norms of loyalty and kinship networks play a crucial role. According to this view, European legal-rational bureaucracy cannot be imported to become dominant; it will be subverted instead (Médard, 1991, p 42). Yet Andvig *et al* argue that corruption is a 'normal' state of affairs and suggest that, as a matter of definition, 'a *de facto* competition between a government and several quasi-governments makes the notion of corruption somewhat unclear' (Andvig *et al*, 2000, p 26).

Other useful concepts from the political literature relate to how the forms of corruption may vary as the world changes. The phrase 'political opportunity structures', originally used by Kitschelt (1986), was borrowed by Mény and Rhodes (1997) for the exploration of differences in political corruption. Heywood states that:

> Opportunity structures do not remain constant, but evolve over time in response to exogenous pressures. Amongst the most significant recent pressures – certainly in western democracies – are those that have derived from transnational developments, often associated with globalisation or internationalisation ... It has become possible to organise transactions of extraordinary complexity, creating in turn new possibilities for a black market in corruption to flourish (Heywood, 1997, p 429).

A further useful idea is that of 'influence peddling' (Heywood, 1997), associated with the introduction of quasi-governmental, non-elected bodies to regulate various economic activities in the wake of privatisation. Since the global economy values information, and this too has become a commodity, the peddling of influence may be seen as a problem from the point of view of classic legal-rational bureaucracies. Both influence and information are intangibles that can be tools for corruption or the object of corruption. Arguably, influence peddling is not new, but information technology and the global networks empowered by it, has expanded the scope for such practices, whilst not necessarily making them more visible to oversight.

Game theory, rationality and trader behaviour

Economists look at corruption from a slightly different angle, using models to represent the decision making of individuals, rather than the social-political conditions. They are interested to understand the decision making processes by which corruption and other criminal activity becomes rational behaviour. One approach to corruption is through game theory, the most oft quoted example of which is the 'prisoner's dilemma' (Platteau, 1994a, 1994b). Briefly, such models suggest that if one has no means of predicting the behaviour of a stranger, that is, reason to trust that another trader will not cheat you or try to take your goods, it is better to try to cheat them first than wait to be cheated. Game theory also suggests that pre-existing ties or knowledge, such as kinship, can mitigate the chance of being cheated and so limit risk exposure; hence reciprocity and ongoing trading relationships are more likely. However, there are certain limits to how personalised networks can be in a transnational market economy. Anthropologists point out that internalised norms of honesty may change the prisoner dilemma into an 'assurance' game, in which it pays to be honest, when and if the other party has already decided to be honest. Bacharach and Gambetta (1997) suggest that these principles can be taken outside strict market conditions and can also apply to the way people behave in organisations, interpreting the stages of offering and seeking employment for a specific task, contracting to undertake that task, being called upon to fulfil the contract, as a kind of sequential prisoner's dilemma or *trust* game. To extend from this, both the contractor and contractee need to believe that they will not be cheated, and that it makes more sense for the contract to be honoured than to be broken. From this perspective, the question becomes how trust may be engendered, what combination of carrot and stick might persuade all involved that law abiding or, at least, contract abiding, behaviours are in their interests.

One solution would be that actors be monitored by a public institution tasked with regulation, enforcement and punishment. This, of course, demands impartial honesty and task efficiency by public officials whose task it is to regulate and enforce. However, if the central state is weak, there will be little trust that contracts can be enforced. Yet, borrowing from the political science literature, the central state may be strong and still corrupt and other (non-bureaucratic) networks may be enmeshed in the state administration and political institutions (for example, clientelist networks in Africa). Under such conditions, what is looked at as a bribe from the point of view of legal-rational bureaucracy, may be understood more as an internal economic transfer within the wider network (Andvig *et al*, 2000, p 28).

Bicchieri and Duffy (1997) have developed a cyclical theory of corruption to explain certain aspects of corruption, namely those that involve the state, via politicians, in contract procurement. Politicians and contractors interact, say, for example, in the process of building new infrastructure, a hospital, roads or transport systems, or other large projects. While the costs of corruption vary, politicians in democratic countries might reasonably expect to 'pay' such costs. Initially costs are high, and so elected politicians will tend to be honest, but as time goes on (for example, when politicians are elected repeatedly to high office) the costs lessen and there will be generalised corruption until they are voted out of office. Thereafter the cycle may be repeated with new politicians. By contrast, Acemoglu and Verdier (1998) suggest a more regulatory vision that sees government officials as the actors who can prevent corruption by supervising competing sets of private contractors.

The state, the market and trust

Analyses associated with Gambetta and his followers relate certain forms of organised criminality to the weakness of the state. Gambetta (1993) argued that historically the Italian government has been weak in the south of Italy and Sicily. Trust between economic actors was low and property and contract relationships were insecure. Under conditions of chronic mistrust, traders turned to the services of Mafia families, able to provide a credible threat should cheating occur during a transaction. Business dealing became possible and initially the cost of hiring Mafia services was lower than that of being cheated. Once established, the Mafia attempted to tax all transactions, a kind of extortion that could be labelled 'corruption' since a price must be paid, which is equivalent to a bribe. It can be noted that under such a system it is not in the interest of any particular Mafia family to cheat, as this would endanger trust and therefore undermine business confidence. Briefly, this is how Gambetta explained the evolution of the Mafia families as quasi-governmental actors who took on the roles of contract guarantee, taxation, justice, punishment and security (Gambetta, 1993).

This perspective sees this model as being transferred from the rural South of Italy, where it also involved groups known as the Camorra, the 'nDragheta and the Corona Sagra, to the USA. There urban variants, perhaps more akin to outright extortion than protection, were created and later copied by such 'terrorist' organisations as the Provisional IRA, ETA, FARC, Northern Ireland Protestant paramilitaries and others. Gambetta's followers would argue that the key phenomenon in all this is 'trust', or the lack of it. According to this theory, then, corruption occurs because the state is weak and individual economic actors cannot trust it to police economic transactions effectively. It is worth stressing here that, globally speaking, in the absence of a transnational state or courts, a set of circumstances analogous to those Gambetta describes exists. What regulator so dominates that global market so as to guarantee contracts and underpin relations of trust?

The modern, global market-based economy operates on a vast scale. Large numbers of transactions involve impersonal encounters between trader and trader, and between trader and government. Because of the problem of building trust, traders fall back on family and friendship networks which are seen as more reliable, although any outsider to a specific network may view such relationships as involving nepotism and favouritism and therefore as corrupt. The problem is to prevent oneself being cheated. This should be the responsibility of government and the courts, but where the government is weak, other mechanisms will arise.

Since nature abhors a vacuum, Gambetta's analysis suggests that some other body or process must fill the gap. The concept that has been used to capture this idea is that of 'the shadow state', and the Chicago school of economics have argued that a shadow state must inevitably emerge from the system of networks in transitional societies (Andvig *et al*, 2000). The emergence of a shadow state is a natural outcome when trust is in chronic short supply in a market. We may glimpse this in contemporary post-authoritarian states, where the state itself is weak and individuals and companies are seeking to become players in the global marketplace. Russia, after the collapse of Communism, is an obvious case, as are most of the other emergent East European nation-states. Iraq, it may confidently be predicted, will be another, as were the post-military dictatorships of Latin America which underwent in the latter years of the 20th century.

Transnational corruption

The attempt to take a transnational approach to corruption is relatively recent. The literature discussed above contains elements that help in looking at corruption occurring in the economic context of globalisation, but there are limitations. Clearly, corrupt behaviour within a state can be explained as rational behaviour on the part of the *indigenous* businesses, in response to the dangers and opportunities that arise as trade opens with other economies. However, the theoretical literature has not been extended to look at the role and motivation of the external players, nor at whether the 'rules' change when things go transnational. How does game theory apply when the stakes are global?

In this context, it may be useful to distinguish between 'old' and 'new' corruption. At some indefinite point in the past, before the creation of world trade, business practices varied from country to country and reflected each society's differing cultural mores. When private companies began trading in countries other than those in which they originated, they had to adapt to the existing business practices of the country in which they wished to operate. As other external competitors came into the same market, the original traders used their knowledge of these practices to maintain their market position. This could be considered 'old' corruption. In many cases trade was a matter of barter and there was no cash economy as there was no way of converting currencies. Only gold and silver or the goods being traded themselves could be used as a means of exchange. Game theory, using the concepts of trust and familiarity in established trading relationships, can help to explain corruption in these circumstances.

'New' corruption arises in the era of transnational corporations (TNCs), when 'external' companies seek to corrupt government officials to obtain a monopoly position, either as a supplier of goods and services or as a purchaser of a primary product. This type of corruption involves local economic and political players dealing with transnational actors, although, as studies of LDCs ('lesser' or 'least developed countries') have argued, the separation of the economic and political spheres in specific countries may not be great. In such circumstances there is a real possibility that power relationships and security internal to the country will be affected, shaping the future direction of economic and political development. Frequently, the World Bank and IMF become involved and influence monetary and fiscal policy. Global financial markets, and the trading of stocks and shares, may also affect the dynamics of economic and political power, not least by affecting the price of stocks and shares of involved TNCs. Ultimately, governmental policy and strategy in the country nominally the home of the TNC may also play a role. In the transnational era, there are vast new opportunity structures for corruption. Representatives from the LDCs might well argue that the present interest in corruption stems from the wish of established TNCs to prevent new competitors seeking to buy their way into their established markets. According to this perspective, the legislation and international conventions discussed below reflect an attempt to preserve the economic status quo rather than to facilitate true market competition.

Can existing analyses of corruption cope with the kinds of issues raised above under the heading of 'new' corruption? If transnational corruption is essentially no different from corruption within a specific country, arguably it does not require any special theoretical attention and existing tools should suffice. As far as policy making is concerned, it could simply be said that corruption is complex, many headed and prone to flourish in new forms as societies change; by its very nature, hard to police, impossible to predict or prevent. However, if transnational corruption is different at *least in part*, it merits further appraisal. On the face of it, it is different both in terms of the transnational geographic 'place' within which it occurs and in terms of the practices and opportunity structures created by the TNCs. TNCs have great resources, wide 'reach' into national economies, far-ranging influence (especially in LDCs), and can operate at high political and governmental levels, both informally and formally. At the outset then, one could posit that transnational corruption occurs because of very specific problems to do with providing the conditions for economic trust, and forms a particular example of the effect of a weak, or indeed, absent, 'state'.

The transnational arena is an ephemeral place, in that it has no clear geographical, political or economic boundaries. We cannot assume that there are culturally shared norms, unless one assumes a Hobbesian view of the moral strategy of the global market's players (that is, the war of all against all). Economic theorists suggest that the desire for trust and security, to minimise risk and cost in trading relationships, requires that some institution provide strong, clear rules that are both enforceable and enforced. In the absence of a legal provider of trust and security, corruption flourishes amidst a variety of illegal providers. Does the transnational arena in which the TNCs operate have a shared set of norms and values that upholds conditions of trust? This would require effective and efficient regulation and policing, such that Gambetta's conditions for decreasing the likelihood that corruption are satisfied. In the absence of a transnational or global state, with what instruments can a sense of trust be built? Can international conventions and policy documents help to supply what is needed?

Corruption and policy

Definitions and concepts

On 15 July 1996, the UN published a Declaration recognising the need to promote social responsibility in the ethical standards of private and public corporations, including TNCs. Notably this primarily referred to public officials rather than TNCs, and other than proposals on tax deductibility and accounting, there was no real attempt to address problems at an institutional level. Also in that year, two other policy initiatives were published: the Council of Europe's Work Programme for 1996–2000, and the Inter-American Convention on Corruption. A year later, in 1997, the EU published a policy document on corruption, COM (97) 192. Two years later, the European Commission was itself in crisis, due to accusations of corruption.

Corruption is clearly a live issue and this is demonstrated by Transparency International's Corruption Perception Index. The index is produced through a process of interviews with resident and non-resident academics, business leaders and risk analysts regarding their perception of levels of corruption among politicians and public officials. In 2003, the index ranked seven out of 10 countries below five on a 10-point scale, where 10 counted as 'clean'. 50% of developing countries scored less than three on the scale. Countries with scores of nine or higher were few and far between: Finland, Iceland, Sweden, Denmark, New Zealand and Singapore (Transparency International, 7 October 2003).

In trying to establish a definition of corruption, policy makers have grappled with the same kinds of conceptual problems that academics have. The World Bank, Transparency International and many other transnational organisations appear to agree that corruption can be defined as 'the abuse of public power for private profit'. Policy usually tries to provide precise definitions of specific corrupt acts, but even with this kind of conceptual refinement a given policy making body may not have legislative teeth and problems arise from this. Then too, creating a generally accepted legal offence of corruption raises cross-cultural complications. As academics have long argued, not unlike every other term in the political lexicon, corruption is an essentially contested term and one person's corruption is another's good business practice. Policy makers appear to proceed on the basis that legislating against particular acts is appropriate, and deciding what to criminalise, what to leave to civil action and what to employers' disciplinary procedures is helpful in reducing the areas of ambiguity. Andvig *et al* (2000) note that five areas are most commonly associated with corruption: bribery, nepotism, embezzlement, fraud and extortion. What is the scope for legislating in these areas?

It might be thought that it would be easy to initiate common legislation and common criminal sanctions against bribery. Yet currently a number of EU states still allow tax exemption for bribes paid to obtain business in a non-EU jurisdiction. The argument has been that, since American and Japanese companies will continue to bribe to obtain contracts, it is handicapping European companies not to allow them to do the same: creating anti-bribery laws would hand a competitive advantage to other companies and countries. Overall, it seems that bribery is an area that is likely to show some interpretative 'drift', even if a framework for legislation could be agreed.

Nepotism is also difficult to tackle. In the private business and industrial sectors the management of family-owned businesses may be parcelled out amongst the next generation with relative impunity; no one complains that the progeny of Henry Ford occupy positions of responsibility in the global TNC that is the Ford Motor Company today. The Darwinian logic of the market is supposed to ensure that companies run by inadequate progeny will become non-competitive. As it is in Hollywood, where the offspring of successful actors may themselves launch successful careers in the movies, in the public sphere it is not necessarily seen as surprising that sons or daughters, wives or husbands follow their father, mother or partner into Parliament or Congress. How can nepotism be proved?

Embezzlement, fraud and extortion are all already defined as offences. Fraud has been difficult to show; for example, distinguishing between compulsory insurance schemes and extortion is conceptually challenging. Most often, the rule of embezzlement seems to be, if you get caught, promise to repay. The relationship between public confidence and profits is so direct that companies that are victims of these practices would normally rather keep them quiet, coming to some private agreement, or at most turning to civil action (see Croall, Chapter 10 this volume). Although police may be called in either as a first resort (that is, in the public sector) or a last resort (that is, in the private sector), criminal action does not result in the return of the monies lost, while civil action may. Resignation on grounds of ill health is often seen as a way of avoiding bad publicity and getting out of a messy situation.

For each concept mentioned above there has been mapped out a particular route through the minefield. The Council of Europe programme focused on procurement, as did the Inter-American Convention, although it also stressed the notion of 'passive' corruption and was fairly even-handed in its acknowledgment of a role for both corrupter and corruptee. The EC approach in 1997 was to focus upon external rather than internal corruption. It discussed the dysfunctional economic effects of corruption on the market, avoiding the thorny topics of nepotism and maladministration completely. The Committee of Independent Experts' (CIE) report to the EC in 1999 was compelled by events to consider internal corruption, as it was set up in response to 'Santergate', and also mentions maladministration. However, the latter is presented as a minor aspect of corruption that is probably best dealt with by civil law, as is 'waste'. In essence, only outright fraud is seen as the criminal, hence more important, form of corruption.

The policies can be read as giving indications of the economic theory prevalent at the time of policy formation. A belief that the market can and should regulate itself does not lend itself to support state supervision, regulation and restriction. A prevalent view is that the state should be principally involved in supervision of public, rather than private, contractors. These tenets tend to be reflected in the degree to which a specific policy making body is willing to be seen as interfering in markets, and the behaviours defined as meriting intervention. Whether a policy making body is making policy to cover private or public spheres obviously depends on its powers and the political pressures it faces. There are differences in the degree to which any of the existing bodies attempting this possess elements of 'statehood' itself. Some have very few legal powers and fairly limited influence over member/signatory states. Yet there may be other factors at work, and this is clearly evident in the context of the EU:

> A far more serious pathology is the way in which *national systems*, controls and norms remain beyond reproach, even when they are fundamentally corrupt or wasteful, or make fraud in the use of EU funds inevitable. Any notion of 'good governance' is undermined by a *communautaire* ethos which makes taboo any suggestion by one Member State that another's national practices might need to be reformed. Fraud will remain one of the clearest failings of EU governance until much that is now unspoken becomes openly debated (Peterson, 1997, p 578).

Transnational responses to corruption

Let us look at this in a little more detail. A number of international conventions and concomitant domestic legislation deal with the criminalisation of corruption. As was previously discussed, the criminalisation of corruption is difficult. It shares many of the problems faced by initiatives to investigate transnational crime groups (see Edwards, Chapter 9 this volume) and those that have arisen from the 'war on terrorism' in the wake of 11 September 2001 (see Sheptycki, Chapter 3 this volume). One of the most fundamental problems is that of reaching agreement on how to define the phenomenon as an offence so that legislation can be framed.

Differences between policies may also arise from factors affecting the policy making bodies themselves:

- different institutional bodies may make policy for the same area of concern, but this may, or may not, be in harmony;
- policy proposals originate both from transnational institutions such as the OECD and the Council for Europe and/or from individual states;
- policy may try to set the same rules for different types of institution;
- the actors involved in the policy making process have different interests;
- policy makers may have narrow, legislative or broader, socio-economic goals; and
- members of policy making bodies may be subject to electoral, or other outside, pressures.

The Inter-American Convention against Corruption 1996

The Organisation of American States has no central bureaucracy, and hence no enforcement apparatus. Its members are primarily recipients of investment rather than investors themselves. The target of the Convention is corruption occurring within and between Member States, and the goal is the removal of opportunities for any country in the Americas to gain competitive advantage over another through the committing of corrupt practices. The means to do this are set out in its Articles, variously as measures, rules and proposals for Latin American governments to follow as individual states.

Specifically, Art 3 proposes 12 preventative measures, whose applicability within their own systems the individual states party to the convention have agreed to consider. The measures are intended to 'create, maintain and strengthen':

- Standards of conduct for public officials, including a requirement that government officials report acts of corruption in the performance of public functions to appropriate authorities.
- Mechanisms to enforce these standards of conduct.
- Training for government personnel to ensure they understand their responsibilities and the ethical rules covering their actions.
- Registration of income assets and liabilities of individuals performing public functions in certain specified posts. Where appropriate, these registrations should be made public.
- System of government hiring and procurement of goods and services to ensure the openness, equity and efficiency of such systems.
- Government revenue collection and control systems that deter corruption.
- Laws denying favourable tax treatment for any individual or corporation for expenditures made in violation of the anti-corruption laws of the state's party to the treaty.
- Systems for protecting whistleblowers.
- Oversight bodies with a view to implementing modern mechanisms for preventing, detecting, publishing and eradicating corrupt acts.
- Deterrents to the bribery of officials including accounting procedures.
- Mechanisms to encourage participation by civil society and NGOs in efforts to prevent corruption.
- The study of further preventive measures that take into account the relationship between equitable compensation and probity in public service.

The first three are similar to the European proposals for steps to create a culture in which corruption cannot flourish, and the seventh concurs with EU attempts to prevent bribes being tax deductible. The fourth point is innovative and would require some enforcement and regulatory mechanism across the Americas. Thinking comparatively with the UK context, it would be akin to the extension to the civil service as a whole of the current provisions for Members of the UK Westminster Parliament to register interests. The fifth point would require the institutional capacity to scrutinise processes of procurement and a body to which complaint could be made. The sixth point needs spelling out in detail, as is also the case for proposals eight to 12. Most of the Convention deals with passive, rather than active, corruption. What has been developed through the Inter-American Convention is therefore vague in crucial respects, is aimed only at a limited variety of corrupt practices, not at the maintenance of trust in the political-economic system generally, and lacks transnational enforcement powers. Nevertheless, this is a serious attempt to address the problem of corruption across an entire region. Whether the Convention sufficiently addresses the key problems of supporting contract enforcement, through the enhancement of both policing and trust, remains moot.

The Council of Europe's Work Programme 1996–2000

In this document, procurement, that is the purchase of goods and services by public bodies, is viewed in terms of the volume of money involved. As such it is understood to be the most important domain of European governance in which corruption may occur. In this document, the aim was to tighten up processes for awarding of contracts to provide goods and services to European public bodies. Three changes in the supervision of this process were put forward:

- attribution procedures which render corruption as difficult as possible. If decision competencies are split between several persons and administrations, bribery becomes more difficult; if submission procedures are correctly carried out, all competitors are put upon an equal footing;

- a high degree of transparency at all stages of the process, including after the procedure has been terminated; and

- reliability checks of the administrator involved in the decision making procedure.

Here, other technical, political, social and economic difficulties were acknowledged but few are addressed in detail. An exception was the suggestion that blacklisting may be a way of dealing with those contractors who revise prices upwards after commencement of works, claiming changes in circumstance. This is a classic and perennial problem in government procurement, and is not one that has yet generated a successful practicable intervention strategy.

In the light of the work by Acemoglu and Verdier (1998), and Bicchieri and Duffy (1997), it is interesting that the question of whether there are differential opportunities for corruption in the private and public spheres arises in this document, which asks whether there is a difference between contracts obtained by corruption in public procurement and contracts between entirely private entities. Do both areas require different rules? And should officials involved in public procurement be forbidden from taking up jobs in companies that have bid for public procurement?

The document notes that offences of corruption, and bribery in particular, are consensual and motivated by mutual interests. Enforcement authorities therefore find it difficult to collect reliable evidence; confessions by the accused subject or testimony by witnesses are rare or non-existent. Although the power to search and seize documents exists, it frequently cannot be invoked unless sufficient background information is already available to the police. The police need to be able to search for financial records, commercial documents or information held by financial institutions. Rules of bank secrecy may become an obstacle to this, especially if financial information is held abroad. On the other hand, the police have the problem of demonstrating that they are not simply engaging in a fishing expedition. Alternative investigative solutions have been put forward, including the use of:

- telephone tapping/bugging and electronic surveillance;

- undercover agents and agents provocateur, including 'sting' operations;

- denunciation-promoting procedures;

- anonymous reports, corroborated by other evidence; and
- redefining the offence in order to make the gathering of evidence easier.

Where civil law remedies are proposed, the law must provide ways and means for litigants to obtain evidence and give them the right to access certain commercial records. On the other hand, legitimate business interests have to be protected.

This has led to the proposal that, as in fraud and money laundering offences, an obligation to report suspicious transactions should be considered in respect of corruption offences. Yet this would lead to a conflict between the duty to report and the duty of confidentiality. How would that conflict be resolved? Should whistleblowers be protected or do they have a fiduciary duty to their employer? To whom, and by whom, should reports be made: the internal auditors, independent auditors, supervisory authorities, financial institutions, or the general public? The document suggests that whoever helps justice should be protected, but as with the material already discussed, it too falls short of providing actionable ideas.

The European Union

In mid-1999, a 144 page report, written by a Committee of Independent Experts, considered allegations of fraud, mismanagement and nepotism in the European Commission. The Commission is the EU's 14,000 member executive civil service and the report listed a devastating catalogue of lax management at the heart of the institution, reaching up to the highest level. The targets of most condemnation were Edith Cresson, a former French prime minister responsible for education and research portfolios in the Commission, and Jacques Santer, the former Prime Minister of Luxembourg and President of the Commission at the time (Bates, 1999). The scandal was given the label 'Santergate' by the media. The conclusions of the report into Santergate stated that, 'Undoubted instances of fraud and corruption in the Commission have thus passed unnoticed at the level of the commissioners themselves', and added that it found 'instances where commissioners or the Commission as a whole bear responsibility for instances of fraud, irregularities or mismanagement in their services or areas of responsibility' (1999a). To date, Santergate probably remains the single largest scandal of its type in the OECD world, although the precise amounts of money involved remain a matter of conjecture.

EU policy before Santergate

The European Commission listed the various cross-national initiatives that were already in place, but pointed out that they were not part of an integrated approach (COM (97) 192). Although all Member States criminalise the bribery of their own public officials, not surprisingly they have done so differently. The Commission noted that all acts of corruption involve at least two parties, the party offering the bribe, which involves the offence of active corruption; and the party accepting the bribe which involves passive corruption, but it is not clear in the documents whether it is the company or the company's employee that is liable when a bribe has been offered or paid. Another uncertainty was whether elected officials would be subject to the same laws as employed public officials. Moreover, some states have historically not included as an offence the payment of a bribe to a person who has influence over an official. Connectedly, the law as written in some states indicates that the official in question must be acting in breach of official duties and, therefore, that no crime is committed when an official accepts a bribe to award a contract to a company that should have got the contract in any event. The Commission also raised problems of territoriality, nationality and other problems of enforcement jurisdiction.

In focusing on bribery, the document did not employ a broad definition of corruption. Rather, it defined how corruption affected the specific interests of the EU. Five, primarily economic, aspects of the interests of the Union were identified as being affected by corruption. Broadly, the interests of the Union were seen as being affected by corruption in that it:

- undermines sound decision making;
- distorts competition and challenges principles of open and free markets, in particular the proper functioning of the internal market;
- it damages the financial interests of the European communities;
- it had various effects upon external policies in respect of a number of states receiving the systems; and
- it is at variance with the transparent and open conduct of International Trade.

Here we find a somewhat different moral emphasis from that found in traditional definitions of corruption, one that stresses the dangers of immoral bureaucratic behaviour. Here, open markets, financial interests and trade are central. However, although both the corrupter and the corruptee are recognised, much of the legislation is aimed at the corrupter rather than at the set of relationships facilitating corruption in the countries where it occurs. Nevertheless, this EU document did represent a movement in the definition of corruption towards the areas referred to earlier in the chapter as the 'new' corruption.

Post-Santergate: practical steps as proposed by the Committee of Independent Experts

The Committee of Independent Experts was set up in response to 'Santergate' in 1999, to examine corruption within the EU.[1] The Committee defined corruption as a special case of fraud, and argued that corruption was related to irregularities, maladministration and waste. Its position can be interpreted as proposing that there is a continuum of seriousness: waste is least serious, next are maladministration and irregularities, and most serious are fraud and corruption. The Committee further argued that the latter two offences should be the subject of criminal sanction, whereas the first three should be dealt with by internal disciplinary procedures, although it also argued that tolerance of slack administrative practices amounts to a tolerance of a relatively high level of fraud.

---

1 Corruption has been legally defined, at least in the case of the interests of the EU, by the first protocol to the Convention on the Protection of the European Communities' Financial Interests. Fraud is defined in the same Convention in Art 1(1).

In its second report, the Committee outlined priorities in combating corruption: a change in culture; codes of conduct; harmonisation of criminal sanctions and a number of administrative and procedural changes.

The new culture wished for is one that stresses integrity, responsibility and accountability, transparency and openness. To achieve this, the Committee focused on changes in three areas:

- standards of personal conduct;
- the chain of responsibility; and
- the *positive* and *negative* institutional accountability of commissioners and officials to the democratic institutions of the EU. *Positive* accountability is the giving of an account, *negative* accountability is being held to account.

The Committee argued that the occupational culture of EU institutions originated in 'shared ethical and political values and priorities flowing primarily from the concept of human dignity'. These were expressed formally in various international and European statements, such as the European Convention on Human Rights, national constitutions and traditions, and Arts 1 and 6 of the Treaty of the European Union in particular (Committee of Independent Experts, 1999b, para 7.2.1). The Committee therefore proposed Codes of Conduct as a solution for some of the problems in the European Institutions (Committee of Independent Experts, 1999b, para 7.4.1). Such codes, it was argued, could provide an ethical reference point for officials and holders of a public mandate. Seven principles, articulated as part of the Nolan Committee's enquiry into standards in public life (which commenced in 1994) were seen as the basis for an appropriate institutional culture: 'Selflessness, integrity, objectivity, accountability, openness, honesty and leadership' (see www.public-standards.gov.uk). The Committee also noted, with approval, material on the OECD website (www.oecd.org) and the adoption by the Council of the OECD, on 23 April 1998, of 12 principles for managing ethics in the public service. From these the Committee deduced a detailed code of behaviour that they then proposed for the Commission.

The Committee also suggested a number of immediate steps that could be taken. In particular, when looking at files and interviewing officials, the Committee found national responses and national networks within the Commission and discovered that some Commissioners and/or their private offices amounted to the creation of national 'fiefdoms' (Committee of Independent Experts, 1999b, para 7.3.3). This institutional process meant that Commission Director Generals and their immediate subordinates were being appointed on the basis of national shares. The Committee suggested that, even though the reason for this is understandable and is not in itself evidence of corrupt activity, it nevertheless needed to be closely monitored (Committee of Independent Experts, 1999b, para 7.3.4).

The Committee stated that criminal sanctions alone are not a sufficient method of combating corruption, although they did recommend that laundering the proceeds of corruption should become a criminal offence (Committee of Independent Experts, 1999b, pp 116, 121). Improved socio-economic conditions, procedures and overall transparency were also advocated. A number of proposals were made, amongst which were changes in auditing and accounting procedures; transparency and equality of access for public procurement; blacklisting; written undertakings not to engage in bribery from competitors for contracts and the protection of whistleblowers from victimisation.

Overall, the thrust of the Committee is quite similar to the proposals of the Organisation of American States, with the addition of an emphasis on fostering an institutional culture that does not support corruption. Unfortunately, the Committee appears to have believed that shared ethical values are evidenced by the existence of the European Convention on Human Rights and other legal texts, and that these would translate into a shared, anti-corruption culture. This hope appears unwarranted, especially since, as the Committee earlier admitted, common, secular, moral values are not shared by the competing cultures that make up the EU.

Conclusions

Creating policies against corruption

The process of identifying corruption in the EU has been important, and is well documented. Although some of the problems faced by the EU are unique, it has illuminated many of the issues faced by transnational bodies more generally. Cultural differences and shared histories both separate and unite the countries participating within the EU, and the technical, legal and procedural steps suggested as means of fighting corruption in that forum have wider relevance. Budgetary committees, the role of auditors, methods of contract and procurement oversight, the problems of gaining evidence that include how to legitimise and defend whistleblowing and the establishment of an effective investigative agency are all illustrative of the complexities involved in stamping out corruption. The reports, discussion documents and Conventions discussed in this chapter show that there is confusion between domestic political priorities and the interests of the commercial sector, both domestic and transnational. In the European context, domestic politicians find it useful to accuse 'Brussels' of being corrupt, wasteful and incompetent while refusing to see the activities of TNCs as a problem, especially since many benefit from the latter's largesse. The discussion rarely starts with the question: who corrupts? The assumption has been simply that bureaucrats (especially Eurocrats) are corrupt to begin with.

Regardless of official or unofficial factors, anti-corruption policies that have a likelihood of success will aim to influence the opportunities for corruption including, but not limited to, cultural facilitators. This is a criminological truism. The institutional context in which corruption occurs can be understood as consisting in 'political opportunity structures' (Kitschelt, 1986; Mény and Rhodes, 1997, p 100). Political opportunity structures are institutional arrangements of political and administrative power, and the extent to which they are transparent and subject to effective regulatory pressure shapes and creates opportunities for corruption (Heywood, 1997, pp 428–29). Although transparency and auditing measures may be suggested, what is as important is the regulatory strength of the body putting forward the policy. Does a particular body, be it the Organisation of American States or the EU, have the power and the inclination to effect the changes and to pursue wrongdoing? These political and cultural structural features are factors that ultimately relate to *trust*: trust that wrongdoing will be discovered, pursued, and prosecuted. In short, trust that corruption and dishonesty will have greater costs than honesty. What also clearly matters is that there is some harmonisation of norms between those of individuals and those of the institution. This may seem more difficult in the transnational context due to cultural differences, but economists would argue that ultimately all actors share the same interest in promoting trust such that market relations can be carried out with a modicum of efficiency.

Each of the policy efforts discussed in this chapter has a slightly different set of difficulties to face here. For example, in the context of the EU, it could be argued that a misplaced respect for differing mores among Member States has provided an opportunity for fraud against the EU; hence the Committee's worry about national 'fiefdoms'. However, it is also obvious that, in the context of the EU, at least there are real institutional arrangements to work in and 'belong' to, which is not the case for the Organisation of American States' Latin American Policy.

To the question 'How does corruption enter into the interface of politics and economics?', the literature presented gives several types of answer. On the one hand are the structural approaches that look to the development of political institutions (and the cultures within them), the degree of separation of state and administration from political parties; and relations of clientelism and dependency. On the other, economists tend to look at the problem in terms of individual rationality and ask questions based on models built on a variety of trust games (such as the prisoner's dilemma). To the question: 'How can corruption be prevented from entering the interface of politics and economics?' the academic literature suggests a variety of answers. There are those who argue that 'corruption' is a normal social practice and hence cannot be wholly prevented. There are those who argue that there is no such thing as a perfect system and hence there is always some opportunity for corruption. Ideological points of view are also brought forward; adherents to neo-liberal principles might argue that the best chance of eliminating corruption comes out of the elimination of government and politics from economics since the market will naturally stop corruption as well as or better than any state intervention could. Alternatively, many argue that, left unregulated, the market actually encourages corruption and that since politics and economics cannot be separated, it is better to make their links explicit and transparent. There is a general recognition that although cultural practices vary and what is corrupt is not agreed, the adoption of the correct shared norms may serve to inhibit corruption and this would be a benefit to all. Having said this, looking at the development of policies aimed at reducing corruption, the pessimist could be forgiven for concluding that, for the most part, transnational actors who have laid claim to policy developments in this sphere have adhered to a vague and unclear admixture of all of these ideas.

What does persuade officials, contract holders and traders to hold to contracts and honest dealing? Rather than simple coercion which probably has, at best, a short-run impact and, over the longer term, may pose heavy costs for any society, rule following behaviours are best supported by trust; trust that all sides will deal fairly because cheating costs more in the long run. But cheating may provide competitive advantage in the short run. That is why enforcement and regulatory mechanisms are needed in order to ensure that the breaking of a contract or engagement in unfair trading practices will be pursued in a way that prevents the cheat from making short-term profits. When contracts are not enforced and fair dealing is not regulated and ensured, contract breakers and dishonest dealers have the competitive advantage, and so corruption is inevitable. Where a contract overseer is an elected official, cyclical corruption is possible: in return for gains at the start of a period in office, the official may use political capital to reward the gain-giver, but costs to the official are high. By the end of a period, where political capital may have been exhausted, the official is more likely to be open to corruption, but will, if the theory and practice of democracy is correct, be voted out. Alternatively, it can be argued that when the political officials oversee the work of those involved in private contracts, corruption is less likely than when there is no oversight. The likelihood of corruption is directly related to the official's level of remuneration relative to that of others in the private sector: a low relative level promotes corruption and bias in the oversight of production (Acemoglu and Verdier, 1998).

These are largely academic considerations that have been given scant attention by policy makers and are hardly, if at all, considered in any of the policies discussed in this chapter. The analysis of policy developments undertaken here shows that enforcement and regulation of corruption, 'the stick', is extremely weak and the rewards for compliance and honest practice are equally so. This is not to suggest that the academics have all the answers. It may well be that academic debate about corruption needs to move beyond the literal focus on trust and contract, when what is being traded may be influence and information as much as a tangible product. The need for more academic work in this sphere is especially evident in the context of transnational corruption and financial crime more generally. In a globalising world, corruption rides on the coattails of the new opportunity structures. Global trading, transnational money markets, and other transnational institutions provide new opportunities for financial crime. For these reasons, a continual re-examination of corruption, in the light of a wide range of academic literatures, remains timely. Politics, economics and policy studies all add valuable perspectives to a criminological problem that, even now, remains inestimable.

References

Acemoglu, D and Verdier, T (1998) 'Property rights, corruption and the allocation of talent: a general equilibrium approach' 108 *The Economic Journal* 1381–1403

Andvig, JC *et al* (2000) *Research on Corruption: A Policy Oriented Survey*, Commissioned by NORAD, Final Report, December, wwwuser.gwdg.de/~uwvw/downloads/contribution07_andvig.pdf

Bacharach, M and Gambetta, D (1997) 'Trust in signs', in Cook, K (ed), *Trust in Society*, New York: Russel Sage Foundation

Bates, A (1999) 'Report strikes at heart of Europe; lax controls at highest levels of EU Commission exposed' *The Guardian*, 16 March

Bicchieri, C and Duffy, J (1997) 'Corruption cycles' 45(3) *Political Studies* 477–95

van Buitenen, P (1999) *Report of Paul Van Buitenen on how the European Commission Deals with its Internal Irregularities and Fraud*, www.sdnl.nl/fraude.htm

Committee of Independent Experts (1999a) *First Report on Allegations Regarding Fraud, Mismanagement and Nepotism in The European Commission*, 15 March, www.europarl.eu.int/experts/report1_ en.htm?redirected=1

Committee of Independent Experts (1999b) *Second Report on Reform of the Commission: Analysis of Current Practice and Proposals for Tackling Mismanagement, Irregularities and Fraud*, 10 September, www.europarl.eu.int/experts/default_ en.htm?redirected=1

Council of Europe (1996) *Programme of Action Against Corruption*, November 1996,

Council of Europe (1999) *Criminal Law Convention on Corruption*, 27 January, Strasbourg,www.conventions.coe.int/treaty/en/Treaties/Html/173.htm

Court of Auditors (1998) *Special Report No 8/98 on the Commission's Services Specifically Involved in the Fight Against Fraud, Notably the 'Unite de Co-ordination de la Lutte Anti-Fraude' (UCLAF) Together with the Commission's Replies*, http://www.eca.eu.int/audit_reports/special_reports/docs/1998/c230_en.pdf

European Commission (1993) *Protecting the Community's Financial Interests: The Fight Against Fraud*, Annual Reports

European Commission (1994) *Protecting the Community's Financial Interests: The Fight Against Fraud*, Annual Reports

European Commission (1995) *Protecting the Community's Financial Interests: The Fight Against Fraud*, Annual Reports

European Commission (1996) *Protecting the Community's Financial Interests: The Fight Against Fraud*, Annual Reports

European Commission (1997) *Communication from the Commission to the Council and the European Parliament on a Union Policy Against Corruption*, COM (97) 192

European Commission (1999) 'Amended Proposal for a Council Regulation concerning investigations conducted by the Fraud Prevention Office', presented by the Commission pursuant to Article 189A(2) of the EC Treaty in Brussels, COM (1999) 140 Final, *Official Journal*, 1999/C21/06

European Council (1997) *Convention on the Fight Against Corruption Involving Officials of the European Communities all Officials of Member States of the European Union*, 26 May, Brussels

Gambetta, D (1993) *The Sicilian Mafia: The Business of Private Protection*, Cambridge, Massachusetts: Harvard UP

Heywood, P (1997) 'Political corruption: problems and perspectives' 45(3) *Political Studies* 417–35

Huntington SP (1968) 'Modernization and corruption', in Huntington, SP, *Political Order in Changing Societies*, New Haven, Connecticut: Yale UP, pp 59–71

Hutchcroft, PD (1997) 'The politics of privilege: assessing the impact of rents, corruption and clientelism on Third World development' 45(3) *Political Studies* 639–58

Kitschelt, H (1986) 'Political opportunity structures and political protest' 16(1) *British Journal of Political Science* 57–85

Médard, J-F (1991) 'L'État n'eo-patrimonial en Afrique', in Médard, J-F (ed), *États d'Afrique Noire. Formations, Mécanismes et Crise*, Paris: Karthala, pp 323–53

Mény, Y and Rhodes, M (1997) 'Illicit governance: corruption scandal and fraud', in Rhodes, M, Heywood, P and Wright, V (eds), *Developments in West European Politics*, London: Macmillan, pp 95–113

Nolan Committee (1996) *First Report on Standards in Public Life*, www.official-documents.co.uk/document/parlment/nolan/nolan.htm

Nye, JS (1967) 'Corruption and political development' 66(2) *American Political Science Review* 417–27

Organisation of American States (1996) *Inter-American Convention Against Corruption*, March, Washington

Organisation for Economic Co-operation and Development (1997) *OECD Convention on Combating Bribery of Foreign Public Officials in International Business Transactions*, 21 November, Paris

Philp, M (1997) 'Defining political corruption' 45(3) *Political Studies* 436–62

Peterson, J (1997) 'The European Union: pooled sovereignty, divided accountability' 45(3) *Political Studies* 559–78

Platteau, J-P (1994a) 'Behind the market stage where real societies exist – Part I: the role of public and private order institutions' 30(3) *The Journal of Development Studies* 533–77

Platteau, J-P (1994b) 'Behind the market stage where real societies exist – Part II: the role of moral norms' 30(4) *The Journal of Development Studies* 753–817

Political Studies (1997) 45(3) Special issue on political corruption

Scott, JC (1969) 'Corruption, machine politics and political change' 63 *American Political Science Review* 1142–58

Scott JC (1972) *Comparative Political Corruption*, New Jersey: Prentice Hall

Tupman, WA (2000) 'The sovereignty of fraud and the fraud of sovereignty: OLAF and the wise men' 8(1) *Journal of Financial Crime* 32–46

United Nations (1996) *Resolution on Action Against Corruption Including the International Code of Conduct for Public Officials*, 12 December

World Trade Organisation (1996) *Government Procurement Agreement*, 1 January

General websites

Committee on Standards in Public Life (successor to the Nolan Committee), www.parliament.uk/works/standards.cfm

Hypertext Websters online dictionary, www.bennetyee.org/http_webster.cgi

Internet Center for Corruption Research, wwwuser.gwdg.de/~uwvw/ (Transparency International reports archived here and there are a number of papers, including Andvig *et al* at wwwuser.gwdg.de/~uwvw/corruption. research_contributions.html)

Legal Information Institute, www.law.cornell.edu/topics/white_collar.html

National White Collar Crime Center, www.nw3c.org

OECD website, www.oecd.org

Public Governance and Management, www.oecd.org/topic/0,2686,en_2649_37405 _1_1_1_1_37405,00.html

Transparency International website, www.transparency.org (Links to: Bribe Payers Index, 2002, www.transparency.org/cpi/2002/bpi2002.en.html and Corruption Perceptions Index annually from 1993 to 2003)

United Kingdom Committee on Standards in Public Life, www.public-standards.gov.uk

Chapter 12
Sex Trafficking in the European Union
Jo Goodey

Introduction

This chapter explores sex trafficking in the EU with a critical eye to undertaking comparative, cross-national research. To this end, the chapter begins by addressing the definition, nature and scale of sex trafficking as it exists in the EU, and highlights some measurement problems associated with 'counting' sex trafficking incidents, which is one of the most illusive organised crime activities. Secondly, the chapter frames the EU's institutional responses to trafficking victims in the context of broader concerns in connection with unwanted immigration and criminality. In contrast, these concerns are set against the increasing profile that has been given over to victims of crime, at the level of the UN and the European Commission, since the mid-1980s. Finally, the chapter outlines research undertaken by the author in selected EU Member States on criminal justice responses to victims of crime, and, specifically, trafficking victims. Findings from the research are compared using a broad-based checklist of possible victim protection and assistance measures. The promise and problems of trying to compare different legal systems with very different victim-centred practices, and different experiences of sex trafficking, are highlighted with regard to the idea of transferable 'good practice' between jurisdictions.

Sex trafficking: definition, nature and scale

Definition

Sex trafficking, or trafficking in women for sexual exploitation, now enjoys an internationally agreed definition under the terms of the Protocol to Prevent, Suppress and Punish Trafficking in Persons, Especially Women and Children, that supplements the 2000 United Nations Convention Against Transnational Organised Crime (TOC).[1] The Convention Against TOC also contains the Protocol Against Smuggling. As trafficking and smuggling are often confused in the public and political imagination, and, as a result, transfer into unhelpful criminal justice

---

1 Under the terms of the Protocol, Art 3(a) states: '"Trafficking in persons" shall mean the recruitment, transportation, transfer, harbouring or receipt of persons, by means of the threat or use of force or other forms of coercion, of abduction, of fraud, of deception, of the abuse of power or of a position of vulnerability or of the giving or receiving of payments or benefits to achieve the consent of a person having control over another person, for the purpose of exploitation. Exploitation shall include, at a minimum, the exploitation of the prostitution of others or other forms of sexual exploitation, forced labour or services, slavery or practices similar to slavery, servitude or the removal of organs' (A/55/383). In comparison, the UN Protocol against the Smuggling of Migrants by Land, Sea and Air (supplementing the UN Convention against Transnational Organised Crime), Art 3(a) states: '"Smuggling of migrants" shall mean the procurement, in order to obtain, directly or indirectly, a financial or other material benefit, of the illegal entry of a person into a State Party of which the person is not a national or a permanent resident' (A/55/383).

practice that tends to 'criminalise' trafficking victims, the Convention has, for the first time, provided a definition of trafficking that clearly distinguishes it from smuggling.

Trafficking and smuggling both involve the illegal movement of people either within or across borders. But, while smuggled people, having paid a fee to their smugglers, are free at the end of the smuggling process, trafficking victims are not. Trafficking fundamentally differs from smuggling as it involves exploitation at every stage of the trafficking process. While some trafficked women undoubtedly know they are being recruited to work as prostitutes, they will not know the extent to which they will be exploited en route and at their destination. In this regard, consent is not an issue in sex trafficking cases. What this means is that women might consent, in their country of origin, to travel abroad and work as prostitutes, but they will not have consented to the abuse or the slave-like conditions under which they are expected to work.

Nature

The bulk of trafficked women in the EU typically come from Eastern Europe, the Balkans, and parts of West Africa, notably Nigeria. Situations of grinding poverty, civil unrest and war, coupled with corruption and established criminal networks, have provided ready channels for trafficking from these regions to the wealthy Member States of the EU. Young women, typically in their late teens to mid-20s, are recruited under false pretences by advertisements for au pairs, waitresses and bar workers, offering lucrative employment in the EU. More recently, as anti-trafficking awareness campaigns have begun to impact in these regions, traffickers have shifted their recruitment methods to other means. These include the befriending of vulnerable young women by traffickers, and by other women who are often former victims of trafficking. More disturbingly, there is evidence to suggest that some family members sell young women onto traffickers for profit.[2]

Economic hardship, coupled with the collapse of civil society, can exacerbate the second class status of women in societies that, under certain conditions, place a low value on the human rights of girls and young women and a high value on their worth as sexual commodities (Bales, 2000). In turn, the EU's sex market has provided the 'pull' to these 'push' factors; with foreign criminals and EU citizens supplying both a prostitution service and the demand for this service from 'clients'. As the penalties for human trafficking are only just being raised across the EU, sex trafficking has provided traffickers with generous profit margins in what has been a low risk criminal activity. The only people not to profit from this business are the women who are variously exploited by traffickers, acquaintances, brothel and nightclub owners, and the men who pay to have sex with them.

Women experience sustained levels of sexual, physical and psychological abuse, both in transit and at their destination. Abuse often starts en route, with rape being a common method used to physically and psychologically break women's resistance. Trafficked women receive little or no money from their work as

---

2 Organisation for Security and Co-operation in Europe, Expert Meeting on Development of an Anti-Trafficking Training Module for Judges and Prosecutors, Sofia, April 2003 – closed meeting; attended by author.

prostitutes. Of the money they do receive, they usually have to pay exorbitant fees for their board and lodging, and, in addition, are often held in debt-bondage to their traffickers, with the debt being their trafficking fee. And trafficked women, as vulnerable foreigners, are expected to perform sexual acts by clients and brothel owners that they would not willingly undertake, and which host country prostitutes will not perform; for example, unprotected anal sex.

It is normal practice for women's passports or means of identification to be taken from them en route to their destination. As illegal immigrants, often with no knowledge of their host country's language, and a mistrust of the police and other authority figures that stems from experience in their home countries, women are in no position to go to the police should they have the opportunity to do so. In this regard, trafficking cases are underreported by victims and are extremely difficult to detect. As with most crime that is related to organised crime, criminal justice agencies can take a figure and extrapolate it by a factor of 10 or more in an attempt to produce a reasonable estimate of the extent of the problem.

Scale

The International Organization for Migration (IOM) came up with the now oft quoted figure of 500,000 women having been trafficked into the EU from central and Eastern Europe in the early 1990s.[3] More recently, the US Department of State estimated that between 700,000 and four million people are trafficked annually worldwide. When looking to publications and websites from inter-governmental organisations (IGOs) and non-governmental organisations (NGOs), ranging from the UN through to Anti-Slavery International,[4] one gets a sense of the same data being circulated with little reference to how this data was obtained. In turn, global figures need cautious interpretation as they often fail to distinguish between trafficking and smuggling, the State Department's data being a case in point.

The United Nation's Global Programme Against Trafficking in Human Beings (GPAT), based in the Crime Programme in Vienna, has recently established a 'database on trafficking flows'. The database gathers information on global trends in trafficking, cross-national trafficking routes, and the volume of trafficking in persons and smuggling of migrants; with the intention being to publish regular reports on national, regional and global trends. The database also has a remit to collect information on offenders and victims that will allow for a clearer picture of 'who' they are. According to GPAT's pages on the UN website: 'This type of database is a first of its kind and is a much needed mechanism to facilitate development of strategies to combat trafficking both nationally and globally.'[5] The database, together with GPAT's forthcoming 'Toolkit' on 'promising practices' against trafficking, sets out to paint a clearer picture of the global nature, extent and responses to human trafficking.

But GPAT's database, in its current guise, has its limitations. As it lacks a critical comparative analysis of data from different sources around the world, it can only be read at face value. In other words, descriptive data that does not engage with the

---

3 See also IOM's regular news bulletins at www.iom.int.
4 See www.antislavery.org.
5 See www.unov.org, for pages on Trafficking in Human Beings.

socio-legal context in which information is gathered, interpreted and reproduced, is limited with respect to what it can offer as transferable ideas for 'good' or 'promising' practice. And, as official and accurate data on organised crime and its victims is hard to source when compared with other criminal activities, it has to be asked *why* counting and description of the phenomenon remain such desirable goals when it is highly unlikely that we will ever know the true extent of the problem? One answer lies with the fact that data-hungry governments are keen to quote UN figures when attempting to quantify the problem of trafficking. In turn, numbers help to clarify, and justify, how much money should be spent on anti-trafficking initiatives.

In support of efforts at counting this particularly illusive crime problem, one can also argue that it is not enough simply to state that there is a 'problem' of trafficking, without first defining it, and its differences with smuggling, and, having done so, determining its scale and trends. The ability of a trafficking database to predict trends in trafficking, and to target criminal justice interventions accordingly, in an effort to pre-empt traffickers, is one of the best uses to which such information can be put. However, as criminals are always one step ahead of the justice system, any open access web-based database can only provide general information about what is commonly known; with examples of practice limited to broad checklists and reference to international instruments such as the UN Convention and Protocol. In other words, the 'real' trends in trafficking and organised crime, and detailed accounts of counter-trafficking initiatives, are always kept as limited access databases by national police forces and intergovernmental organisations such as Europol and Interpol.

Within the EU, the German police, the *Bundeskriminalamt* (BKA), and the Dutch Rapporteur's Office on Trafficking, now produce regular situation reports on the extent and nature of the problem in their respective countries. With the BKA's 1999 situation report indicating 801 official cases of trafficking, there is a significant gap between global estimates of the problem, which run into the thousands per country, and official statistics. However, the BKA's figures don't appear so low when compared with the 71 official cases of sex trafficking recorded in 1998 for a Home Office report on the situation in England and Wales (Kelly and Regan, 2000). However, as the report's authors spell out, the actual extent of sex trafficking in England and Wales may be anywhere from two to 20 times greater. While official data on sex trafficking in the EU is, like all crime statistics, limited in what it can tell us about the extent of the problem, it is no worse than government and NGO 'guesstimates' which paint a picture of trafficking that often appears exaggerated or based on spurious 'data'.

The 'real' figures on trafficking obviously lie somewhere along a scale, with official statistics at one end, and NGO and IGO estimates at the other. What we do know more about, given the accounts of trafficked women, is the varied but equally heinous nature of the crime. Efforts at providing more accurate statistics on the phenomenon, if undertaken as a means to pre-empt traffickers, and with consideration for the budgets of criminal justice and social agencies that must respond to the problem, can be considered as worthwhile undertakings. Monitoring the problem of trafficking, if unaccompanied by any real sense of progress against it, is not a worthwhile undertaking in itself. As Kelly and Regan comment (2000, p 12), with respect to the number of international instruments, from Conventions through to 'good practice' guidelines, that have been written in recent years in response to the problem of trafficking: '[there is a sense of] much talk but limited action.' In this regard, the next section explores the place of international instruments against trafficking, in the context of the EU, with this critique in mind.

Recognition of victims of crime, and specifically trafficking victims, at the level of the EU

The EU has been actively engaged in anti-trafficking initiatives since the mid-1990s, and responds to the problem of trafficking in the general framework of action concerning immigration and asylum control. The various criminal, humanitarian and social problems associated with trafficking are interpreted by EU governments along a continuum that readily associates illegal immigration with criminality (Goodey, 2002). In this regard, there is a two pronged approach to trafficking in the EU that, first, sets out to tackle the problem in relation to organised crime and traffickers, and secondly, responds to the humanitarian needs of trafficking victims.

The development, since the mid-1990s, of a justice and home affairs policy that welds the human rights abuses associated with trafficking to concerns surrounding the threat of organised criminality and illegal immigration, is neatly illustrated by a range of funding initiatives that have emerged from the Commission. The first of these, running from 1996–2000, was the STOP programme, or STOP I.[6] This set out to improve international co-operation in the fight against trafficking, and sexual exploitation of children, through, primarily, training of criminal justice personnel in these matters. In 2000, the DAPHNE programme was established, with funding available for NGOs to combat violence against children, adolescents and women; including victims of trafficking. STOP II, for the brief period 2001–02, was set up in an effort to more directly tie the activities of the STOP initiative with the DAPHNE programme, and with applicant EU countries also eligible for funding. In turn, since 2003, the AGIS programme has replaced a number of criminal justice programmes in the EU, including STOP II.[7] Its remit is to facilitate co-operation between the police, judiciary and other professionals in different Member States and candidate countries in the fight against crime and, in particular, organised crime involving, among other activities, trafficking. The work of AGIS is mirrored by the ARGO programme, which was established at the beginning of 2002. Its remit is to build a common European asylum system, with control on visas, immigration and the EU's external borders.

These action-oriented programmes are supported by a number of legally and non-legally binding instruments that have emerged from the Council of the European Union, the European Parliament, and the European Commission. The first of these to specifically target trafficking, from February 1997, was the Council of the European Union's Joint Action to combat trafficking in human beings and the sexual exploitation of children; the onus being on Member States to review their legislation in this area, and to enhance judicial co-operation against trafficking.

---

6 For an introduction to European Commission Justice and Home Affairs programmes see http://europa.eu.int/comm/justice_home/index_en.htm.
7 AGIS replaced the following programmes: Grotius, Oisin, STOP, Hippocrate and Falcone.

Overshadowing the specific remit of this Joint Action, and reflected in the development of the comprehensive AGIS and ARGO programmes, are the Union's broader concerns regarding border control, illegal immigration and associated criminal activity. In this regard, the Commission's efforts to create an area of 'freedom, security and justice' within the EU are, more accurately, limited in their application to EU citizens. Undesirable outsiders, namely poor non-EU citizens, be these illegal immigrants, refugees or trafficked women, present the inconvenient face of a control policy that has tightened the EU's external borders in an effort to ease internal freedom of movement for EU citizens. The relevant parts of The Amsterdam Treaty (May 1999) and the Vienna Action Plan, on the implementation of the Treaty's provisions on an area of freedom, security and justice, together with the conclusions of the Tampere European Council (October 1999), have addressed trafficking, with the main aim of harmonising definitions and judicial co-operation across Member States in an effort to apprehend traffickers as 'undesirable outsiders'. Arguably, until very recently, the welfare of trafficking victims has been a secondary consideration in the EU's justice and home affairs policy which has focused on the criminality of trafficking rather than its impact on victims.

In 2000, following on from the UN Convention and Trafficking Protocol, the European Commission introduced a proposal for a 'Council Framework Decision on Combating Trafficking in Human Beings'. The UN Protocol and the European Commission's Framework Decision are, to a large extent, identical instruments. But, once again, the Framework Decision only devotes one article out of 12, Art 8, directly to victims. The onus, as ever, is on fighting crime. Victims of trafficking have typically been regarded by EU criminal justice agencies, and the Commission, as tools through which criminal justice agencies might be able to secure convictions of traffickers. To date, the needs and rights of trafficking victims have been addressed by European organisations and NGOs, such as the Council of Europe and IOM, that have a humanitarian stance but which do not have the power to pass binding legislation on Member States. This is not to deny the influence of these organisations on the Commission's Justice and Home Affairs policy, but to place the humanitarian focus on trafficking in a political framework that has only recently introduced these concerns as part of binding legislation.

Accompanying specific measures against trafficking, and for trafficking victims, has been a global undercurrent of victim-centred criminal justice developments. Since the mid-1980s, the international community has put victims' rights on the political agenda, with the 1985 UN Declaration of Basic Principles of Justice for Victims of Crime and Abuse of Power being the benchmark instrument to which all others refer. Once again, following hot on the heels of the UN, Europe outlined its own victim-centred instrument in the guise of the Council of Europe's Recommendation (85)11 on the Position of the Victim in the Framework of Criminal Law and Procedure. These two instruments reflected a social and political groundswell toward recognition of victims' rights that had been put in motion with the development of state compensation schemes for victims of violent crime from the mid-1960s, and the influential work of the feminist movement in highlighting violence against women. But, these victim-centred instruments were both explicitly and implicitly aimed at citizens of individual states. Only recently, through the European Court of Human Rights, have EU citizens challenged their treatment as second class victims in Member States other than their own. With the recent recognition of trafficked women as victims, and the introduction of binding legislative reform to this effect, the EU will have to adjust its victim services to accommodate trafficked women (van Dijk, 2002). However, the application of victim-centred justice to trafficked women is hampered by the fact that victims of crime, who are EU citizens, do not currently enjoy equal access to victim-centred justice in different Member States.

The fact of uneven and unequal distribution of victim-centred justice across the EU should come as no surprise. However, there is a yawning gap between what criminal justice reform is currently promising trafficked women, as a 'soft' right, and what it will be able to deliver them in practice. Given that it is now 18 years since both the 1985 UN Declaration for Victims and the Council of Europe Recommendation came into being, with, in some European countries, very little evidence of significant developments towards victim-centred justice, one has to cautiously welcome the latest wave of victim initiatives that centre on trafficked women. As non-EU citizens who are more often than not associated with illegal immigration and criminal activity, the extent to which trafficked women will be afforded special criminal justice services as particularly vulnerable victims remains to be seen. Given that other vulnerable and at risk victims, such as victims of domestic violence and sexual assault, do not experience the degree of victim-centred criminal justice service that one might expect across the EU, it has to be asked if trafficking victims will fare any better. To this end, the author's research in selected EU Member States has highlighted the distance between the law in theory and the law in practice with respect to the treatment of vulnerable and at risk victims of crime in general, and trafficking victims in particular.

Undertaking comparative cross-national research on criminal justice responses to trafficking: promises and problems

Research background

Based in the Crime Programme at the United Nations in Vienna, the author has undertaken a two year study on criminal justice responses to vulnerable and at risk victims of crime in the EU, with a special focus on responses to victims of sex trafficking. The mainstay of the research is devoted to the place of theoretical and policy discussions in the EU in consideration of organised crime, migrants, sex trafficking, and victimisation (Goodey, 2000, 2002, 2003a and 2003b). The research also explored the theory and practice of criminal justice responses to trafficking victims and other categories of vulnerable and at risk victims, through evidence-based research in selected EU Member States. What the research did not set out to produce was a black letter lawyer's comparative review of the law in the books as it is supposed to impact upon vulnerable and at risk victims, and in particular, trafficking victims. Other researchers have already undertaken this task (Brienen and Hoegen, 2000; Kartusch, 2001). What the research did set out to accomplish was a critique of criminal justice practice with respect to how vulnerable and at risk victims actually experience criminal justice, and any special provisions that might apply to trafficking victims.

The main research tool for this exercise consisted of a research questionnaire that was distributed to criminal justice personnel, government ministries, NGOs and academics. The questionnaire is divided into six parts that variously ask about criminal justice provisions for vulnerable and at risk victims, and specifically, victims of trafficking. The questionnaire was distributed either in whole or in part to respondents according to their particular area of expertise. Experts were identified to take part in the research using established contacts with the UN Secretariat in Vienna, and through attendance at various meetings and conferences where people were approached and asked to take part in the research.[8] Respondents were asked to identify other experts who might be able to contribute to the research exercise. Approximately 130 detailed questionnaires were distributed to identified expert respondents in all 15 Member States. The request received a 50% response rate; with some countries returning up to eight completed questionnaires, and others only one or two. As a result, eight Member States were selected for detailed comparison, namely: Austria; Belgium; England and Wales; Finland; France; Germany; Italy; and the Netherlands. The questionnaire findings were supplemented by research interviews and attendance at meetings that addressed the problem of organised crime and human trafficking.[9] Interview schedules specifically addressed special programmes for victims of sex trafficking that interviewees had identified in the course of questionnaire completion.

The questionnaire was originally planned with the possibility of undertaking a comparative statistical analysis of findings between each Member State. However, the following factors made this unfeasible in practice: (a) the number of responses per country was insufficient; (b) ambiguous responses to pre-ordained response categories; and (c) submission of additional material and responses that did not comply with the questionnaire format. However, the questionnaire did provide ample scope for respondents to supply their own comments, unrestricted by pre-ordained categorisation. The questionnaire, together with the research interviews, has furnished the research with qualitative findings that supplement the research's theoretical and policy-based critique of current criminal justice practice in the EU concerning vulnerable and at risk victims and, specifically, trafficking victims.

The theory and practice of victim assistance

Having supplied a range of criminal justice experts in different Member States with a questionnaire enquiring about the application of the law in practice, three conclusions can be drawn from the variety of answers both between and within

---

8 Meetings and conferences attended included, for example: 10th UN Congress on the Prevention of Crime and Treatment of Offenders, Vienna, April 2000; British Society of Criminology Conference, Leicester, July 2000; 10th International Symposium on Victimology, Montreal, August 2000; Expert Meeting on State Compensation to Crime Victims in the EU, Sweden, October 2000; American Society of Criminology Conference, San Francisco, November 2000.

9 For example: Economic and Social Council organised meeting on Transnational Organised Crime, Home Office, London, December 2000; Europol Expert Meeting on Trafficking in Human Beings for the Purpose of Sexual Exploitation, The Hague, March 2001 – closed meeting; meeting with representatives from the Dutch Rapporteur's Office on Trafficking, The Hague, March 2001; meeting with Anti-Trafficking Team of the Federal *Bundeskriminalamt*, Wiesbaden, March 2001; see BKA (1999); International Organisation for Migration Meeting on Trafficking, European Parliament, Brussels, September 2002; Organisation for Security and Co-operation in Europe, Expert Meeting on Development of an Anti-Trafficking Training Module for Judges and Prosecutors, Sofia, April 2003 – closed meeting.

Member States. First, the practice of law, unsurprisingly, is anything but uniform across the EU. While a point of law can be tracked down in the appropriate legal texts, its application will reflect a number of context-specific factors. Secondly, there is often little consensus among legal experts in each Member State about the circumstances under which a law can be applied. Thirdly, the impact of victim-centred international instruments, be these legally or non-legally binding, is not apparent in the treatment that vulnerable victims, including trafficking victims, are likely to encounter if they enter the criminal justice system in the EU. Theoretically, if the combined impact of international instruments were adhered to by Member States – such as the 1985 UN Victims Declaration, the 2000 UN Convention and Trafficking Protocol, and the European Commission's Council Framework Decision on Combating Trafficking – a comprehensive range of measures should be available to vulnerable and at risk victims, including trafficking victims, in one form or another; that is, either as binding legislation or as 'soft law' guidelines. In practice, victims encounter a system of justice that is determined by each jurisdiction and the discretionary application of law at the level of individual courts.

Here, four Member States, with very different legal systems, have been selected for comparison with respect to a comprehensive list of criminal justice measures: England and Wales (EW); Finland (FI); France (FR); and Germany (GE). England and Wales exemplifies the common law system of justice, Finland, Nordic law, and France and Germany, variations on civil law. In turn, the criminal justice process in each Member State can be classified with respect to adversarial or inquisitorial justice; with England and Wales falling into the former category, and the other three the latter. The classification of systems of justice can help us to understand the 'place' afforded victims in each system. So, based on crude characterisations, the following can be assumed. In the adversarial system of common law, the victim has no part to play other than that of witness for the prosecution, and can expect an aggressive cross-examination should their case come to trial. In comparison, the victim in the inquisitorial system can play a more active role in criminal proceedings as the *partie civile*, or through what is otherwise known as the adhesion principle, and does not have to endure cross-examination. And the Nordic system of law demonstrates elements of both systems, though it leans towards the civil.

At the same time, the taxonomy of justice, based as it tends to be on stereotypes, can be misleading with regard to how victims are actually treated in practice. Therefore, while it is typically held that the adversarial or common law system is not victim-centred, and the inquisitorial or civil system is, there is comparative criminal justice research available that challenges this polarised depiction of each system (Brienen and Hoegen, 2000). In this regard, common law systems, recognising the harm that can be inflicted on victims through aggressive cross-examination, have endeavoured to rectify this through, among other things, the provision of video links and screens in court to assist the testimonies of vulnerable victims. Similarly, the absence of the victim's right to act as *partie civile*, and bring a civil claim for compensation during the course of a criminal trial, has led to England and Wales having the most generous state compensation scheme for victims of violent crime in the EU.[10] In comparison, while the victim's right to play an active

---

10 For the year 2000, it has been estimated that 340,926,000 Euros was provided in state compensation to victims of violent crime in England, Wales and Scotland; and for 1999, the estimated amount for France was 147,550,000 (Mikaelsson and Wergens, 2001).

part in criminal proceedings exists in inquisitorial or civil law systems, this right is not commonly invoked in practice, and, when it is, victims are often unsuccessful in securing claims for compensation against offenders. In addition, although France has the second most generous state compensation scheme for victims of violent crime in the EU, it distributes less than half the sum of money that is made available under the scheme in England and Wales.

The questionnaire listed a number of protection and assistance measures that could, theoretically, be available to victims in the run-up to, during and after a criminal trial, if international victim-centred guidelines were followed. Using a subjective interpretation of the questionnaire results and available interview commentaries, Table 1 lists these measures according to their application or non-application in the four Member States selected for comparison. The following symbols indicate the level of consensus among respondents over a specific victim assistance or protection measure: (•) Experts were in consensus that a measure exists in practice for victims; (?) Experts disagreed about whether a measure was available in practice for victims; (No) Experts were in consensus that a measure did not exist in practice for victims.

Protection and Assistance Measures	EU Member States			
	EW	FI	FR	GE
Information available to victims in form of leaflet	•	•	•	•
Special police unit for specific victim categories	•	•	•	•
Psychological counselling and/or victim support	•	•	•	•
Victim's identity can be hidden in case file/dossier	?	No	?	No
Recorded statements admissible as evidence in court	?	?	•	?
Anonymous statements admissible as evidence in court	No	No	?	?
Victim's evidence can be heard '*in camera*' away from court	•	•	•	?
Victim can wait separately in court from defendant	?	?	•	?
Victim can wait away from court until called to give evidence	?	?	?	?
Screens in court to shield victim from defendant's gaze	•	No	No	No
Video link between courtroom and room where victim testifies	•	No	No	?
Rearrangement of courtroom furniture possible	?	No	?	?
The defendant can directly cross-examine any victim	?	No	?	?

The victim has ready access to an interpreter if needed	•	•	•	•
Civil claim for compensation can be brought during criminal trial	No	•	•	•
Compensation can be awarded to victim as part of sentencing	•	No	No	No
Victim of violent crime has access to state compensation	•	•	•	•

Table 1: The practice of protection and assistance for victims of crime in four EU Member States.

Table 1 shows that there is some consensus over certain provisions between the four Member States: namely, all experts in each Member State agreed that the following measures were available to victims: information about victim services in the form of a leaflet; access to a special police unit for certain victim categories such as children and victims of sexual assault; access to psychological counselling and/or some form of victim support service; ready access to an interpreter; and availability of state compensation for victims of violent crime. In contrast, there was a range of responses between Member States for other victim-centred measures. For example, it was indicated by experts in England and Wales that use of live video link, between the courtroom and a witness room where the victim testifies, is made available for specifically vulnerable or at risk victims, such as children and intimidated witnesses. In comparison, experts in Finland and France indicated that no such provisions were generally available, but that vulnerable victims could be protected from defendants by other means such as evidence being held 'in camera'; that is, typically in a judge's chambers, away from the courtroom and the defendant, but with the defendant's lawyer present. Experts in Germany indicated that while provisions for video link existed in law, its use in practice was inconsistent across the different German *Länder*, and between individual courts.

It is possible to challenge the evidence presented in Table 1, given that it represents an interpretation of experts' subjective accounts of criminal justice in practice. But the variation in responses in Table 1 is an indication of the extent to which victims of crime in general, and trafficking victims in particular, do not enjoy a full range of victim-centred criminal justice provisions in practice at the pre-trial, trial and post-trial stage of justice in selected Member States. Given that EU citizens who are victims of crime do not have access to a full range of measures that could, in theory, be available to them, it is highly unlikely that most victims of trafficking, as the least 'desirable' of victim categories, will receive these services unless emphasis is put on their plight as particularly vulnerable and at risk victims. The EU's signature to various victim-centred Commission and UN Conventions, Declarations and Recommendations, including specific ones focused on trafficking, might lead us to think that the situation is otherwise.

Perhaps what Table 1 most usefully reveals is not what criminal justice practice for victims can be in each jurisdiction, but, rather, the inherent problems of trying to characterise practice in each jurisdiction, and in turn, between jurisdictions. Each expert's experience and interpretation of criminal justice practice can differ widely. Furthermore, at a basic but important level, it is extremely difficult to categorise legal and criminal justice practice as there are so many exceptions under which

Table 2: The theory and practice of selected victim protection measures in Germany.

Victim Protection Measure	Practical Application of Law According to Experts
Recorded pre-trial statements as evidence in court	Experts indicated this measure is, theoretically, admissible in cases involving victims up to age 16 (StPO (German Code of Criminal Procedure), s 255a); however, there was disagreement about its application in practice.
Anonymous pre-trial statements as evidence in court	Experts generally indicated that this measure is inadmissible under German procedural law; however, police respondents indicated that this measure could be applied in exceptional cases involving state witnesses/informers, and, in theory, all 'serious' cases of importance to the state.
Victim's evidence can be heard *'in camera'* away from court	Experts indicated this measure is, theoretically, available in consideration of victims who would be endangered if testifying in open court (StPO, s 247a); however, there was disagreement about its application in practice to a range of victims.
Victim can wait separately in court from defendant; and victim can wait away from court until called to give evidence	Experts indicated these measures are, theoretically, available (StPO, s 214), but that practice is highly dependent on local courtroom facilities and practice.
Video link between courtroom and room where victim testifies	Experts were in consensus that this measure is available in theory in the following cases (StPO, s 247a): child victims up to age 16; when intimidation of the victim is highly probable; when it is considered that the victim will not tell the truth due to fear of intimidation. However, some experts indicated that the application of these measures is not consistent in practice.

certain laws and guidelines can be applied. In this regard, Table 2 lists five victim protection measures that, according to German law, can be utilised in the pre-trial and trial stage of a criminal trial, but which, according to expert respondents, are not applied uniformly in practice.

In reference to Table 2, while experts referred to child victims, state witnesses/informers, and the general category of intimidated witnesses, no direct reference was made to victims of trafficking as the law does not specifically accommodate their needs. According to police respondents in Germany,[11] measures could be evoked for trafficked women, particularly if the case in question warranted heightened security. And, at the time of writing, of the four Member States listed, only Germany has a dedicated witness protection programme in place for trafficked women. The other Member States could, in theory, put into action special protection measures for certain high profile trafficking cases. However, given that the vast number of trafficking cases do not warrant an extensive witness protection programme involving change of a woman's identity and round the clock protection, there are other basic measures, such as the ability to wait in court away from the defendant, or to wait away from court until called to give evidence, that could be of more benefit to trafficked women.

Towards transferable ideas of 'good practice'

Criminal justice responses to victims of crime and trafficking victims are embedded in the particular socio-legal culture of each country or region. Accordingly, suggestions for transferring victim-centred criminal justice 'good practice' between jurisdictions must account for context-specific differences between legal systems.

Looking at the list of measures in Table 1, each one could be selected as a 'good practice' for vulnerable and at risk victims, including victims of sex trafficking, as together they variously comply with the standards set out for victim-centred justice in international instruments such as the 1985 UN Declaration for Victims, and the 2000 UN Trafficking Protocol. In this regard, where experts have indicated that a Member State currently does not practice a particular victim-centred measure, or where there is no consensus about the application of this measure in practice, then the example of another state can be drawn upon where this measure is applied in practice. In turn, the possibility of transferring practice examples of victim-centred justice, such as use of video link in cases involving child victims, can be explored in relation to sex trafficking cases.

There are a number of steps that need to be considered when looking to utilise victim-centred 'good practice'. First, when borrowing 'good practice' examples from other jurisdictions, careful consideration should be given to 'matching' jurisdictions with respect to: (a) similar legal cultures and criminal justice practices; (b) similar recognition and practice of victim-centred justice; and (c) comparable problems with sex trafficking. While no two legal systems and no two countries are exactly alike, it is more likely that the transfer of 'good practice' ideas will work when consideration is given to the above factors. For example, to try and adapt victim-

---

11 Meeting with Anti-Trafficking Team of the Federal *Bundeskriminalamt*, Wiesbaden, March 2001.

centred criminal justice practice between England and Wales and Greece, let alone to try and adapt practice for the specific category of trafficking victims, would prove to be a far harder task than attempting the same between England and Wales and Ireland, or Greece and Germany. In the first instance, England and Wales share a common law system with Ireland, while the Greek system is based on Germanic law. Secondly, victim-centred criminal justice is well developed in England and Wales and Ireland, relatively well developed in Germany, and underdeveloped in Greece. And, thirdly, the extent and nature of trafficking between these countries is very different, so that the transfer of a particular victim-centred measure needs to accommodate the particular circumstances and needs of different groups of trafficked women, and the relationship they have both to traffickers and the criminal justice system in each country.

If examples of 'good practice' are to be more than descriptive accounts of what works in one jurisdiction, as is the case with the European Commission's latest efforts at 'good practice' indicators,[12] then efforts at 'matching' jurisdictions can be welcomed as a step towards ensuring that 'good practice' examples might actually work outside the jurisdiction in which they were developed. Given that victim-centred criminal justice practice is very different in each of the EU's 25 Member States, it is very difficult to talk in general terms about a 'good practice' measure without some understanding of how this might or might not work in practice in each jurisdiction. If 'good practice' for victims, including trafficking victims, is to be anything more than a practice ideal, in the nature of the UN Trafficking Protocol, then due recognition and knowledge of criminal justice practice has to be taken on board.

In turn, interpretations of what constitutes 'good practice' differs from group to group, and from country to country. If the police consider a victim-centred measure, such as witness protection, as 'good practice' because it resulted in an increase in the number of convictions, victims might not consider the same measure as 'good practice', as it tends to place undue strain on victims to co-operate with the authorities and testify in a case. Still other jurisdictions might consider witness protection as an excessive and costly undertaking for their jurisdiction's few trafficking cases. In other words, 'good' practice needs careful definition and critical interpretation by its instigators and end users, including trafficked women, before it can be held up as a model example.

Conclusion

Criminal justice responses to victims of sex trafficking need to be interpreted at a number of levels with regard to both the theory of law and the practice of criminal justice.

In the first instance, the definition, nature and 'counting' of sex trafficking can only reveal a partial picture of the true extent of the phenomenon, as the quality and interpretation of data, both official and unofficial, differs between jurisdictions. Secondly, the EU, through the Commission, has traditionally responded to sex

---

12 See the European Crime Prevention Network, http://europa.eu.int/comm/justice_home/eucpu/home.html.

trafficking in the framework of broader concerns regarding border control, illegal immigration, and organised crime. More recently, attention has been paid to sex trafficking with regard to the needs and rights of its victims. But, while legally binding and non-legally binding international instruments promote checklists of 'good practice' guidelines in an effort to apprehend traffickers and assist trafficking victims, victim-centred criminal justice practice differs widely across the EU. The difference between the theory and practice of law is neatly illustrated by the range of victim-centred criminal justice provisions that currently exist across the EU. As the research presented here shows, given that victims of crime in general do not receive due access to victim-centred justice in the EU (as international instruments indicate they should), it is hardly surprising that a range of services are not available to trafficking victims. Trafficking victims' construction in the same framework as illegal immigrants and organised criminals has not aided their due recognition as particularly vulnerable victims. However, increasing emphasis on the impact of trafficking on victims, coupled with increased international recognition of victim-centred justice, should do much to promote criminal justice responses for trafficking victims in the next few years.

Research that sets out to look beyond the theory of what 'good practice' for trafficking victims should be, according to international checklists, must take account of the socio-legal realities of criminal justice practice. In this regard, 'good practice' checklists are only meaningful if they can be readily transferred into practice, and from one jurisdiction to the next. As the author's research has shown, criminal justice practice varies greatly within the EU and, to this end, international instruments can only offer ideal checklists of what practice should be. The transfer of practice within and between jurisdictions can become a practical reality if efforts are made to 'match' jurisdictions with similar experiences of trafficking and victim-centred criminal justice practice.

References

Bales, K (2000) *Disposable People: New Slavery in the Global Economy*, Berkeley: California UP

BKA (1999) *Trafficking in Human Beings, Situation Report 1999*, Wiesbaden: Bundeskriminalamt

Brienen, M and Hoegen, E (2000) *Victims of Crime in Twenty-Two European Jurisdictions*, unpublished PhD thesis, Katholieke Universiteit Brabant, Nijmegen, the Netherlands: Wolf Legal Productions

Council of Europe (2001a) *Proposal for a Council Framework Decision on Combating Trafficking in Human Beings*, 2001/0024(CNS)

Council of Europe (2001b) *Proposal for a Council Framework Decision on Combating the Sexual Exploitation of Children and Child Pornography*, 2001/0025(CNS)

van Dijk, JJM (2002) 'Empowering victims of organized crime: on the concurrence of the Palermo Convention with the UN Declaration on Basic Principles of Justice for Victims' 9 *International Review of Victimology* 15–30

European Commission (1997) *Official Journal*, L 063, 4 March

European Commission (2000) *Communication from the Commission to the Council and the European Parliament on Combating Trafficking in Human Beings and Combating the Sexual Exploitation of Children and Child Pornography*, COM(2000) 854 final/2

European Commission (2001) *Green Paper on 'Compensation to Crime Victims'*, COM (2001) 536 final, p 18

Europol (1999) *General Situation Report on 'Trafficking in Human Beings'*, The Hague: Europol

Goodey, J (2000) 'Non-EU citizens' experiences of offending and victimisation: the case for comparative European research' 8(1) *The European Journal of Crime, Criminal Law and Criminal Justice* 13–34

Goodey, J (2002) 'Whose insecurity? Organised crime, its victims and the EU', in Crawford, A (ed), *Crime and Insecurity; the Governance of Safety in Europe*, Cullompten: Willan, pp 135–58

Goodey, J (2003a) 'Organised crime, its victims and the EU: the case of human trafficking', in Edwards, A and Gill, P (eds), *Transnational Organised Crime*, London: Routledge

Goodey, J (2003b) 'Migration, crime and victimhood: responses to sex trafficking in the EU' 5(4) *Journal of Punishment and Society* 415–31

International Organisation for Migration (1995) *Trafficking and Prostitution: The Growing Exploitation of Migrant Women from Central and Eastern Europe*, Geneva: IOM

Kartusch (2001) *Reference Guide for Anti-Trafficking Legislative Review: With Particular Emphasis on South Eastern Europe*, Vienna: Ludwig Boltzmann Institute of Human Rights/OSCE

Kelly, L and Regan, L (2000) *Stopping Traffic: Exploring the Extent of, and Responses to, Trafficking in Women for Sexual Exploitation in the UK*, Police Research Series, Paper 125, London: Home Office

Mikaelsson, J and Wergens, A (2001) *Repairing the Irreparable*, Umeå: The Swedish Crime Victim Compensation and Support Authority

Office to Monitor and Combat Trafficking in Persons (2002) *Trafficking in Persons Report*, 5 June, www.state.gov/g/tip/rls/tiprpt/2002/10653.htm

Part 4

Transnational Control Responses

Chapter 13
Understanding Global Trends in Policing: Explanatory and Normative Dimensions[1]

Jennifer Wood and Michael Kempa

Introduction

Over time, there have been shifts in how scholars have conceived of 'policing'. These shifts have emerged in the form of conceptual 'waves',[2] wherein practical discoveries in who undertakes policing, how they do so, and with what impacts, have led to modifications in theoretical accounts. For scholars concerned with understanding global, cutting edge trends, a central challenge has been to ensure that our conceptual waves do not lag far behind the constant innovation of practical actors. Without contemporary and comprehensive explanatory theory,[3] the development of sound normative proposals in the form of new policies and practices is compromised.

This chapter will begin with a brief overview of key practical and conceptual waves in policing, with an emphasis on how scholars have adjusted their theoretical concepts and narratives. This brief 'history of the present' (Foucault, 1977; Castel, 1994) will begin with the 'modern', state-centred conception of policing and will end with where we are currently, a time in which scholars are depicting the 'plural' (Loader, 2000; Button and John, 2002; Sarre and Prenzler, 2000), 'multilateral' (Bayley and Shearing, 2001) or 'nodal' (Shearing, 2001a; Johnston and Shearing, 2003) nature of policing. This review will provide a basis for discussing what the immediate future of scholarly research questions could look like; building upon the progress that has been made into central research questions during the course of previous waves.

The central argument of this chapter is that contemporary scholarship on the 'plural' or 'nodal' nature of policing has opened up new and interesting conceptual spaces within which innovative explanatory and normative projects can be undertaken. A central component of a future research agenda should be a more comprehensive 'mapping' of both the nature and implications of this plural policing landscape. Just as much research needs to be done in determining how precisely a 'nodal' analysis can be translated effectively into policy advice and/or practical policing initiatives.

---

1 We are grateful to Clifford Shearing, Philip Stenning and Peter Grabosky whose ideas have contributed significantly to this paper.

2 We use the metaphor of 'waves' in order to stress the continuities as well as discontinuities in policing trends and scholarly understandings of this concept. Rather than locating ruptures or breaks at the level of practice and theory, it captures the fluidity of policing forms and scholarship. Waves do not necessarily occur in sharp chronological order – rather, they tend to overlap and flow concurrently.

3 We draw here from John Braithwaite's understandings of both 'explanatory theory' as a set of 'ordered propositions about the way the world is' (2002, p ix) and 'normative theory' as a set of 'ordered propositions about the way the world ought to be' (*ibid*).

We also suggest that a nodal analysis has considerable potential to guide comparative work by generating new insights into both global trends and local variation in the nature and impacts of policing arrangements. In developing this argument, we will draw from the work that each of us, along with others, are undertaking in different places including Argentina, Canada, Northern Ireland and South Africa.

We should note that this chapter draws on the English literature devoted primarily to developments in Western liberal democracies. As such, the claims we make in developing our argument refer specifically to such contexts as well as to countries in political 'transition' that are aspiring to the core democratic values we discuss throughout this paper. With that in mind, we will speculate as to the utility of the nodal framework for studies of trends in other contexts and locales.

Policing and democracy

A current conception of policing that attempts to synthesise much existing scholarship is captured in a recent report to the Law Commission of Canada (LCC), which states that policing is 'any activity which is expressly designed and intended to establish and maintain (or enforce) a defined order within a community' (Hermer *et al*, 2002, p 9). Within this conception, notions of 'order' and 'community' are further defined. A 'defined order' is understood as:

> a set of explicit or implicit norms designed to regulate behaviours (conduct), relationships or expression, and to provide for the establishment of institutions and procedures (Hermer *et al*, 2002, p 10).

'Community' is then defined as:

> a collectivity, whether it be defined in terms of a specific geographic area, by a sense of shared identity on the basis, for instance, of gender, nationhood, race, ethnicity or sexual orientation, or by a shared sense of goals organised through economic, political or cultural activity (Hermer *et al*, 2002, p 13).

For policing to be 'democratic', the report states that:

> Implicit in [the] idea of *'effective and acceptable policing'* must not only be the requirement that policing recognises and meets the community's needs for order, security, safety and justice, but also, and equally importantly, that it recognises and conforms to the core democratic values … [of] *fairness, equity, respect for fundamental human rights, inclusiveness, access to justice and accountability* (Hermer *et al*, 2002, p 72; emphasis added).

The above quotations contain several core explanatory concepts and normative values pertaining to policing in liberal democracies, ranging from 'order' and 'community', to 'equity', 'justice' and 'accountability'. For the remainder of this chapter we will examine changes in the ways in which these core concepts and values have been understood and approached in view of significant practical developments in policing over time. This will allow us to consider the implications of these changing conceptions for the future of explanatory and normative theory building.

Policing and the 'public': a state-centred conception

The first key wave in sociological studies of policing expressed a 'state-centred political consciousness' (Shearing, 1992, p 404) that equated 'modern policing' with policing by the state. This political consciousness is expressed in the writings of Thomas Hobbes, who argued that effective, acceptable and efficient governance must be guaranteed in the form of a sovereign power, standing over and above us, that upholds laws through its defining capacity and means: its recourse to coercion and punishment (Hobbes, 1651/1968). In the area of policing policy and scholarship, this broader political consciousness engendered 'police fetishism': 'the ideological assumption that the police are a functional prerequisite of social order and that without a police force chaos or "anarchy" would ensue' (Reiner, 1994, p 716).

Within this view, the central 'auspice' (sponsor) and 'provider' (deliverer) (Bayley and Shearing, 2001) of policing is the sovereign state that both recognises and meets the needs for order, security and justice of 'society' or the 'nation'. The legitimacy of this system of policing and governance is traced to the notion of the 'social contract', wherein each and every citizen gives up certain liberties in return for order and security. (For an overview of the social contract in political theory, see Hindess, 1996; and on its application to policing practice, see Eng, 2002.) This social contract both expresses and constitutes a distinction between the 'public' and 'private' spheres, seeing policing, and governance more generally, as being a matter of 'public' interest and 'public' responsibility (see Shearing, 1992). Accordingly, 'equitable' and 'inclusive' policing is in theory guaranteed by the mere fact of being publicly delivered as part of the expectations of 'social citizens' or citizens of a nation.

This state-centred view also expresses a particular conception of 'access to justice', another democratic principle articulated above in the LCC report. 'Justice' has particular features which embody, according to Johnston and Shearing (2003), a 'punishment mentality ... focused primarily, though by no means exclusively, on past events, [which] emphasises coercive physical force, involves direct governance through the state and consists of an imposed process prescribed through general rules' (p 38). This mentality contains both instrumental and symbolic dimensions. Its instrumentality (future oriented focus) is rooted in the conception of deterrence (both general and specific) and is achieved through the threat of coercive force by the institutions of the state including the police. The symbolic dimension is its retributive character, focusing on condemnation and restoring a 'moral balance' that has been upset (Shearing, 2001b; see Zehr, 1990).

From within this state-centred view,[4] policing research focused on studies of the 'police', classically defined as 'institutions or individuals given the general right to use coercive force by the state within the state's domestic territory' (Klockars, 1985, p 12). In particular, researchers were concerned with honing their explanations of policing 'on the ground', determining how precisely coercive force was exercised

---

4   As Shearing explains, researchers from different sides of the political spectrum expressed the state-centered political consciousness. Thus, while critical/Marxist scholars argued that policing did not promote the public good for all, they nonetheless assumed that 'modern policing meant state policing and this, in turn, did and should mean state use of force to preserve the peace' (1992, p 408).

and in what contexts. These studies involved inquiries into police behaviour and decision making (see Reiss, 1971; Ericson, 1982; Bordua, 1968; Bittner, 1974; Bayley, 1994), the nature of police deviance (see Skolnick, 1966; Rubinstein, 1983; Punch, 1979) and the distinctive features of police subculture (see Wilson, 1968; Reuss-Ianni and Ianni, 1983; Manning, 1977). What researchers discovered was that while police constables were constituted as impartial and fair agents of law enforcement, a range of *informal* factors influenced their judgments and discretion.

The apparent discrepancies between the 'law in the books' and the 'law in action' (Holdaway, 1979; Cain, 1973; Ericson, 1982) provided rich empirical grounds for normative concerns about threats to democratic values posed by highly discretionary policing practices. Issues related to human rights infringements and threats to civil liberties were foremost on the agenda (Reiner, 1994). Normatively, scholars, policy makers and practitioners were concerned with ways to shape and structure police decision making in order to come closer to the 'modern' ideal of effective, acceptable policing that protected human rights, granted access to justice and ensured equitable and fair treatment.

A key component of this normative agenda was the enhancement of adequate mechanisms of accountability, the spirit of which is captured below by Doreen McBarnet:

> Citizens should be subject to the rule of law not of men, to established law not individual whim or retrospective decision, with all citizens equal before the law and free from arbitrary arrest or imprisonment. An essential ingredient is that state officials, especially the police, operating the most explicitly oppressive of routine state powers, criminal law, should themselves be subject to laws that protect these civil rights. This imposes recognised limitations on the effectiveness of police work, but the rhetoric goes that it is better for ten guilty men to go free than for one innocent man to be wrongly convicted (1979, p 24).

Underlying this conception of accountability is an emphasis on the rights and expectations that social citizens have to be protected from the malign potential of state violence. In other words, efficiency of policing must be trumped by the protection of citizenship rights. Emphasis was, and is, placed on citizen complaint mechanisms and other remedial mechanisms both internal to, and external to, the police organisation itself (on accountability see, for example, Stenning, 1995, 2000; Goldsmith and Lewis, 2000).

Another component of accountability was the notion that 'equitable' and 'fair' policing can only be achieved if individual citizens do not interfere with (that is, bias) operational matters – hence the development of the notion of the 'operational independence' of the Chief Constable (Lustgarten, 1986; Marshall, 1965, 1979). From this view, the state is understood as both the embodiment of society's interest and a guarantor of the 'public good' and the 'public order'. What is important, therefore, is the establishment of mechanisms, such as 'police boards', for ensuring sufficient political input into overarching policing *policy* rather than day-to-day practice (Reiner, 2000; Loveday, 2000, 1991, 1987).

While researchers discovered that the 'reality' of public policing did not measure up against the 'ideal', normative responses were, and largely continue to be, sought from within the established state-centred view. Put simply, the state is seen as the most appropriate location for democratic policing (see Shearing, 1992). The public/private distinction, central to liberal democratic thought, buttresses the notion that democratic policing is a public responsibility and a 'public good' (see Loader and Walker, 2001).

Policing and the 'private': expanding conceptions

Shearing and Stenning were among the first to direct scholarly debate toward the 'quiet revolution' (1981, 1983) that was occurring in the form of policing practices sponsored and/or delivered by private actors within 'mass private property' – spaces that are privately owned yet grant varying degrees of access to the public, including shopping malls, theme parks, industrial complexes, and more recently, gated communities (Shearing and Stenning, 1983; Reichman, 1987; Hermer *et al*, 2002; Blakely and Snyder, 1997).

The discovery of policing within the 'private' sphere called for a conceptual move on the part of researchers. Policing was now conceived (at least by some) as either a 'public' or 'private' function. The public/private dichotomy, remaining central during this wave, provided the political basis for conceiving of private policing as operating to promote 'private' interests (see Shearing, 1992, 2003) and 'private' goods. The emergence, or 're-birth' (Johnston, 1992) of *private policing* auspices within privately owned spaces served to challenge the 'police fetishism' described above, but nonetheless understood the system of public policing as a normative benchmark against which the democratic implications of private processes and practices would be understood and assessed.

Interestingly, the idea of private auspices and providers of security and order is seen from this view as being perfectly compatible with the liberal democratic principle of individual autonomy and freedom from state intrusion. Consistent with this principle, both individuals *and* corporations are understood as similarly entitled to this sphere of freedom (Shearing, 1992, p 407). What the public/private distinction couldn't account for was the precise nature of the collectivities being policed in these spaces, collectivities that were neither 'public' nor 'private' in the Hobbesian sense. While the notion of 'mass private property' seemed to be the most compelling conceptual option for describing the spatial character of policing, Shearing and Stenning also spoke of a 'new feudalism' (Shearing and Stenning, 1983, p 503), invoking a return to new forms of 'communal' governance.

Depicted in subsequent research were the ways in which the 'social contract', as a figurative basis for governmental legitimacy, was being supplanted by forms of 'community' or 'parochial' contracts (Shearing and Wood, 2000; Crawford, 2003). Individuals, as either permanent or temporary members of these 'mass private properties', are bound by the rights and expectations guaranteed by these contracts (Shearing and Wood, 2000). It was found, for example, that in some cases, such as gated communities or even condominium complexes, it is usually the case that there are formalised and indeed very precise behavioural requirements for community members. Other contracts are less formal, but nonetheless explicit, such as when one shops among a community of consumers within a shopping mall (see Hermer *et al*, 2002). As Crawford describes:

> ... the 'new social contract' ... may be less the Hobbesian compact by which society (at the level of the nation state) is united, but rather consists of a complex mesh of 'parochial contracts' into which people are embedded and across which people pass in their everyday encounters and interactions. Often they do so without ever realising it. These 'parochial contracts' constitute the regulatory framework for the diverse 'zones of governance' that, through loose chains and interlaced networks, constitute contemporary social order (2003).

Given the hegemony of the state-centred view, it was difficult to conceive of forms of 'justice' being delivered by these 'private governments' (Macauley, 1986). Early research discovered, however, a considerable focus on 'instrumental ordering' (Shearing and Stenning, 1985) within these common spaces and a less explicit emphasis on the kind of 'symbolic ordering' expressed in the 'punishment mentality' (Johnston and Shearing, 2003). More recently, this instrumental focus has been explained in terms of a 'risk mentality' concerned primarily with 'loss' and 'shrinkage' of assets and profits (Shearing and Stenning, 1981, 1983). In other words, a future-oriented, instrumental understanding of 'justice' in the form of harm reduction and profit maximisation dominated. This instrumental logic was found to be given concrete effect in the strategies and practices of private policing. Coercive force and access to the criminal law were not central to these private governments in the furtherance of policing objectives. For example, the 'means' of policing with these mass private spaces were described as non-coercive and embedded in other tasks and functions of private actors, ranging from bank tellers to the gatekeepers of Disneyworld (Shearing and Stenning, 1985). Security and order promotion was also embedded in the physical landscape of privately owned spaces (Shearing and Stenning, 1983; Hermer *et al*, 2002).

This growth in private policing revealed a tension within liberal democratic thought itself. On the one hand, by virtue of being privately sponsored and privately delivered, it was nearly impossible to conceive of private policing as operating in the 'public interest' (see Shearing, 2003). On the other hand, it is in the public interest to cherish the sphere of liberty that the public/private distinction is itself an expression of. As Tim Hope put it:

> ... in any society which values the right of its members legitimately to possess and enjoy private property, and for anyone who derives an identity from membership in such a society, then the security of private property may be thought of as a citizenship right reflecting human need (2000, p 84).

While the right to private protection, and hence private policing, has been difficult to contest from within a liberal democratic frame, the resultant inequities in the distribution of these 'private' goods have been more controversial. For instance, it has been argued – based on the fact that only particular kinds of communities benefit from private forms of policing (for example, members of corporate communities, members of university communities, or members of gated communities, etc) – that the distribution of this service is structured along the lines of buying power or other methods of access to 'private', or 'club' goods (Crawford and Lister, 2003; Webster, 2002). How the growth of 'private governments' might lead to a 'succession of the successful' – by attempts to discontinue contributions to the public tax base – has also been raised as a normative concern (Bayley and Shearing, 2001).

In a similar vein, the potential for exclusion from these mass private spaces has been described as 'spatial sorting' (Kempa *et al*, 1999; Rigakos and Greener, 2000; Wakefield, 2000; Caldeira, 1996, 2000; Davis, 1990; Hermer *et al*, 2002) that similarly reveals a deeper concern with 'equitable' policing. As indicated, the fundamental character of property relations and property rights within liberal democratic societies provides both the political and legal basis for such sorting to occur.

Policing and the 'transnational'

The discovery of 'transnational' forms of policing served to further challenge the state-centred political consciousness. The Hobbesian conception of the sovereign state as sole auspice and provider of policing and governance has been challenged through practical developments taking place 'above' nation states (Sheptycki, 1998, 1995). The phenomenon of 'globalisation'[5] prompted researchers to explore the ways in which 'transnational' interests, instead of, or in addition to 'public' or 'national' interests, were now configuring policing objectives. The territorial basis for policing could no longer be conceived exclusively as the nation-state:

> ... the territoriality of political, economic and cultural life has been shattered in recent decades. The particular ways in which most aspects of our lives have been bundled or packaged in containers called nation-states have been increasingly challenged and subtly eroded (Elkins, 1995, p 15; see also Held, 2000).

Researchers thereby 'discovered' and explained new forms of 'public' and 'private' transnational policing. In reference to the growth of paid private policing organisations interacting with other commercial and non-commercial providers, Les Johnston argued that:

> their activities ... both transcend and penetrate the state. On the one hand, they perform security functions 'both in between and outside of state spaces' (Kempa *et al*, 1999, p 213). On the other hand, they are called upon by governments to undertake what are, traditionally, considered to be core state functions (2000b, p 22).

For scholars, collective life was becoming increasingly difficult to conceive of in reference to the public/private distinction. New realms of existence were not only emerging 'above' and 'below' national states, but were taking on new dimensions altogether. Of particular interest to researchers has been the emergence of new *virtual* realms of collective existence, commonly referred to as 'cyberspace' (Wall,

---

5 Scholars from a range of disciplines have described the phenomenon of 'globalisation'. Economists have been observing the accelerating 'internationalisation' of economics and the emergence of broadened international capitalist market relations. International relations theorists have noted an intensification of interstate relations and the development of a form of global politics previously unheard of (Held *et al*, 1999; Elkins, 1995). Sociologists have attempted to describe the new 'world society' and new forms of global consciousness (Bateson, 1990). Key drivers of these developments have been advancements in information and communications technologies, allowing for faster and cheaper movement of capital and labour (Camilleri, 1990). These structural shifts have produced new global pressures, including new threats to local, national and global security (Bateson, 1990). Activities including terrorism, drug trafficking, arms trafficking, fraud, money laundering, computer crime, environmental crime, kidnapping and extortion, industrial espionage and the theft of valuables such as arts and antiques have all taken on a 'transnational' dimension (Anderson, 1989; Johnston, 1999) which James Sheptycki and others have sought to describe and explain (1997, 1998, 2000, 2002a).

1997; Manning, 2000). In contrast to the singular 'social order' underlying the modern conception of policing, researchers realised with the ascension of globalisation that multiple conceptions of order – rooted in both physical and virtual collectivities – were being articulated and promoted. In some cases these new forms of policing were expressing 'supranational' orders such as in the case of the EU (Bigo, 2000; Walker, 2000; Johnston, 2000a) and in other cases, orders became fractured and localised, uncoupled from national identities. Such developments led Reiner to conclude that 'the rise of *the* police – a single professional organisation for handling the policing function of regulation and surveillance, with the state's monopoly of legitimate force as its ultimate resource – was itself a paradigm of the modern. It was predicated upon the project of organising society around a central, cohesive notion of order' (1992, p 779).

'Justice' as practised within these different transnational forms was difficult for researchers to describe. In contrast to forms of justice bound to sovereign laws with sovereign territories, a 'functional integration or "melding"' (Johnston, 2000a, p 51) between public and private policing was being theorised in relation to 'a risk-logic ... that is reshaping the governance of security within both state and non-state terrains' (Shearing, 2001b, p 217; Beck, 1992; Giddens, 1991):

> State sovereignty gives way to fragmentation in risk management across myriad public and private sector institutions. Certainty resides less in the imagined will of strong central authority and more in the certainties that each risk institution promises. Risk society promises a world in which fail-safe risk technologies rather than fallible people rule. It promotes any technology of governmentality that might reduce uncertainty, foster self-regulation, and prevent loss (Ericson and Haggerty, 1997, pp 52–53).

In contrast to previous concerns with the malign potential of coercive capacity, scholars were now concerned with the malign potential of risk-based technologies. Such concerns remained rooted within a state-centred view that emphasised citizenship rights as inscribed within sovereign systems of governance. Particular concern was noted in regard to the ways in which the gathering, compilation and dissemination of intelligence could threaten individuals' rights as citizens, particularly those rights pertaining to privacy (Daniels *et al*, 2001; Maguire, 2000). In this regard, there is an emphasis on ensuring a balance between the possible effectiveness and efficiency of intelligence-led policing activities and the protection of individual liberties and human rights (see Brodeur, 2000). This debate has been particularly intense in relation to the policing of terrorism (Daniels *et al*, 2001), where 'transnational' interests can be seen as in tension with established citizenship rights.

What a new 'transnational' and/or 'postmodern' model of policing would look like is far from resolved, mainly due to the hegemony of the state-centred view. Effective mechanisms of 'accountability', for example, are difficult to conceive of outside of a state-centred framework (Sheptycki, 2002b, 2002c). Central to the debate has been the cross-jurisdictional nature of transnational policing which uncovers a multiplicity of issues relating to differences in criminal statutes, criminal law and procedure and police standard operating procedures (Brodeur, 2000), not to mention the involvement of private policing organisations in the mix (Johnston, 2000a, 2000b; Sheptycki, 1998; McLaughlin, 1992).

The 'new regulatory state' conception

The established Hobbesian view of states monopolising policing and governance was further challenged through a set of practical developments from within states themselves. Practical discoveries of nation-state reforms in different parts of the Western industrialised world revealed that practical actors were reinterpreting conceptions of 'effective and acceptable' policing. Pressures to 'reinvent government' (Osborne and Gaebler, 1992), to the end of reducing the costs of state governance (Sheptycki, 1997), reflected a deep concern over efficiency of policing. While spurred on by the imperatives of globalisation, this emphasis on efficiency was driven by ideological arguments, namely that states had created 'dependency' in citizens by relying on public government as the sole auspice and provider of policing and other 'social' services (Miller and Rose, 1992; Rose, 1996; for exemplars of normative texts, see Osborne and Gaebler, 1992; Eggers and O'Leary, 1995).

State actors were now speaking more 'in the name of community' and less 'in the name of society', to borrow phrasing from Rose (1996). A set of practical programs gave life to this conception, including 'community policing' (O'Malley and Palmer, 1996), and another variant, 'broken windows' or 'disorder-based policing' (Wilson and Kelling, 1982; Kelling and Coles, 1997; Herbert, 2002). Researchers found further evidence of a 'functional melding' between state and corporate mentalities in the form of different arrangements for carrying out 'risk-based' policing. Focused on the endgame of optimal efficiency, disorder-based policing centred on banishing 'communities of risk' (Johnston, 1997, 2000a), including the homeless, transients and subsistence beggars from particular kinds of public spaces, on the presumption that cracking down on 'disorderly people' will further crime prevention objectives (Hermer et al, 2002; Hermer and Mosher, 2002; Herbert, 2002).

New forms of 'justice' were being expressed that did not conform to the state-centred view. Given the emphasis on enhanced state efficiency, alternatives to the expensive system of retributive justice were being sought, ranging from community-based corrections (Tonry and Lynch, 1996; Landreville, 1995) to the now widely discussed 'restorative justice' movement (Braithwaite, 1989, 2002).

New practices of accountability also revealed the 'functional melding' between public and private forms of policing and governance. Within the state sector, accountability was being reconfigured in line with the 'rationality of the marketplace' (O'Malley and Palmer, 1996; O'Malley, 1997) and realised through mechanisms like audits, business plans and other technologies of accounting and financial practices (Rose, 1996; Power, 1994). Researchers also discovered that citizens were being reconstituted as 'consumers' of policing and other government services in line with state attempts to 'customise' their service delivery to local needs and priorities (McLaughlin and Murji, 1995; Lacey, 1994; Stenson, 1996; Wood, 2000; Loader, 1999). Such 'consumers' were being encouraged to exercise 'responsible citizenship' (Johnston, 1992) and to be active and entrepreneurial in ensuring security for themselves and their loved ones (O'Malley and Palmer, 1996; Garland, 1996, 2001).

While sovereign states were still striving to act as guarantors of order and security – through recognising and meeting collective needs – they did so by 'hiving off' of 'rowing' (Osborne and Gaebler, 1992) or provider functions to the paid private security sector, such as hiring private guards to protect state assets/buildings and to transport prisoners (Johnston, 1992, 2000a). Furthermore, public police were recovering their costs through charging fees for events that do not benefit the entire public, such as sporting events, concerts, and parades (Bayley and Shearing, 2001; Grabosky, 2003).

States sought to maintain their 'steering' or auspice function by continuing to safeguard 'public' interests. In so doing, the established state-centred conception of governance could be fundamentally retained and reasserted. States have encouraged the public to get involved in the business of the public police, but not, except in rare instances, to take it over outright (Hudson, 2001; Jones and Newburn, 1998; Garland, 1996; Crawford, 1994, 1997). In noting these various dimensions of state devolution, researchers now conceive of a 'new regulatory state' (Grabosky, 1994; Braithwaite, 2000; Scott, 2001) that aspires, wherever possible, to 'govern "at a distance"' (Miller and Rose, 1992, p 181) in the delivery of collective goods, including security. Given the emphasis in liberal democracies on rights to private property and private protection (discussed earlier), the ideal of safeguarding 'steering' functions for the state could never be fully achieved. While states and the public police have sought to direct explicit strategic partnerships with non-state entities, recent years have also seen the emergence of cases wherein private or joint public-private entities have captured both the steering *and* rowing aspects of policing, such as local business associations who pool resources and take advantage of zoning bylaws to establish Business Improvement Districts (Murphy, 1997; Greene *et al*, 1995) or residential communities that engage the services of private patrols (Noaks, 2000). Overall, private providers of policing have emerged to satisfy the 'insatiable demand' that the cash strapped, cost conscious public police have been unable to meet (Loader, 1997), producing a new phenomenon in 'parapolicing' (Rigakos, 2002). 'Citizen patrols' have also emerged, ranging from student patrols on campus to violent forms of vigilantism (Johnston, 1996, 1999, 2000a; Hermer *et al*, 2002; Leach, 2003). Research has shown that these forms of 'autonomous' non-state policing sometimes emerge with the tacit support of the state and public policing agencies (Johnston, 2000a); in other cases, such initiatives are in conflict with the wishes of such agencies (Johnston, 2000a; Mopas, 2002).

This overall reconfiguration of both auspice and provider functions has raised even more challenges to researchers assessing the democratic implications of policing. For the most part, the problem of accountability for both public and private providers is largely seen to be resolved through the implementation of 'new regulatory' strategies, involving the state setting uniform standards of police service delivery (see, for example, the Adequacy and Effectiveness of Police Services Regulation of the *Ontario Police Services Act*, Ceyssens *et al*, 2002; see Wood, 2000). Others have devised strategies for ensuring that the public police occupy a central place in the security market – particularly the market for patrols. A recent example is the 'Community Support Officers' scheme implemented by the London Metropolitan Police. The argument is that by offering a second tier (and cheaper) police patrol presence that is controlled by the public police, effective, efficient and democratic policing services will be ensured (see Johnston and Shearing, 2003).

The incorporation of risk-based thinking within the state sphere has generated normative concerns similar to those expressed during the ongoing wave of research into private policing. Issues of 'equity' and 'spatial sorting' have been raised anew in view of increasingly widespread efforts to banish marginalised populations from public spaces in the name of risk minimisation. This example has served to raise a broader issue of whether risk-based thinking with the public sector has not lessened the punitive impulse, but rather rendered punishment more harsh and threatening to citizenship rights (Herbert, 2002; Maguire, 2000; Hughes, 1998). But perhaps more importantly, as we will discuss below, it has become increasingly difficult to both understand and address such 'democratic deficits' from within a state-centred political consciousness.

Plural and nodal conceptions

The most recent wave in scholarship acknowledges the now 'plural' (Loader, 2000) or 'multilateral' (Bayley and Shearing, 2001) nature of policing. In contemplating ways in which to extend this wave, Shearing, along with others, has introduced the notion of 'nodal governance' as a framework to guide future explanatory and normative work (Shearing, 2001b; Hermer et al, 2002; Johnston and Shearing, 2003; Shearing and Wood, 2000; Kempa and Shearing, 2002; Kempa et al, 2004). Within this framework, a 'node' is understood as an auspice, provider or both (Bayley and Shearing, 2001). Within and across nodes, policing processes and practices give concrete expression to different conceptions of 'community', 'order', 'justice', 'accountability', 'equity', and so on.

From this nodal conception, there may be dominant features of auspices and/or providers that remain salient for long periods of time, such as a retributive conception of justice even though, for example, risk-based thinking may be incorporated. We see this, for example, in the aforementioned case of zero tolerance policing, where the public police node has enfolded risk-oriented thinking within their largely reactive law enforcement dominant world view and methods (Johnston, 1997, 2000a; Johnston and Shearing, 2003).

At an explanatory level, this framework does not give conceptual priority to particular nodes as objects of inquiry. It may indeed be the case that particular nodes – for example, the public police – remain central as auspices and/or providers of policing. As such, scholars may choose to focus their inquiries on these entities, but an *a priori* emphasis on state nodes is not a requirement of the framework itself.

The nodal view is also intended to move scholars away from the assumption that there is a particular nature and degree of co-ordination between nodes. In fact, the nature of co-ordination (if such co-ordination exists at all) is an open empirical question. For example, co-ordination between nodes could be tacit, regulated, or even competitive (see Bayley and Shearing, 2001; Grabosky, 1996; Johnston, 2000a).

As a collective body of work, the literature on plural policing and nodal governance has brought to the fore different tensions in relation to the public/private distinction that is so fundamental to liberal democratic thought. Accordingly, Shearing has begun to explore whether future explanatory and normative work would benefit from the introduction of new conceptual pillars, including 'common goods' (Shearing, 2003), 'common spaces' (von Hirsch and Shearing, 2001; Hermer et al, 2002; Kempa et al, 2004), and 'community denizenship' (in contrast to 'social citizenship') (Shearing and Wood, forthcoming). Shearing is not suggesting scholars abandon the public/private distinction altogether: he is suggesting that these new conceptual pillars could assist in lending clarity to the changing nature of policing and governance.

The potential contribution of these conceptual pillars to comparative policing research has only begun to be explored. For example, the notion of 'communal space' may provide the conceptual breadth required to capture a range of territories of policing that the public/private distinction fails to capture. This became clear following Jones and Newburn's critique of the 'mass private property' hypothesis (1999). They argued that, while 'mass private property' of the form initially described by Shearing and Stenning may be proliferating in North America, and is extensively policed by paid private security agencies, such property forms are relatively limited in the UK and Western Europe, and virtually non-existent further afield (Jones and Newburn, 1999, 2002). However, if one moves beyond the notion of 'mass private property' (which still seeks to work within the public/private distinction) to 'communal space', one can 'discover' a range of unfamiliar forms of space that are controlled to varying degree by rules set and enforced by non-state nodes both within and outside of established democratic contexts (Kempa et al, 2004).

As an example, in the unsettled political context of Northern Ireland, which is gradually emerging, through an ongoing peace process, from a long history of civil conflict (which has been particularly pitched over the last 30 years), there exist pockets of urban space that are virtually closed by force to the public police. These pockets are thereby governed in summary and brutal fashion by paramilitary organisations whose alleged 'relationship' with special divisions of state security agencies has been a matter of extreme controversy (see, for example, Hillyard, 1993). Similar developments have been noted in the post-authoritarian transitional political context of Russia and Eastern Europe more generally, where some pockets of urban areas are policed by paid private security agencies that have, in some cases, connections to organised crime and/or to discredited (and in some cases disbanded) special (for example, 'secret') public police bureaux (Johnston, 1992; Los, 2002; Los and Zybertowicz, 2000). In South Africa, there exist entire rural villages of poor people who largely police themselves through both pacific and violent autonomous means, which have variously co-operative and antagonistic relationships with state security services (Aitkenhead, 2000; Baker, 2001). At the same time, there are remotely located gated towns in South Africa, replete with institutions of 'communal government' and populated by the well-to-do, that are policed by paid private security agencies (Kempa et al, 2004). None of these property forms, or the types of policing that occur there, are easily classified or probed according to the public/private dichotomy.

How this conceptual shift to 'communal space' could be useful in assessing whether forms of policing promote 'common goods' instead of, or in addition to, strictly 'public', 'private', or 'club' goods, requires much further attention (Shearing, 2003; Crawford and Lister, 2003).

On future research

Research on the nature of plural policing or nodal governance is in the earliest stages, and in fact, opens up more questions than it has so far answered. For the remainder of this chapter, we will organise our discussion around the core democratic values spelled out at the beginning of this chapter in the excerpts from the LCC report. For each value we will provide a very preliminary exploration of how the nodal governance view could assist in the development of innovative explanatory and normative theory building. We will then provide some suggestions as to how to move from theory to the development of innovative policy and practices.

Efficiency

Research into how policing 'efficiency' has been understood and implemented by practical actors has tended to focus on either state nodes or corporate nodes. Peter Grabosky has contributed significantly to theoretical explanations of how state institutions have been devolving responsibilities and harnessing other resources to the end of enhanced governmental efficiency (1995, 1996). Building on these studies, much work remains to explore how the entire range of auspices and providers are sharing their resources and networking their capacities. As it stands, such analyses tend to be state-centred, whilst neglecting the ways in which non-state entities, for example, harness the resources of state institutions. 'Resources' refer not only to the formal operating budgets of formal providers like the public or private police, but also indirect resources in the form of in-kind contributions (human resources, equipment, space, etc). It is important therefore to map the flow of resources from their original source(s), and to map the ways in which these resources are contributing (or not) to efficient policing on the whole.

Once again, Peter Grabosky's work has been instructive. He suggests that much more explanatory work is required around the question of whom is 'paying' for policing (and how) and who is 'benefiting' (2003). As an explanatory guide, he suggests conceiving of three broad kinds of, in this instance, public/private co-sponsorship: *coercion*, *sale* and *gift*. 'Coercion' refers to instances in which the state commands private entities to undertake certain functions, such as reporting cash transactions over a particular dollar amount, in order to contribute to public law enforcement. 'Sale' refers to acquisition by the state sector of goods and services from the private sector such as, for example, technological or forensic expertise. 'Gift' refers to private sponsorship of public policing in the form of provision of grants or complimentary goods and services such as office space or vehicles (Grabosky, 2003).

Enhancing our understanding of both who pays for, and who benefits from, policing services, will allow scholars to develop more sophisticated normative stances. As Grabosky puts it:

> The notion of policing as a public good, available to all, and paid for by all through the system of taxation and government appropriation, seems to have faded considerably ... [G]overnment's ability or willingness to provide what was once known as 'the basics' seems unlikely to expand in the short term. What are the limits of corporate sponsorship of public policing? How much is desirable? How much is feasible? As Davis (2000, p 9)

reminds us, there are good gifts and bad gifts, and those that are not really gifts at all (Grabosky, 2003, pp 12–13).

Another reason why it is important to examine the flows of resources between nodes, is that it may be possible to identify 'co-ordination deficits' that detract from the quality of policing as a whole (Crawford and Lister, 2003). For example, some nodes may operate in complete 'benign neglect' of one another, unaware of the range of knowledge and capacities that could be mobilised in furtherance of policing objectives. Such a scenario may raise the issue of duplication and overlap, and reveal in some cases that certain entities have more appropriate knowledge, capacities and resources to undertake particular policing functions than others. Such an argument is of course not new, and indeed the police have argued for decades that they do not possess the appropriate capacities and resources to meet all policing objectives. Nonetheless, such analyses tend to be state-centred as well, focusing on how non-state resources can be captured for state ends. A comprehensive mapping of all auspices and providers of policing, and the ways in which they harness the resources of others, requires much more scholarly attention.

Equity

The Law Commission of Canada report cites 'inclusiveness' as a core democratic value. Within a nodal framework, the research involved in exploring the nature and degree of exclusions and inclusions in policing would have several dimensions. To date, research has tended to either focus on the exclusionary character of state policing or corporate policing, with less of an emphasis on their 'additive outcomes' (Kempa et al, 2004).

Furthermore, the nodal framework prompts one to suspend one's judgment as to whether all forms of exclusion are necessarily, by virtue of being exclusionary, a 'bad thing' and contrary to the enhancement of democracy. For instance, from a strict economic standpoint, an efficiently delivered good is one where everyone who pays also benefits. In other words, there is no 'free riding' problem. 'Gated communities' can thus be seen as optimally efficient in the delivery of policing, since only those who pay benefit (except for visitors of gated communities who receive an extra level of security while they are visiting).

This exclusionary form of policing can be seen as very efficient, but is it in keeping with the democratic value of inclusion? From within a state-centred framework, the answer would be unequivocally 'no', since not all citizens benefit equally from the guarantee of order and security within this particular communal space which fits with the traditional definition of 'mass private property'. However, if one examines other forms of policing within other kinds of communal spaces that may only benefit particular communities, the outcome of exclusion may be less worrisome. For example, if a small portion of public taxes were diverted into democratic forms of communal policing within, for example, shantytown communities, the fact that these resources may only benefit these communities may be seen as promoting equity, rather than threatening it.

Of course, the inclusions and exclusions produced by different forms of 'communal policing' would have to be considered in tandem for the purposes of understanding 'additive outcomes'. Taken together, separate research findings from

North America could serve as a preliminary basis for exploring this broader question. As a hypothetical starting point, we could begin with an analysis of residential gated communities and their exclusionary potential in a particular city. In this instance, non-members of these communities, by virtue of being non-members, are excluded from the policing services delivered there (except in instances where they are temporary visitors) (Blakely and Snyder, 1997).

One could then build on this analysis by exploring other forms of policing and their impacts within surrounding communal spaces. There are, for instance, less extreme examples of enclaves of wealth, such as shopping malls. As has been suggested, people unable to flow through these spaces as 'consumers', such as the homeless or mentally ill, tend to be excluded from these spaces (Hermer et al, 2002). Often operating in tandem with these forms of communal policing are disorder-intolerant policing strategies undertaken by the public police outside of these enclaves of wealth. Further research could then determine the degree to which the same individuals and collectivities that are banished from these communal governments are also banished from the 'conduit spaces' surrounding these enclaves (as hypothesised by Shearing, 1999).

One could add to such a research project an analysis of other forms of community-directed policing that serve to further intensify these 'additive outcomes', which are, in this scenario, selectively exclusionary in relation to marginalised groups. An example could be a community-based association, representing the interests of property owners in an economically diverse urban centre, that are mobilising the resources of the public police to intensify the banishment of 'disorderly' people from their 'communities' (see Fischer, 2001). From a nodal perspective then, forms of exclusion are additive and the target and degree of exclusion depends on the different kinds of nodal policing arrangements that are in place.

This kind of research could then lead scholars to determine which nodal arrangements for policing are more normatively unattractive in terms of their additive processes and outcomes than others. In the comparative context, the additive impacts of 'spatial sorting' would be different outside of the forms of property relations that characterise the Western democratic context. For example, in the contexts of South Africa and Brazil, the lines delineating enclaves of privilege are much more extensive and rigidly demarcated and guarded, with the effect that many of the spaces in between them approximate feudal 'badlands' nearly wholly outside of the control of the public police, who foray into such spaces only as a matter of emergency and with tremendous recourse to force (on Brazil, see Caldeira, 2000, 1996; on South Africa, see Aitkenhead, 2000; Baker, 2001).

Access to justice

The Law Commission of Canada report also mentions 'access to justice' as a democratic value. Within a nodal framework, research on how 'justice' is understood and given concrete effect by practical actors would be more broadly conceived than it would otherwise be within a state-centred, or conversely, corporate-centred perspective. Based on findings from previous waves, the nodal framework suggests that 'justice' as a concept has no singular connotation, but is dependent on how it is conceived within and across particular nodes (see Shearing *et al*, forthcoming). This can be seen in the example of institutions of criminal justice that have sought to accommodate, in some instances 'restorative', and in other cases 'risk-minimisation', modes of thinking within an otherwise hegemonic paradigm of retribution.

To date, established analyses of restorative or other 'alternative' forms of justice have tended to work within a state-centred framework. The ways in which 'justice' is conceived, articulated, and practised within and across a range of policing nodes calls for much further attention. Similarly, research into 'access to justice' would involve not only the question of who has access to 'criminal justice' and in what conditions, but also who has access to the benefits of *different* forms of justice and in what conditions. The descriptive theory produced through such research could lead to more sound normative positions as to whether, for example, some collectivities have varying degrees of access to retributive justice while others have different justice options (for example, third party mediation, civil remedies, community-based conflict resolution). An additional important question could be whether different systems/processes of justice complement or compete with one another in particular cases – and whether their additive outcomes may be detrimental to certain segments of the population.

Accountability

The traditional emphasis – within a state-centred framework – on describing and assessing legal and political forms of accountability would be considered too limited from a nodal perspective. Ensuring that agents of security act within the law is of course fundamental to democracy and human rights. As such, the ways in which different policing nodes are accountable for acting within the laws of the state requires further research. Philip Stenning (2000) has made important progress in this regard, having argued that it is insufficient for researchers to assess the accountability of private policing in relation to criteria established for the public police. To do so would be to underestimate the numerous accountability mechanisms that exist for private policing and to overestimate the degree to which accountability mechanisms for public policing are effective.

With respect to political accountability, the research question from a plural perspective is more complex. This is because, as we have previously suggested, the nature of 'political community' (see Held, 2000) has itself been transformed through pluralisation: a wide variety of groups whose identities are not connected to physically located communities are asserting themselves within and across contemporary states, and demanding that their interests be reflected in policing policies. Thus, the established conception of 'operational independence', and question of checks and balances over political influence into policing policy, continues to be central to the accountability of the public police as an institution of the 'social'. Within a nodal conception, however, the nature of political direction over policing has itself been pluralised.

This is to say that a range of 'communities' may also be playing a role in shaping the operational decision making of the public police (and indeed across the gamut of policing nodes), to the extent that 'operational independence' is an even more elusive and fraught notion than it has already proven to be (see especially Lustgarten, 1986). From a nodal perspective, the question of what degree of community control over policing is normatively desirable depends on a context-specific analysis of established nodal relations and their additive outcomes. In some cases, community direction may be promoting forms of biased, exclusionary policing (see Fischer, 2001). In other cases, the fracturing of political direction may be serving to deepen democracy because it is enhancing community self-direction and allowing individuals and groups to have more input into the processes and practices that affect them. The challenge in all cases will be to strike a balance between the independence of policing agencies and the infusion of community interests that is appropriate to the particular context under consideration.

An example of an innovative approach to striking such a balance comes from Northern Ireland, where a new policing governance agency – the Policing Board for Northern Ireland – has recently been created (November 2001) as part of the programme of policing reform that is a central pillar in that society's ongoing peace process. The Board has been given a mandate[6] to promote the 'operational responsibility' of the Chief Constable of the public police service and to ensure a democratic plural policing system more generally. 'Operational responsibility' signifies an explicit shift in thinking about the relationship between the Chief Constable and his or her governing authorities. First, rather than being understood as totally 'independent' in the planning and execution of operational matters – as has been the conceptual drift within the doctrine of 'operational independence' in the western world in recent decades (Lustgarten, 1986) – the broader objectives which define the parameters of his or her decision making are to be negotiated and set with other authorities. Secondly, the Chief Constable's decisions are understood as rightly subject to scrutiny by oversight agencies after they have been taken – and either sanctioned or identified as inadequate. Working within this framework, the Policing Board for Northern Ireland has powers to both set mid-term policing objectives and require the Chief Constable to account for operational decisions that have been taken after the event – but not to tell the Chief Constable how he must undertake particular investigations or initiatives. Additionally, the Board is empowered through controlling the policing budget (in co-operation with the Chief Constable and the Secretary of State) and through monitoring local initiatives, through district level sub-authorities, to regulate the involvement of civil agencies in the process of policing.

It is hoped that such a holistic approach to policing governance in Northern Ireland will undermine what is at present resigned support in some communities for vigilante activities, through providing efficacious democratic policing alternatives. Within the context of Northern Ireland's legacy of bitterly contested politics and too often interrupted peace processes, the very preliminary impacts of

---

6 It must be stressed that the precise powers that have been awarded to the Policing Board through legislation are regarded as inadequate by some segments of Northern Irish society, to the extent that these powers remain a central point of contention in the ongoing negotiations surrounding the acceptance of the policing dispensation by the Republican community – which for many would signal the 'official' beginning of 'conventional' politics in Northern Ireland. The way in which these powers are finally defined in formal legislation and various government issued 'codes of practice', and are ultimately exercised in practice, remains to be measured.

the Policing Board indicate that it – along with the Police Ombudsman's Office which handles public complaints regarding misuse of police powers – has thus far helped to begin to inspire public confidence in the policing system by striking a balance between allowing for local input, while limiting political control of the police.[7]

The nature of such different aspects of policing governance (that is, 'accountability') – legal, financial and political – and their impacts must be researched further. In this regard, different conceptions and aspects of accountability are not assumed to have priority over others in explanatory accounts. Each is examined on its own terms and in relation to its contribution to democratic values.

Respect for human rights

A nodal framework would obviously call for an assessment of the ways in which the range of auspices and providers embrace, promote, or conversely hinder, the promotion of human rights. Human rights violations on the part of state institutions obviously continue to be the focus of attention, and some studies have addressed the human rights implications of private policing providers (see Rigakos, 2002). Notwithstanding, and in relation to the issue of inclusions and exclusions in policing, a mapping of human rights implications would require consideration of 'additive effects'.

Here we can again briefly consider the case of Northern Ireland. Underpinning the massive program of policing reform that is a vital part of that territory's peace process, an independent Commission recommended the adoption of a human rights emphasis into every aspect of the public policing composition, training and practice (Independent Commission on Policing Reform in Northern Ireland (ICPNI), 1999). The Commission also recognised that policing in Northern Ireland regretfully involves a high degree of violent vigilante activity in marginalised neighbourhoods, which subjects a substantial portion of the population to the threat of brutal and summary 'justice' and undercuts the quality of such communities' interaction with the public policing experience. The Commission thus attempted to put into place mechanisms that would undermine support for such vigilante agencies and to enable the expansion of democratically accountable forms of state regulated civil policing, along with public policing, into these spaces. This would help to ensure the spread of human rights-oriented policing as a whole (not just public policing) into all communities of Northern Ireland. Thus, in considering the human rights implications of current policing practices and efforts towards reform, it is vital to assess the additive impacts, and their distribution, of the various policing nodes in operation in a particular locale.

From theory building to practical innovation

The explanatory and normative theory building achieved through such lines of inquiry would ideally lead to an agenda for policing and governance reform, both

---

7 It must be pointed out that it is far too early for the lasting impacts of the policing reform process (and of the broader peace process itself) in Northern Ireland to be assessed.

in the form of policy suggestions and specific practical projects. In order to move from theory building to practical innovation, one must determine not only what is *normatively desirable*, but also what is *practically realistic* in a particular place and time, or as Braithwaite puts it, to 'work with [established] sensibilities and seek to harness them in a transformative way' (2000, p 231). This requires a mapping of the 'conditions of possibility' (Foucault, 1997, p 8; Gordon, 1980, p 236) for change.

In part, a waves-based analysis of policing allows scholars to understand what is within the realm of 'thinkable' and 'doable' at both practical and conceptual levels. It may be the case that radically new models of policing cannot be introduced at particular places and during particular times. One may find radical proposals translated into conservative beginnings, as was the case in Northern Ireland, where a more radical reading of the *Policing* Board concept laid out in the initial report of the Independent Commission (ICPNI, 1999) was translated at the Bill stage into a *Police* Board concept, which fit more closely with state-centred sensibilities of how to resolve conflicts over policing in Northern Ireland. On the basis of relatively humble legislative beginnings, the Board was subsequently able to assert itself. Its developing track record was established in a tumultuous political context and the unfolding demands of the developing peace process, prompted the government to affirm its faith in the institution by realigning its powers with those initially envisaged in the report of the Independent Commission. This reflects a case where more radical ideas for policing reform only had practical 'bite' in a context where, on the one hand, political representatives of widely divergent constituencies proved themselves able to set aside emotive and symbolic aspects of policing reform to work together on practical policing issues (which had not been a broadly held expectation at the inception of the Board); and, on the other hand, the faltering peace process required a dramatic legislative gesture signifying an 'act of completion' by the British Government.[8]

As another example of 'conditions of possibility', we can refer to an international development project devoted to policing reform that one of us, along with others, is implementing in Argentina.[9] This project is based on the premise that Canadian know-how in both policing and community development, in the form of models, technologies and practices – can be transferred and adapted to relevant institutions and groups in Argentina in furtherance of democratic policing and governance reform.

In exploring whether certain normative projects would resonate in the Argentine context, one of our observations was that established thinking around policing reform in the north-western hemisphere tended to focus on initiatives developed within a state-centred or 'new regulatory' perspective. This thinking therefore understood policing reform as involving change 'from within' the public police, or change in the form of a 'new regulatory' agenda. Therefore, considerable emphasis

8 The process of the development of the system of policing governance in Northern Ireland is the subject of an ongoing detailed investigation by one of us as the basis of a doctoral thesis. In keeping with existing agreements with study respondents, the brief analysis presented at this early stage of the research process draws upon publicly available data.

9 This is the 'Project for Safe and Just Communities' administered by the Centre for International Studies, University of Toronto in conjunction with the Centre for Studies and Research in Human Rights, Faculty of Law, National University of Rosario. This project is sponsored by the Canadian International Development Agency.

was, and is, placed on initiatives such as enhanced police training or the implementation of state-led community policing.

Our team wanted to think more broadly about the possibilities for innovative policing reform and accordingly chose to work within a nodal perspective. This is not to suggest that we abandoned standard approaches to policing reform entirely. In fact, we undertook reviews with different institutions and groups in Argentina of the kinds of public policing models and technologies that existed in Canada, and subsequently determined which models would resonate with Argentine policing needs and available policing resources (for example, 'use of force' training modules and the 'how to's' of community-based policing that could be deployed within the existing public police services). In addition to this, our normative agenda focused on the enhancement of democratic policing by working with poor communities (shantytown dwellers) who have been bearing the brunt of an exclusionary and brutal system of public policing. From within a nodal perspective, we took what we understood to be the most innovative developments in policing from among those reviewed above and set out to implement a model for deepening democracy. In particular, we worked within a model that focused on innovative ways of both realising restorative justice values (Shearing *et al*, forthcoming) and of enhancing community self-direction (for details on this model, see Shearing, 2001c; Wood and Font, 2003).

Central to our stance in this project is the argument that in situations where established forms of policing are producing undemocratic outcomes, agendas for producing change need not work within the framework that produced these outcomes in the first place (Shearing, 1997). Put another way, in the context of Argentina, exclusionary and brutal policing is so hegemonic both within the formal police and private institutions of security, that the 'conditions of possibility' for substantial change within those formal sets of policing institutions were limited. By embracing the potential for other entities to produce democratic policing outcomes (that is, poor collectivities), we carved out a space for change and imagined positive prospects for democracy that would be most likely to achieve significant democratic gains in the near future. By focusing our explanatory and normative analyses exclusively on the state sphere, the possibilities for democratic renewal would seem much more remote.

The above discussion only captures a small and tentative sample of lines of inquiry that could be pursued from within a plural or nodal perspective. That being said, what we would stress is the need for core democratic values to be at the centre of explanatory work, whilst remaining more open-ended about the possible contribution of different policing and governance arrangements to these values. The excerpt below, again from the report to the Law Commission of Canada, captures this argument:

> It is particularly important ... to try to move the debate over policing reform beyond its current parameters, which tend to polarise discussion of both state and non-state policing institutions and practices. Thus, for instance, in our view the question is not whether policing is most appropriately undertaken by the state or under non-state auspices – a conversation which almost always ends in controversy about the undoubted failings of both – but rather, how the multiplicity of state and non-state

resources for policing can be harnessed to provide the most effective and acceptable policing for communities (whether at the local, regional, national, or international level).

In order to develop innovative normative agendas that seek to harness the 'multiplicity of state and non-state resources', it is essential to provide an exhaustive map of such resources, taking into account both global trends and local variation.

Conclusions

Through an analysis of waves of change at the level of practical developments and scholarly understandings of policing, we are reminded that the domain of 'policing' is in a constant process of innovation. Practical actors innovate by establishing new ways of 'doing' policing, from the establishment of new institutions and programs to the implementation of new practices and mundane routines. Scholars are in a constant process of 'conceptual innovation' involving a questioning of previously held assumptions about the nature of that which they seek to describe. As Castel says:

> ... the present reflects a conjunction of elements inherited from the past and current innovations. In other words, the present bears a burden, a weight that comes from the past, and the task of the present is to bring this burden up to date in order to understand its current ramifications ... (1994, p 238).

At present, we suggest that a 'plural' or 'nodal' framework allows us to challenge the 'burdens' we have carried in the form of established conceptions and understandings about what policing is, who undertakes it, how they do so, and with what impacts that may not resonate with present realities. In particular, the nodal framework moves us outside of the state-centred framework and its fundamental public/private distinction – deeply connected concepts that do not capture many of the most recent 'discoveries' in policing canvassed in this paper. As we've outlined, these concepts are poorly suited to probing policing developments in Western democracies, are less useful for comparative work in nations undergoing political transition, and, in turn, are completely inappropriate for analysing policing in authoritarian and/or theocratic political contexts. By introducing new ideas and conceptions, the plural or nodal framework has the potential for producing new research questions and normative projects that are more closely aligned with the practical experiences and concerns of those who engage in and are the recipients of policing.

References

Aitkenhead, D (2000) 'Rough justice', *Daily Mail and Guardian*, Johannesburg, South Africa, 15 December

Anderson, M (1989) *Policing the World*, Oxford: Clarendon

Baker, B (2001) 'Taking the law into their own hands: fighting crime in South Africa', paper presented at the 29th Joint Sessions of Workshops, ECPR, 6–11 April, Grenoble

Bateson, MC (1990) 'Beyond sovereignty: an emerging global civilisation', in Walker, RBJ and Mendlovitz, SH (eds), *Contending Sovereignties: Redefining Political Community*, Boulder, and London: Lynne Rienner Publishers

Bayley, D (1994) *Police for the Future*, Oxford: OUP

Bayley, D and Shearing, C (2001) *The New Structure of Policing*, Washington, DC: The National Institute of Justice, US Department of Justice

Beck, U (1992) *Risk Society: Toward a New Modernity*, London: Sage

Bigo, D (2000) 'Liaison officers in Europe: new officers in the European security field', in Sheptycki, JWE (ed), *Issues in Transnational Policing*, London and New York: Routledge, pp 67–99

Bittner, E (1974) 'Florence Nightingale in pursuit of Willy Sutton: a theory of the police', in Jacob, H (ed), *The Potential for Reform of Criminal Justice*, Beverly Hills, California: Sage

Blakely, EJ and Snyder, MG (1997) *Fortress America: Gated Communities in the United States*, Washington, DC: Brookings Institute Press

Bordua, D (1968) 'Police', in *International Encyclopedia of the Social Sciences*, Vol 12, New York: Macmillan

Braithwaite, J (1989) *Crime, Shame and Reintegration*, Cambridge: CUP

Braithwaite, J (2000) 'The new regulatory state and the transformation of criminology' 40 *British Journal of Criminology* 222–38

Braithwaite, J (2002) *Restorative Justice and Responsive Regulation*, Oxford: OUP

Brodeur, J-P (2000) 'Transnational policing and human rights: a case study', in Sheptycki, JWE (ed), *Issues in Transnational Policing*, London and New York: Routledge, pp 43–66

Button, M and John, T (2002) '"Plural policing" in action: a review of the policing of environmental protests in England and Wales' 12(2) *Policing and Society* 111–21

Cain, M (1973) *Society and the Policeman's Role*, London: Routledge

Caldeira, T (2000) *City of Walls: Crime, Segregation, and Citizenship in Sao Paulo*, Berkeley: California UP

Caldeira, T (1996) 'Building up walls: the new pattern of segregation in Sao Paulo' 48(1) *International Social Science Journal* 55–65

Camilleri, JA (1990) 'Rethinking sovereignty in a shrinking, fragmented world', in Walker, RBJ and Mendlovitz, SH (eds), *Contending Sovereignties: Redefining Political Community*, Boulder, and London: Lynne Rienner Publishers

Castel, R (1994) '"Problematization" as a mode of reading history', in Goldstein, J (ed), *Foucault and the Writing of History*, Oxford, UK and Cambridge, USA: Basil Blackwell, pp 237–52

Ceyssens, P, Dunn, SC and Childs, S (eds) (2002) *Ontario Police Services Act*, Fully Annotated, 2002–2003 edn, Saltspring Island, British Columbia: Earlscourt

Crawford, A (2003) 'Contractual governance of deviant behaviour' 30(4) *Journal of Law and Society* 479–505

Crawford, A (1997) *The Local Governance of Crime: Appeals to Community and Partnerships*, Oxford: Clarendon

Crawford, A (1994) 'The partnership approach to community crime prevention: corporatism at the local level?' 3 *Social and Legal Studies* 497–518

Crawford, A and Lister, S (2003) 'Integrated local security quilts or frayed, fragmented and fragile tangled webs? The patchwork shape of reassurance policing in England and Wales', paper presented at the conference titled 'In Search of Security: An International Conference on Policing and Security', hosted by the Law Commission of Canada, Montreal

Daniels, RJ, Macklem, P and Roach, K (eds) (2001) *The Security of Freedom: Essays on Canada's Anti-Terrorism Bill*, Toronto: Toronto UP

Davis, M (1990) *City of Quartz*, London: Vintage

Davis, N (2000) *The Gift in Sixteenth Century France*, Madison: Wisconsin UP

Eggers, WD and O'Leary, J (1995) *Revolution at the Roots: Making Our Government Smaller, Better and Closer to Home*, New York: Free Press

Elkins, D (1995) *Beyond Sovereignty: Territorial and Political Economy in the Twenty-First Century*, Toronto: Toronto UP

Eng, S (2002) 'Policing for the public good', commentary prepared for the Law Commission of Canada Study Panel on Order and Security, October

Ericson, R (1982) *Reproducing Order: A Study of Police Patrol Work*, Toronto, Buffalo, and London: Toronto UP

Ericson, R and Haggerty, K (1997) *Policing the Risk Society*, Toronto and Buffalo: Toronto UP

Fischer, B (2001) 'Community policing – some observations and reflections on its social, legal and democratic implications', in Einstein, S and Amir, M (eds), *Policing, Security and Democracy: Special Aspects of 'Democratic Policing'*, Huntsville, Texas: Office of International Criminal Justice, pp 35–62

Foucault, M (1977) *Discipline and Punish: The Birth of the Prison*, New York: Vintage

Foucault, M (1997) 'Candidacy presentation: Collège de France, 1969', in Rabinow, P (ed), *Ethics, Subjectivity and Truth: Essential Works of Foucault 1954–1984*, Vol 1, New York: The New Press

Garland, D (1996) 'The limits of the sovereign state: strategies of crime control in contemporary society' 36(4) *British Journal of Criminology* 445–71

Garland, D (2001) *The Culture of Control: Crime and Social Order in Contemporary Society*, Chicago: Chicago UP

Giddens, A (1991) *Modernity and Self-Identity: Self and Society in the Late Modern Age*, Cambridge: Polity

Goldsmith, A and Lewis, C (eds) (2000) *Civilian Oversight of Policing: Governance, Democracy and Human Rights*, Oxford and Portland, Oregon: Hart Publishing

Gordon, C (1980) 'Afterword', in Foucault, M, *Power/Knowledge*, Brighton: Harvester, pp 229–59

Grabosky, P (1994) 'Beyond the regulatory state' 27 *The Australian and New Zealand Journal of Criminology* 192–97

Grabosky, P (1995) 'Using non-governmental resources to foster regulatory compliance' 8(4) *Governance: An International Journal of Policy and Administration* 527–50

Grabosky, P (1996) 'The future of crime control' 63 *Trends and Issues in Crime and Criminal Justice Series*, Canberra: Australian Institute of Criminology

Grabosky, P (2003) 'Private sponsorship of public policing', paper prepared for the conference titled 'In Search of Security: An International Conference on Policing and Security', hosted by the Law Commission of Canada, Montreal

Greene, J, Seamon, T and Levy, P (1995) 'Merging public and private security for collective benefit: Philadelphia's centre city district' 14(2) *American Journal of Police* 3–20

Held, D (2000) 'The changing contours of political community: rethinking democracy in the context of globalization', in Ericson, R and Stehr, N (eds), *Governing Modern Societies*, Toronto: Toronto UP, pp 42–59

Held, D, McGrew, A, Goldblatt, D and Perraton, J (1999) *Global Transformations: Politics, Economics and Culture*, Cambridge: Polity

Herbert, S (2002) 'Policing the contemporary city: fixing broken windows or shoring up neo-liberalism?' 5(4) *Theoretical Criminology* 445–66

Hermer, J and Mosher, J (eds) (2002) *Disorderly People: Law and the Politics of Exclusion in Ontario*, Halifax, Ontario: Fernwood Press

Hermer, J, Kempa, M, Shearing, C, Stenning, P and Wood, J (2002) *Policing in Canada in the 21st Century: Directions for Law Reform*, report to the Law Commission of Canada, Ottawa: Law Commission of Canada

Hillyard, P (1993) 'Paramilitary policing and popular justice in Northern Ireland', in Findlay, M and Zvekic, U (eds), *Alternative Policing Styles: Cross Cultural Perspectives*, Deventer and Boston: Kluwer, pp 139–56

Hindess, B (1996) *Discourses of Power: From Hobbes to Foucault*, Oxford: Blackwell

von Hirsch, A and Shearing, C (2001) 'Exclusion from public space', in von Hirsch, A, Garland, D and Wakefield, A (eds), *Ethical and Social Perspectives on Situational Crime Prevention*, Oxford and Portland, Oregon: Hart Publishing, pp 77–96

Hobbes, T (1651/1968) *Leviathan*, Macpherson, CB (ed), Harmondsworth: Penguin

Holdaway, S (ed) (1979) *The British Police*, London: Edward Arnold

Hope, T (2000) 'Inequality and the clubbing of private security', in Hope, T and Sparks, R (eds), *Crime, Risk and Insecurity*, London and New York: Routledge, pp 83–106

Hudson, B (2001) 'Punishment, rights and difference: defending justice in the risk society', in Stenson, K and Sullivan, RR (eds), *Crime, Risk and Justice: The Politics of Crime Control in Liberal Democracies*, Cullompton: Willan Publishing, pp 144–72

Hughes, G (1998) *Understanding Crime Prevention: Social Control, Risk and Late Modernity*, Buckingham, UK and Philadelphia: OU Press

Independent Commission on Policing Reform in Northern Ireland (ICPNI) (1999) *A New Beginning: Policing in Northern Ireland*, www.belfast.org.uk/report.htm, accessed 29 April 2003

Johnston, L (1992) *The Rebirth of Private Policing*, London: Routledge

Johnston, L (1996) 'What is vigilantism?' 36(2) *British Journal of Criminology* 220–36

Johnston, L (1997) 'Policing communities of risk', in Francis, P, Davies, P and Jupp, V (eds), *Policing Futures: The Police, Law Enforcement and the Twenty-First Century*, London: Macmillan, pp 186–207

Johnston, L (1999) 'Private policing in context' 7(2) *European Journal on Criminal Policy and Research* 175–96

Johnston, L (2000a) *Policing Britain: Risk, Security and Governance*, Harlow: Longman

Johnston, L (2000b) 'Transnational private policing: the impact of global commercial security', in Sheptycki, JWE (ed), *Issues in Transnational Policing*, London and New York: Routledge, pp 21–42

Johnston, L and Shearing, C (2003) *Governing Security: Explorations in Policing and Justice*, London and New York: Routledge

Jones, T and Newburn, T (1998) *Private Security and Public Policing*, Oxford: Clarendon

Jones, T and Newburn, T (1999), 'Urban change and policing: mass private property reconsidered' 7(2) *European Journal on Criminal Policy and Research* 225–44

Jones, T and Newburn, T (2002), 'The transformation of policing? Understanding current trends in policing systems' 42 *British Journal of Criminology* 129–46

Kelling, G, and Coles, C (1997) *Fixing Broken Windows: Restoring Order and Reducing Crime in Our Communities*, New York; London; Sydney; Singapore: Free Press

Kempa, M, Stenning, P and Wood, J (2004) 'Policing communal spaces: a reconfiguration of the "mass private property" hypothesis' 44 *British Journal of Criminology* 562–81

Kempa, M, Carrier, R, Wood, J and Shearing, C (1999) 'Reflections on the evolving concept of "private policing"' 7(2) *European Journal on Criminal Justice Policy* 197–223

Kempa, M and Shearing, C (2002) 'Microscopic and macroscopic responses to inequalities in the governance of security: respective experiments in South Africa and Northern Ireland' 29 *Transformation: Critical Perspectives on Southern Africa* Special Issue on Crime and Policing in Transition 55–74

Klockars, C (1985) *The Idea of Police*, Vol 3 of Law and Criminal Justice Series, Beverley Hills, California: Sage

Lacey, N (1994) 'Government as manager, citizen as consumer: the case of the Criminal Justice Act 1991' 57 *The Modern Legal Review* 534–54

Landreville, P (1995) 'Prison overpopulation and strategies for decarceration' 37 *Canadian Journal of Criminology* 39–60

Leach, P (2003) 'Citizen policing as civic activism: an international inquiry', paper presented at the conference titled 'In Search of Security: An International Conference on Policing and Security' hosted by the Law Commission of Canada, Montreal

Loader, I (1997) 'Private security and the demand for protection in contemporary Britain' 7 *Policing and Society* 143–62

Loader, I (1999) 'Consumer culture and the commodification of policing and security' 33(2) *Sociology* 373–92

Loader, I (2000) 'Plural policing and democratic governance' 93(3) *Social and Legal Studies* 323–45

Loader, I and Walker, N (2001) 'Policing as a public good: reconstituting the connections between policing and the state' 5(1) *Theoretical Criminology* 9–35

Los, M (2002) 'Post-communist fear of crime and the commercialisation of security' 6(2) *Theoretical Criminology* 165–88

Los, M and Zybertowicz, A (2000) *Privatizing the Police-State: The Case of Poland*, London: Macmillan, and New York: St Martin's Press

Loveday, B (1987) 'The joint boards' 3 *Policing* 196–213

Loveday, B (1991) 'The new police authorities in the metropolitan counties: the costs and consequences of the abolition of the metropolitan county authorities' 1 *Policing and Society* 193–212

Loveday, B (2000) 'New directions in accountability', in Leishman, F, Loveday, B and Savage, S (eds), *Core Issues in Policing*, 2nd edn, Harlow: Longman, pp 213–31

Lustgarten, L (1986) *The Governance of Police*, London: Sweet & Maxwell

Macauley, S (1986) 'Private government', in Lipson, L and Wheeler, S (eds), *Law and the Social Sciences*, New York: Russell Sage Foundation

Maguire, M (2000) 'Policing by risks and targets: some dimensions and implications of intelligence-led crime control' 9 *Policing and Society* 315–36

Manning, P (1977) *Police Work*, Cambridge, Massachusetts: MIT Press

Manning, P (2000) 'Policing new social spaces', in Sheptycki, JWE (ed), *Issues in Transnational Policing*, London and New York: Routledge, pp 177–200

Marshall, G (1965) *Police and Government*, London: Methuen

Marshall, G (1979) 'Police accountability revisited', in Butler, D and Halsey, A (eds), *Policy and Politics*, London: Macmillan

McBarnet, D (1979) 'Arrest: the legal context of policing', in Holdaway, S (ed), *The British Police*, London: Edward Arnold

McLaughlin, E (1992) 'The democratic deficit: European Union and the accountability of the British police' 32(4) *British Journal of Criminology* 473–87

McLaughlin, E and Murji, K (1995) 'The end of public policing? Police reform and "the new managerialism"', in Noaks, L, Maguire, M and Levi, M (eds), *Contemporary Issues in Criminology*, Cardiff: Wales UP, pp 110–27

Miller, P and Rose, N (1992) 'Political power beyond the state: problematics of government' 43(2) *British Journal of Sociology* 173–205

Mopas, M (2002) 'Policing in Vancouver's downtown east side: report of case study', Appendix to Hermer, J, Kempa, M, Shearing, C, Stenning, P and Wood, J *Policing in Canada in the 21st Century: Directions for Law Reform*, Report to the Law Commission of Canada, Ottawa: Law Commission of Canada

Murphy, J (1997) 'The private sector and security: a bit on BIDs' 9 *Security Journal* 11–13

Noaks, L (2000) 'Private cops on the block: a review of the role of private security in residential communities' 10 *Policing and Society* 143–61

O'Malley, P (1997) 'Policing, politics and postmodernity' 6(3) *Social and Legal Studies* 363–81

O'Malley, P and Palmer, D (1996) 'Post-Keynesian policing' 25 *Economy and Society* 137–55

Osborne, D and Gaebler, T (1992) *Reinventing Government*, New York: Penguin

Power, M (1994) *The Audit Explosion*, London: Demos

Punch, M (1979) *Policing the Inner City*, London: Macmillan

Reichman, N (1987) 'The widening webs of surveillance: private police unravelling deceptive claims', in Shearing, C and Stenning, P (eds), *Private Policing*, Beverly Hills and London: Sage Publications

Reiner, R (1992) 'Policing a postmodern society' 55(6) *Modern Law Review* 761–81

Reiner, R (1994) 'Policing and the police', in Maguire, M, Morgan, R and Reiner, R (eds), *The Oxford Handbook of Criminology*, Oxford: Clarendon, pp 705–72

Reiner, R (2000) *The Politics of the Police*, 3rd edn, Oxford: OUP

Reiss, A Jr (1971) *The Police and the Public*, New Haven, Connecticut: Yale UP

Reuss-Ianni, E and Ianni, FAJ (1983) 'Street cops and management cops: the two cultures of policing', in Punch, M (ed), *Control of the Police Organization*, Cambridge, Massachusetts: MIT Press, pp 251–74

Rigakos, G (2002), *The New Parapolice: Risk Markets and Commodified Social Control*, Toronto: Toronto UP

Rigakos, G and Greener, D (2000) 'Bubbles of governance: private policing and the law in Canada' 15(1) *Canadian Journal of Law and Society* 145–84

Rose, N (1996) 'The death of the social? Refiguring the territory of government' 25(3) *Economy and Society* 327–56

Rubinstein, J (1983) *City Police*, New York: Farrar, Strauss and Giroux

Sarre, R and Prenzler, T (2000) 'The relationship between police and private security: models and future directions' 24(1) *International Journal of Comparative and Applied Criminal Justice* 91–113

Scott, C (2001) 'Analysing regulatory space: fragmented resources and institutional design' *Public Law*, Summer, 329–53

Shearing, C (1992) 'The relation between public and private policing', in Tonry, M and Morris, N (eds), *Modern Policing*, Chicago: Chicago UP, pp 399–434

Shearing, C (1997) 'The unrecognised origins of the new policing: linkages between private and public policing', in Felson, M and Clarke, RV (eds), *Business and Crime Prevention*, Monsey, New York: Criminal Justice Press, pp 219–30

Shearing, C (1999) 'Remarks of Professor Clifford Shearing' (on zero tolerance policing) 35(4) *Criminal Law Bulletin* 378–83

Shearing, C (2001a) 'A nodal conception of governance: thoughts on a policing commission' 11 *Policing and Society* 259–72

Shearing, C (2001b) 'Punishment and the changing face of governance' 3(2) *Punishment and Society* 203–20

Shearing, C (2001c) 'Transforming the governance of security: a South African experiment', in Strang, H and Braithwaite, J (eds), *Restorative Justice and Civil Society*, Cambridge: CUP, pp 14–34

Shearing, C (2003) 'Refiguring the public and private within a nodal governance framework', paper presented at the conference titled 'In Search of Security: An International Conference on Policing and Security', hosted by the Law Commission of Canada, Montreal

Shearing, C and Stenning, P (1981) 'Modern private security: its growth and implications', in Tonry, M and Morris, N (eds), *Crime and Justice, An Annual Review of Research*, Vol 3, Chicago: Chicago UP, pp 193–245

Shearing, C and Stenning, P (1983) 'Private security: implications for social control' 30(5) *Social Problems* 493–506

Shearing, C and Stenning, P (1985) 'From the Panopticon to Disney World: the development of discipline', in Doob, AN and Greenspan, EL (eds), *Perspectives in Criminal Law*, Toronto: Canada Law Book, pp 335–49

Shearing, C and Wood, J (2003) 'Nodal governance, democracy, and the new "denizens"' 30(3) *Journal of Law and Society* 400–19

Shearing, C and Wood, J (2000) 'Reflections on the governance of security: a normative inquiry' 1(4) *Police Practice* 457–76

Shearing, C, Wood, J and Font, E (forthcoming) 'Nodal governance and restorative justice' *Journal of Social Issues*

Sheptycki, JWE (1995) 'Transnational policing and the makings of a postmodern state' 35(4) *British Journal of Criminology* 613–35

Sheptycki, JWE (1997) 'Insecurity, risk suppression and segregation: some reflections on policing in the transnational age' 1(3) *Theoretical Criminology* 303–15

Sheptycki, JWE (1998) 'Policing, postmodernism and transnationalism' 38(3) *British Journal of Criminology* 485–503

Sheptycki, JWE (ed) (2000) *Issues in Transnational Policing*, London: Routledge

Sheptycki, JWE (2002a) *In Search of Transnational Policing*, Aldershot: Avebury

Sheptycki, JWE (2002b) 'La problème de la responsabilité et de l'action policière sous tous ses aspects, Pout une cartographie général de la responsabilité en matière de police à l'ére post-moderne' 48 *Cultures et Conflits*, Hiver, 81–108

Sheptycki, JWE (2002c) 'Accountability across the policing field: towards a general cartography of accountability for postmodern policing' 12(4) *Policing and Society Special Issue on Police Accountability in Europe* (Guest Editor Monica den Boer) 323–38

Skolnick, J (1966) *Justice Without Trial*, New York: Wiley

Stenning, P (ed) (1995) *Accountability for Criminal Justice: Selected Essays*, Toronto: Toronto UP

Stenning, P (2000) 'Powers and accountability of private police' 8(3) *European Journal on Criminal Policy and Research* 325–52

Stenson, K (1996) 'Communal security as government – the British experience', in Hammerschick, W, Karazman-Morarvetz, I and Stangl, W (eds), *Jahrbuch fur Rechts und Kriminalsoziologie*, Baden Baden: Nomos

Tonry, M and Lynch, M (1996) 'Intermediate sanctions', in Tonry, M and Morris, N (eds), *Crime and Justice: A Review of the Research*, Vol 20, Chicago: Chicago UP

Wakefield, A (2000) 'Situation crime prevention in mass private property', in von Hirsch, A, Garland, D and Wakefield, A (eds), *Ethical and Social Perspectives on Situational Crime Prevention*, Oxford and Portland, Oregon: Hart Publishing, pp 125–45

Walker, N (2000) 'Transnational contexts', in Leishman, F, Loveday, B and Savage, S (eds), *Core Issues in Policing*, 2nd edn, Harlow: Longman

Wall, D (1997) 'Policing the virtual community: the Internet, cyberspace and cyber-crime', in Francis, P, Davies, P and Jupp, V (eds), *Policy Futures: The Police, Law Enforcement and the Twenty-First Century*, London: Macmillan, pp 208–38

Webster, C (2002) 'Property rights and the public realm: gates, green belts, and *gemeinschaft*' 29 *Environment and Planning B: Planning and Design* 397–412

Wilson, J (1968) *Varieties of Police Behavior*, Cambridge, Massachusetts: Harvard UP

Wilson, J and Kelling, G (1982) 'Broken windows: the police and neighbourhood safety' *The Atlantic Monthly*, March, pp 29–38

Wood, J (2000) *Reinventing Governance: A Study of Transformations in the Ontario Provincial Police*, unpublished PhD thesis, University of Toronto

Wood, J and Font, E (2003) 'Building peace and reforming policing in Argentina: opportunities and challenges for shantytowns', paper presented at the conference titled 'In Search of Security: An International Conference on Policing and Security', hosted by the Law Commission of Canada, Montreal

Zehr, H (1990) *Changing Lenses: A New Focus for Crime and Justice*, Scottdale, Pennsylvania: Herald Press

Chapter 14
The Evolution of European Policing Strategies in Response to Transnational Crime

Paul Norman

Introduction

> Few events have galvanised the international system into action so completely in so short a time as the horrific attacks of 11 September in the United States. In the immediate aftermath, the Union expressed its full solidarity with the United States and its support for the action, including military action, which it was taking. The fight against terrorism is more than ever a major policy objective of the European Union (Presidency of the Council of the EU, 2001b, para 1).

The elevation of counter-terrorism to the status of a 'major policy objective' of the EU was a seminal event in the development of European institutions of governance. September 11th launched the EU and its Member States into a significant programme of criminal police and judicial policy development, operational action and institution building. The speed and cross-pillar breadth of the EU's response following the attacks was remarkable, especially given the discontinuous pattern of crises and institutional inertia that had previously characterised EU Justice and Home Affairs (JHA) co-operation. However, despite the rhetorical reference to September 11th, many of these measures were already on the table, having been set out at a European Council summit in Tampere in 1999. This raises questions about whether or not the EU's response to September 11th is yet another indicator of an already established pattern of discontinuous development, or a genuinely enhanced governmental capacity to act against transnational crime affecting the EU. Such questions are crucial at the present juncture, as the EU expands to include 25 Member States.

The ratification of the Treaty on European Union (TEU) in 1993 created what were to be Byzantine and fluid arrangements for the EU's third pillar of JHA co-operation. Initially, most Member States saw JHA as tangential to the mainstream integration project of economic and monetary union, with the third pillar's inter-governmental features resting on rules of unanimity, and power laying firmly in the hands of Member States, not the European Commission or the European Parliament. Throughout the 1990s the pace of JHA integration was unsurprisingly at that of the 'slowest' Member State. The difficulty of the task, together with increasing expectations and the demands of accession of 10 new Member States must be set against the objective set out in the Treaty of Amsterdam, to establish an Area of Freedom, Security and Justice (AFSJ). By 2001, major elements of the vision of establishing the AFSJ lay dormant. Arguably, the foundering vision was rescued by the Member States' determination to respond to the attacks by Al-Qaeda in America. The EU's response to September 11th transformed the prospective legislative and institutional order and extended the practical breadth of European policing strategies in integrating JHA with action in the spheres of foreign policy and within the financial system in tackling terrorist financing (den Boer, 2000, pp 218–22; Council of the EU, 2002a; European Council, 2002, Annex V). As den

Boer and Monar state, 'September 11 must be regarded as the first truly "cross-pillar" test of the Union's role as a security actor' (2002, p 11).

This chapter will show that the development of EU policing against transnational crime has been slow and largely the result of specific 'pushes', key events or crises. A discontinuous pattern of legislative, institutional and operational development betrays the weaknesses of third pillar governance. This is part of the case for substantial change in the arrangements for European governance, reflected in attempts to draft a constitution for the EU (European Convention on the Future of Europe, 2003). Even after the reforms of the Treaty on European Union brought in by the Treaty of Amsterdam, the domain of criminal police co-operation retained strong inter-governmental features, whereby rules of unanimity in decision making undermined what could be agreed and realistically achieved by all – the lowest common denominator. Approaching a period of major expansion in membership of the Union and the development of a third pillar, JHA external relations dimension, the need for a major overhaul of the third pillar was a key theme of the European Convention on the Future of Europe and its resultant draft constitution. The post-September 11th impetus for EU–USA co-operation, and international co-operation against terrorism, further enhanced the importance of the external relations effects on the EU's approach to transnational crime. The resulting agreements between the EU and the USA on extradition and mutual legal assistance are the most prominent examples of this.[1] These agreements help in understanding European policing strategies as these set out prospective parameters of the EU's global response to transnational offending and organised crime.

The chapter examines the EU's ambitions to develop effective policing strategies to combat serious cross-border and organised crime affecting the EU. It looks at the new EU institutions of Europol and EuroJust and efforts to deepen police and judicial co-operation in criminal matters. Attention is paid to three areas: the development of strategic guidance over the third pillar of justice and home affairs co-operation and its 'working methods'; third pillar institutional development, in particular in the criminal police and judicial spheres; and finally the development of operational enforcement capacities for tackling transnational offending and organised crime within the EU.

Third pillar governance and external relations: developing strategies to counter organised crime

The development of third pillar governance since 1993 has come about in a series of 'fits and starts' in which treaty changes or Presidency initiatives have overcome legislative blockages. During this period, many of the Council Presidency initiatives have been the most 'politicised' attempts to move the Union forward in the field of JHA, the stimuli often being unforeseen 'events', with the EU's response to September 11th (examined below) being the most recent. Prior to September 11th, there were three main phases in the development of third pillar governance. The first was a decision that anticipated ratification of the Maastricht Treaty on

---

1 For the full text of the agreements see: Statewatch Legislative Observatory, www.statewatch.org/semdoc/observatory/observatory4.htm.

European Union. This created the original formal EU inter-governmental co-operation machinery for police, customs and immigration services in 1992.[2] The pressure for such change came from the abolition of internal border controls under the terms of the Single European Act. Pressure to maintain perceived levels of 'internal security' led to the emphasis on transnational security and law enforcement co-ordination across a range of agencies in order to secure the 'external frontiers' of the Union (Home Affairs Committee, 1990). Ratification of the TEU in November 1993 formalised a relatively incoherent group of policy forums into a hierarchical and more transparent system of governance (Hayes-Renshaw and Wallace, 1997, p 94). This structure remained fractured by the three 'pillars' – the community method within the European Community treaties (first pillar) and inter-governmental co-operation within the Common, Foreign and Security Policy (second pillar) and Justice and Home Affairs (third pillar). Article K6 established a formal framework for EU co-operation and a justicable legal basis for international agreements between the Member States of the EU. Decision making under the new third pillar was strictly inter-governmental and reliant upon unanimous agreement between Member States. This had only an attenuated role for the Commission, and no meaningful practical role for the European Parliament, in scrutinising legislative initiatives, let alone national parliaments (Art K11). Sheptycki described this Byzantine structure initially as a 'transnational state system' (1997) and later as a 'post-modern state system' (1998). Given the political complexity of the machinery of European governance, his suggestive analysis could only but raise further questions about ways in which policy decisions were manufactured within them.

The policy domain of JHA co-operation was capped by the collective political authority of the justice and interior ministers from the Member States in a new JHA Council. Whilst this seemingly moved away from the inchoate patchwork of informal co-operation that pre-dated the TEU, these arrangements for EU co-operation proved to be disappointing. The early decision making processes of the third pillar were characterised by tortuous negotiations and extended delays in drafting two key instruments, the Europol Convention and the Convention on Mutual Legal Assistance. Decision making based on unanimity principles (TEU, Art K4.3) resulted in a lack of agreement on the appropriate role of the European Court of Justice, the inability to agree uniform standards of data protection, the demand for meaningful external accountability mechanisms, and ultimately no common view on Europol's future development.[3] Somewhat later, the Council's own assessment accepted that the system of JHA governance 'has proved very cumbersome and has slowed down the decision making process' (Council of the EU, 1995, p 17). The growing crisis in third pillar governance was clearly illustrated by the disruption to JHA co-operation caused by the UK's obstructionism during the BSE crisis (Statewatch, 1996), and its ideological resistance to the European Court of Justice (Duff, 1997, pp 186–87). It was widely understood that a flawed

---

2   This is not strictly inter-governmental as Title VI cites connections between the third pillar and other EU institutions such as the European Parliament, the Commission and the Court of Justice. In addition, expenditure under this pillar *may* be charged to the Community budget (O'Keefe, 1995, pp 903–04).

3   The Treaty of Amsterdam partly addressed this by allowing conventions to come into force upon completion of national ratification procedures in half the Member States (Art K6.2(d)).

system of JHA governance had encumbered Member States, where a single 'Eurosceptic' administration could exploit the weaknesses of inter-governmental co-operation, prevent agreement and ultimately block the attainment of the objectives of the Union.

The review of the TEU (ultimately informing the treaty changes agreed within the Treaty of Amsterdam) provided the opportunity for reappraisal (Council of the EU, 1995). The Treaty of Amsterdam introduced a revised legislative process with a number of attractive innovations that forged links between the JHA Council with other EU institutions, including a formal consultation role for the European Parliament (Art 39.1). The political will to improve what had become an embarrassing EU policy process spurred the Irish Presidency to initiate change in advance of the Treaty of Amsterdam in the latter half of 1996. A second policy push came about as a result of the Irish Presidency's response to a seemingly domestic issue – the assassination of an investigative journalist Veronica Guerin (International Press Institute, 2000). That event spurred the Irish Presidency to promote domestic legislation within the context of broad-based EU action against 'organised crime', the creation of the EU's first JHA High Level Group (on organised crime), the subsequent EU *Action Plan on Organised Crime* (Norman, 1999; 2001, pp 186–88) with its enhanced focus on the achievement and implementation of agreed policy outcomes. This sustained Irish Presidency initiative established the institutional space for the General Secretariat of the Council, servicing national Member States co-operating in the Council of the EU, to develop expertise in the field with the seconding of 'eight national experts and practitioners' (Council of the EU, 1997, p 6), thereby providing the technical prerequisites for increased continuity between, and support for, the rotating Presidencies – a role performed by the Commission under the first pillar.

Crucial to the success of this push by the Irish Presidency was the effective de-politicisation of policy formation, legislative development and institutional construction in the decisive move to selective horizontal policy integration, underpinned by the informal devolution of executive responsibility to a number of key 'expert' or 'High Level' groups. For the first time there was strategic orientation to the third pillar, which rested on concrete action on a wide operational front. The 1996 Irish Presidency focus on action against 'organised crime' was key to changing third pillar governance and gained high level endorsement at the European Council (Dublin II) in December 1996. The initiative circumvented the problematic third pillar structures by creating the 'High Level Group on Organised Crime' which provided the policy 'cement' for the co-ordination of JHA policy development and implementation across the three pillars.

The Council's review of the effectiveness of the *Action Plan on Organised Crime* (updated at Vienna in December 1998) acknowledged that 'the Plan of Action helped to create the political and professional climate required on both the EU level and the national level to take and implement the necessary decisions' (Council of the EU, 2000, p 2). The packaging of a wide range of stalled legislative initiatives under the auspices of ordinary criminal police and judicial co-operation was a deft manoeuvre that assuaged anticipated domestic political opposition to deepening JHA integration and brought much needed strategic direction to the JHA Council in the Action Plan's 15 Political Guidelines. The JHA Council created a successor to the

High Level Group, the Multidisciplinary Group (MDG) on Organised Crime, in July 1997, providing for a continued focus on strategy and its implementation. The MDG rapidly developed a close working relationship with the 'Group of Eight' (or G8) Senior Experts Group on Transnational Organised Crime, facilitated by the UK's concurrent Presidency of both the EU and the G8 (Norman, 1999, pp 110–14; Wrench, 1997). The resulting overlapping networks of state actors 'possessing specialist skills and expertise' focusing on 'transnational organised crime' (and later 'cybercrime') were further empowered within the transnational context of EU-G8 solidarity (Norman, 1999). Remarkably, some of the EU 'working methods' during this period included the presentation of G8 agreements at JHA Councils for adoption, bypassing the third pillar policy making processes entirely (Norman, 1999, p 113). This was the start of the EU's nascent external relations ambitions in JHA. This in turn affected the negotiating position of the EU Member States in the drafting of both the UN Convention on Transnational Organised Crime and the Council of Europe's Cybercrime Convention (Norman, 2001).

Thus, we see during this period a move away from the formal inter-governmentalism of the third pillar to a reliance on mechanisms that sought to enhance effectiveness and efficiency of the JHA policy domain and thereby its 'output legitimacy' (Horeth, 1999, p 251). Further, these exhibited a transnational orientation towards globalised crime concerns as articulated within transatlantic partnerships with the USA and Canada, the G8 and to a lesser extent the Council of Europe (Norman, 1999, pp 114–17). The period of the Irish and UK Presidencies was the precursor to the development of a more systematic and gradated network of transnational relationships that moved from informality to a formal basis in the first JHA external relations strategy document (Presidency of the Council of the EU, 2000). The developing external orientation for European policing strategies came with the next phase, which significantly broadened the scope of the EU JHA integration. Following ratification of the Treaty of Amsterdam, a special Justice and Home Affairs European Council (Tampere) in October 1999 focused upon cross-border crime issues. Given the above Council mechanisms focused upon organised crime, the overall coherence of third pillar policy development, implementation and institution building was now underpinned by two parallel lines of activity concerning organised crime on the one hand and, on the other, an Area of Freedom, Security and Justice (Monar, 2001, pp 758–60). There was significant overlap between the police and judicial co-operation components of the Action Plans, ultimately resulting in a decision to merge the twin track approach with a new *Strategy for the Beginning of the New Millennium*, published in May 2000. In common with the original High Level Group's approach, this sought to provide overall strategic coherence to the Union's strategy with a series of Political Guidelines, linked to specific recommendations and clearly delineated institutional responsibilities. The Commission's cross-pillar role under the provisions of the Treaty of Amsterdam introduced another pressure point to ensure Member State implementation and achievement of JHA policies. The Commission instituted a twice yearly 'scoreboard' for measuring improvements made by individual Member States towards attaining the 'Area of Freedom, Security and Justice' (European Commission, 2002a).

The evolution of third pillar governance since 1993 has come in fits and starts. More recently, policy formation, institution building and national implementation of legislative instruments has been considered in general by the EU, stimulated by the Commission's *White Paper on European Governance* (European Commission, 2001a). Surprisingly, the White Paper only tangentially considered third pillar governance issues (Curtin, 2001) despite the Commission's shared right of initiative (with Member States) under Titles IV and VI. Nevertheless, key issues were raised (predominantly to be resolved by the Council) including strategic guidance for the third pillar, consultation in legislative processes and the discipline provided by continuing 'impact assessment' of legislative proposals. Clear strategic guidance to the JHA Council on the Union's ultimate integration ambitions has recently come to the fore, provided first by the High Level Group and latterly in the ambitions in the Treaty of Amsterdam. Contrary to the Second Pillar (TEU, Art 13), the European Council is not formally cited in the provisions of the TEU and thus does not have a routine obligation to provide strategic guidance to the third pillar/JHA Council (Curtin, 1993, p 27; O'Keefe, 1995, pp 895–97). This increased the significance of the rotating Presidency, most particularly in the phase prior to the Treaty of Amsterdam when the Commission had limited powers of legislative initiative (excluding police and judicial co-operation in criminal matters and customs co-operation (TEU, Art K2)). The pitfalls of a reliance upon Presidencies which rotate on a six-monthly basis, and who have no treaty-based authority to represent or lead Member States in the third pillar (O'Keefe, 1995) was recognised implicitly in the push initiated during the Irish Presidency. That initiative, to mandate a High Level Group on Organised Crime, was an approach elevated after ratification of the Treaty of Amsterdam in the special Tampere European Council setting out how to attain an Area of Freedom, Security and Justice. This 'de-politicised', and thereby facilitated, EU action (Norman, 1999, pp 106–10). As Curtin observed, this approach has since continued, exacerbating the perception of diminished accountability and reduced transparency, not something the authors of the *European Governance White Paper* were evidently much concerned with. Thus:

> an increasing number of (sensitive) tasks of public administration are arguably carried out by a growing number of independent bodies such as Europol, pro-EuroJust, etc ... there is a marked growth in position and tasks and influence of informal committees with no legal basis ... [and where] the General Secretariat of the Council exercises power comparable to a public administration (Curtin, 2001).

This chimes with Anderson and Burns' analysis of the EU as 'an instance of post-Parliamentary governance' where 'negotiations, policy making and implementation takes place in thousands of specialised policy settings' (1998, pp 227, 229). What is more, this process is found at ever higher levels of transnational governance (Sheptycki, 1996). This places greater responsibility upon political executives to provide strategic guidance (and legitimacy), which is why the absence of a routine broad-based strategic orientation to the European Council was an area identified by the Commission for further development in the governance of the Union (European Commission, 2001a).

Legislative blockages had been an outcome of the problematic operation of the third pillar, an area where in the Commission ventures a position in its follow up proposals on 'better lawmaking'. These sought to:

form a whole centred on *the basic lawmaking framework of the European Union*, including the way EU law is transposed into national law. They are designed to apply to all the EU's regulatory areas – not just the Community 'pillar', but also the third 'pillar' that relates to justice and home affairs, bearing in mind the institutional framework and the decision making arrangements proper to each 'pillar' (European Commission, 2001b, p 2).

Further, the Commission stated that 'Member States should also carry out consultations and impact assessments when they exercise their right of initiative and make legislative proposals under Title VI of TEU and IV of the Treaty establishing the European Communities' (European Commission, 2002c, pp 17–18). This might be expected to reduce the number of impractical proposals that have contributed to third pillar legislative blockages. Perhaps that is why the Council of the EU lent its support to these developments (Council of the EU, 2002a, p 3), since these could *potentially* draw upon the Commission's 'better law making' proposals on consultation and the use of impact assessments within the third pillar.

By the time of the June 2002 Seville European Council, the Council's efforts at reform in advance of enlargement had been accepted with immediate effect (Council of the EU, 2002f, Annex II). For the European Council this entailed a 'substantial change to present practices in the direction of enhancing the efficiency of the institution' (2002, p 2). The reforms included the development of a 'multi-annual strategic programme' by December 2002, linked to an 'annual operating programme of activities' for each of the Councils. Crucially, this was agreed by the next two Presidencies. Strategic guidance to the third pillar was initially weak, and a range of internal and external JHA activities made matters more complicated. The increasingly cross-pillar nature of EU policing and security, the shared right of initiative for both the Commission and the Council, prospective enlargement of the Union in 2004, and the developing external relations dimension to JHA where long-term focused political and administrative action is required, have all had an impact on the 'vision' of the EU's third pillar. But it was the anticipated pressures due to enlargement, and continued unanimity requirements, that focused the third pillar institutions on reform prior to September 11th.

Institutional development and operational capacities

Since ratification of TEU in November 1993, the development of operational capacity to counter cross-border and organised crime has largely focused on the European Police Office (Europol). Europol gained a formal place as a police intelligence agency within the EU's institutional architecture in the Treaty on European Union (Art K1(9)) and it was the first EU enforcement body within the third pillar. This took time to build. It was more than three years before the Council could agree on the legal basis for the organisation (Council of the EU, 1995). Moreover, national ratification was an extended process and it was an additional three years before Europol could be officially launched in July 1999 (Europol, 2003). Europol's areas of competence were outlined in an Annex to the original Convention, but the categories covered were only gradually activated. It was only in the immediate aftermath of September 11th that Europol's competence was fully activated in all areas (Council of the EU, 2001b). Thus, by 2003, Europol's 500 staff were well positioned to perform five main roles: acting as a central point for EU

Member States' exchange of criminal information; operational intelligence analysis with a central analytical database; conducting strategic intelligence analysis; spreading best investigative practice; and finally, supporting transnational operations conducted by the Member States (Europol, 2003, p 1).

In examining Europol's contributions to European policing strategies, particularly against organised crime, it is useful to reflect back to the period of the Single European Act, when the policing and security impact of the abolition of internal border controls first focused attention on the Community's external borders. The eventual goal was to deepen co-operation and EU-wide criminal investigation capacities in order to overcome the perceived 'security deficit'. This meant that efforts to enhance police co-operation between the Member States were directed both at the effectiveness of border controls to create a 'hard outer shell', as well as the detection, surveillance and prosecution of transnational offenders. Europol was to 'add value' to the intelligence effort of each Member State, pooling intelligence and information for Europol's intelligence analysts to develop. In addition to this central point for intelligence analysis, Europol was a convenient site for the co-ordination of operations, working principally through national units in each Member State via the seconded Europol liaison officers based at Europol's headquarters in The Hague. Under this system, each Member State creates a single national unit to function as a point of contact for transnational enquiries, as well as delegating liaison officers to facilitate inter-agency communication and co-operation (Council of the EU, 1995). An early example of this practice was the UK's National Criminal Intelligence Service (NCIS) which was comprised of seconded officers from the full range of national enforcement agencies including police constabularies, UK Customs, the Immigration Service and the Secret Intelligence Service. This is the model of practice for liaison policing, where seconded personnel, working alongside personnel employed directly by NCIS, Europol or other similar dataveillance hub, liaise with their parent agencies and with personnel in designated national units in other countries. Both Interpol and Europol are part of this system (NCIS, 2002, pp 35–36). Up until the early years of the present decade each country in the 15 Member States was in the process of developing analogous systems for liaison policing, but practices varied (den Boer, 2002). These developments, which as of this writing are continuing apace, are intended to facilitate trans-European police co-operation (and indeed transnational policing generally) and have, in effect, transferred policing capacity from the local to the national level in each of the Member States (Sheptycki, 2002).

Europol became a key site for further EU criminal police development after September 11th. Its budget increased by 50% in 2002, reflecting the increased demands from the creation of the EU Counter Terrorist Task Force, the Counter Terrorist Analytical Unit, the enhancement of computing facilities and the deployment of Europol officers, for the first time, in other countries. Reflecting both the focus on EU-USA co-operation, as well as the need to further develop the network of information exchange and operational liaison mechanisms, Europol opened liaison offices in Washington, the USA and at Interpol's Headquarters in Lyon, France (Monar, 2003, p 128; Europol, 2003, p 2). This was made possible by the joint agreements between Europol and the respective third countries and organisations. By the end of 2003 there were three agreements in force with

International Organisations[4] and eight with third countries,[5] with another 13 being negotiated (Statewatch, 2003). Extending Europol's intelligence and information network was understood to be a key element in increasing its effectiveness. The Council of the EU went one step further at the end of 2003, when it agreed to allow Europol to participate in specific operations within the agreed EU framework of Joint Investigative Teams comprising two or more Member States (Monar, 2003, p 128).

This is a significant increase in transnational police operational capacities. Although the arrangement clearly falls short of the initial ambitions of some Member States (notably Germany) in the early 1990s, of a Euro-FBI with full operational powers, it does provide a fully fledged operational law enforcement structure at the EU level. It is too early to tell what the outcome of this will be, particularly for those Member States performing below what has been deemed to be optimal levels of effectiveness.

The strategic agenda for tackling organised transnational crime also focused on judicial co-operation in criminal matters, not only between the Member States, but also with regard to third parties. In 1998, a decentralised European Judicial Network was established to improve judicial procedures between Member States, to provide information to parochial judicial authorities about other Member States and to spread good judicial practice in mutual legal assistance (Council of the EU, 1998). The gathering and transfer of evidence and the transfer of alleged offenders and witnesses, is an important aspect of successful prosecution of trans-European crime. The need to deepen judicial co-operation was recognised in the Conclusions of the 1999 Tampere European Council, which announced plans for a judicial co-operation unit, EuroJust, to work alongside Europol. As it turned out, hot on the heels of the EuroJust initiative came the effective abolition of extradition between Member States and the extension of mutual recognition of judicial decisions. Mutual recognition required a programme of 'harmonisation' of sanctions and a detailed EU legislative programme in the criminal policy sphere. Progress on this was slow despite early 2001 agreement on a *Programme of Measures to Implement the Principle of Mutual Recognition of Decisions in Criminal Matters* (Council of the EU, 2001a) – that is, until the September 11th attacks in the USA (Monar, 2002, pp 129–32).

Overnight the domain of EU counter-terrorist co-operation became one of the most high profile areas of co-operation between EU Member States, significantly deepening judicial co-operation in criminal matters and enhancing practical policing capacities. Within days of the declaration of the 'war on international terrorism', the Commission prepared two key proposals on *Combating Terrorism* which established common EU definitions of terrorist offences, and the European Arrest Warrant (EAW), which effectively abolished extradition between EU Member States (European Commission, 2001b, 2001c). The JHA Council met on 20 September to agree the 'EU counter-terrorism roadmap', endorsed on 21 September by a special European Council meeting. The JHA Council *Conclusions* of 20 September 2001 set out a far-reaching 'roadmap' of EU action in four main areas: counter-terrorism within the EU, co-operation between EU police and intelligence agencies, the financing of terrorism, and lastly EU-USA co-operation (JHA Council, 2001).

4　Interpol, World Customs Organisation and the European Central Bank.
5　Iceland, Norway, Poland, Hungary, Slovenia, Estonia, USA and Czech Republic.

Since then, the roadmap has been continuously updated[6] with allied initiatives and actions, recording progress made by the EU institutions and the Member States (Presidency of the Council of the EU, 2002).

Operationally the EU responded quickly to early indications of European links to the Al-Qaeda terrorist suspects. This dovetailed with the need to replace traditional extradition arrangements with the EAW, although the list of crimes to which the EAW pertained extends well beyond terrorism to include 32 different offences, among them crimes as various as fraud, embezzlement, racism and xenophobia. The EAW facilitates fast and easy extradition of suspects between EU Member States. This legislation built upon two earlier EU extradition conventions, the 1995 Convention on Simplified Extradition between Member States of the EU (covering 'voluntary' agreement to extradition) and the 1996 Convention Relating to Extradition (covering 'involuntary' extradition). Previous experience using these Conventions demonstrated how problematic implementation of EU Conventions could be, with extended delays in securing national ratification. On September 11th only two-thirds of Member States had ratified both, but by July 2002, only two States (France and Italy) had yet to commit themselves. These conventions have now come into force, and indeed, since then this measure has been coupled with 'mutual recognition of measures on the taking of evidence' in the electronic sphere (Presidency of the Council of the EU, 2002, p 14).

The roadmap was a most significant boost to third pillar institution building, as evidenced by the commitment to the full launch of EuroJust, already committed to at Tampere (JHA Council, 2001). It was July 2002 before rules of procedure and agreement on Community funding had been settled (Presidency of the Council of the EU, 2002, p 12). Comprising essentially of a single representative of each Member State, EuroJust is a system for the provision of legal advice to investigators, prosecutors and judges. It assists with requests for international judicial assistance and liaises with the EU's Anti-Fraud Office on prosecutions (Council of the EU, 2002e). EuroJust can act in a number of 'formations': either as a whole 'College', or with two or more Member States representatives, or even with just one Member State representative providing assistance (Council of the EU, 2002e; Monar, 2003, p 127). EuroJust was empowered not only to work with Joint Investigation Teams, but may also take the initiative and ask individual Member States to launch operations (but it may not compel such action). EuroJust's *modus operandi* is essentially threefold: to provide operational legal advice to law enforcement agencies; to maintain an index of investigations; and to facilitate the exchange of relevant data with international organisations and third countries (Council of the EU, 2002e).

In the key area of EU-USA relations, the roadmap sought to enhance policy co-operation within the 'Transatlantic Dialogue' (EU-USA, 1995). JHA co-operation was a long-standing feature of the (secret) EU-USA Transatlantic Dialogue but, subsequent to September 11th, there was a clearer focus on operational police and judicial activities. This facilitated US participation in EU counter-terrorist task forces and the counter-terrorist analytical unit established at Europol. It enabled

---

6 By COREPER. Versions include those of October 2001 (12800/01 REV 1), April 2002 (7686/02), May 2002 (8547/02), July 2002 (10773/02 REV 2).

intelligence gathering, analysis and co-ordination of police operations, as well as the extension of contacts with EuroJust. Informal exchange of intelligence with the US authorities preceded formal agreements on information exchange (JHA Council, 2001). The first such agreement dealt with strategic intelligence exchange with Europol and was signed in December 2001. This extended beyond terrorism to include other forms of serious crime. Following this came two more legal agreements. First, a joint agreement on the exchange of intelligence, including personal data (Council of the EU, 2001f, pp 1–2), was approved at the November 2002 JHA Council following discussions with the Joint Supervisory Body responsible for overseeing data protection issues at Europol (Council of the EU, 2002a, p 25). Secondly, there were complementary agreements based on Art 38 of the TEU which concerned EU-USA extradition and mutual legal assistance. This was the first of its kind, and again it extended beyond terrorism to serious crime in general (Statewatch, 2002). The latter agreement was regarded as somewhat controversial because the USA still makes use of the death penalty – anathema to many European countries. But again, this kind of agreement was already envisaged at Tampere (Council of the EU, 1999, para 60). These agreements were sealed in July 2003 (Council of the EU, 2003).

The post-September 11th developments should be seen in the context of the longer-standing development of practical operational capacities for EU police co-operation. Reflecting back, it can be seen that the 1995 *New Transatlantic Agenda* was a wide-ranging co-operation agreement accompanied by a detailed Joint Action Plan. The Plan details measures including 'establishing interim co-operative measures between competent US authorities and the Europol Drugs Unit and [to] begin implementing the possibilities provided for in the convention on Europol' (EU-USA, 1995, p 24). In 1996, the JHA Council was already considering a formal Protocol entitled 'Access of the United States to the Data Held by the Europol Drugs Unit' (Statewatch, 1996, p 2) but, due to the Byzantian nature of EU decision making, no agreement was sealed. After September 11th, the operational imperative is palpable: the EU Task Force on Counter Terrorism began operating within Europol (with American officers based there). Following the agreement on the EU-USA Mutual Legal Assistance Treaty, prior agreements between EU Member States to allow the formation of Joint Investigation Teams for specific operational projects could be extended to allow participation of US personnel. These can take place in connection with a fully-fledged EuroJust.

The extension of legal and investigative powers across the territory of the EU, and under the rubric of counter-terrorism, is significant. These initiatives have significantly deepened integration of the 'security' aspects of the EU's project to create an Area of Freedom, Security and Justice (Monar, 2000, pp 140–41; Grabbe, 2001, pp 73–75). It has also transformed the nature of the Union's external relations vis-à-vis Justice and Home Affairs. Achieving these outcomes has required significant cross-pillar co-ordination. The high priority given to counter-terrorism undoubtedly provided the EU policy makers with a facilitative environment to achieve already established plans and objectives set out in the 1997 Treaty of Amsterdam and the Tampere European Council on JHA.

Conclusion

Developing European policing strategies against transnational and organised crime continues to be a key challenge for the Union. The period after September 11th was one of substantial institutional and legislative development. However, what this chapter shows is that the majority of these achievements were already mapped out at the Tampere Summit in 1999. This raises questions about the longer-standing pattern of development of JHA issues within the EU, ongoing since 1993. Why has the governance of the third pillar been so problematic? Is the EU now in a position to make sustained progress in the implementation of European strategies to counter transnational and organised crime?

Prior to September 11th, the pace of JHA integration was slow and sporadic but nevertheless achieved a number of major breakthroughs. The initial formalisation of JHA police, customs and immigration co-operation was a good beginning, but the ambitions for the development of Europol were slow in coming. In the mid-1990s, under the Irish Presidency, the EU push against organised crime was accelerated and this was, at least to some extent, sustained in the Treaty of Amsterdam. However, implementation of the AFSJ, was slow in the lead up to the most high profile EU event for JHA – the Tampere Summit. The *Conclusions* of Tampere demonstrated that the heads of state had learnt the lesson of the Irish Presidency – the expediency of a strategic focus on threats such as organised crime. However, it was also clear that the EU policing strategies could not be effective in tackling transnational offending into the Union if Europol's reach could not be developed to other third countries and major international police organisations. The developing external relations strategy in justice and home affairs, pushed to the fore with the Irish and subsequent UK Presidencies in 1996–97, was a necessary precursor to the major developments in the post-September 11th context. Significant operational police and judicial engagement now exists between the EU and the USA, which includes agreements for mutual stationing of liaison officers, extradition, mutual legal assistance and prospective American involvement in pan-European Joint Investigation Teams. The relationship between EU and USA criminal police and judicial authorities is one thread in a web of global relationships that comprise a global strategy against transnational and organised crime.

Questions as to whether the EU can sustain the pace of progress are ultimately based on an assessment of third pillar governance. Is it capable of continued development in this sphere? The evidence from the post-1996 period seems to suggest that action plans, deadlines and Commission and Council monitoring of individual Member States' obligations to implement policy and legislative agreements contributed substantially to the effectiveness of the governance regime. Further, the commitment to multi-annual strategic planning of work, spanning a number of Presidencies, was established during this time, thus anticipating key reforms in the draft Constitution that, as of this writing, is yet to be agreed and ratified. These can be regarded as evidence of a development away from previous pattern of discontinuous JHA integration.

It is likely that the ongoing development of the operational capacities of Europol and EuroJust (which now extends to third parties, that is, the EU-USA agreements) have passed the point of no return. National criminal justice systems could not easily be detached from this web of co-operation agreements. The political impetus for continued growth in the sphere of transnational policing remains clear even some time after September 11th, and the prospects of the further extension of this web of co-operation to other countries seem clear. Perhaps at that point, an unambiguous assessment of the effectiveness of transnational policing strategies against transnational crime and other sources of insecurity can be made.

References

Anderson, SS and Burns, TR (1998) 'The European Union and the erosion of parliamentary democracy: a study of post-parliamentary governance', in Anderson, AS and Eliassen, KA (eds), *The European Union: How Democratic Is It?*, London: Sage, pp 227–51

den Boer, M (2000) 'The fight against terrorism in the second and third pillars of the Maastricht Treaty: complement or overlap?', in Reinares, F (ed), *European Democracies Against Terrorism: Governmental Policies and Intergovernmental Co-operation*, Aldershot: Ashgate, pp 211–26

den Boer, M (ed) (2002) *Organized Crime; A Catalyst in the Europeanisation of National Police and Prosecution Agencies?*, Maastricht: European Institute of Public Administration

den Boer, M and Monar, J (2002) '11 September and the challenge of global terrorism to the EU as a security actor' 40 *Journal of Common Market Studies* (Supplement 1) 11–28

Council of the EU (1995) *Report on the Council of Ministers on the Functioning of the Treaty on European Union*, Cmnd 2866, London: HMSO

Council of the EU (1997) *Achievements in the Field of Justice and Home Affairs in 1997*, Report for the Council to the European Council, 13191/1/97, Brussels: Council of the EU

Council of the EU (1998) 'Joint Action of 29 June 1998 adopted by the Council on the basis of Article K3 of the Treaty on European Union, on the creation of a European Judicial Network (98/428/JHA)' 1 *Official Journal*, L 191, 7 July, Brussels: Commission of the European Communities, pp 4–7, http://europa.eu.int/eur-lex/pri/en/oj/dat/1998/l_191/ l_19119980707en00040007.pdf, accessed 25 February 2005

Council of the EU (1999) *Presidency Conclusions: Tampere European Council*, Brussels: Council of the EU, http://europa.eu.int/european_council/conclusions/index_en.htm, accessed 25 February 2005

Council of the EU (2000) *The Prevention and Control of Organised Crime: A European Union Strategy for the Beginning of the New Millennium*, Note from Article 36 Committee to COREPER/Council, 6611/00, Brussels: Council of the EU, http://ue.eu.int/ueDocs/cms_Data/docs/dynadoc/jo/jai/EN/ST006611_00ORI EN.pdf, accessed 25 February 2005

Council of the EU (2001a) 'Programme of measures to implement the principle of mutual recognition of decisions in criminal matters', *Official Journal*, C 012, 15 January, Brussels: Commission of the European Communities, pp 10–22

Council of the EU (2001b) 'Council Decision of 6 December 2001 extending Europol's mandate to deal with the serious forms of international crime listed in the Annex to the Europol Convention', *Official Journal*, C 362, Brussels: Commission of the European Communities, p 1

Council of the EU (2001c) 'Council Common Position of 27 December 2001 on the application of specific measures to combat terrorism', *Official Journal*, L 344, 28 December, Brussels: Commission of the European Communities, pp 93–96, http://europa.eu.int/smartapi/cgi/sga_doc?smartapi!celexapi!prod!CELEXnum doc&lg=EN&numdoc=32001E0931&model=guichett, accessed 25 February 2005

Council of the EU (2001d) *Working Methods in the JHA Area*, Outcome of Proceedings: Article 36 Committee to COREPER, 10336/01, Brussels: Council of the EU

Council of the EU (2001e) *Presidency Conclusions: European Council Meeting in Laeken*, Brussels: Council of the EU, http://europa.eu.int/european_council/conclusions/index_en.htm, accessed 25 February 2005

Council of the EU (2002a) *European Union Action to Combat Terrorism – Update of the Roadmap*, Presidency Note to the Council (General Affairs), 10773/2/02, Brussels: Council of the EU, www.statewatch.org/news/2002/jul/rm10773-r2.pdf, accessed 25 February 2005

Council of the EU (2002b) *Working Methods in the Council (JHA Area): JHA Activities other than Legislative Work*, Note from General Secretariat to COREPER, 5515/02, Brussels: Council of the EU

Council of the EU (2002c) 'Council Framework Decision of 13 June 2002 on Joint Investigation Teams', *Official Journal*, L 162, 23 May, Brussels: Commission of the European Communities, pp 1–3

Council of the EU (2002d) *Council Decision on the Signing of the Euro-Mediterranean Agreement Establishing an Association Between the European Community and its Member States and the People's Democratic Republic of Algeria*, 6786/02, Brussels: Council of the EU

Council of the EU (2002e) 'Council Decision of 28 February setting up EuroJust with a view to reinforcing the fight against serious crime (2002/187/JHA)', *Official Journal*, L 63/1, Brussels: Commission of the European Communities, http://europa.eu.int/eur-lex/pri/en/oj/dat/2002/l_063/l_06320020306en00010013.pdf, accessed 25 February 2005

Council of the EU (2002f) *Presidency Conclusions: Seville European Council 21 and 22 June 2002*, Brussels: Council of the EU, http://europa.eu.int/european_council/conclusions/index_en.htm, accessed 25 February 2005

Council of the EU (2003) 'Council Decision of 6 June 2003 concerning the signature of the Agreement between the EU and the USA on extradition and mutual legal assistance in criminal matters', *Official Journal of the European Communities*, L181, 19 July, Brussels: Commission of the European Communities, pp 25–26

Curtin, D (1993) 'The constitutional structure of the Union: a Europe of bits and pieces' 30 *Common Market Law Review* 17–69

Curtin, D (2001) 'The European Commission's White Paper on governance: a vista of unbearable democratic lightness in the EU?' 11(6) *Statewatch Bulletin* 4–7

Duff, A (ed) (1997) *The Treaty of Amsterdam: Text and Commentary*, London: Federal Trust

European Commission (2001a) *European Governance: A White Paper*, COM (2001) 428 final, 2 July, Brussels: Commission of the European Communities

European Commission (2001b) *Proposal for a Council Framework Decision on Combating Terrorism*, COM (2001) 521 final, 19 September, Brussels: Commission of the European Communities, http://europa.eu.int/comm/justice_home/unit/terrorism/terrorism_sg_en.pdf, accessed 25 February 2005

European Commission (2001c) *Proposal for a Council Framework Decision on the European Arrest Warrant and the Surrender Procedures Between the Member States*, COM (2001) 522 final, 19 September, Brussels: Commission of the European Communities

European Commission (2001d) *Proposal for a Council Regulation on Specific Restrictive Measures Directed Against Certain Persons and Entities with a View to Combating International Terrorism (Presented by the Commission)*, COM (2001) 569 final, 2 October, Brussels: Commission of the European Communities, www.statewatch.org/news/2001/ oct/FINANCE.PDF, accessed 25 February 2005

European Commission (2002a) *Biannual Update of The Scoreboard to Review Progress on the Creation of an 'Area of Freedom, Security and Justice' in the European Union (first half 2002)*, COM (2002) 261 final, 30 May, Brussels: Commission of the European Communities

European Commission (2002b) *European Governance: Better Lawmaking*, COM (2002) 275 final, 5 June, Brussels: Commission of the European Communities

European Commission (2002c) *Action Plan: Simplifying and Improving the Regulatory Environment*, COM (2002) 278 final, 5 June, Brussels: Commission of the European Communities

European Commission (2002d) *Regional Co-operation Programme in the Field of Justice, in Combating Drugs, Organised Crime and Terrorism: Framework Document*, EuroMed Report Issue No 44, Brussels: Commission of the European Communities

European Convention on the Future of Europe (2002a) *Convention on the Future of Europe*, Brussels: European Convention, european-convention.eu.int/bienvenue. asp?lang=EN, accessed 25 February 2005

European Convention on the Future of Europe (2002b) *Justice and Home Affairs: Progress Report and General Problems*, Cover Note from Praesidium to Convention, CONV 69/02, Brussels: European Convention

European Convention on the Future of Europe (2002c) *Mandate of Working Group X 'Freedom, Security and Justice'*, Note from Secretariat to the Convention, CONV 258/02 WG X3, Brussels: European Convention

European Convention on the Future of Europe (2003) *Draft Treaty Establishing a Constitution for Europe*, CONV 850/03, 18 July, Brussels: European Convention, european-convention.eu.int/docs/Treaty/cv00850.en03.pdf, accessed 25 February 2005

EU-USA (1995) *New Transatlantic Agenda and Action Plan*, General Secretariat of the Council of the EU, Press Release 12296/95, Brussels: Council of the EU

EU-USA (2001) *Joint US-EU Ministerial Statement on Combating Terrorism*, Press Release, 20 September 2001, Brussels: Council of the EU

Europol (2003) *Factsheet on Europol*, January, The Hague: Europol, www.europol.eu.int/ataglance/facts/files/2003/2003-01-01-E-EN-FactSheet.doc, accessed 25 February 2005

Grabbe, H (2001) 'Breaking new ground in internal security', in Bannerman, E, Everts, S, Grabbe, H, Grant, C and Murray, A (eds), *Europe After September 11th*, London: Centre for European Reform, pp 63–75

Hayes-Renshaw, F and Wallace, H (1997) *The Council of Ministers*, Basingstoke: Macmillan

Home Affairs Committee (1990) *Practical Police Co-operation in the European Community*, 7th Report, House of Commons, Session 1989–90, HC 363-I and II, Vol I and Vol II, London: HMSO

Horeth, M (1999) 'No way out for the beast? The unsolved legitimacy problem of European governance' 6(2) *Journal of European Public Policy* 249–68

International Press Institute (2000) *Veronica Guerin: International Press Institute Report*, Missouri, USA: International Press Institute, 6(2), www.freemedia.at/IPIReport/Heroes_IPIReport2.00/20Guerin.htm, accessed 25 February 2005

JHA Council (2001) *Conclusions Adopted by the Council (Justice and Home Affairs) Brussels*, SN 3926/6/01, Brussels: Council of the EU

Monar, J (2000) 'Justice and home affairs' 38 *Journal of Common Market Studies* (Supplement 1) 747–64

Monar, J (2001) 'The dynamics of justice and home affairs: laboratories, driving factors and costs' 39(4) *Journal of Common Market Studies* 747–64

Monar, J (2002) 'Justice and home affairs' 40 *Journal of Common Market Studies* (Supplement 1) 121–36

Monar, J (2003) 'Justice and home affairs' 41 *Journal of Common Market Studies* (Supplement 1) 119–36

Muller-Graff, P-C (1994) 'the legal bases of the third pillar and its position in the framework of the Union Treaty' 31 *Common Market Law Review* 493–510

NCIS (2002) *National Criminal Intelligence Service Annual Report 2001–2*, London: NCIS, www.ncis.gov.uk/downloads/NCISAnnualRep2002.pdf, accessed 25 February 2005

Neunreither, K (1994) 'The democratic deficit of the European Union: towards closer co-operation between the European Parliament and the national parliaments' 29(3) *Government and Opposition* 299–314

Norman, P (1999) 'European Union police policy-making and co-operation', in Carr, F and Massey, A (eds), *Public Policy in the New Europe: Eurogovernance in Theory and Practice*, Aldershot: Edward Elgar Publishing, pp 104–22

Norman, P (2001) 'Policing "high tech crime" in the global context: the role of transnational policy networks', in Wall, DS (ed), *Crime and the Internet*, London: Routledge, pp 184–94

O'Keefe, D (1995) 'Recasting the third pillar' 32 *Common Market Law Review* 893–920

Presidency of the Council of the EU (1998) *Progress Report on Organised Crime to the Cardiff European Council*, Note from the Presidency to European Council, 7303/3/98, Brussels: Council of the EU

Presidency of the Council of the EU (2000) *European Union Priorities and Policy Objectives for External Relations in the Field of Justice and Home Affairs*, Item Note from COREPER to General Affairs Council/European Council, 7653/00, Brussels: Council of the EU

Presidency of the Council of the EU (2001a) *Evaluation of the Conclusions of the Tampere European Council*, Note from Presidency to General Affairs Council/European Council, 14926/01, Brussels: Council of the EU

Presidency of the Council of the EU (2001b) *European Union Action Following the Attacks in the United States*, Presidency Report to European Council, 14919/1/01, Brussels: Council of the EU

Presidency of the Council of the EU (2002) *European Union Action Plan to Combat Terrorism – Update of the Roadmap*, Presidency Note to Council (General Affairs), 10773/2/02, Brussels: Council of the EU

Sheptycki, JWE (1996) 'Law enforcement, justice and democracy in the transnational arena' 24(1) *International Journal of the Sociology of Law* 61–75

Sheptycki, JWE (1997) 'Transnationalism, crime control and the European state system; a review of the literature' 7 *International Criminal Justice Review* 130–40

Sheptycki, JWE (1998) 'Policing, postmodernity and transnationalisation' 38(3) *British Journal of Criminology* 485–503

Sheptycki, JWE (2002) *In Search of Transnational Policing*, Aldershot: Ashgate

Statewatch (1996) 'Council of Justice and Home Affairs: beef ban conflict dominates the meeting in Luxembourg on 4 June' 6(3) *Statewatch Bulletin* 18–19

Statewatch (2001) 'Letter from the US Mission to the EU to President Prodi', in *US Letter to from Bush to EU*, 16 October, Statewatch Analysis No 2, London: Statewatch, pp 2–5

Statewatch (2002) 'Secret EU-US agreement on criminal co-operation being negotiated', *Statewatch Analysis* No 12, London: Statewatch

Statewatch (2003) *SEMDOC Legislative Observatory*, updated 28 November 2003, London: Statewatch, www.statewatch.org/semdoc/observatory/legobs4contents.html, accessed 25 February 2005

Wallace, H (2001) *The Future of Europe Debate: Opportunities for British Policy*, One Europe or Several Policy Paper, May, Brighton: University of Sussex, www.one-europe.ac.uk/pdf/p5wallace.pdf, accessed 25 February 2005

Wrench, P (1998) 'The G8 and transnational organised crime', in Cullen, PJ and Gilmore, WC (eds), *Crime Sans Frontiers: International and European Legal Approaches*, Hume Papers in Public Policy, 6(1 & 2), Edinburgh: Edinburgh UP, pp 39–43

Conclusion

Chapter 15
Globalisation, Reflexivity and the Practice of Criminology
Janet Chan

Introduction

Criminology at the end of the 20th century was said to be in a state of fragmentation (Ericson and Carriere, 1994), stricken by a chronic sense of failure (Hogg, 1996), identity crisis (Pavarini, 1994) and recurring ambivalence (Garland, 1996). This chapter examines recent theorising of broader social and political trends in modern societies and discusses their implications for the practice of criminology. It is suggested that processes of globalisation and reflexivity have already led to changes in both the status of criminology and the politics of criminal justice policy. First of all, globalisation has facilitated the 'free trade' of criminological knowledge and ideologies and accelerated the deterritorialisation of culture and politics. Under 'reflexive modernisation' (Beck, Giddens and Lash, 1994), in which social processes are 'turned back' upon themselves, criminology as science is increasingly being challenged, not only from within the discipline in the form of academic critique, but also from without, in the arena of law and order politics. At the same time, criminologists and criminal justice policies are increasingly being 'governed' by 'technologies of performance' and the 'technologies of agency' as part of 'reflexive government' in advanced liberal societies (Dean, 1999). While these interpretations of social and political trends should not be read as deterministic, they provide ways of seeing and understanding the challenges facing criminology in the new millennium.

The state of criminology

Let us explore the 'crisis' of criminology, as evidenced by the instability and fragmentation of the discipline and the contradictory and ambivalent tendencies of contemporary policy. The notion that criminology is in crisis is not new. The 'failure' of criminology has been a 'recurrent motif within debates concerned to evaluate the contemporary state of criminology' (Hogg, 1996, pp 43, 47; see also Cohen, 1988; Braithwaite, 1989). This failure is alternately seen as related to criminology's inability to 'prescribe policies that will work to reduce crime' (Braithwaite, 1989, p 133) or the absence of a critical edge among its 'mainstream' practitioners (Taylor, Walton and Young, 1973; Cohen, 1981). But the crisis of criminology is not limited to its lack of impact on policy or politics, it relates more crucially to the self-image of the discipline. Pavarini pronounced some years ago that criminology 'is now facing a situation of crisis of identity so profound that we may have serious doubts about its capacity for survival as presently constituted' (1994, p 43). For Pavarini, part of this identity crisis relates to the repetitive and banal exercise of unmasking the 'naturalistic fallacy' of crime and punishment that criminology has engaged in over the past 20 years. But this 'permanent state of precariousness and crisis, this recurrent temptation towards suicide' is also a consequence of criminology's 'confused claims to knowledge', its 'parasitic' relation to other branches of science and the unregulated fluidity of its disciplinary boundaries (Pavarini, 1994, pp 50–51).

Another manifestation of this crisis is found in the contradictory nature of criminal justice policy. Garland (1996) has observed in the UK and elsewhere a trend in official criminology that is 'increasingly dualistic, increasingly polarised, and increasingly ambivalent':

> There is a *criminology of the self*, that characterises offenders as rational consumers, just like us; and there is a *criminology of the other*, of the threatening outcast, the fearsome stranger, the excluded and the embittered. One is invoked to routinise crime, to allay disproportionate fears and to promote preventive action. The other is concerned to demonise the criminal, to excite popular fears and hostilities, and to promote support for state punishment (Garland, 1996, p 461).

The result of this ambivalence is that punitive policies coexist with strategies aimed at 'normalising crime, responsibilising others and defining deviance down', but while the latter are 'premised upon consolidated research results and clear administrative rationalities', the former are driven by political considerations (Garland, 1996, p 462; see Chan, 1999).

In order to better understand the challenges facing criminology in the millennium that stretches before us, it is useful to examine recent theorising about the broader social and political trends in modern societies. Processes of globalisation and reflexive modernisation are particularly interesting because of the consequences entailed for criminology as a science, criminal justice policies and the politics of law and order.

Before studying these broader trends, however, it is important to emphasise the existing diversity of criminological practices across the OECD countries. Instead of making the usual distinction between 'administrative criminology' and 'academic criminology', I have found it useful (see Chan, 1996)[1] to conceptualise the practice of criminology in terms of the Bourdieuian framework of the 'field' (of power and capital) and 'habitus' – those taken for granted aspects of research practice which 'delimit the thinkable and predetermine the thought' – of criminology (Bourdieu and Wacquant, 1992, pp 39–40). Ericson, who defines a criminologist as 'someone who uses abstractions of crime and security to establish institutional and professional jurisdiction over social problems' (1996, p 19), has provided a survey of the 'field' occupied by criminologists, both within and outside of the academy. Ericson found that the production of academic criminology takes place in a diversity of 'university organisation, paradigms, research funding, publication outlets and professional association', although the 'field' of academic criminology is not a 'pluralistic and level playing' one (Ericson, 1996, p 17). Rather, it is a 'space of conflict and competition' (Bourdieu and Wacquant, 1992, p 17) over power and resources: winners of 'criminological jurisdiction' owe much of their success to the strength of their location in academic institutions, the dominance of their theoretical or political paradigms, the access they have to research funding, the prestige of their publishers and the power of their professional associations (Ericson, 1996). Criminologists also occupy a hierarchy of organisations outside the academy.

---

1 Several excerpts from Chan (1996) are integrated into this text without attribution to avoid the use of cumbersome and extended quotations.

Within government agencies, for example, power and resources are usually more available in units with connection to criminal law, courts, the judiciary, police or the legal profession, compared with units dealing with community services, juvenile justice or corrective services. Similarly, differences in status and resources between criminologists who work for private consultancy firms and those who are employed in community organisations are particularly stark.

In terms of habitus, it has been pointed out that criminologists do not operate under a homogeneous set of theoretical traditions (Chan, 1996). For example, criminologists who work under a predominantly positivist tradition make different assumptions, employ different methods of data collection and analysis, and abide by different criteria of validity from those working under a social constructionist, feminist or poststructuralist tradition. Such variations may also be found among different disciplines: for example, historians, psychologists, economists and lawyers are likely to develop research practices that overlap only minimally. Similarly, the habituses of university academics are not likely to share many common features with those of policy analysts in government agencies and private firms, although the competitive pressure for policy-relevant research funding may have narrowed these gaps (O'Malley, 1996).

In the following sections I will draw on recent theoretical analyses of modern societies to describe the broader social and political trends which may have implications for the practice of criminology. Three major bodies of work will be drawn upon: the literature on globalisation; theories of reflexive modernisation; and studies of 'governmentality'. While there have been concerns that these bodies of work are not compatible,[2] and hence it is inappropriate to bring them together in one paper, I am persuaded by Garland's argument that there is no reason why governmentality studies and sociological theories should be regarded as mutually exclusive, and that much can be gained from encouraging a 'more fruitful dialogue ... between these forms of work' (Garland, 1997, p 205).

Globalisation

Globalisation has become, as Bauman (1998, p 1) suggests, 'a fad word fast turning into a shibboleth'. Giddens (1990, p 64) defines globalisation as 'the intensification of worldwide social relations which link distant localities in such a way that local happenings are shaped by events occurring many miles away and vice versa'. Globalisation is therefore a two way process. Tomlinson's notion of 'complex connectivity' best captures the condition of globalisation: 'the rapidly developing and ever-densening network of interconnections and interdependencies that characterise modern social life' (1999, p 2). These connections or linkages exist in a variety of 'modalities' – social, institutional, material, symbolic as well as technological. Globalisation, for Giddens, is not simply an 'out there' phenomenon

---

2 O'Malley (1996, p 36) has criticised the type of analysis which 'render criminology merely an effect of determining social forces' as 'profoundly disabling' since it assumes such social forces as 'unproblematic realities'. His preference was to study the links between criminological thinking and political rationalities, because 'the placing of criminology in the realm of the political renders the terrain of the discipline far more contingent and thus constestable' (O'Malley, 1996, p 36).

(that is, the development of social relations of a worldwide kind far removed from the concerns of everyday life), but also an 'in here' matter (that is, related to even the most intimate aspects of our lives).

When globalisation is mentioned in the context of criminal justice, the usual concern is how to deal with the threat of transnational or organised crimes (Nelken, 1997, p 253); this chapter is, however, more concerned with the extent to which criminology and criminal justice policies have been affected by globalisation. This is not to deny that some connection exists between crime trends and trends in criminal justice policies, but globalisation's effect on criminology and policy is not necessarily related to its effect on crime.

Globalisation and criminology

As an 'expert system', criminology has always been global in its orientation. As Giddens has argued, expert systems form one type of 'disembedding mechanism' in late modernity, that is, a mechanism which 'lifts out' social relations from local contexts and then restructures them across 'indefinite spans of time-space' (Giddens, 1990, p 21):

> In its modern guise at least, expertise is in principle devoid of local attachments. In an ideal-typical way, it could be said that all forms of 'local knowledge' under the rule of expertise become local recombinations of knowledge derived from elsewhere. Obviously in practice things are more complicated than this, owing to the continuing importance of local habits, customs or traditions ... [E]xpertise is disembedding because it is based upon impersonal principles, which can be set out and developed without regard to context ... Expert systems decontextualize as an intrinsic consequence of the impersonal and contingent character of their rules of knowledge-acquisition; as decentred systems, 'open' to whosoever has the time, resources and talent to grasp them, they can be located anywhere. Place is not in any sense a quality relevant to their validity; and places themselves ... take on a different significance from traditional locales (Giddens, 1994, pp 84–85).

It may be that the increased popularity of the English language and advances in modern transport and communication technologies has made a difference to the extent to which knowledge is globalised, but criminology has always had a transnational and even transcontinental existence.[3] Van Swaaningen's (1999) observation that the centre of criminological thinking has shifted from Europe to America since the 1940s is illustrative of this (albeit unidirectional) globalising tendency:

> Since its emergence in the second half of last century until World War II, European criminology was the major source of inspiration for Anglo-American students of crime and crime control. The Belgian Adolphe Quetelet, the Italian Enrico Ferri, the Frenchman Gabriel Tarde, the Dutchman Willem Bonger: which self-respecting criminologist would not know them? ... After World War II, the dominant stream of

---

3 A small illustration of this is found, quite by accident, in a second-hand copy of the English translation of Raffaele Garofalo's *Criminology* (published by Heinemann in London in 1914, under the auspices of the American Institute of Criminal Law and Criminology) I picked up in a Sydney bookshop. The book once belonged to the Queensland Parliamentary Library, whose stamp, dated 23 July 1914, was found in several pages of the book. The acquisition of this book by an Australian library within the same year of its publication in England in 1914 is truly remarkable, something not always achievable even in these days of Amazon.com.

influence and inspiration turned around. From now on the wind would blow from the 'new' to the 'old' world. New developments on the European continent were no longer introduced in the English-speaking world. Now English succeeded French as the academic *lingua franca*, Anglo-American studies became much more widely read in Europe. Which European criminologist would currently not know Shaw and MacKay, Edwin Sutherland, Howard Becker or indeed Travis Hirschi? Many North American scholars have left their traces in continental European criminology and criminal justice policy alike (van Swaaningen, 1999, pp 8–9).

Van Swaaningen's observation is consistent with the general perception that American criminology pays little attention to developments elsewhere, as it sees itself as the centre of globalised knowledge.[4] Nevertheless, Giddens maintains that, unlike its earlier phase, today's globalisation is a two way process, and not synonymous with Western imperialism:

> Although still dominated by western power, globalisation today can no longer be spoken of only as a matter of one way imperialism. Action at a distance was always a two way process; now, increasingly, however, there is no obvious 'direction' to globalisation at all, as its ramifications are more or less ever present. The current phase of globalisation, then, should not be confused with the preceding one, whose structures it acts increasingly to subvert (Giddens, 1994, p 96).

The global influence of John Braithwaite's work (see Cohn and Farrington, 1998, p 167, where Braithwaite ranked as the fifth most cited scholar between 1991 and 1995 in the four international criminology journals analysed) lends support to Giddens' conclusion that the traditional centre-periphery distinction may have become less clear cut.

Globalisation and criminal justice

If criminology has always been global in orientation, what about criminal justice policy and practice? As Nelken has warned, it is important to distinguish between two consequences of globalisation, homogenisation and interdependence, since 'interdependence does not necessarily presume or produce homogeneity' (1997, pp 260–61). Sheptycki (1998) reminds us that transnational policing has always been around and it involves both interdependence and homogenisation. Nevertheless, more recent developments such as the 'opening up of global markets, the information revolution, and the end of the Cold War' have contributed to an exponential growth of transnational policing (Sheptycki, 1998, pp 496–97).

The homogenising influence of globalisation on criminal justice is most evident: from the traditional use of prisons, juvenile courts, fines, probation, parole, to the modern introduction of community service orders, situational crime prevention, community policing, private jails and restorative justice, it is obvious that global exportation of criminal justice policies has been around for a very long time (see Nelken, 1997, p 263). Zimring predicts that as a result of growing economic and cultural interdependency between nations in the developed world, 'common

---

4   Cohn and Farrington's (1998) tables show that the vast majority of 'most-cited scholars' cited in the American journal *Criminology* are American, whereas many more 'foreign' scholars appeared in the corresponding lists for the British, Canadian and Australian/New Zealand journals studied.

normative standards and technology transfer will push toward convergence in criminal justice practices and standards':

> What the police and prisons do in Texas or Brisbane to criminals can be a matter of great concern to citizens and government in foreign nations because of high mobility. In the United States, executions in Texas of Latin-American nationals cause riots in Mexico and South America. In Australia, death sentences for drugs in Singapore or Malaysia are a *cause célèbre* when Australian nationals are involved, and American media go into states of high arousal for months when an American teen is sentenced to caning [in Singapore].[5] But it is not just the punishment of foreign nationals that makes a nation's criminal punishment and policy into other people's business. To the extent that nations group themselves into communities of common interest and function, minimum standards of decency and fairness in policy, in justice system procedures, and in punishment are of increasing importance (Zimring, 1999, pp 3–4).

Examples of 'normative convergence' cited by Zimring include the abolition of capital punishment and the convergence in national imprisonment rates in many developed countries, except the United States. While technological pressure is not considered to be as strong as normative pressure, Zimring predicts, nevertheless, that 'technology transfer' is an important force behind the convergence of criminal justice policy:

> The other great force for convergence in criminal justice policy is international flow of information and rhetoric. Part of this is technological transfer as the best practices in policing and forensics get known in international circles. DNA is important in Sydney within two years of being important in Los Angeles. Part of this is transmission of trends and styles. This year's fashions in criminal justice travel almost as fast as this year's skirt length does from Paris to Perth (Zimring, 1999, p 6).

Convergence of criminal justice policy is, of course, not always seen as a positive development. For example, the 'exporting' of inappropriate criminal justice policy from powerful nations to others is a controversial area (see Chan, 1994, in relation to the privatisation of prisons in New South Wales). Nelken points also to the threat of transnational policing to democracy:

> [The fear] is that police forces are in fact using these fears about transnational crime to forge alliances which are not democratically accountable. America has long been in the lead here in exporting abroad its war against drugs and terrorism, but in Europe this is also well illustrated by the interstate TREVI or EUROPOL policing arrangements; the European Commission itself only has observer status, the European Parliament still less say. Criminal justice is thus globalising along with everything else (and in the same way) and efforts at transnational police action represent a real danger to democratic structures which themselves presuppose the national state (Nelken, 1997, p 254).

---

5   In May 1994 an American youth by the name of Michael Fay, living an expatriate lifestyle with his parents in Singapore, was found guilty of vandalism. Fay was arrested in Singapore in October 1993 on 53 counts of vandalism, including spray painting cars. After pleading guilty to reduced charges, he was sentenced to four months in prison and given a $2,230 (Singapore dollars) fine. He was also given four strokes with a ratan cane in Queenstown Remand Prison, Singapore. At the time, the sentence and caning caused immense international media interest. In Singapore, the event was news because the boy involved was American, as well as being young, good looking and having highly vocal parents. Although the sentencing of a young American drew the practice of corporal punishment for criminal wrongdoing into the international spotlight for some months, canings far worse than his were, and still are, daily events in Singapore and other places in south-east Asia.

Bauman goes as far as to suggest that the escalation of punitive 'law and order' policies may be a cultural consequence of globalisation:

> The complex issue of existential insecurity brought about by the process of globalisation tends to be reduced to the apparently straightforward issue of 'law and order'. On the way, concerns with 'safety', more often than not trimmed down to the single issue worry about the safety of the body and personal possessions, are 'overloaded', by being charged with anxieties generated by other, crucial dimensions of present day existence – insecurity and uncertainty (Bauman, 1998, p 5).

The 'condensation' of the problems of insecurity and uncertainty brought about by (economic) globalisation into anxiety about personal safety is attractive for politicians, who 'can be supposed to be doing something about the first two just because being seen to be vociferous and vigorous about the third' (Bauman, 1998, p 117). Governments are therefore reduced to the role of fighting crime to provide a 'safe environment' for market forces to operate in a global economy:

> In the world of global finances, state governments are allotted the role of little else than oversized police precincts; the quantity and quality of the policemen on the beat, sweeping the streets clean of beggars, pesterers and pilferers, and the tightness of the jail walls loom large among the factors of 'investors' confidence', and so among the items calculated when the decisions to invest or deinvest are made … The care of the 'orderly state', once a complex and convoluted task, reflecting the multiple ambitions and wide and multi-faceted sovereignty of the state, tends as a result to narrow to the task of fighting crime (Bauman, 1998, p 120).

Deterritorialisation of culture and politics

The homogenising effect of globalisation should not be exaggerated, especially in relation to cultural practices such as criminal justice policy. People still live in physical localities, even if they are connected to global events and actions (Tomlinson, 1999, p 9). What globalisation does is to transform 'the relationship between the *places* we inhabit and our cultural practices, experiences and identities' (Tomlinson, 1999, p 106). In other words, the 'local' is transformed as a result of the processes of globalisation, but not in the crude sense of losing its identity totally to the 'global'. Rather, the major cultural impact of globalisation is *deterritorialisation* – the 'local' is losing its capacity to define people's 'terms of existence':

> … complex connectivity weakens the ties of culture to place. This is in many ways a troubling phenomenon, involving the simultaneous penetration of local worlds by distant forces, and the dislodging of everyday meanings from their 'anchors' in the local environment. Embodiment and the forces of material circumstance keep most of us, most of the time, situated, but in places that are changing around us and gradually, subtly, losing their power to define the terms of our existence (Tomlinson, 1999, p 29).

Tomlinson admits, however, that deterritorialisation is by no means a universal or linear phenomenon – it is uneven and may be accompanied by resistance and countervailing tendencies – nor is it necessarily alienating or destructive in its consequences. Globalisation can widen people's awareness and experience, from an awareness of how global events can affect their lives to the experience of sampling other cultures through travel, food, entertainment and other consumer products. For most people, this 'weakening or dissolution of the connection between everyday lived culture and territorial location' is experienced as a mixed bag 'of familiarity and difference, expansion of cultural horizons and the increased perception of vulnerability, access to the "world out there" accompanied by penetration of our own private worlds, new opportunities and new risks' (Tomlinson, 1999, p 128).

Robertson's (1995) concept of 'glocalisation' helps capture the complexities of the relationship between the global and the local. Robertson seeks to transcend the debate about global homogenisation/heterogenisation by noting that both tendencies exist in late modernity and are 'mutually implicative' (1995, p 27). Borrowing the term from its business origin in micromarketing ('the tailoring and advertising of goods and services on a global or near global basis to increasingly differentiated local and particular markets'), Robertson does not see the local and the global as oppositional or having an 'action-reaction' relationship (1995, pp 28–29):

> ... globalisation has involved the reconstruction, in a sense the production, of 'home', 'community' and 'locality' ... To that extent the local is not best seen, at least as an analytic or interpretative departure point, as a counterpoint to the global. Indeed it can be regarded, subject to some qualifications, as *an aspect* of globalisation ... the concept of globalisation has involved the simultaneity and the interpenetration of what are conventionally called the global and the local, or – in more abstract vein – the universal and the particular (Robertson, 1995, p 30).

Globalisation, then, involves not simply the 'linking of localities', as in Tomlinson's notion of connectivity, but also the 'invention' of locality, indeed an institutionalised global creation of locality (Featherstone and Lash 1995, p 4).

How does the global construct the local? In spite of the relative ease and affordability of international travel in recent times, most people experience the outside world through the media (Giddens, 1991; Tomlinson, 1999). Mediation, particularly in the form of televisual systems, has the capacity to reproduce local conditions of 'intimacy' over distance and involve people 'emotionally and morally with distant others, events and social-cultural contexts' (Tomlinson, 1999, p 151). Mass-mediated 'quasi-interaction' (Thompson, 1995) is, however, by its nature a limiting experience because it is essentially a one way (monological) form of communication and hence, the audience are limited in their ability to engage in the events presented. People respond to televisual communications in a variety of ways: some people are 'shocked', 'emotionally touched', 'moved to compassion and even to action', while others turn away (Tomlinson, 1999, p 176). In effect, people selectively relate to those experiences that matter to them in constituting their self-identity, so that, even though globalisation may have brought remote events closer to home than before, the local, direct experience still predominates (Tomlinson, 1999, pp 177–78; Thompson, 1995). As it turns out, law and order, to rewrite Nelken's (1997, p 251) observation about law, is 'both the most local and the most universal or globalised of cultural phenomena'. In fact, as Garland (1996, p 446) points out, 'the threat of crime has become a routine part of modern consciousness, an everyday risk to be assessed and managed'. The media, then, reinforce the sense of commonality of risk faced by people from different localities and pave the way for apparently successful solutions to be exported from one locality to another.

One example of the 'glocalisation' of criminal justice policy relates to the so called 'New York Miracle' – 'zero tolerance' policing strategies which claimed to have led to a dramatic decline in crime and violence in New York City. Within a short time of its 'success story' being known to the world, zero tolerance had captured the imagination of some Australian politicians who became enthusiastic supporters of such a style of policing (Dixon, 1998, p 96). On the surface this looks like a simple case of cultural exportation from America, aided by global communications technology (see, for example, Giuliani, 1997) and the ease of international travel (a number of Australian public officials including police managers have gone on 'study tours' to visit New York). However, there has not been a blanket adoption of zero tolerance policing in any Australian jurisdiction. Rather, elements of the NYPD model (Brereton, 1999) such as Compstat (the use of crime mapping to allocate resources and monitor local police performance) and saturation policing, certainly found their way into the operation and management of the New South Wales Police Service (see, for example, Chan, Dixon, Maher and Stubbs, 1998; Darcy, 1999). Globalisation may have resulted in some of the NYPD policing methods becoming disembedded from their original location and re-embedded in New South Wales. In turn, New South Wales' adoption of these strategies played a part in constituting zero tolerance policing as a global trend in policing. What may have been a local policing issue now has its reference point half a world away. Supporters and critics alike can no longer debate policing strategies purely in terms of local issues; in this way the local and the global have penetrated each other. This example illustrates that to the extent that a local or national criminology or criminal justice policy orientation exists, it is increasingly defined in relation to the global.

Reflexive modernisation

The theory of 'reflexive modernisation' was developed independently by Giddens (1990) and Beck (1992; see also Beck, Giddens and Lash, 1994). In his influential book *Risk Society*, Beck (1992, p 10) postulates that 'we are witnessing not the end but the *beginning* of modernity – that is, of a modernity *beyond* its classical industrial design'. Beck argues that classical (simple) modernisation, which involves the demystification of 'privileges of rank and religious world views', is being replaced by reflexive modernisation, which is concerned with the demystification of science and technology and the 'modes of existence in work, leisure, the family and sexuality' (1992, p 10). Giddens, who also theorised a 'radicalised' phase of modernity, considers the twin processes of globalisation and the 'disinterring and problematising of tradition' as having become 'particularly acute in the current era' (1994, p 57). For Giddens, reflexivity has become an integral feature of modern social life, as 'social practices are constantly examined and reformed in the light of incoming information about those very practices, thus constitutively altering their character' (1990, p 38).

The word 'reflexivity' does not, however, mean the same thing to every writer. For example, Nelken has found at least five different uses of the word 'reflexive' in contemporary social theory:

... a way of overcoming the domain assumptions of one's theoretical starting point ...;
second, a defining characteristic of the operations of post (or late) modern society, or of

the individuals or systems in it ...; third, a method of giving attention to persuasive tropes in the writing of social science ...; fourth, a call for a different form of social investigation which involves greater collaboration between the researcher and the subjects of research ...; or fifth, the key to a new reflexive method of regulating modern societies by stimulating self-regulation ... (Nelken, 1994, p 9).

Nevertheless, reflexivity is usually understood in one of two senses: 'The first invites the theorist to be more *reflective* about the point and manner of his or her theorising, the other draws attention to the *recursiveness* which characterises the way contemporary systems, discourses and agents actually reproduce themselves' (Nelken, 1994, p 9). For Beck, the concept of 'reflexive modernisation' does not imply 'reflection, but (first) self-confrontation' (1994, p 5). In other words, it is not a self-conscious, intentional process, but one which 'occurs undesired, unseen and compulsively', although he does not rule out reflection as a secondary process (Beck, 1994, pp 5, 177). Beck insists that this new stage of modernisation, 'in which progress can turn into self-destruction' is not related to a crisis or a revolution; rather, it 'occurs surreptitiously and unplanned in the wake of normal, autonomised modernisation and with an unchanged, intact political and economic order' (1994, pp 2–3). Reflexive modernisation – the 'modernisation of modernisation' (Beck, 1994, p 4) – marks the transition from industrial society to risk society, in which the 'threats produced so far on the path of industrial society begin to dominate' (Beck, 1994, p 6).

How does reflexive modernisation affect the practice of criminology? It does so in three ways. First, criminology as a science is demystified or at least its status as an authoritative source of truth is undermined as a result of further scientisation. Secondly, users of criminological research have become 'co-producers' of criminological knowledge and shoppers in the supermarket of ideas and arguments. Thirdly, new forms of law and order politics begin to emerge which defy old political categories.

Demystification of science

Beck postulates that under reflexive modernisation, methodological scepticism – the hallmark of science – is applied to science itself, with the result that 'its claim to enlightenment are demystified' (1992, p 154). Science, which in an earlier modernity functioned as a tradition whose truth was once respected and accepted unquestioningly by non-scientists, is, under reflexive modernity, treated as contestable and open to 'discursive articulation' and critique (Giddens, 1994, 1999; Lash, 1994). For Beck, this demystification of science has meant the loss of science's claim to authoritative truth:

> In the past three decades science has changed from an activity *in the service* of truth to an activity *without* truth, but which has to make the most it can socially of the benefits of truth. Scientific practice has definitely followed scientific theory into conjecture, self-doubts and *convention*. Internally, science has retreated to making decisions. Externally the risks proliferate. Neither internally nor externally does science still enjoy the blessings of reason. It has become *in*dispensable to *and in*capable of truth. ... The truth claim of science has not withstood penetrating self-examination, neither empirically, nor in the theory of science. On the one hand, science's claim to be able to explain things has retreated to the *hypothesis*, the conjecture subject to recall. *On the other hand* reality has

sublimated into *data* that are *produced*. Thus 'facts' – the former centrepieces of reality – are nothing but answers to questions that could just as well have been asked differently, products of rules for gathering and omitting (Beck, 1992, p 166).

The almost universally accepted fallibility of scientific knowledge – 'scientific knowledge is always tentative and open to refutation' – has meant that the acceptability of scientific results can only be established by convention: 'through a consensus of experts in the field and the fulfilment of certain methodological and professional norms' (Majone, 1989, p 43). At the same time, the critiques of science have themselves become scientised, so that 'alternative' sciences, which reflect different principles or interests, have begun to emerge. As Ericson and Haggerty observe, 'Doubt [about science] becomes institutionalised because knowledge is always under revision in the reflexive practice of science, the reflexive use of expertise, and the reflexive monitoring of everyday life' (1997, p 98).

It may be argued that criminology, in spite of its short history of existence as a 'science' (Pavarini, 1994, p 43), has had its fair share of reflexivity, both in terms of self-confrontation and self-reflection. From the critique of administrative criminology by Taylor, Walton and Young (1973) to the left realist, feminist and postmodern critiques of recent years (see Pavlich, 1999), reflexive criminology may have come perilously close to Beck's (1994) notion of progress turning into self-destruction. Nevertheless, these exercises of self-confrontation were largely restricted to a small section of the practitioners of criminology, and amounted to little more than the usual disagreement or critique among experts. Such disagreements are not likely to destabilise academic criminology, since critique is in fact the 'motor of their enterprise' (Giddens, 1994, p 86). A more damaging form of reflexivity involves the criminologies of policy, where the initial promise of positive criminology to individualise punishment to prevent crime gave way to the 'nothing works' cynicism of the 1970s, which was then replaced by the euphoria and subsequent doubts over community corrections in the 1980s (Cohen, 1985), and new enthusiasm and controversy in relation to restorative justice in the 1990s (Alder and Wundersitz, 1994). Just as the public is increasingly aware of the hazard of environmental pollution brought about by progress in science and technology, there is a growing concern that criminology has not produced policies that control crime (see Braithwaite, 1989). At times like this, the 'recourse to scientific results for the socially binding definition of truth is becoming more and more necessary, but at the same time less and less sufficient' (Beck, 1992, p 167, italics removed). The reaction of mainstream criminology is to salvage this situation by reclaiming scientific authority through experimental research (Strang, Barnes, Braithwaite, and Sherman, 1999), meta-analyses (Sherman, Gottfredson, MacKenzie, Eck, Reuter and Bushway, 1998), and risk management strategies, while seeking 'foreground' (Katz, 1988), 'opportunity' (Clark, 1983), as well as background (Currie, 1988) explanations. Left realist criminology (Matthews and Young, 1992) was also born out of this desire to redefine criminology and reclaim its authority in law and order politics.

Such efforts may already be too late as the decline of expert authority has already begun. Zimring has provided a remarkable case study in relation to the passage of the 'Three Strikes' legislation in California, which represented 'an extreme example of populist pre-emption of criminal justice policy making' (1996, p 243). The law was rushed through without consulting any criminal justice professionals or experts to assess its likely impact. Although the 'Three Strikes' law may have been no more than a 'one-time California fiasco', Zimring is concerned that there appears to be a decline of expert authority evident in criminal justice policy making in the United States:

> ... the sheer amount of expertise available on questions of crime and punishment has expanded rapidly. There are well over 500 college and university criminal justice programs in the United States and bumper crops of new PhDs each year. So we have more experts. But expert influence on the process and expert involvement in the process has declined ... Part of the problem is that most academic lawyers are not much interested in criminal justice policy processes. Most of the problem is that there is no demand for what experts have to offer, which is information about the implications and consequences of policy choices (Zimring, 1996, p 253).

This trend can also be found further afield. For example, in 1999 Australia's Prime Minister made headlines for himself over his preference to consult an American FBI chief rather than listen to Australian drug research experts on ways to deal with the heroin problem (*Sydney Morning Herald*, 1999).

Non-experts as co-producers of knowledge

While the demystification of science has its positive side in terms of freeing people from the '"patronising" cognitive dictates of the experts' (Beck, 1992, p 168), it can be disturbing since 'there are no super experts to turn to' (Giddens, 1994, p 87). The authority of science is increasingly established on the basis of political compatibility, 'presentation, personal persuasive power, contacts, access to the media' or other techniques for the 'mobilisation of belief' (Beck, 1992, pp 168–69). Reflexive scientisation challenges the contrast between 'lay people' and 'experts' (Beck, 1992, p 154). Users of scientific results – including policy makers, the media and other non-experts – are no longer simply consumers, but 'co-producers' of 'valid knowledge', while the sciences are 'transformed into *self-service shops* for financially well endowed customers in need of arguments' (Beck, 1992, p 173):

> It is not uncommon for political programs to be decided in advance simply by the choice of what expert representatives are included in the circle of advisers. Not only are practitioners and politicians able to choose between expert groups, but those groups can also be *played off against each other* within and between disciplines, and in this way the autonomy of the customers is increased (Beck, 1992, p 173).

Consumers also learn that 'unwelcome results can be blocked *professionally* (by methodological criticism, for instance)' (Beck, 1992).

This has certainly been the trend in policy-oriented research, including criminology. Social science research is rarely used to fill a 'knowledge gap' and provide policy makers with authoritative data to make rational decisions (see Weiss, 1991, 1995; Chan, 1995; Brereton, 1996). At best, it percolates into people's consciousness subtly as ideas and shapes their assumptions and definitions; more often it enters into the policy arena as arguments, often supplied by interest groups or advocates of certain positions (Weiss, 1995). In general, 'Political actors select their ideas and arguments from the supply that happens to be available at a given time' (Majone, 1989, p 164). Policy issues are rarely 'purely technical' – they are often 'trans-scientific', that is, 'questions of fact that can be stated in a language of science but are, in principle or in practice, unanswerable by science' (Majone, 1989, p 3; see also Brereton, 1996). When the issues are 'trans-scientific', scientific experts are likely to be questioned by generalists in public debates. Beck even speaks of public discussion as a type of science, which is 'related to everyday life, drenched with experience and plays with cultural symbols', 'media-dependent, manipulable, sometimes hysterical', as distinct from 'standard science' (1994, pp 30–31). Researchers increasingly have to learn to communicate their findings to a wider audience, including through the media, in order to have impact on policy (Weiss, 1995; Haslam and Bryman, 1994; Daly, 1995).

Emergence of new politics

Reflexive modernisation also leads to a 'reinvention of politics' in the sense that 'The forms of political involvement, protest and retreat blur together in an ambivalence that defies the old categories of political clarity':

> ... a contradictory multiple engagement arises, which mixes and combines the classical poles of politics so that, if we think things through to their logical conclusion, everyone thinks and acts as a right winger and left winger, radically and conservatively, democratically and undemocratically, ecologically and anti-ecologically, politically and unpoetically, all at the same time. Everyone is a pessimist, a passivist, an idealist and an activist in partial aspects of his or her self. That only means, however, that the current clarities of politics – right and left, conservative and socialistic, retreat and participation – are no longer correct or effective (Beck, 1994, p 21).

It is likely that with criminal justice issues, the emerging politics is strategic rather than programmatic. For example, Hogg and Brown's (1999) reply to their critics reflects a deliberate lack of political clarity:

> ... we resist the idea that there is any useful way in which we may lay down a transformative trail or a political blueprint in relation to a future law and order strategy ... The politics of effecting progressive change always involve conditions, possibilities and constraints that are unwarranted and unchosen by their protagonists. Progressive outcomes are never guaranteed; unintended consequences always threaten to thwart the best laid plans and theories. Politics is by its nature a realm of conflict, compromise and contingency. All effective politics – whether electoral or issues based – involve coalition building, often among interests and groups who share limited common ground. Therefore the actual direction, composition, priorities, strategies and chosen allies in movements, campaigns and projects for progressive reform are likely to vary enormously for different issues and contexts (Hogg and Brown, 1999, pp 331–32).

Hogg and Brown (1998) see Hirst's (1994) notion of 'associative democracy' as a promising alternative. Similarly, Giddens has advocated 'The Third Way', which seeks 'the renewal of social democracy' (Giddens, 1998).

Reflexive government

Beck's account of reflexive modernisation and risk was criticised by Dean (1999) because it rests on totalising and realist assumptions; nevertheless, he suggests ways of salvaging the theory by 'focusing on the concrete and empirical and analysing specific types of risk rationalities and practices' (Dean, 1999, p 182). By adopting a nominalist position, Beck's notion of reflexivity can be useful for analysing the rationality of government in advanced liberal democracies. Thus, Dean introduces the term 'reflexive government' to describe the 'governmentalisation of government' or the 'turning of the state upon itself':

> The imperative of reflexive government is to render governmental institutions and mechanisms, including those of the social itself, efficient, accountable, transparent and democratic by the employment of technologies of performance such as the various forms of auditing and the financial instruments of accounting, by the devolution of budgets, and by the establishment of calculating individuals and calculable spaces ... (Dean, 1999, p 193).

Dean suggests that 'reflexive government' is facilitated by 'technologies of agency' and 'technologies of performance'. Technologies of agency include various forms of contracts (for example, contracting out of public services, performance contracts, learning contracts) and techniques of empowerment, consultation and negotiation (Dean, 1999, pp 167–68). Technologies of performance are 'designed to penetrate the enclosures of expertise fostered under welfare state and to subsume the substantive domains of expertise ... to new formal calculative regimes' (Dean, 1999, pp 168–69). Examples of these are familiar: 'the devolution of budgets, the setting of performance indicators, "benchmarking", the establishment of "quasi-markets" in expertise and service provision, the "corporatisation" and "privatisation" of formerly public services, and the contracting-out of services' (Dean, 1999, p 169). These technologies allow for control from 'above' by using performance contracts, indicators and audits; they also facilitate regulation from 'below' by empowering users and consumers to contest professional practice and knowledge. As part of the neo-liberal political rationality, these technologies seek to govern by combining self-regulation with external accountability (Power, 1997; see Chan, 1999).

In relation to the governance of criminologists, these technologies have already been observed by O'Malley (1996), who argues that the distinction between 'administrative' criminology and academic criminology, once sharply demarcated, is becoming less clear cut in the 'post-social' era. He offered several reasons for this change:

> First, and perhaps most crucial, the move toward rendering the state more independently accountable, and increasingly in market-like terms, has delivered a greatly increased volume of state-originated consultancy-based work to academic criminologists ... Second, as universities also begin to partake of marketising drives and drives toward accountability, so they propel academic criminologists in the direction of seeking and gaining consultancies and grants ... Likewise, university research grants are beginning to occupy a new terrain. As part of the increasing pressures for external auditing and market practices, academics increasingly are required by their institutions to apply for national competitive grants. The granting agencies, in turn are increasingly influenced by demands for accountability, and this in turn, implies 'relevance' ... Finally, expertise in the post-social is more generally marketised, and all of these changes may be seen to reinforce and partake of this shift ... In short, pressures created in the post-social environment are beginning to eliminate a once clear distinction between administrative and academic criminology, tending to push the latter in the direction of the former, and thus creating unfamiliar alignments and fissures, reinforcing the sense that criminology is fragmenting (O'Malley, 1996, p 35).

Similarly, there has been a new emphasis on evaluation of criminal justice programs and policies as part of the policy process (O'Malley, 1996, p 35; see also Hogg and Brown, 1998, p 193).

Conclusion

The social and political trends described in this chapter – globalisation, reflexive modernisation and reflexive government – are useful for providing ways of seeing and understanding the challenges facing criminology in the new millennium. However, they should not be read as deterministic or universal. There is much that criminologists can do to reverse any undesirable trends.

Globalisation has had its fair share of critics (for example, Gray, 1998) and there is no denying that there is a dark side to its economic dimension. For criminology and criminal justice, the challenge is to resist the types of interdependence and homogenisation that are inappropriate or detrimental to justice (see Smart, 1999). The debates surrounding zero tolerance policing in New South Wales, for example, have shown that criminologists do have a role to play in educating policy makers and the general public about the dangers of mindless importation of foreign products (see Dixon, 1998; Brereton, 1999). By studying the particular and the local, criminologists are able to promote the best of the global and contest its less desirable influences. When the best already resides in the local (for example, Australia's success in harm reduction strategies against heroin), the challenge is not only to protect it from being invaded by inferior, foreign products, but also to ensure that it becomes globally recognised.

Reflexive modernisation may have been responsible for a decline of authority among criminological experts. The loss of a position of privilege in the politics of knowledge is frustrating but inevitable given that critique is part of the criminological enterprise. Beck suggests that the 'round table' model is one way of building consensus among scientists, politicians and the general public:

> Negotiation and mediation institutions of this type must experiment with novel procedures, decision making structures, overlaps of competence and incompetence and multiple jurisdictions. They can no more be had without breaking up monopolies and delegating power than with the old demands and models of efficient non-ambiguity. Everyone, the involved authorities and companies, as well as the trade unions and the political representatives, must be prepared to jump over their own shadows, just as, conversely, radical opponents must be willing and able to make compromises ... (Beck, 1994, pp 29–30).

The New South Wales Drug Summit was a relatively successful example of using novel procedures and structures, creating a dialogue between experts and non-experts, while providing the space for scientific evidence, direct contact with drug users and families, debates and compromises. Sessions were partly open to the public and the source materials, transcripts of speeches and recommendations posted on the internet, thus facilitating the dissemination of information in an alternative form to traditional news media (see NSW Drug Summit 1999 website).

The technologies of reflexive government can be oppressive for criminologists in reinforcing the 'iron cage' of administrative rationality (see Smart, 1999). They may even be detrimental to policies if they are too narrowly evaluated (O'Malley, 1996).

Power (1997) has noted some of the unintended consequences of the 'audit explosion' which are counterproductive (see also Ericson and Haggerty, 1997; Chan, 1999). The challenge for criminologists is to relentlessly contest inappropriate performance indicators or evaluative criteria. The proliferation of contract research and the rise of criminologists in the private sector must be subject to close scrutiny, because, more than anything else, there is a distinct danger that the acceleration of these trends will spell the end of critical reflexive criminology.

References

Alder, C and Wundersitz, J (eds) (1994) *Family Conferencing and Juvenile Justice: The Way Forward or Misplaced Optimism?*, Canberra: Australian Institute of Criminology

Bauman, Z (1998) *Globalisation: The Human Consequences*, Cambridge: Polity

Beck, U (1992) *Risk Society: Toward a New Modernity*, London: Sage

Beck, U (1994) 'The reinvention of politics: towards a theory of reflexive modernisation', in Beck, U *et al*, *Reflexive Modernisation: Politics, Tradition and Aesthetics in the Modern Social Order*, Cambridge: Polity, pp 1–55

Beck, U, Giddens, A and Lash, S (1994) *Reflexive Modernisation: Politics, Tradition and Aesthetics in the Modern Social Order*, Cambridge: Polity

Bourdieu, P and Wacquant, L (1992) *An Invitation to Reflexive Sociology*, Cambridge: Polity

Braithwaite, J (1989) 'The state of criminology: theoretical decay or renaissance?' 22 *Australian and New Zealand Journal of Criminology* 129–35

Brereton, D (1999) 'Zero tolerance and the NYPD: has it worked there and will it work here?', paper to the Australian Institute of Criminology Conference, 'Mapping the Boundaries of Australia's Criminal Justice System', Canberra, 22–23 March 1999

Brereton, D (1996) 'Does criminology matter: crime, politics and the policy' 8(1) *Current Issues in Criminal Justice*, Special Issue, 'The Future of Criminology' 82–87

Chan, J (1994) 'The privatisation of punishment: a review of the key issues', in Moyle, P (ed), *Privatisation of Prisons and Police in Australia and New Zealand*, London: Pluto

Chan, J (1995) 'Systematically distorted communication? Criminological knowledge, media representation and public policy' *ANZ J of Criminology*, Special Supplementary Issue 23–30

Chan, J (1996) 'The future of criminology: an introduction' 8(1) *Current Issues in Criminal Justice*, Special Issue, 'The Future of Criminology' 7–13

Chan, J (1999) 'Governing police practice: limits of the new accountability' 50(2) *British Journal of Sociology* 251–70

Chan, J, Dixon, D, Maher, L and Stubbs, J (1998) *Policing in Cabramatta*, Final Report to the New South Wales Police Service

Clark, RV (1983) 'Situational crime prevention: its theoretical basis and practical scope', in Tonry, M and Morris, N (eds), *Crime and Justice: An Annual Review of Research*, Chicago: Chicago UP, pp 225–56

Cohen, S (1981) 'Footprints on the sand: a further report on criminology and the sociology of deviance in Britain', in Fitzgerald, M, McLennan, G and Pawson, J (eds), *Crime and Society: Readings in History and Theory*, London: Routledge

Cohen, S (1985) *Visions of Social Control*, Cambridge: Polity

Cohen, S (1988) *Against Criminology*, New Brunswick: Transaction Books

Cohn, EG and Farrington, DP (1998) 'Changes in the most-cited scholars in major international journals between 1986–90 and 1991–95' 38(1) *British Journal of Criminology* 156–70

Currie, E (1988) 'Two visions of community crime prevention', in Hope, T and Shaw, M (eds), *Communities and Crime Reduction*, London: Home Office Research and Planning Unit, pp 280–85

Daly, K (1995) 'Celebrated crime cases and the public's imagination: from bad press to bad policy?' *ANZ J of Criminology*, Special Supplementary Issue, 6–22

Darcy, D (1999) 'Zero tolerance – not quite the influence on NSW policing some would have you believe' 10(3) *Current Issues in Criminal Justice* 290

Dean, M (1999) *Governmentality: Power and Rule in Modern Society*, London: Sage

Dixon, D (1998) 'Broken windows, zero tolerance, and the New York miracle' 10(1) *Current Issues in Criminal Justice* 96–106

Ericson, R (1996) 'Making criminology' 8(1) *Current Issues in Criminal Justice*, Special Issue, 'The Future of Criminology' 14–25

Ericson, R and Carriere, K (1994) 'The fragmentation of criminology', in Nelken, D (ed), *The Futures of Criminology*, London: Sage, pp 89–109

Ericson, R and Haggerty, K (1997) *Policing the Risk Society*, Toronto: Toronto UP

Featherstone, M, Lash, S (1995) 'Globalization, modernity and the spatialization of social theory', in Featherstone, M, Lash, S and Robertson, R (eds), *Global Modernities*, London: Sage

Featherstone, M, Lash, S and Robertson, R (eds) (1995) *Global Modernities*, London: Sage

Garland, D (1996) 'The limits of the sovereign state: strategies of crime control in contemporary society' 36 *British Journal of Criminology* 445–71

Garland, D (1997) 'Governmentality and the problem of crime: Foucault, criminology and sociology' 1(2) *Theoretical Criminology* 173–214

Giddens, A (1990) *The Consequences of Modernity*, Cambridge: Polity

Giddens, A (1991) *Modernity and Self-Identity: Self and Society in the Late Modern Age*, Cambridge: Polity

Giddens, A (1994) 'Living in a post-traditional society', in Beck, U *et al*, *Reflexive Modernisation: Politics, Tradition and Aesthetics in the Modern Social Order*, Cambridge: Polity, pp 56–109

Giddens, A (1998) *The Third Way: The Renewal of Social Democracy*, Cambridge: Polity

Giddens, A (1999) 'Risk', BBC Reith Lectures *Runaway World*, Week 2, http://news.bbc.co.uk/hi/english/static/events/reith_99/default.htm, accessed 25 February 2005

Giuliani, R (1997) *Mayor Rudolph W Giuliani's Testimony before the House Committee on Government Reform*, 13 March 1997, www.nyc.gov/html/rwg/html/97a/reform.html

Gray, J (1998) *False Dawn: The Delusions of Global Capitalism*, London: Granta Books

Haslam, C and Bryman, A (eds) (1994) *Social Scientists Meet the Media*, London and New York: Routledge

Hirst, P (1994) *Associative Democracy – New Forms of Economic and Social Governance*, Cambridge: Polity

Hirst, P and Thompson, G (1996) *Globalisation in Question: The International Economy and the Possibilities of Governance*, Cambridge: Polity

Hogg, R (1996) 'Criminological failure and governmental effect' 8(1) *Current Issues in Criminal Justice*, Special Issue, 'The Future of Criminology' 43–59

Hogg, R and Brown, D (1998) *Rethinking Law and Order*, Sydney: Pluto

Hogg, R and Brown, D (1999) 'Rethinking law and order: a rejoinder' 32(3) *Australian and New Zealand Journal of Criminology* 331–33

'Howard's FBI war on drugs' (1999) *Sydney Morning Herald*, 22 February

Katz, J (1988) *Seductions of Crime*, New York: Basic Books

Lash, S (1994) 'Reflexivity and its doubles: structure, aesthetics, community', in Beck, U *et al*, *Reflexive Modernisation: Politics, Tradition and Aesthetics in the Modern Social Order*, Cambridge: Polity, pp 110–73

Majone, G (1989) *Evidence, Argument, and Persuasion in the Policy Process*, New Haven and London: Yale UP

Matthews, R and Young, J (1992) *Issues in Realist Criminology*, London: Sage

Nelken, D (1994) 'Reflexive criminology?', in Nelken, D (ed), *The Futures of Criminology*, London: Sage, pp 7–42

Nelken, D (1997) 'The globalisation of crime and criminal justice: prospects and problems' 50 *Current Legal Problems* 251–77

New South Wales Drug Summit, www.druginfonsw.gov.au/drug_summit

O'Malley, P (1996) 'Post-social criminologies: some implications for current political trends for criminological theory and practice' 8(1) *Current Issues in Criminal Justice*, Special Issue, 'The Future of Criminology', 26–38

Pavarini, M (1994) 'Is criminology worth saving?', in Nelken, D (ed), *The Futures of Criminology*, London: Sage, pp 43–62

Pavlich, G (1999) 'Criticism and criminology: in search of legitimacy' 3(1) *Theoretical Criminology* pp 29–51

Power, M (1997) *The Audit Society*, Oxford: OUP

Robertson, R (1995) 'Glocalisation: time – space and homogeneity – heterogeneity', in Featherstone, M, Lash, S and Robertson, R (eds), *Global Modernities*, Sage, London

Sheptycki, JWE (1998) 'Policing, postmodernism and transnationalisation' 38(3) *British Journal of Criminology* 485–503

Sherman, L, Gottfredson, DC, MacKenzie, DL, Eck, J, Reuter, P and Bushway, SD (1998) *Preventing Crime: What Works, What Doesn't, What's Promising*, Washington DC: US Department of Justice, National Institute of Justice

Smart, B (ed) (1999) *Resisting McDonaldisation*, London: Sage

Strang, H, Barnes, GC, Braithwaite, J and Sherman, LW (1999) *Experiments in Restorative Policing: A Progress Report on the Canberra Reintegrative Shaming Experiments (RISE)*, www.aic.gov.au/rjustice/rise/progress/1999.html

van Swaaningen, R (1999) 'Reclaiming critical criminology: social justice and the European tradition' 3(1) *Theoretical Criminology* 5–28

Taylor, I, Walton, P and Young J (1973) *The New Criminology*, London: Routledge

Thompson, JB (1995) *The Media and Modernity*, Cambridge: Polity

Tomlinson, J (1999) *Globalisation and Culture*, Cambridge: Polity

Waters, M (1995) *Globalisation*, London: Routledge

Weiss, C (1991) 'Policy research as advocacy: pro and con' 4(1–2) *Knowledge and Policy* 37–55

Weiss, C (1995) 'The haphazard connection: social science and public policy' 23(2) *International Journal of Educational Research* 137–50

Zimring, F (1996) 'Populism, democratic government, and the decline of expert authority: some reflections on "three strikes" in California' 28(1) *Pacific Law Journal* 243–56

Zimring, F (1999) 'Crime, criminal justice, and criminology for a smaller planet: some notes on the 21st century', plenary paper to the Australian and New Zealand Society of Criminology Annual Conference, Perth, 27–30 September

Index